COLONIALISM IN AFRICA 1870–1960

GENERAL EDITORS

PETER DUIGNAN, *Senior Fellow, Hoover Institution,*
Stanford University

L. H. GANN, *Senior Fellow, Hoover Institution,*
Stanford University

VOLUME 3

HOOVER INSTITUTION PUBLICATIONS

COLONIALISM IN AFRICA
1870–1960

VOLUME 3
PROFILES OF CHANGE:
AFRICAN SOCIETY AND
COLONIAL RULE

Edited by

VICTOR TURNER

Committee on Social Thought
University of Chicago

CAMBRIDGE
AT THE UNIVERSITY PRESS
1971

Published by the Syndics of the Cambridge University Press
Bentley House, 200 Euston Road, London N.W.1
American Branch: 32 East 57th Street, New York, N.Y.10022

© Cambridge University Press 1971

Library of Congress Catalogue Card Number: 75–77289

Standard Book Number: 521 07844 X

Printed in Great Britain
at the University Printing House, Cambridge
(Brooke Crutchley, University Printer)

CONTENTS

v

CONTENTS

ILLUSTRATIONS

PREFACE

The first two volumes of Colonialism in Africa were designed to provide an analysis, as well as a convenient summary, of major problems bearing on the history and politics of the imperial era. The contributors to our preceding volumes covered many aspects of the colonial past. They paid attention to social as well as to historical and political questions. But unavoidably, many gaps remained. Colonial Africa experienced major culture clashes which derived from the impact of complex economic, social, political and religious forces on the indigenous societies of Africa. These involved issues merit further elucidation.

The present work is thus intended to provide additional information concerning the social problems of colonial Africa, to examine afresh certain widely held preconceptions, and also to make an independent contribution to the study of African societies. Professor Victor Turner, the Editor, has drawn on experts from several disciplines, representing different schools of thought. He has assembled a distinguished team of collaborators, whose labours show how far anthropology, sociology and sociological history can contribute to a better understanding of the past and the present.

The Editor has consulted the *Index-gazetteer of the world* published by *The Times* of London for the spelling of geographical names. He has also drawn on Joseph H. Greenberg's *The languages of Africa* and George P. Murdock's *Africa: its peoples and their culture history* for the spelling of linguistic and ethnic terms. But wherever authors have expressed a special preference for any particular version, the individual writer's wishes have been respected. Editorial practices vary a good deal in different countries. Also contributors often have a strong preference for their own usage and style. Hence the collaborators have been allowed as much freedom as seemed consistent with the standards set by Cambridge University Press. The final responsibility for the accuracy of the statements made, for the bibliographical information provided and for the citations rests with the individual authors. (Additional bibliographical information concerning the general background of the imperial era will be found in the bibliographical volume to be published in the *Colonialism in Africa* series.)

We should like to express our thanks to the various contributors, and

PREFACE

to Professor Victor Turner, to whom the sole credit and responsibility
for the completion of this volume are due. We owe much to Miss Mildred
Teruya for her bibliographical labours. We are grateful to Dr W.
Glenn Campbell, Director of the Hoover Institution, Stanford University, for the kind co-operation which he has extended to us. Once
again, we should like to acknowledge the financial generosity of the
Relm Foundation of Ann Arbor, Michigan, whose assistance has made
this project possible.

PETER DUIGNAN, L. H. GANN
General Editors

1969

INTRODUCTION

by

VICTOR TURNER

The contributors to the present volume, with the exception of the historians Klein and Welbourn, are all seasoned anthropologists who did field-work in Africa during the colonial period. From certain points of view, including those of some administrators both of the colonial and the post-colonial régimes, anthropologists are still regarded as the last people who should be entrusted with the task of making a survey of the 'colonial situation'. It used to be argued by officials of the *ancien régime* that anthropologists, immersed as they were in the specificities of African life, came to accept the structural perspective of their informants, became their spokesmen, and by their words and works impeded the efforts of district and provincial administrators to govern efficiently. Some were even accused by white settlers and European civil servants of being 'Reds', 'socialists' and 'anarchists'. It is now asseverated by African leaders and administrators, down to the district level, that anthropologists before independence were 'apologists of colonialism' and subtle agents of colonial supremacy who studied African customs merely to provide the dominant white minority with information damaging to native interests but normally opaque to white investigation. Thus yesterday's 'socialist' has become today's 'reactionary'. Sir Alan Burns (1957) and Frantz Fanon (1961) are improbably allied.

It is true, of course, that in their personal capacity anthropologists, like everyone else, have a wide spectrum of political views. Some are known 'conservatives'; others lean far to the 'left'. But as professionals, anthropologists are trained, over almost as many years as doctors, to collect certain kinds of information as 'participant observers' which will enable them, whatever may be their personal views, to present as objectively as the current level of their discipline's development permits, a coherent picture of the sociocultural system they have elected to spend some years of their lives in studying, and of the kinds of processes that go on in it. It is their ultimate duty to publish their findings and expose them, together with an exact description of the means by which they were obtained, to the international public of their

I

anthropological colleagues and beyond that to the 'world of learning'. Eventually, news of their work and analyses, through their own 'popular' writings or through citations, résumés (not infrequently bowdlerized) and digests by non-anthropologists, seeps through to the general reading public. Time thus winnows their reports and rids them of much that is biased and 'loaded'. There is no point in special pleading or tendentious argument; there are professional standards against which all reports are measured, and, in the end, the common sense of the common man.

Some sociologists, historians and political scientists have claimed that anthropologists cannot see the forest for the trees—they study peoples and groups that can hardly be seen on a world map without a magnifying glass, or even on a map of Africa. It may be admitted that on this 'micro'-level their 'intensive' findings are exact, that they discover many fascinating interconnections between social and cultural events and relationships. But it is denied that they can say anything significant about the major political, economic and social processes that intertwine to make up the 'histories' of colonies, nations and continents. They are 'immersed in matter', thick with specificity. Their data 'can be used' by the sophisticates who know how to compare on the scale of nations and the span of decades, but their theories are scarcely adequate beyond the level of kinship and local relations.

This volume is itself a lively refutation of such a critique. Anthropologists have limned various profiles of the latest 'colonial' period—sixty to eighty years of European overlordship in sub-Saharan Africa—in terms either of broad topics such as land tenure, religion and education or of studies in depth of the history of particular peoples, such as the Gogo, the Lugbara or the Kanuri. Each profile implies or exemplifies the comparative method. This is because anthropology (however uneasily) straddles the sciences and the humanities. In their training, anthropologists are taught to employ the rhetoric both of the sciences and, increasingly, of history. On the one hand, they are encouraged to proffer 'general-law type explanations' where 'the principle of coherence is supplied by subsuming the data under general laws supposedly standard in scientific discourse' (Jack Hexter, 'Historiography', in *International Encyclopaedia of the Social Sciences*, 1968, VI, 373). On the other, they are trained to write narratives of events not only lucidly but also evocatively—to convey to others, for example, 'the riches of...a great happening' (*ibid.*). As more anthropologists use the extended-case method, they go to school with the historian and try to learn from him how best to practise historiography.

Yet the anthropologist's earlier and enduring commitment to the quest for general laws, to quantification, to the comparative method and the search for 'structural regularities' (whether at the level of observation or of ideas), and to the rhetoric of the sciences as a vehicle for communicating his findings, gives his work a dual character seldom found in that of either the historian or the sociologist *pur sang*. Although he is devoted to—even belabours—the particular, he loses no opportunity to generalize. Yet like William Blake he believes that 'General Forms have their Vitality in Particulars'. When he goes into the field he takes with him a baggage of assorted generalizations and hypotheses about the nature of society and culture, structure and process. His observations on children playing, women pounding millet in groups, men judging cases, are made with these in mind and not from mere jackdaw collectorship. He seeks out the principles underlying customary behaviour, the regularities (if any) underlying behaviour not ordered by clear rules. When he has thought about his case material and processed his quantitative data, he tries to give as systematic an account as he can of the 'people' or community within a 'people' who have formed the objects of his depth investigation. What is 'systematic' in his account is largely the product of the findings (and suppositions about those findings) of the international body of anthropologists. Yet a small increment, to be added to this total, is his own, the result of his trafficking with a particular aggregate of men, usually of a culture and language alien to his own. His 'dual mandate' from science and history confronts a dual human situation where a shared humanity tries to solve the problems presented by sharp cultural and historical mutual repugnancies.

Sociologists, working with questionnaires, and historians, working from archives and documents, do not have the anthropologists' problems of sustained encounter with people at once both sympathetic and antipathetic, both exotic and familiar. The shock and joy of discovering the common in the different has sometimes led anthropologists to champion strongly the people they study against whatever authorities, black or white, rule the nation. The difficult task of working out an alien structure of ideas and beliefs has led to a similar result, though here it is the cognitive capital invested, rather than the affective 'shock of recognition', that generates quixotic support of what is often a lost or losing cause. The thrust of my argument here, of course, is that anthropologists are existentially involved, by the nature of their discipline, since Malinowski (at much personal cost) laid down its present field lines, with the peoples they study, and do not think about them in libraries or studies in terms of the descriptions of others or of scribbled or typed replies to questions about particular aspects of their lives or attitudes. This engagement in some ways destroys detachment from the object of study; but when other societies are considered it may give additional insight, since the anthropologist is constantly relating the data he reads about to the experiences he has had.

I mention these matters to indicate that when anthropologists move into the field of wider generalization they do so in ways appropriate to their ambiguous profession. They are no strangers to the 'general law' approach, but, on the other hand, they are steeped in concrete particularity. Some anthropologists migrate mentally to one pole and ignore the opposite pole; others try to relate the poles in various ways. Instances of all three approaches will be found in the present volume, sometimes within the article of a single author. In a first draft of this introduction I followed the very common procedure of trying to summarize the argument of each author, then comparing them, and, as a grand finale, of attempting to abstract some regularities of form and change in the history of the 'colonial era'. But on mature considera-tion I see that this was a fruitless project. The essays, written by acknowledged experts, with many books and papers under their belts, diverge widely in orientation and in content. All I can say is that as an anthropologist who was himself for more than two years involved deeply, indeed almost 'baptized', in the complex life of a village society, I can vouch for the 'smack' of truth that pervades all these pieces. The touchstone or lodestone won by anthropologists after years of living with villagers and tribesmen can, in no mystical way, be applied to cognate documents, and find out in them the truths of a specific human situation, if not of *the* human condition. I believe that the reader of this book will gain the special kind of penetrative understanding of peoples and problems that can be given only by those who have lived their thinking about man among men with an utterly different social and cultural tradition from their own. The reader may have sharp political or religious disagreements with certain of the authors, but he cannot but recognize that there is an authentic ring about what they say, even if the words and the philosophical slants are unacceptable to him.

I would like, finally, to say that generalizations based largely on the accounts of trained observers of 'other cultures' should not be considered less veridical than those based on 'documents' written or compiled in the first instance by persons either untrained in the analysis of social relations or with axes to grind handed to them by the authorities of particular groups in their native cultures, religious, political, social, economic, or all compounded. Admittedly, some might think these 'woodnotes wild' (or domesticated in particular aviaries) more authentic than any professional tradition of social study; but if man's continuing effort to know himself by taking thought as well as revelation has any worth, our hypothetical reader has much to ponder over in the profiles of change portrayed for him in this volume.

BIBLIOGRAPHY

Burns, Sir Alan Cuthbert (1957). *In defence of colonies; British colonial territories in international affairs.* London.

Fanon, Frantz (1961). *Les damnés de la terre.* Paris.

Hexter, Jack (1968). 'Historiography', in *International Encyclopaedia of the Social Sciences*, David Sills, ed., VI.

Sills, David, ed. (1968). *International Encyclopaedia of the Social Sciences.* 17 vols. New York.

CHAPTER I

SOME EFFECTS OF COLONIAL RULE AMONG THE LUGBARA

by

JOHN MIDDLETON

This essay is an account of the changes that occurred among the Lugbara of Uganda and the Congo as a consequence of some sixty years of colonial rule.[1] I studied these people after fifty years of colonial administration.[2] I devote most attention to the more obvious effects of this rule: some changes occurred which can only indirectly be regarded as its consequences. Because of their remoteness from the main colonial centres of the region, the Lugbara were relatively little affected by the colonial episode; and their traditional organization and culture were not greatly changed. I realize that to write of 'traditional' society here may imply that it had never changed before the advent of colonial government. I do not assume that at all. But it is difficult, given the present state of our knowledge, to reconstruct changes in the period much before the end of the nineteenth century; and it is irrelevant to this particular essay.

The traditional society and culture

It is not possible now to reconstruct in detail the forms of Lugbara society and culture before the advent of colonial rule. It is a reasonable assumption that neither the society nor the culture had changed mark-

[1] The Congo (Leopoldville) became independent in 1960 and Uganda in 1962. The Sudan had become independent in 1956.

[2] I worked among the Lugbara from the end of 1949 until early 1952, with assistance from the Worshipful Company of Goldsmiths and the Colonial Social Science Research Council, London. The initial writing-up of field data was assisted by the Wenner–Gren Foundation for Anthropological Research, New York.

Some of the material presented here has been taken from earlier papers. I am grateful to Dr A. I. Richards and Messrs Faber and Faber for permission to reprint material from my chapter in *East African chiefs* (London, 1960); to Professors P. J. Bohannan and G. Dalton and the Director of the Northwestern University Press to use material from *Markets in Africa* (Evanston, 1962); and to the Editor of the *Journal of the Royal Anthropological Institute* to use material from vol. 93, no. 1, 1963.

edly for very long periods, and Lugbara society of today has not changed appreciably from what it was at the end of the last century. The way of life of the older men of today—or at least of the period of my stay among the Lugbara—is very similar to that of their fathers, according to the men themselves, with two important reservations: the colonial administrations introduced taxation and they altered the traditional jural system by the prohibition of warfare and feud. But I found that Lugbara men still talked as though feud and warfare still occurred—they conceived of their society as though feud and warfare still supplied important jural sanctions and, of course, the older among them had taken part in feuds and wars. Old women could also remember these episodes and talked of retrieving the corpses of their kin from the fields of battle; but they, unlike the men, were less aware of feud and war as social mechanisms that could interrelate groups having certain remote lineage connections.

Lugbara awareness of the effects of colonial rule is considerable. Older people maintain that the country, its people and their culture, have been largely destroyed; whereas younger men are more aware of some of the advantages brought about by colonial rule. In the early 1950s most Lugbara thought that if the Europeans left, the Baganda and other southerners or, even worse, the Arabs of the Sudan, whom Lugbara remembered as slave-traders, would take over. They were thus ambivalent about the merits and demerits of colonialism: being one of the smaller and more remote peoples of eastern Africa, they knew that their place was likely to be one of subjection in either event.

They could describe to me their society as they remembered it to have been at the end of the previous century; and although this description was always subject to some distortion and romanticization, I think we may assume it was a fair picture. The initial stages of colonial impact had a deep effect upon the Lugbara (as presumably upon all peoples anywhere). In fact, the early events of colonial rule could have affected directly only a relatively few people (and the dreadful treatment meted out to many people of the region by the Arab slavers had been spared the Lugbara); but these events are remembered today with vividness, whereas later events, from about 1920 to the present day, are merged together in people's memories. This means essentially that it is possible to date the early events with some precision; but later events merge together and dating is much more difficult. I therefore present this essay in two main sections: the early events from the end of the last century to the Udupi revolt in 1919 comprise the first section, and later events the second. First, however, it is convenient to describe, very briefly, the outlines of Lugbara traditional society.

At the time of the 1948 census the Lugbara people numbered some 244,000, of whom 161,000 lived in the West Nile district of Uganda and 58,000 in the Mahagi district of the Congo. In addition, 22,000 Uganda Lugbara and 2,500 Congo Lugbara lived in southern Uganda. There were also some 500 in the Yei district of the Sudan. The Lugbara and the Madi to the east are the most easterly of the Sudanic language speakers and are thus linguistically unrelated to their neighbours to the south, the Nilotic-speaking Alur, and to the north, the Nilo-Hamitic Kakwa and Kuku. Only to the west are there linguistically related peoples, the Keliko and Logo, and to the south-west, the Ndu and 'Bale. The Lugbara areas are about the most remote and inaccessible of all three territories in which they live today. The nearest large town in Uganda is Kampala, 500 miles away by road and river steamer. Kisangani (Stanleyville) in the Congo is 600 miles to the west and Juba in the Sudan 120 miles to the north. Besides the distance, the system of rivers and roads makes it impossible for produce to be exported if it is at all bulky; and in recent years the Lugbara have been able to export only their labour and tobacco, which can be processed to some extent locally. The effects of colonialism in the form of direct contact with large urban centres of communications have therefore been relatively slight. At the time of my stay very few Lugbara women had ever seen a European at close quarters, let alone spoken to one, and few older men had done so. The younger men for the most part had gone south as labour migrants, and so had become aware of the outside world from their own experience; also a great many Lugbara had served in the army in the Second World War.

The country of the Lugbara consists of part of the high and open watershed between the Nile and the Congo river networks, between 4,000 and 5,000 feet above sea level. It is well watered, with well distributed rains and many permanent rivers and streams, and is fertile enough in the central areas of the country to support a population of over 200 persons to the square mile. The Lugbara are peasant farmers. They say that they once had large herds of cattle that were almost wiped out in a series of cattle epidemics between 1890 and 1925. Today, although socially important, cattle are not prominent in the economy.

Traditionally the Lugbara lacked a king or chiefs. They are divided into some sixty clans, each defined by reference to a clan founder many generations ago. Clans are dispersed, and do not form political entities. In theory they are exogamous, but this is by no means always so. The largest traditional political units are what I call subtribes, each based upon a core consisting of a subclan. This is a segment of a clan, typically the core of a clan from which smaller groups have periodically split off to attach themselves to related groups elsewhere. A subtribe is segmented into constituent territorial groups, which may be called major, minor and minimal sections; each of these in turn is based upon a lineage core, the major, minor or minimal lineage. This is, of course, a common form of organization in Africa. I use the term 'family cluster' for the minimal sections, so that the smallest of these local groups is a family cluster based upon a minimal lineage. The head of this lineage, whom I call the Elder, is also the head of the family cluster. Heads of wider lineages have certain ritual duties, but have no authority within these wider lineages except over the members of their own minimal lineages. The system of effective lineage authority is thus at a very low level of segmentation (see Middleton, 1958, 1960a, 1965).

Traditionally a subtribe occupied a series of large clusters of huts and compounds. Each compound was the home of a family cluster, and was divided among the constituent joint and elementary families of the group. Near each family cluster's compound were its 'home fields', under a system of permanent farming. Outside the compounds of the subtribe lay the 'outside fields' under shifting cultivation. These provided a belt of country which acted as a no-man's land, from half a mile to ten miles wide, between the subtribe and neighbouring subtribes. In addition, there were also riverine irrigated fields, the most fertile and the most prized. They were also in the shortest supply. A wife should be given all types of field, and most of the disputes within local groups seem to have been over the equitable distribution of field types by the elder. Grazing is traditionally on fallow fields; and there were also grazing grounds on land too shallow for cultivation, usually in the poorer areas between subtribes (See Middleton and Greenland, 1954).

Most natural resources needed in everyday life are found throughout Lugbaraland. These include such products as clay for pots, iron for smithing (done by Ndu smiths who live peaceably among the Lugbara), ochre for personal and hut decoration, reeds for matting, grass and

9

leaves for women's apparel, gourds for household vessels. All parts of Lugbaraland produce the same crops, although there are many differences in variety, and people are well aware of the best types for their particular types of land. In the past, rainstones of quartz, superior types of iron, and oracle poisons were the most important items of trade. These were obtained by small parties of men who could travel in comparative safety along kinship routes, or by the few influential men whose status gave them safe-permit throughout the area. There were, as a consequence, few disputes over natural resources.

Traditionally, and still in theory, subclans are exogamous. A man may marry a girl of a lineage of a different subclan within the same subtribe. This is usually in a different major section, since within that section there are close ties of uterine kinship which prohibit marriage. The traditional pattern of disputes is therefore simple: within the major section they are mostly over land rights, and between major sections and subtribes over women.

Before the prohibition of intergroup fighting, disputes were settled within the major section (and certainly within the minor section) by arbitration by respective elders or by duelling; beyond the major section and within the subtribe by feud; and beyond the subtribe by warfare. The distinction between feud and warfare was simply that there was a recognized obligation that feuds should quickly be settled by agreement, but warfare could not permanently be settled—men merely waited for tempers to die down, and when the next hoeing season began open fighting would cease and men take up hoes instead of spears and arrows. Arbitration within the subtribe was typically by rainmakers. Each subclan had its own rainmaker, the senior man of the senior descent line of the subclan. He had powers of cursing men engaged in feud, and his person was regarded as a sanctuary for an evildoer. But rainmakers could not act beyond the subtribe. There were also men known as 'ba rukuza ('men whose names are known'), who were regarded as being like 'big trees in the forest'. They were men of wealth and influence and had powers of persuasion, and thus rudimentary political authority. They could occasionally act as arbiters in inter-subtribe disputes. Both rainmakers and 'ba rukuza acted only when asked to do so by the participants in feud or warfare. Fighting was the concern of men only (although women had the task of collecting corpses). Women could travel with reasonable safety between hostile groups, and often acted as go-betweens.

Lugbara traditional religion is based upon the cult of the dead (Middleton, 1960*a*). The unit of ritual is the family cluster, whose members worship their patrilineal ghosts and to a lesser extent their matrilateral dead also. There are a few wider rites, performed by rainmakers and involving prayer to Divine Spirit: these are at the first harvests and at times of drought, of famine or of epidemic. They seem never to involve more than a subtribe, and today have fallen largely into desuetude.

There were in the past, therefore, few direct ties between subtribes. All Lugbara have—and had—the same myths and cosmological beliefs, and recognize themselves as a single people distinct from their neighbours. But before colonial rule the scale of direct relations was narrow, and people had little knowledge as to the boundaries of their society. This has always been a very small-scale society, and old men say that it was rare for anyone during the course of his lifetime to travel more than ten miles or so from the place in which he had been born.

Colonial rule began in 1900. Lugbaraland was in the Lado Enclave, which was administered as part of the Etat Indépendant du Congo under the 1894 agreement between King Léopold II of the Belgians and Great Britain.[1] Actual administration by the Belgians began in 1900, and the area was divided at his death in 1909. The western third remained under Belgian control and was administered from Aru, but in 1910 the remainder passed to the Sudan and was administered from Kajo Kaji. In 1914 this area became part of Uganda, and it was at this date that any firm administration commenced, from the small town of Arua. The line between Uganda and the Congo was drawn as the line of the Nile–Congo watershed, today marked along much of its length by a road. It runs between related settlements and even compounds, and in some places even cuts scattered compounds in half. Administration and taxation have always been different in the two colonial territories. The border has been the scene of continual local movement, and there has always been a largely unoccupied belt of secondary forest along much of its course. Control of the border has been in the hands of the customs officials at the one Ugandan and the one Congolese customs posts, both set up along the road between the respective administrative centres of Arua and Aru. A similar situation has existed in the north, along the Uganda–Sudan border.

[1] For the history and description of the Lado Enclave, see Stigand (1923), which includes a copy of the 1894 Agreement; see also Collins, 1960, 1962*a*, 1962*b*; Lotar, 1946.

The early history of contact: 1880–1920

The period between 1880 and 1920 witnessed the appearance in Lugbaraland of Arabs and Europeans and the spread of their economic and political power over the area and its people. Although we cannot say for certain that these were the first important outside contacts experienced by Lugbara, they were the first contacts of which we can still trace the effects. They were almost certainly also the first external contacts by forces so markedly more powerful than the Lugbara themselves. The Lugbara could not merely absorb them, but were forced to adapt their own society to the new forces.

This span is also the earliest period that could be remembered in detail by people alive in 1950. The Belgians first set up an administration in Lugbaraland in 1900, an occurrence that provides a convenient base line for the memories of old Lugbara men and women. Events before that cannot be dated to within a year or so; but subsequent events can be, at least up to the Yakan revolt of 1919, another important date in Lugbara history. After 1919 it is in fact more difficult to establish the order of events in Lugbaraland. For the moment we may say that this first period, from about 1880 to the 1919 revolt, was a highly traumatic one for the Lugbara. It marked for them the beginning of the destruction of their traditional way of life. Or it would be more accurate to say that it marks for the living, who remember it, the beginning of this destruction: how they regarded it at the time is, of course, quite another matter.

This period also marked the beginning of the extension of the limits of Lugbara society: the Lugbara became part of a wider social system. We may assume that in fact they had always been a part of some wider system, and had never lived in complete isolation; but it seems that this period marks the first time that the Lugbara themselves became aware of so belonging. This came about as a consequence of the Arab slaving and ivory-trading activities in the southern Sudan. This is not the place to attempt to give a history of the Arab and Egyptian colonization and despoliation of the Sudan, since it has been described by many people (e.g., Schweinfurth *et al.*, 1888; Junker, 1892; Schweitzer, 1898). Most of the southern Sudan, occupied by Negro peoples, had been laid waste by Arab slavers and traders during the second part of the nineteenth century; but they had not penetrated the Lugbara highlands to any extent. They had taken slaves from the Kakwa, Kuku, Madi and the other peoples to the north, but not from among the Lugbara themselves. Though early reports of the Sudan government mention that Kakwa slavers were at times active among the northern Lugbara, this occurred after the turn of the century.

The Egyptian slavers and government officers, most of whom were little more than slavers, set up posts in Kakwa country, at Janda and Kenyi's, and others at Kalika's and Bagbei's in Keliko country. All these posts were only a few miles from Lugbaraland. Today the Lugbara speak of Arabs and Europeans (they do not distinguish between them when speaking of early travellers) who travelled through their country before the Belgians came in 1900, but we do not know their identity. In 1877 Dr Junker entered western Lugbaraland, but soon retired. In 1892 the Belgians Van Kerkhoven and Milz entered the country. Van Kerkhoven was accidentally shot there, and Milz crossed to the Nile (Lotar, 1946: 132 ff.). The Nile Valley had been visited by Europeans and Arabs from the time of Miani's visit to Dufile in 1860; but this was not in Lugbaraland proper. The presence of Emin Pasha at Wadelai from 1885 until 1889 was important: although he himself never entered their country, he employed some Lugbara as servants and his troops raided them.

Apart from these external contacts, which were in themselves very slight, the Lugbara were more seriously affected by other events. These were the appearance between 1890 and 1895 of cerebrospinal meningitis, smallpox and rinderpest. There seem always to have been recurrent famines, but there was a particularly severe one about 1895. I have also heard Lugbara say that there were outbreaks of plague and smallpox about this time. These disasters resulted in serious changes in both the human and animal populations, and in considerable movement of people from one area to others. The Lugbara believed that these disasters were connected with the advent of Europeans and Arabs, and also with the movements of African peoples to their north.

There is a third set of factors which marked the beginning of radical external contact. These events followed the spread of the Azande and Mangbetu kingdoms to the north-west and the rise of the Mahdi to the north, and were followed by much population movement by the small tribes of the region. The Mahdi, Muhammad Ahmad ibn al-Sayyid Abdulla, defeated Hicks Pasha in 1883 and General Gordon in 1885, and set up a theocracy at Khartoum (see Holt, 1958; Collins, 1962a). In 1883 the Agar Dinka rose against the then Egyptian government and killed the garrison at Rumbek, a place which had suffered severely at the hands of the Arab slavers. The Dinka possessed a magic water which they drank before battle, and which was generally thought in the area to make them invincible. The water spread among the peoples of the region, who with its aid fought against the government, the Mahdi and the Azande. I have described these struggles elsewhere and need not repeat details here (Middleton, 1963 a; also Driberg, 1931).

The reaction of the Lugbara to these events, all of which affected them to some extent even though they occurred outside the boundaries of Lugbaraland, was to want to obtain this magic water for themselves. About 1891 some important Lugbara visited Kakwa country, where they obtained water from a Kakwa called Rembe who lived near Loka, in Chief Donju's territory near the Kaia river. They returned with the water to Lugbaraland and dispensed it among their followers. It was used, probably among other occasions, by Lugbara who wiped out two patrols of Sudanese troops from Wadelai in 1892, after the departure of Emin Pasha. The Sudanese suffered heavy losses, the Lugbara almost none. The eastern Lugbara women still wore bracelets made of the iron from the guns captured from the Sudanese in the 1920s. The bracelets are said to exist today, though I have not seen one myself (Driberg, 1931). Older Lugbara still tell of these battles and point out the actual sites. I know the names of the Lugbara who visited Rembe, and of some of those who received the water. They were almost all later to be appointed as chiefs by the Belgians.

BELGIAN ADMINISTRATION. The Belgians set up a small post at Ofude in northern Lugbaraland as the headquarters of the administrative district known as Mont Wati. In 1905 a second post was set up at Alenzori, a few miles to the west, and a farm established there for breeding transport oxen. By 1907 there were five Europeans at Ofude and two at Alenzori. There were smaller staging camps elsewhere in Lugbara country and in the neighbouring areas.[1] At Ofude there were also about 250 Congolese troops, whom the Lugbara much feared and whom they called Tukutuku.[2] The administration was little more than nominal; only the Kakwa and the Alur submitted easily to the Belgians, the

[1] These details come from Sudanese Government Intelligence Reports of 1907 and 1908, prepared mainly by members of the survey commission for the proposed Nile–Congo railway, which was never built. The reports were kindly made available to me by Professor Collins. Some further details from them are included in Middleton (1963 a).
[2] So called from the Lingala word for muzzle-loading gun.

Lugbara maintaining a sullen independence. However, the Belgians appointed a few chiefs, whom they called *makoto*. These were the same men who had earlier obtained Rembe's water. Since they knew how to deal with Europeans, with the aid of their magical water, they were put forward as chiefs. The rainmakers stayed in the background. The Belgians used these chiefs, most of whom were related by kinship, to gather grain and other tribute; and they paid them in cattle, making them far wealthier than any Lugbara had ever been before. Their names are still mentioned today with dislike as traitors, but also with respect as men who could tackle the Belgians and could make a profit from them. The Belgians themselves are recalled as pleasant enough men who did little but talk and drink; but the Tukutuku are remembered as evil people.

These *makoto* were mostly the men who had earlier visited Rembe, as I have said. They were able to travel safely through subtribal territories other than their own among the Lugbara, and also among the Kakwa. They seem all to have been 'men whose names are known', but I do not know by what criteria they had acquired that status. Later in the colonial period many chiefs tried to convince the British and Belgian administrations that they were in fact hereditary, but this is certainly untrue. However, the Belgian administration, in an unpublished 'Ethnographic survey' of the Lugbara made in 1933, stated that Lugbara chiefs were members of a traditional aristocracy, and treated them as such (Quix, 1933).

The Belgians withdrew from the posts in 1907, and most of the area later became part of the Sudan, administered from Kajo Kaji. The western part remained under Belgian control, administered from Aru. The Sudanese administration was very slight, and the area was overrun by ivory poachers and other riffraff. Efforts were made to build roads, and some taxes were levied; but in general until the area passed to Uganda in 1914 there was virtually no colonial administration and the chiefs lost their former power.

THE BEGINNING OF BRITISH ADMINISTRATION. The next period in this early traumatic era was that of the early British administration The 'New Areas' came under Uganda control at the beginning of 1914, and Mr A. E. Weatherhead was sent as district commissioner to introduce effective administration. He settled first at Ibrahim's (Laropi) on the Nile, but soon moved inland and set up a post at what is now Arua, in the centre of Lugbaraland and some ten miles from the Congo border. The area under his control included peoples other than the Lugbara—Alur, Madi and Kakwa, with small enclaves of Ndu and 'Bale. For a year or two he was aided by an Indian doctor and a few police only, but was able to subdue the local peoples and to create an administrative organization. His early records, which are still extant in the District Office in Arua, show that whereas the Alur soon accepted his authority, it took a good deal of careful work to bring the Lugbara under administrative control. He referred to them as 'wild and untractable' and as 'shy and unorganized', who needed 'severe measures' before they ceased their perpetual feuding. The older Lugbara still remember Weatherhead with respect and affection: 'Ejerikedi' is regarded in a way that no other European has ever been, as a brave and honest man whom they could trust and who trusted them. I have heard tales about him by the hour, and he is remembered as all that a European and a man of authority should be (and the Lugbara have had a high regard for most of their administrators).

The stages by which the Lugbara were introduced to a cash economy cannot now be traced in detail. The most significant events were the introduction of taxation and the growth of a demand for consumer goods which could only be acquired for cash. Neither the Belgians nor the Sudanese introduced money taxation while they administered the Lado Enclave, although both collected grain and livestock as tribute, mainly to feed their troops. The Belgians introduced taxation in western Lugbara in 1912, and Weatherhead introduced it among the Uganda Lugbara in 1918. The 1915 Report of the provincial commissioner for the Northern Province of Uganda stated that there were 45,000 estimated potential taxpayers in the West Nile District (including Alur and others besides the Lugbara).

The first Baluchi, Arab and Indian traders reached Arua by 1915, bringing salt and cloth to sell. The first store was opened in Arua in the same year and the second at Aru in 1919. One of the oldest storekeepers told me that in the first years his profit came from barter of small amounts of oil crops (mainly simsim) for salt, soap and cloth. The same pattern, that of storekeepers also being middlemen in the trade in cash-crops for export, has persisted to the present day.

Arua Township, which was established in June 1914, consisted then of a couple of small government huts and some tents. The new British administration began to build roads and houses. The work was done by imported Banyoro, since the Lugbara could not be prevailed upon to act as labourers. After a few years, however, local people were substituted for the Banyoro. In 1916, the military authorities sent a strong recruiting party to the district, but with little success; after several weeks they had managed to recruit only fourteen Lugbara. I have been told by several surviving Lugbara soldiers of the First World War that they were forcibly recruited by chiefs and that six deserted almost immediately. However, three hundred more Lugbara were recruited in 1918.

I wish to discuss the later economic development of the district in a following section: here it is enough to say that until about 1920 the outside world had little direct economic impact upon the Lugbara, although some of them were becoming aware of such things as consumer goods and cash crops. After 1920 the sale of their labour was to attain great importance, but this had to wait for the rapid development of Uganda as a whole after the First World War.

THE CULT OF YAKAN. What did occur was a further set of natural disasters, the ever-increasing influence of Weatherhead and the reappearance of the Yakan water cult (Middleton, 1963 a; Driberg, 1931).

Severe outbreaks of cerebrospinal meningitis and rinderpest occurred again about 1912. In addition there was at least one outbreak of smallpox in the years immediately following, and also further cattle epidemics. Finally, in 1918 there was an outbreak of Spanish influenza. These various epidemics are not always very clearly differentiated by the Lugbara. They refer to meningitis as *ndindia* and to smallpox as *mmua*, both words meaning 'secret' or 'sickness sent secretly'. They are regarded as being sent by Divine Spirit, and meningitis is still an epidemic which comes to Lugbaraland with varying intensity almost every dry season, to die out with the first rains in March.

This period was, therefore, marked both by further severe outbreaks of human and cattle sicknesses, and also by the appearance of Weatherhead, who, unlike the earlier administrators, started to control the area with considerable firmness. The result was that the Lugbara turned again to the Yakan water, and on this occasion the prophet Rembe actually came to Lugbaraland to dispense his water and also to organize the cult. He wandered around northern Lugbara setting up cult lodges; and although he was probably in the country for only a few months, he is still remembered vividly by Lugbara who saw him and became

17

cult adherents. Rembe is by now a mythical hero of the Lugbara. He was taken to the Sudan and hanged at Yei in 1917, but Lugbara believe that he in fact escaped death and will return to their country one day to lead them back to a primeval life of happiness and plenty. Rembe had an assistant called Yondu, who stayed for a longer period and who was concerned more with cult organization than with the mystical aspect of the dispensing of water. He too travelled throughout the country setting up lodges. By 1918, when the cult came to the notice of the district commissioner, it was clear that there was much unrest. Police were brought in from southern Uganda; and in April 1919 there was a serious affray at Udupi, in north-eastern Lugbara, in which eleven police and a subcounty chief were killed. Most of the government chiefs were implicated, and were deported to Ankole until 1925; some of them died there. After this the cult died out, although there are traces of it in later years, and it still exists today as one of several spirit cults. Details of the cult symbolism need not concern us here (Middleton; 1960a, 1963a, 1968), but it is pertinent to mention certain points having to do with its organization and its place in Lugbara religious belief.

Rembe was a prophet. His power to lead men and to dispense the water that contained divine power was thought to come directly from Divine Spirit. The original water came from a pool in northern Lugbara in which was thought to live a snake with a human head that could give oracular verdicts. The power in this water could pass to other water if a small amount was diluted with fresh water. Those who drank it were promised certain things: they would not die; their ancestors would come back to life; their dead cattle would do likewise; they could disobey the government and not pay tax; they would be immune against Europeans' rifles, which would fire only water; and they would later get rifles themselves with which to drive the Europeans from the country. At first the cult was not anti-European, nor even markedly anti-government. Men who remember the cult say that they drank the water because they wanted peace, and Rembe told his followers not to disobey the Europeans, who would leave the country of their own accord. At the beginning the main aims of the cult were to remove sickness and bring the dead back to life. The more political aims seem to have developed after Rembe's departure.

The organization of the cult, membership of which became virtually universal in northern and central Lugbara (frequently through terrorization), was very different from any traditional organization of the Lugbara. Almost every subclan had its 'chief' (*opi*) of the cult, who was in no case a rainmaker. Within each subtribal territory there was an organization of three grades of adherents, of which the two highest consisted of men known also as *opi*. The highest grade consisted of those who had acquired water from Rembe himself or from one of his immediate assistants, who seem all to have been Kakwa. These *opi* knew all the special cult songs and so acquired particular ritual knowledge, and they carried small staves of *inzu* wood. Members of the second grade had acquired water from members of the first grade; they did not know all the songs and did not carry sticks. Ordinary adherents composed the third grade. Both men and women became members, although as far as I know women belonged to the lowest grade only. It is said that men and women attending the lodges slept together irrespective of their clan affiliation, a marked departure from traditional Lugbara practice. At the lodges they drank water, sang songs, drilled with dummy rifles made of reeds or wood, and ate and slept, often for long periods.

It is said that 'chiefs' could travel round the countryside in safety, and were regarded as partaking to some extent of the divine power that gave the water and the prophet their power. It is significant that many of these 'chiefs' were not genealogically important men in the traditional lineage system, and none of them were rainmakers. The whole provided a new form of social organization for the Lugbara, one in which neither descent, age, nor sex was significant. Although the lodges seem to have been dispersed on a subtribal basis, at least the 'chiefs' were linked in a network of wealthy men (they received fees for dispensing the water) who enjoyed both power and considerable prestige. This organization died out after 1919.

Rembe was regarded by the Lugbara as coming from Divine Spirit. He was a prophet, with the example before him of the Mahdi, the self-styled Messiah who set up his theocracy in Khartoum. The peoples of this region, who had for so long been subjected to Sudanese influence, could accept this concept. Rembe was a leader who never had the chance to rise to the heights of his power. This was both because he was captured and killed and also because the scale of his leadership was too small. He was a focal figure for this very small-scale society in their need to adapt a new form of social organization to cope with the disasters which overcame them. But he had too far to go to create a viable organization that could compete with European power on equal terms. It is probable also that the changes he was trying to bring about were too foreign to traditional Lugbara culture. If the ancestors had been brought back to life, as he wished to do, this would have destroyed both the traditional cult of the dead and the basis of family and lineage authority. He was supported far more by the younger people than by the elders and especially the rainmakers. The Yakan cult was not an attempt to revert to the traditional way of life of the Lugbara (Rembe was, after all, a Kakwa, not a Lugbara) but to return to what might be called an original Paradise. Rembe tried to lead his adherents to a 'pre-social' phase when the dead would live again and Divine Spirit would rule men through his prophets, without other forms of social ranking or authority. The cult was thus by its very nature foredoomed to failure.

But there were also other relevant factors. The main one was the changing position of younger men and women, who formed the bulk of the adherents. Their independence from their lineage seniors was implicitly recognized in the cult organization. By 1920 the beginnings of the opening up of Lugbaraland to the outside world were being felt; as we shall see, by 1925 labour migration was becoming an integral part of Lugbara economy. With lack of money at home, and also with increasing land shortage, younger men began to emigrate, although only temporarily. From this time on they began to accept the new order introduced by the Europeans instead of trying to fight it and return to the old days. Once having tasted independence from their elders they did not wish to return to dependence upon them. Also they no longer wished to give money and chickens to cult leaders but to keep their wealth themselves. The problems facing young men could henceforth better be solved by labour migration and cash-crop growing than by cult adherence. The teaching of the Christian missions was soon also to have its effects.

The later period of slow change: 1920 to the present day

After the decline of the Yakan cult, the Lugbara seem to have accepted colonial rule and to have adjusted themselves to it and to the changes that it brought. When talking to Lugbara about their experiences, I have been struck by the difficulty of fixing dates of events after the Yakan cult. Of course, different Lugbara have different recollections of this later period. The older chiefs and subchiefs remember events mainly in connection with particular district commissioners whose names they can recall; teachers remember the names of particular missionaries and events associated with them. But ordinary men and virtually all women find it impossible to date events with any degree of exactitude. In this section I shall therefore discuss the main aspects of change rather than try to present a chronological account. It is convenient to discuss first economic development, then political, religious and other changes. These are all closely interrelated but it is possible to show the main outlines in each area. In addition, most older men see these changes as regrettable, as events that have 'destroyed the land', whereas young men see them as providing opportunities to escape from parental and chiefly control.

MONEY AND LABOUR. The main economic developments that affected the Lugbara during their colonial experience were aspects of the change from a former subsistence economy to a peasant economy, with the use of money and the exchange of surplus and consumer goods by market transactions.

Early in this period there were several epidemics which had serious effects on the economy of local groups. Meningitis appeared almost annually, and until controlled by strict (and unpopular) measures sleeping-sickness became a serious problem. There were droughts and crop failures in 1918 and in 1922. There were outbreaks of rinderpest in 1917 and in 1924-5, and there was a serious outbreak of East Coast Fever in 1923 resulting in what the district commissioner's report for that year described as 'colossal' mortality. The seriousness of the outbreaks in 1923, 1924 and 1925 may be gauged from the experience of one typical lineage group in north-central Lugbara which had only three cattle left out of a former total of some hundred and twenty. Formerly wealthy lineages often lost their entire wealth at a single stroke. This resulted in changes in their relative political position vis-à-vis other lineages and necessitated their acquiring cash for taxation and other needs by means other than the sale of hides and skins, which was at first an obvious and easy way of acquiring money.

The country of the Lugbara is too high for many cash-crops. Cotton can be grown only in parts of eastern Lugbara, near the Nile Valley, and oil crops such as simsim have proved inadequate as cash-crops because of the distance of Lugbaraland from the markets of southern Uganda. Besides, facilities for processing oil plants locally have been lacking, although a few Indian traders have occasionally tried to set up mills. Tobacco has been a useful crop and the acreage devoted to it has increased steadily throughout the years. Tobacco factories, owned by Europeans, were set up in the area in 1932; and by 1950 the East African Tobacco Company, which supplied seed and bought leaf, had paid out some £20,000 in tobacco prices and wages. The total income brought into the Lugbara areas in 1951 from sales of cash-crops and hides or skins amounted to over £88,000.

The main source of money for the Lugbara, however, has been the sale of their labour. This became increasingly important as West Nile District became involved in the economic development of the remainder of Uganda. Large-scale railway construction took place in southern Uganda in the early 1920s. Lugazi Sugar Works, in Busoga, was opened in 1924. Other large employers who have since relied largely on Lugbara labour began to operate later in the period: Kakira Sugar Works and the sisal estates at Masindi Port opened in 1929, and the tobacco factories in Bunyoro in 1931. Until the 1931 depression the European- and Indian-owned timber and other estates in Bunyoro increased in numbers and in their demands for labour.

In 1922 the district commissioner, West Nile, wrote in his annual report that the Alur and Madi were going south, staying there only three or four months to earn money for their poll tax, but that very few Lugbara did so. By 1925, however, the situation was altering, and many Lugbara were responding to calls for labour. They went mainly to the railway construction at Masindi Port, Mbulamuti, and Namasagali, and to the Bunyoro plantations.

Since that period there has been a general conflict between the local administration in West Nile and the demands of the southern labour employers. The local administration recognized that Lugbara had to go south to earn needed cash, but also realized that unlimited migration would lead to rapid destruction of Lugbara social life. In 1925 the first accredited labour recruiters arrived at Arua; in 1948 the West Nile Recruiting Organization was formed by the big three Indian companies which used most of the labour (the sugar works at Kakira and Lugazi and the sisal estate at Masindi Port). The Bunyoro plantations ceased to recruit labour in West Nile after the depression, obtaining what labour they wanted from free-lance Lugbara already working in Bunyoro.

Lugbara migrants come and have always come from both Uganda

and Congo counties, although recruiting in the Congo for work in southern Uganda has been nominally forbidden, since the demands in the Congo of the Kilo Moto gold-mines (which were in operation during the First World War) and other employers have been regarded as paramount. But the greater attraction of Uganda (including higher wages, better treatment, lack of forced labour, lack of brutal punishments for desertion and other offences) meant that Congolese Lugbara have in fact worked mainly in Uganda rather than in the Congo. In 1951 over 5,000 Uganda Lugbara and over 2,500 Congo Lugbara went south. Migrants have either been recruited by the labour recruiting organizations or have gone south independently, the proportion of independents increasing regularly over the years.

The main employers of contract labour, the Indian-owned sugar and sisal estates, employed only a minority of Lugbara labour. At the time of the 1947 census half the total migrants lived in Bunyoro and about a third in Buganda; almost all worked in employment other than these Indian-owned firms. Most worked as sharecroppers and tenants of various kinds, growing cotton and other crops for Nyoro and Ganda landlords; and many also worked for themselves in the newly settled areas of northern Bunyoro. They would often work for more than one employer. The migrants, with a fair proportion of Lugbara women, lived for the most part in small settlements of Lugbara. Many of the settled migrants in southern Uganda went south on contract, paid for by the recruiters, and would desert as soon as possible after arrival. Although they thus forfeited their free repatriation at the termination of their contract, they found it worth while, since they could earn far more money as tenants for Ganda landowners or working independently in small shops and firms in Kampala and other urban centres.

Most men who went south on contract came back fairly soon with comparatively little money; and they tended to return again when they felt the need for more. The usual length of stay was eight or nine months, although some stayed on after completing their contract with recruiting employers, spending some time as independent migrants. But few stayed away for much longer than a year.

The men who went south independently stayed away longer but brought back greater amounts, and did not return south so often. The independent migrants provided most of the permanently 'lost' men who never returned to their homes or who did so only after several years, often having married and established families in the south.

Migrants returned after a year or so in southern Uganda with money and goods, usually cloths, blankets, various trinkets and small gifts. In addition, some money was usually sent home during the migrant's absence. In the early 1950s the total cash value of money and goods brought and sent home by any migrant was about shs. 60/- for a single year's work. This figure takes into account that migrants who went south to work for Nyoro and Ganda cotton-farmers earned rather more than those who went on contract to the sugar and sisal estates; but it must be remembered that contract migrants were also fed and housed at their place of work, and had their passage paid in both directions. A very approximate estimate of the annual income per head among the total Uganda Lugbara population of West Nile District in 1951 from labour migrancy was about shs. 19/-.

In addition the Lugbara had a cash income from sales of produce within West Nile District. Local sources of employment, which were virtually nil, may be ignored. The cash income per head of population in 1951 from the sale of animal products (hides and skins), tobacco, sunflower seed (introduced in 1950) and cotton amounted on average to shs. 10/60.

The total cash income per head from both sales of produce and labour migration was therefore about shs. 30/-. This figure refers to income per head of population, and not merely to those men who went south as labour migrants. It does not include income from local wage labour, nor to money acquired from sale of crops or livestock to other Lugbara, but only to money in the form of earnings or of receipts for crops or livestock sold to traders who exported them. Since 1951 the income from tobacco growing has increased very considerably, but I do not have detailed figures.

The average Lugbara elementary family consists of 4·5 persons. The average elementary family income was, therefore, about shs. 135/- from extra-district labour or cash sale. Wage labour and sale of crops and livestock within the district probably amounted to about shs. 100/- for an average elementary family. The amount of foodstuffs exchanged by barter cannot be known with any degree of reliability, nor can that exchanged in the form of gifts between kin. The latter was certainly important, since men who earn wages or who grow a considerable surplus of goods are expected to distribute much of their earnings and surplus among their closer kin. A few labour migrants would return after three or four years with up to shs. 1,000/-, and many men earned wages which might amount to shs. 200/- or 400/- a year. Although I have included these high money-incomes in the figures given above, these earnings were usually distributed among kin and neighbours, and the same applied to any extra large amounts of foodstuffs grown. This distribution was effected at markets and at kinship feasts.

It is not possible to compute with any accuracy whether or not the amount of home-produced supplies consumed by the household is greater or less today than it was before European impact. The density of population is greater, and today there is virtually no unused nor long-fallow land. Today the land used for cash-crops has presumably reduced that available for food crops, but the average acreage per head does not seem to have diminished to any marked extent. The fact that some modern crops have higher yields than some traditional ones is significant here. It may be said that including home-produced income the average total income per head is greater today than it was formerly, but the amount cannot be stated with much accuracy.

A last point about labour migration that must be mentioned is that there is a congruence between the number of labour migrants and the degree of population pressure, as indicated in the following tabulation:

Table 1. *Absentee rates for Lugbara labourers, 1951*

County	Absentee rate (%)	Density of persons to the square mile
Maraca	26·5	240
Ayivu	20·9	240
Terego	17·8	80
Vura	13·7	65
Aringa	12·4	15

The figures for Terego, Vura and Aringa are deceptive, since these counties include large tracts of empty or almost empty land. The densely occupied central subcounties of Terego average 154 persons to the square mile, and the centre of Vura averages 140 persons to the square mile.

People thus went on labour migration not only to earn cash, but also to ease the pressure on the land, while still keeping their rights to lineage land. The factors that are relevant here, and the effects of labour migration, may better be understood after consideration of land shortage and changes in patterns of settlement in recent times.

LAND AND SETTLEMENT. Labour migration is one of the most obvious factors observable in Lugbara society today that has developed as a consequence of the introduction of a cash economy, as one aspect of a complex of changes in the economy of the area. It is a partial consequence of land shortage and of changes in patterns of settlement and farming. It enables the Lugbara at least partially to accept these changes, over which they have little or no control, without having to change the form of their society too radically or too suddenly.

During the present century there has developed an ever-increasing pressure upon the land. There is no doubt that the total population has increased with the enforcement of peace and improved medical facilities under the colonial governments. In addition, the enforcement of peace has meant that there is no longer the need for people to live together in large settlements for mutual defence against human enemies and wild animals.

The traditional pattern of settlement of the compounds of a subtribe has now vanished in every part of central Lugbaraland, although it is still found in some of the outlying areas of the east and north where there is some spare land (although of poor fertility) and many wild animals. In place of the old pattern there is virtually continuous settlement across the country, the former zones of outside fields between subtribes being filled with compounds and home fields. Formerly there was a continual slow movement from north to south by a process of migration-drift, and slow but continual adjustment of subtribal boundaries by warfare. By these means the optimum population to a given area of land was maintained. One of the consequences of the establishment of colonial administration was the appointment of chiefs over subtribal and smaller areas (see below), and the boundaries between them were demarcated. Instead of a subtribal centre with its land stretching outwards until the boundaries met those of neighbouring subtribes, the lines were drawn and regarded as important, both by European administrators and by chiefs. Movement of local groups across these boundaries was no longer permitted. The fixing of boundaries between subtribes and between smaller territorial units where they happened to be in the years between 1914 and 1920 has led to an increasing disparity between population and carrying capacity of the land. Some areas have become far more crowded than immediately neighbouring areas. This situation has been mitigated in three ways—by the emigration of individuals who attach themselves to matrilateral kin living elsewhere, by movement to the outlying and emptier parts of Lugbaraland, and by labour migration to the south from the most crowded areas.

The consequence of the disparity between population and the carrying capacity of the land has been that the traditional distribution of types of fields between women of a settlement can no longer be made. Indeed the scarcest type, the irrigated field in the valley bottoms, is frequently no longer available at all. Fields are cultivated for longer periods without fallow than they would traditionally have been. This tendency has also been accentuated by the absence of so many younger men on labour migration, since it is chiefly they who traditionally do the arduous work of opening the fields at the beginning of the agricultural year. Crops that involve lighter labour and have heavier yields have been substituted for the traditional staples. Today cassava has the largest acreage of any crop planted, although it is disliked by the Lugbara as a food. It was not even mentioned in a list of crops grown in the district in 1931, and extensive planting of it as a famine crop was started only in 1944–5.

Maize was introduced into the area about 1925, and today has a large acreage, as has the sweet potato, another crop recently introduced. Cassava and sweet potato are ideal crops for families many of whose men are absent on labour migration. Both have high yields, need little weeding, and can be stored in the ground for long periods.

The traditional domestic economic unit was the family cluster, under the authority of its elder, and the traditional field working group consisted of the men and women of the cluster. Although each wife had fields of all the types I have mentioned, there was considerable exchange of produce between the wives of any one man or of sets of brothers. But in most areas this traditional pattern has changed. The domestic economic unit is now the compound and often the elementary family (only 37 per cent of Lugbara men have more than one wife), although the authority of the elder is still held to be proper and is still largely effective. A woman finds it more difficult to ensure a regular supply of all types of foodstuffs that she may normally need. In the past she and her co-wives could draw upon one another's supplies (although each wife had control of her own stores), but nowadays she is much less likely to be able to do so. She must therefore obtain extra supplies of particular foods, as well as supplies for unforeseen occasions, from markets, which did not exist in the traditional system. Not all foods are in equal demand at markets. The most wanted grains are maize and white sorghum. These are used almost entirely for beer, and the demand for beer is the most difficult of any to foresee. It is needed in almost all religious rites and for many ceremonial occasions, as well as for casual visiting of kin. Since most of these occasions cannot be foreseen, maize and sorghum for the essential beer have usually to be obtained from markets. Any beer left over is sold for cash at beer drinks, the woman keeping the money as she thinks fit. The introduction of maize, the scarcity of irrigated land (on which maize and white sorghum are grown) and the growth of markets are interconnected.

Women also exchange cassava for other foodstuffs which are preferred, especially as relishes; these are particularly ground-nuts, peas, beans and simsim. Cassava is wanted by poorer women and those who lack large fields. It is thought rather shameful to give guests cassava, and it is eaten mainly by large families in which many children have to be fed. It is bought by women who sell the rarer foodstuffs and buy cheaper food in exchange, thereby deriving a profit in cash from the transaction as well as food for their children.

TRADE AND MARKETS. The small townships of the area date from about 1920, although a few petty traders had entered the area earlier. Except for the administrative centres of Arua and Aru, these gazetted townships are very small, only one other having more than half a dozen shops at the time of my stay. The shops are kept by Indians and Arabs, and offer a vast array of petty consumer goods, including cloth. The traders usually supplement their incomes by acting as buyers of tobacco, hides and skins and other commodities produced in the area, travelling around the countryside for the purpose. They may also act as labour recruiters and as hawkers. There are also non-gazetted centres, in which there are small shops owned by Africans—few of them Lugbara—who are mainly tailors or keepers of 'hotels' or beer clubs. Their range of goods is more limited and their profits much smaller. Traders, whether African, Indian or Arab, play certain important economic roles in Lugbaraland. They provide imported consumer goods, offer certain skills (particularly tailoring), and cater for the welfare of travellers along the few roads. They also buy the less important cash-crops, providing a source of cash to the local population (Middleton, 1962).

Besides the shops, large and small, and a few peripatetic traders and hawkers, there are markets throughout Lugbaraland. The market is now a recognized institution. The first one was opened about 1925. Before then exchange had been carried on solely by traditional means. Markets are found near all subcounty headquarters and at a few other places. They are open one or two days a week and are attended by most people in the neighbourhood. Markets are controlled by licensed local entrepreneurs, who charge a small entrance fee to women wishing to sell crops, pots, grinding-stones or other commodities. The market 'owner' has to keep it clean and to maintain order. He usually makes a handsome income, and many owners control several markets.

Women who sell in the market are both ordinary housewives who come to sell small surpluses of foodstuffs and to buy others, or who are semi-specialists selling pots, baskets and other items. The medium of exchange is cash. Besides catering for the needs of women to buy foodstuffs, markets also act as distributing centres for cash. People could not produce the cash for taxes if there were no markets, since money is still scarce in Lugbaraland and enters from only a few sources. Much of it is soon removed in the form of taxes. All adult men must have cash for taxes, but not all of them can acquire it themselves; they do so through their wives' transactions at the market-place. Markets thus are the means by which small amounts of locally produced foodstuffs and commodities such as pots and gourds are distributed within a neighbourhood. They are a source of money income to the local population as well, and they permit a wide distribution of imported consumer goods.

The market in Lugbaraland may be seen as an accommodating institution. It is a response to changes in the size of the basic residential group and in patterns of settlement and farming; and it offsets the effects of labour migration in that it enables the Lugbara to avoid drastic modifications in their way of living caused by the impact of the outside world. The large self-sufficient family clusters of traditional Lugbara society can give way relatively smoothly to the small, non-self-sufficient households of today only if housewives can rely upon a frequent exchange of small local surpluses. This has been achieved through the growth of the small local market.

Although most women who go to a market both enter and leave it with foodstuffs, they also bring away money. They may keep the money for future needs, to buy domestic utensils or to buy their children clothing. In addition they may hand over some of it to their husbands and their brothers, who need it for taxes, consumer goods and cattle for bridewealth. Formerly a young man had a formally defined status, associated with his age, his marital status, his genealogical position in his lineage, and factors of personality and influence. Today he may increase his status, or more accurately, may hasten its increase, by the acquisition of money. He may acquire a wife before his fellows; he may buy beer for his seniors; and he may also become more independent of the authority of his elders by lessening his economic dependence upon them. The commonest way for a man to get money is to go to southern Uganda as a labour migrant or to grow cash-crops, mainly tobacco. Young men can grow tobacco and earn their own money from it merely by opening land in the outlying areas of the country, where in fact poorer land makes for better crops of tobacco. But labour migration and moving away to the outskirts of the country have certain disadvantages. If they can, men prefer to stay in their own homes, since their women and kin are there. If they go away for too long they may be regarded as 'lost' and may lose both chances to acquire higher status and even rights in their lineage land. Many say that the cash rewards are not commensurate with the disadvantages. An alternative way of acquiring money is for a man to be given it by his sisters or his wives. The former method is virtually universal, the latter less so because wives have other financial responsibilities, especially towards their children. Almost all unmarried girls make money in markets and give it to their brothers, who look after their sisters' personal interests in return.

The desire for a higher, or at least a more independent, status than their traditional one is a reason why many women trade at markets. They can earn money to buy themselves clothes and ornaments, so that they are seen to be progressive and desirable to young men who have been to southern Uganda and observed the outside world there. This applies particularly to unmarried girls and to divorced women, the latter said to be an increasing category in Lugbara society. Women and girls who hang around too much at markets and at the small shops where tailors are sewing clothes are often said to be loose and merely looking for lovers. Some of these trading women (especially the divorced women among them) form informal associations to protect their interests against shopkeepers and hawkers, and to maintain their good names against gossip. They may also form small groups specializing in a particular set of commodities over a small area, moving from one market to another and not underselling one another. These groups are very informal, and it is significant that they consist of women from different lineages, a marked break with tradition.

TECHNOLOGY. Shops and traders have been introducing imported consumer goods to the Lugbara since the First World War, and specialist government departments have been urging the Lugbara to grow better crops, to improve their hygiene, to use modern medical facilities and so on. Many consequences are visible in the everyday life of the ordinary Lugbara family, especially among those who have been south as labour migrants and have seen other countries. In the domestic sphere metal pots are replacing local clay pots, and imported hoes and matchets are widely used (although for domestic purposes women still use traditional knives made by Ndu smiths). Almost every household uses small tin lamps and kerosene for lighting, matches for fire making, soap for washing, and simple imported drugs for medical purposes. Most men possess some kind of European clothing, and most younger women own a few pieces of coloured cloth or even Ganda-style clothing for special occasions, although the traditional leaves are usually worn by all women. Men often smoke cigarettes and drink European-type beer, although the expense of these and similar items limits their use to special occasions. Many younger men have bicycles.

More basic, perhaps, have been the consequences of the introduction of new seed by the Agricultural Department, of the sleeping-sickness and other health regulations enforced by the Medical Department, of eucalyptus and cassia trees to provide building material and fuel, and the teaching of skills such as carpentry by the missions. Compared to many parts of Africa, radical technological change has hardly begun in this region; but it is on the threshold of appearing and of making rapid development.

The establishment and development of the administrative structure

Four main problems faced the first administrators in Lugbara. They had to end the state of almost continuous feud and warfare between small groups; they had to obtain food; they had to recruit labour to build roads; and they had to create a permanent local administration that could be represented by recognized chiefs. Weatherhead put an end to serious fighting by a system of policing and of making 'alliances' with certain tribes, which were placed under his protection on the condition that they did not initiate hostility. Communication was not easy, largely because of difficulties of language—Lugbara and Madi are so different in every respect from the other languages of Uganda that interpreters were almost unobtainable. Use was made of the remnants of Emin Pasha's Sudanese troops, some of whom were Madi and a few Lugbara. They were used as 'agents', each responsible for an area. Later a single Nubi 'agent' was appointed to be responsible for the Lugbara. He was not withdrawn until the late 1920s.

The problem of setting up local administrative units was difficult. The largest indigenous units were subtribes, small aggregates of some 4,000 people. There were about forty-five of them in that part of Lugbaraland under Weatherhead's authority. A senior man from each subtribe was appointed as a representative, and several subtribes were grouped into chiefdoms. Chiefdom boundaries were drawn on geographical grounds, or according to main cultural and dialectal divisions, or in some cases according to local traditions which recognized an early mythical connection between clan groups that lived in one vicinity. There was thus considerable uncertainty as to which chiefdom many subtribes belonged to, and subtribes would change their chiefdom according to the personality of their chief and other factors. This continual realignment went on for several years.

However, by the early 1920s the situation had attained some degree of stability. There were a dozen 'counties', each under a chief, the *sultan*. Each of these was divided into three or four 'subcounties', each under a subchief, the *wakil*. Within the subcounty were 'parishes', under a chief called *mukungu*; and under him were several 'headmen' or *nyapara*. The subchiefs were the highest authorities set over indigenous units, in that in most cases a subcounty was coterminous with a subtribe. Parishes seem usually to have been coterminous with major sections (see Middleton, 1956, 1960 b).

This organization has persisted to the present day, with continual amalgamation of units at all levels for greater administrative convenience. There are now five counties in Uganda Lugbara, each with from three to five subcounties. Whereas the average population of one of the originally created counties was about 15,000, it is now between 25,000 and 40,000. County chiefs are now known as *opi*, a Lugbara word used for rainmakers and 'men whose names are known' generically, and subchiefs as *joago*, a Nilotic word. Parish chiefs and headmen are called by their original titles.

With the amalgamation of administrative units has gone the growth of local government staff at the chiefly and subchiefly levels; parish chiefs and headmen have no official staff. The first chiefs appointed advisers from their own kin and close friends. Although they were unpaid and unrecognized by the government, they wielded considerable authority. They also had tribal police, chosen from among kin and friends, and quite distinct from the Uganda police stationed at district headquarters and a few other posts and under direct control of the Uganda government.

Above this level at the time of my stay were the district commissioner and his staff (European), and that of the district council, with a district paramount chief, judge, secretary and other officials (all African). These officials were drawn from the chiefly bureaucracy, by rotation or more permanent appointment, and chiefs were formally responsible to the council. West Nile District includes peoples other than the Lugbara, and these officials were drawn from all the tribes in an unofficial rotation.

The roles of these various functionaries differ considerably. Chiefs and subchiefs have officially recognized courts, and only they can award officially recognized punishments of fines and imprisonment. Above them are district courts, which are primarily appeal courts but with sole jurisdiction in respect of certain offences that cannot be dealt with by chiefs' courts. County chiefs' courts are primarily appeal courts from subchiefs' courts, which usually meet once a week. Chiefs at both levels have lock-ups in which to incarcerate remand and short-term prisoners. They are also responsible to the Uganda government and to the district administration for measures such as tax-collection, inspection and collection of famine crops, sleeping-sickness inspection and bush-clearing, latrine and waterhole digging. Many are the agents not only of the administration in their areas, but also of specialized services of the central government. They act as representatives of their people and guardians of their interests at district and other councils. Chiefs and subchiefs are salaried officials, liable to promotion and demotion, to movement from one area to another within both Lugbara and West Nile District, as well as to dismissal.

The lower administrative functionaries are different, in that they act as agents of the chiefs and appear to the people to be directly responsible to the chiefs. Certainly in most cases it is the chiefs who appoint them. They have neither institutionalized courts nor power of fining, although they may have considerable authority. They hold informal meetings, which we may call 'moots', at which matters of judicial and administrative importance are discussed.[1] Any civil case is discussed at a moot before being taken to the subchief's court, and at this first stage the parish chief and headmen usually try to settle cases by amicable agreement. If they cannot do so, then they act as sponsors for the people concerned at the court, and a subchief may rely largely on their opinions as to the merits of a case. Parish chiefs and headmen are responsible to the chiefs for apprehending criminals, for ensuring that taxpayers and labourers on work of public importance appear where required at the proper time, and for acting as their people's general representatives to the chiefs. Much of their work is done at beer-parties and on other informal occasions. Councillors are selected from men of local importance. They often include representatives of special interests, such as mission schools, or they are ex-headmen and ex-subchiefs who have been dismissed or have retired. They meet regularly and play an important part in the system of communication between chief and people.

Lugbara distinguish between the two grades of higher chiefs on the one hand and the parish chiefs and headmen on the other. The former are known generically as 'chiefs' (*cifu*); and at the time of my stay they were also known as *mundu*, the term used for both Europeans and Africans with authority and status in the present governmental system. Chiefs are distinguished as a category apart from the lower functionaries, who are not called by these terms—although the position of parish chief, *mukungu*, is often marginal. I shall refer to county and subcounty chiefs as 'chiefs' and to parish chiefs and headmen as 'headmen', since they form two clearly distinguishable categories.

THE SETTLEMENT OF DISPUTES. The most important aspect of the political role of the chiefs, as far as Lugbara are concerned, is its judicial one. There have always been disputes to settle, both before and after the coming of the Europeans, but Lugbara see the chiefs' purely administrative actions as being extraneous to everyday life at the local level.

In the indigenous system disputes were settled by the exercise of

[1] The term 'moot' is used by myself; these meetings are referred to by Lugbara as the 'words' (*e'yo*) of a headman.

force or by religious sanctions, depending on the lineage relationship between the parties concerned. The nature of the remedial action was determined by that relationship rather than by the intrinsic nature of the offence. The traditional principle is still operative, but another has been added, dependent upon the nature of the offence itself, this being the only interest of the administration. As a result, both factors are now significant. Certain traditional offences, such as homicide, are treated as criminal actions by central government courts. Other actions, which did not exist traditionally, such as tax evasion, are also regarded by the government as crimes, on account of their nature. We may say that today those offences traditionally dealt with by the use of socially approved force (e.g., homicide, adultery, divorce and other cases to do with bridewealth, etc.—all between groups whose kinship tie is non-existent or irrelevant in the given situation) and new administrative offences (e.g., tax evasion) are tried by government courts supported by sanctions introduced by the government. But those traditionally resolved by religious or mystical sanctions, and concerned mainly with the maintenance of domestic and kinship authority, in which the government has no primary interest or responsibility (e.g., disobedience to senior kinsmen, impiety to the dead) are still dealt with by the use of traditional sanctions.

The new judicial machinery consists of two parts which interact. One includes the courts of chiefs and district commissioners; the other consists of the moots summoned by headmen, at which councillors and elders of the area usually attend. Most cases, except those reserved for district courts only and administrative offences such as tax evasion, are first discussed in moots. Discussion there may take place even where the parties are of different administrative divisions. Headmen try to settle as many cases as they can before the parties go to the courts proper. A case discussed at a moot is not formally recognized as being a case at law until the headman informs the chiefs' court that it will soon be brought before it. Often public discussion at the moot leads to mutual agreement to settle. In many or most of the cases that are sent up to chiefs' courts two headmen are concerned, one representing each party. They assemble the evidence and accompany their parties to the court as sponsors.

There are no figures for the number of cases that are discussed and settled at moots and of those that subsequently go to higher courts. Records are not kept at moots, as headmen cannot award official penalties. I estimate that about half are settled there. Administrative offences are dealt with by direct summons to a chief's court and are not discussed at moots.

From figures collected from certain subcounty chiefs' court records for 1953, a total of about 40 per cent were in respect of seduction of an unmarried girl. Next were those brought by a chief for failure to obey government order or to pay tax, about 30 per cent of the cases. Third in numerical importance were cases of assault brought by one person against another, some 15 per cent of the total. There were only a few cases of debt and of other offences.

In the civil cases, where the clan and lineage affiliation of the parties is known, about two-thirds were between members of the same subtribe and one-third between members of different subtribes. About two-thirds were between members of different major sections (including those between different subtribes), the groups between which relations are primarily political in the indigenous Lugbara system, and which were traditionally settled by fighting and not by religious sanctions.

Traditionally the major factor that determines whether sanctions based on force or those based on mystically caused sickness should be brought into operation is the lineage relationship between the parties. Today moots and courts deal with matters that were traditionally resolved by organized intergroup fighting, which is now prohibited. The main function of moots is to check hostility of the kind that might lead to violence, so that it can be settled by the chiefs' courts. Neither courts nor moots are primarily concerned with relations between persons of the same major section. In the figures mentioned the majority of the civil cases were between members of different major sections, whose relations with one another lack ritual content and which were traditionally controlled by force.

It can be seen that today the chiefs' courts have taken over one of the more important functions formerly performed by the institution of intergroup fighting. In the sense that fighting provided a sanction for intergroup relations, so today does the power of these courts. In both cases organized force is used to settle disputes, but the source and control of the force has changed.

There is a direct relationship between this situation and the difference in status and role of chiefs and of headmen. Until Lugbara society changes its structure radically, a headman cannot be in charge of a unit greater at the most than a subtribe. These and major sections are the principal political units in the sense that they are concerned in conflicts that are channelled upwards at moots. It is chiefs who settle disputes (concerned mainly with rights in women) between these political units, and there is a minimum size for the units over which they have direct authority. They must be above the parties and so impartial, in a structural sense; whereas headmen need not be so—and in fact cannot be so—since they act as sponsors or representatives for political units.

THE ROLE OF CHIEF. The judicial role of chiefs is only one aspect of their total political role, although for Lugbara it is the most important. Lugbara do not see the present political system as a single whole, although they are caught up in it in every part of their lives. The political structure has changed during this century as a result of the creation of a centralized administrative system, with the district commissioner at the apex of the administrative pyramid. Yet Lugbara themselves still conceive of politics in traditional terms, as consisting of relations between units in a system without centralized political authority. Chiefs play new roles, for which the Lugbara have no place in their conception of their own society. On the whole, they consider their chiefs to be on the side of the central government in any conflict of interests that may arise between the government and the people. In this context it is the headmen who are thought to be their representatives, while the chiefs are considered rather as the agents of a government set above the people.

The position of the chief—and especially of the subchief, who comes into greater everyday contact with the people than does the county chief—is a difficult one. Chiefs must try cases impartially that would formerly have been settled by force and must therefore be above the interests of local groups; yet they are expected to behave as true Lugbara, as kin and neighbours. The ideal is that of some of the past county chiefs, who were local men with smaller chiefdoms than the present ones. They saw the relationship of chief and followers in terms of kinship and neighbourhood and could play their roles in these terms. But the modern chief has had to become a bureaucrat. His relations with his people are impersonal and allow no room for kinship and neighbourhood considerations. The fact that his people may be his kin is not recognized by the government, although the chief and his kin are only too aware of these ties; and kinsmen expect their chief to give them preferential treatment. With the greater development of an administrative bureaucracy the difficulty of the chief's position increases. Formerly administrative, kinship and general social roles were hardly kept apart. Today there is an increasingly sharp distinction between them. As this difficulty increases, so does the rate of movement of chiefs—and especially of subchiefs—both from one post to another and also from subchieftainship to positions outside the chiefly hierarchy altogether.

Until very recently all appointments as chief, of either grade, were made by the district commissioner, who also confirmed or vetoed the appointments of headmen made by the chiefs. Today appointments at the highest level are made by the district council and district commissioner in consultation, and lower appointments by various elective procedures. In effect, however, headmen are still appointed by the chiefs in consultation with their councils.

It is clear from past district records that there has been a general tendency to make the senior chiefs' posts hereditary. Hereditary succession has occurred in several instances. In 1950, of the five present county chiefs two were sons of former county chiefs and one of a very important 'man whose name is known', who was also a subchief in the early days of the administration. The first county chiefs appointed at the beginning of the century were soon regarded as being in the pay of the Europeans and became highly unpopular. As I have said, they were originally put forward by the people because they had been among the leaders of the Yakan cult. The leaders of the revolt at Udupi in 1919 were almost all these same chiefs, who seem to have acted thus partly in an effort to regain prestige and the confidence of their people. Many of them were dismissed after the revolt, and some were deported outside the district. This apparently helped them regain their popularity. Some chiefs remained in office for as much as twenty years, and this aided their pretensions to hereditary status. They tried to prolong high status by ensuring that their sons should succeed them. They also tried to select subchiefs and parish chiefs from among their kin. In fact, two of the five county chiefs who had succeeded their fathers in those posts tried to choose all their subcounty and parish chiefs from close kin. They were not able to do so, owing to the district commissioner's refusal to confirm obviously incompetent young men in high positions, and owing also to popular feeling against some of the appointments. They have had more success in cases where the appointee is not formally set over the people. At the time of my stay, for example, three of the five non-commissioned officers in the local police, in charge of detachments at county headquarters, were near kin of the chiefs concerned and had followed their eminent relatives from one headquarters to another. Today, with the greater mobility of subchiefs, these kin appointments are becoming increasingly difficult. Also, whereas in the past such nepotic appointment had been accepted by the people as being apparently the way of the Europeans, more recently it has been explained to them by the government that they may choose their own subchiefs. In such cases the sons of one or two important chiefs have been beaten at the polls. All the same, these county chiefs have close ties of kinship with other chiefs and in some cases more than one tie simultaneously.

Not unnaturally it has been government policy to select efficient chiefs. Over the years chiefdoms have been reduced in number and the more inefficient chiefs have been discarded. The original county chiefs were all 'men whose names are known' and whose names became more known as their wealth increased during their tenure of office. Most were kin; a few were originally Sudanese soldiers. They seem all to have been illiterate and uneducated, though by no means hostile to education, which they recognized as essential to political advancement. They took the chance to educate their sons and close kin, who thereby became eligible for high position. At the time I worked in Lugbaraland every county chief had been to school (although not all had more than primary education). They had moved upwards through a mission education that often included several years of teaching followed by training in junior grades of the local government service within the district. One or two accepted traditional religious beliefs, but the missions provided their means of advancement. They were in frequent and confidential contact with Europeans and exercised very considerable and often autocratic authority. They were among the few wealthy men of the community.

There have always been many subcounty chiefs, and originally they represented the larger subtribes. The administration apparently paid a good deal of attention to local public opinion in selecting them, and many of the earlier ones were chosen on account of genealogical status, personality and other factors, but hardly for educational ability (their clerks took care of registers and records). In 1950 they were mostly under forty, with at least primary education. Several had secondary education. Like the county chiefs they tended to have worked in government and missions. Most were related to other chiefs, but few had ties of kinship with their subjects; and there was considerable movement from one post to another.

THE BEGINNINGS OF SOCIAL STRATIFICATION. Chiefs also have attributes that emphasize their difference from and their opposition to traditional functionaries and headmen. Chiefs and their clerks and senior police (both the latter having considerable power) are literate members of a bureaucracy. They are representatives of the *'ba odiru*, the 'New People', the educated and semi-educated protégés of the Europeans. New People are becoming a distinct group found in every Lugbara chiefdom and they regard themselves as members of a class and as distinct from the local inhabitants. They tend to regard clan and lineage ties as comparatively unimportant. Their families intermarry, they attend the same schools and they are even becoming conscious of having ties with similar people outside the borders of Lugbaraland. They move from one area to another in the course of their work. They provide the lower administrative officials of the central government, the teachers and the traders, and are of necessity associated with either the government or the missions, the sources of power and education. They are differentiated from other people also by their ordinary behaviour, by their way of life and dress, and, if they are government servants, by occupying the new tiled brick houses built for them by the district council.

At a lower level the parish chiefs and headmen are the relatively uneducated and 'traditional' members of the administrative system. They have ties with local groups which rarely extend outside traditional limits and are associated with traditional Lugbara groupings and not with a single class which spreads across them. In contrast to the New People, they are often referred to as 'our people', *'ba amani*. Lugbara assume, sadly, that the numbers of such parish chiefs and headmen are declining and that they must give way to younger New People. But any attempt by chiefs to install New People at this level is met with considerable hostility. The loyalties of New People are thought to have changed and they themselves to have risen above the sense of personal responsibility towards members of their own kin groups.

With the present-day development of local government from a system concerned primarily with the transmission of orders downwards to a more complex one concerned with the new and manifold tasks of modern local administration and social development, there goes the greater transfer of power to the New People. Change in Lugbara is generated from above, and the New People are the only ones in contact with its source. They are the people who can manipulate the new bureaucratic machinery of government. At present it is government policy to appoint promising young chiefs and officials to temporary posts at the African local government headquarters in Arua. After a period they return to chiefly duties and may be promoted.

Also, it is only the New People who can move out of the administrative system to gain power in other ways. So far in West Nile District there has been little opportunity for people to acquire money or power outside government and missions, and it is only the government that has been able to provide a reasonable official salary. But it may be assumed that if the wealth of the area increases there will be more outside work; this will be open only to New People, however. At present the only spheres other than petty trading open to men who wish to break away from traditional occupations are centred on supporting or opposing mission activities, and here New People hold the power. Also, as I mention in the following section, all such endeavours have originated outside the district, among non-Lugbara, whom local opinion links with the New People.

CHRISTIANITY AND ISLAM. The Christian missions have had a considerable effect upon traditional Lugbara social life and institutions. It is not easy to measure this impact, but the observer in Lugbaraland at the time of my stay soon became aware of their virtually all-permeating influence upon everyday Lugbara life. The Lugbara were not, of course, always aware of mission influence any more than they were always aware of the activities of the government. Besides, the effects of the missions were perhaps noticeable less in the field of religion itself than in almost any other field, since the missions were significant primarily as carriers of Western culture rather than as Christian evangelizing organizations. This is, of course, a personal impression only, and not one that would be accepted by members of the missions themselves. And to say it is not in any way to denigrate the effects of the missionaries' activities or their worth. Indeed, Lugbara have often said to me that if it had not been for the memory of Weatherhead and the personal behaviour of some of the better-known missionaries, their notions of

Europeans would have been very much less favourable than they were. But whether or not a European was a missionary seems to have had little significance as to the degree of respect or affection in which he was held by Lugbara—some missionaries were unpopular and feared; others were respected and much liked.

In the Uganda part of Lugbara, two Christian missions have been at work: the Verona Fathers, who entered the area in 1918 from the Sudan and whose personnel consists of Italians; and since 1922 the Africa Inland Mission (AIM), most of whose stations in Africa are staffed by Americans (as in the neighbouring areas of the Congo), but whose staff in West Nile District were English members of the Church of England. The Catholics were at the time of my stay under the control of the Bishop of Gulu in Acholiland; the AIM were under the administration of the Bishop of the Upper Nile stationed at Buwalasi, far away in eastern Uganda. The AIM staff, being British, were generally accepted both by the administration and the Lugbara as being 'official', whereas the Italian priests of the Verona Fathers were 'foreign' (many of them had, in fact, been interned during the Second World War).

The organization of the Verona Fathers mission is based upon a central station at Arua, with some half-dozen main out-stations scattered throughout the district and serving both Lugbara and members of other tribes. Almost all the out-stations as well as the central station have Italian personnel. Each station has a church, a small hospital and primary schools; and in addition the central station has a large secondary school. There is also a large technical school at Arua, and a higher secondary school manned by Americans at Nyapea, in Alur country. The AIM also has its central station at Arua, with many small out-stations; only the central station is manned by Europeans. The Protestants have small primary schools at their out-stations, controlled by Lugbara teachers and evangelists, but few large churches. They have a small secondary school at Arua.

The situation among the Congo Lugbara is similar, with American-staffed Protestant stations and Belgian-staffed Catholic stations.

The internal organizations of the missions are somewhat different. In everyday matters the Catholic mission is far more strictly controlled and administered by European priests than is the Protestant mission, which has fewer European staff, less money, and gives considerably greater authority to its Lugbara clergy and lesser officials. The material 'efficiency' of the Catholic mission appeared to me far greater than that of the Protestant mission; but in general the Lugbara maintained that life for them was easier under the Protestants, since they were able more to control their own affairs. But the greater doctrinal strictness of the Protestants (who consider drinking and smoking to be sinful) weighs against them in the eyes of the Lugbara. In addition, the Catholics permit, or at least do not actively forbid, the inheritance of widows, which is forbidden by the Protestants.

In general the missions do not directly compete in most parts of Lugbaraland. The stations are rarely built in obvious competition, and any given subtribe or cluster of subtribes considers the local Catholic or Protestant mission to be its 'own'.

All schools in the district are mission schools, the government paying teachers' salaries and certain other expenses and maintaining an inspectorate. Very large numbers of Lugbara children attend primary school. A good proportion of the primary education consists of evangelistic teaching in Christianity. Some of it deals with the three Rs, and some with personal hygiene, simple farming techniques and the like. In general, Lugbara want their children to receive the second, but recognize that the first is a prerequisite. In many Lugbara families I know, few of the children who attended school failed to attend traditional rites and to learn details of their traditional religion: the fact that in their translations of the Bible the missions translate God by the Bantu term *Mungu* rather than the Lugbara term *Adroa* gave Lugbara parents the rationalization that both faiths were equally valuable and true. The proportion of children with more than a couple of years' primary schooling was relatively small, and only a few acquired a secondary education.

Both missions maintain hospitals, and the AIM also has a leper hospital and settlement a few miles outside Arua. The government has a large central hospital at Arua, with a string of dispensaries throughout the district; and almost all health work is controlled by the government medical services.

The effects of mission teaching upon traditional Lugbara religion (Middleton, 1960*a*) are difficult to estimate. In any lineage there are one or two practising Christians, but most of those who have been to school are also followers of traditional religion. They merely follow the course set them by their traditional roles in the kinship and lineage systems. I have known elders, who should actually perform or supervise the more important rites, who are Christians. Most of them still supervise the performance by deputies, and do not themselves make sacrifices to the dead. But missionary attempts to explain that Lugbara traditional religion is the work of 'Satan' generally fall on deaf ears. Certain enthusiastic missionaries have at various times tried to destroy shrines, an act that is resented by the Lugbara, including the practising Christians. The intolerance of certain missionaries is extremely unpopular, and they are often considered cannibals and even sorcerers. Traditional beliefs in witches and sorcerers continue largely unaffected by Christian teaching, since these beliefs are responses to situations of lineage, family and neighbourhood tension which did not decrease in either severity or in frequency (Middleton, 1963 b).

At the time of my stay there were also a few separatist Christian sects and schools. The most vociferous were the emissaries from the south of the Balokale sect, descended ultimately from the Oxford Movement. These attempted to convert Lugbara, but apart from some adherents in the central Protestant station in Arua they had little direct success. In fact, many Lugbara had already adopted this movement as in some way associated with a spirit cult known as Balokale: a man could be affected by a spirit of that name which would assail him with trembling. He would then erect a shrine where he would make periodic offerings (Middleton, 1963 a).

There were also a few small and struggling independent schools, mostly run by dissident Protestants who attempted to give a traditionally based Lugbara Christian education. These schools were still too new at that time for their future to be foreseen, and I do not know their fate since my departure.

Lastly, something should be said here about the influence of Islam among the Lugbara. The earliest contacts with the outside world were with Arab slave- and ivory-traders and with the Muslim Sudanese troops of Emin Pasha. At the time of my stay most of the survivors of the earliest period of outside contact who had themselves had direct contact with its agents were Muslims. Arua Town is a town of almost 8,000 inhabitants, most of whom are Muslim, and the same is true of the smaller centres. These Muslims are known as *Nubi* and maintain that they are the descendants of Emin Pasha's troops, who were scattered after Emin's departure and most of whom were involved in the Uganda Mutiny of 1897–8. In fact, there are very few of these men left; and most Nubi are Lugbara, Alur, Kakwa and other tribesmen who have become converted to Islam or whose fathers were so converted. Lugbara girls who marry Nubi immediately adopt Muslim dress as well as religion and become Nubis over night. The Nubis form a markedly distinct population: besides being Muslim, with their own mosques and schools, they deal in the trade in hides and skins or follow other urban occupations. They maintain close ties with Nubi communities elsewhere in Uganda (Bombo, Masindi, and so on) and regard themselves as distinct from other people. There have always been a few Muslim chiefs appointed in certain areas among the Lugbara, and the subchief of Arua Town has always been a Muslim. They are handicapped by their distinction from the government and mission officials; and it is recognized by all Lugbara that the road to the new power of the outside world no longer lies with the Muslims. Their former power and influence have greatly declined, and in recent years the atrocities reported from the southern Sudan, which bring back the stories of Arab slavery, have made their position even weaker.

Conclusion

The basis of the traditional social organization of the Lugbara was the family cluster, formed round its core minimal lineage at one extreme, and the system of dispersed clans and lineages at the other. The former group was—and still was in 1950—the basic residential, economic, political and ritual unit in which Lugbara lived and which a Lugbara regarded as the centre of his society. The latter system provided a sense of tribal unity and a sense of stability within a wider world (Middleton, 1958, 1960a).

The bonds that kept the family cluster and its core lineage together, as well as the sanctions associated with them, have weakened. No alternative social bonds have as yet been accepted by the majority of Lugbara. The former sanctions were primarily religious. But the decline in the cult of the dead and the growing importance of status measured by money income and education have initiated a process of secularization. Secular sanctions have always been effective at the level of the major section and above. This is still so, although the actual nature of the secular sanctions has changed from feud and warfare to chiefs' jural powers. The main areas in which change is apparent are in the relationship between old and young and, to a lesser extent, between men and women. In brief, the old have grown poorer and the young richer. The old have become weaker and less able to maintain their traditional authority over their dependents, who have found that they can live in society without having to accept all the authority of their elders and seniors. At the time of my stay most younger men were, in fact, still accepting such authority. But it was clear then that as the older men died out and the younger became more educated, more able to earn their own money and livestock, and more able to found and maintain their own elementary families, so the traditional system would crumble ever more rapidly. The teaching of the missions, despite the intention of many missionaries, only accelerates the process.

The new organization of the Yakan cult, although it did not last for very long, provided the necessary spurt towards this change. Later the 'horizontal' organization that was a part of the cult, as contrasted to the traditional 'vertical' organization of the lineage system, began to provide the basis for new kinds of organization in which new concepts concerning authority and the relative status position of young and old had more play. At one level the appearance of the' New People' is an example of this development. By the early 1950s men who shared similar experiences of the new world, even though they lacked common lineage affiliations, were setting up new organizations. Former soldiers banded themselves together; Christians and Muslims formed religious groupings which soon concerned themselves also with many non-religious activities (for example, growing special food crops to provide the fare for Christian feasts and meetings); there were a few small independent schools; there were attempts to start a trade union among the workers at the tobacco factory. And there were many informal associations, formed by ex-labour migrants, ex-schoolboys, dance teams, football teams, drinking clubs, clusters of chiefs' hangers-on, and so on. Many of these essentially comprised people with similar expectations rather than similar experiences, and had hardly begun to be very meaningful or effective. But a beginning had been made.

Likewise women were beginning to form new groupings, in which they sometimes held views counter to those upholding the traditional place of women. There had always been special women's dances at which men were prohibited and ridiculed, but during my stay these were proliferating. Christian women set up informal groups for domestic and literary self-improvement, including the wearing of clothing instead of leaves. Specialist women producers and traders were beginning to form market groupings. All this was strengthened by the increasing freedom of wives from their husbands. Women were beginning to win divorce actions in chiefs' courts, and divorced women were able to live their own lives freely without having to mind the gossip that usually surrounded them. Again, the missions frequently provided the rationalizations for these changes, often without fully realizing it. It was significant that almost all women's associations were based on the missions; ties were important between mission headquarters and out-stations, but hardly affected the mass of the population.

Associated with these changes came a gradual widening of the scale of Lugbara society as a whole. People could now travel about in safety. Labour migrants could seek work abroad; students could leave for secondary schools outside Lugbaraland. People mixed more freely with members of other tribes, both as labour migrants and as soldiers during the Second World War: many Lugbara soldiers had served in Burma and the Middle East as well as in other parts of East Africa. Older people regard this widening of scale as something regrettable and evil, expressed in terms of the increase in sorcery (Middleton, 1963 b), but the younger people think differently.

A last event that took place before the end of the colonial rule was the introduction by the colonial government of elective processes for the appointment of chiefs and of parliamentary representatives. I myself was able to witness only the election of chiefs.[1] Lugbara suddenly found themselves able to play a large part in the wider political system; and although when I was there this process had hardly begun, the general direction of the change and the growing importance of younger and educated people were clear. Once the present senior generation, whose members can recall the pre-colonial period, has died out, traditional Lugbara society seems likely to change very rapidly.

BIBLIOGRAPHY

Collins, Robert O. (1960). 'Ivory poaching in the Lado Enclave', *Uganda Journal*, **24**, no. 2.

(1962a). *The southern Sudan, 1883–1898: a struggle for control.* New Haven, Yale University Press.

(1962b). 'Sudan–Uganda boundary rectification and the Sudanese occupation of Madial, 1914', *Uganda Journal*, **26**, no. 2.

---

[1] A ministerial system for the central government was introduced in 1955, and the first direct elections for African Representative Members of the Legislative Council were held in 1958.

Driberg, J. N. (1931). 'Yakan', *Journal of the Royal Anthropological Institute*, **61**.

Holt, P. M. (1958). *The Mahdist state in the Sudan, 1881–1898: a study of its origins, development and overthrow*. Oxford, Clarendon Press.

Junker, W. (1892). *Travels in Africa, 1882–1888*. London.

Lotar, L. (1946). *La grande chronique de l'Uele*. Brussels, Institut Royal Colonial Belge.

Middleton, John (1956). 'The role of chiefs and headmen in Lugbara', *Journal of African Administration*, **8**, no. 1.

(1958). 'The political system of the Lugbara of the Nile–Congo divide', in *Tribes without rulers*, J. Middleton and D. Tait, eds. London.

(1960a). *Lugbara religion: ritual and authority among an East African people*. London, Oxford University Press.

(1960b). 'The Lugbara', in *East African chiefs*, A. I. Richards, ed. London.

(1962). 'Trade and markets among the Lugbara of Uganda', in *Markets in Africa*, P. Bohannan and G. Dalton, eds. Evanston, Northwestern University Press.

(1963a). 'The Yakan or Allah water cult among the Lugbara', *Journal of the Royal Anthropological Institute*, **93**, no. 1.

(1963b). 'Witchcraft and sorcery in Lugbara', in *Witchcraft and sorcery in East Africa*, J. Middleton and E. Winter, eds. London.

(1965). *The Lugbara of Uganda*. New York.

(1968). 'Some categories of dual classification among the Lugbara of Uganda', *History of Religions*, **7**, no. 3.

and D. Greenland (1954). 'Land and population in West Nile District, Uganda', *Geographical Journal*, **120**, no. 4.

Quix, Administrateur (1933). Unpublished Report on Lugbara, Office of Chef de Poste, Aru, Congo.

Schweinfurth, G., F. Ratzel, R. Felkin, and G. Hartlaub (1888). *Emin Pasha in Central Africa*. London.

Schweitzer, G. (1898). *Emin Pasha*. London.

Stigand, C. H. (1923). *Equatoria: the Lado Enclave*. London.

CHAPTER 2

CHIEFSHIP IN SINE-SALOUM (SENEGAL), 1887–1914

by

MARTIN A. KLEIN

Robert Delavignette, writing in the years just before the Second World War, said about French policy towards African chiefs:

We are caught up on certain necessary contradictions; on the one hand, we feel strongly that it is indispensable that we leave unchanged the traditional nature of the *chef de canton*'s authority and take advantage of the feudal spirit which persists; on the other hand, we are led by the force of the same colonization to bend him to our administrative mentality (1946).

The present essay describes the way in which these contradictory imperatives were worked out in the Sine-Saloum region of Senegal. When first brought under French authority in 1887, the region contained the Serer states of Sine and Saloum as well as the Muslim Wolof state of Rip. The discussion will ignore certain smaller areas attached to the region as an administrative convenience.

Traditional political systems

Sine and Saloum were states of from 60,000 to 100,000 people. In theory, the king, called the Bour, was absolute. In practice, power was collegial, and the king was often dominated by his entourage, chosen from among his relatives and the slaves of the crown. The Bour himself was elected from among the *guelowar*, descendants in the maternal line from Mande-speaking conquerors, who five centuries earlier had imposed a political system on the apparently stateless Serer. The Bour's will, however, was expressed through the *tiédo*, the warrior class, who controlled most political offices and received most of the rewards in a highly elaborate political structure. Beneath the *tiédo* in a hierarchical social system were the *diambour* (literally, the free men), the slaves and the artisan castes. Each of these groups had its own rights and privileges. The peasantry were in general not easily imposed upon and were

49

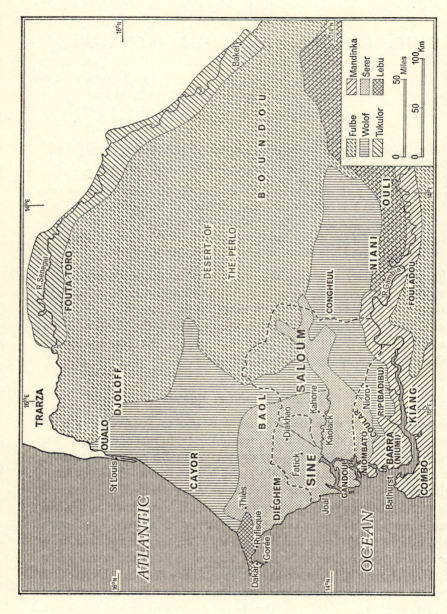

Figure 1. The nineteenth-century states of Sine and Saloum in Senegal, and surrounding areas, showing present population distribution.

likely to send their women and herds into the woods and fight back if excessive demands were made on them by the *tiédo*.

In theory the Bour was chosen by the *grand diaraff*, the chief of the free men, and approved by an assembly of *tiédo* and *diambour*; but in practice there was generally a succession struggle resolved on the field of battle. The *grand diaraff* and the popular assembly merely confirmed the strongest in power. Legitimacy and traditional personal ties played an important role in any power struggle, but so too did a man's ability to support an entourage and to distribute wealth extracted from the peasantry. Once in power, a Bour could usually maintain himself through his control over subsidiary chiefships and tax revenues, but chiefs were deposed and the struggle for power was ruthless. The traditional political structure had two important implications for the French. First, because of the constant struggles for power, the country was subject to outside influence during any succession conflict. The contestants for power sought aid where they could find it and made concessions to traditional enemies that they regretted when the succession was secure. Second, once the conquest was complete, the French found themselves dealing with accepted political authorities, with methods and relationships tested over the centuries (Gamble, 1957: 97–103; Aujas, 1931: 293–333; Bourgeau, 1933: 1–62).

Superficially similar, the structures of Sine and Saloum were different in many ways. Sine was the smaller and older. It was also more homogeneous and more centralized. With the exception of small groups of Fulbe pastoralists, the population was solidly Serer. Even more important, almost all authority was bestowed by the Bour. In almost every village not assigned to one of the major title-holders, there was a representative of the Bour who served as both judge and tax-collector. There were no large hereditary territorial commands.[1]

Saloum was far more heterogeneous—it contained Fulbe, Wolof and Mandinka minorities and it incorporated within its political structure many smaller chiefships that were never completely digested. In the solidly Serer core area, near the present city of Kaolack, the only remnants of these early chiefships were titles that the Bour Saloum bestowed. However, in the west, the subchiefship of Djilor possessed a political structure parallel to that of Saloum and had a limited control

---

[1] The first census in 1891 contains a list of the villages which supported each chief. Revenue and power were clearly fragmented, leaving the kingship the one potent centre of power (*ARS*, 1891 *a*).

over the choice of its own chief. In 1895, a chief chosen by the Bour Saloum was chased from the area three times before the local people were prevailed upon to accept the outsider.[1] In the east, there were four major chiefships, each numbering from 6,000 to 10,000 people, that were primarily Wolof. Each of these chiefs was chosen from the descendants in the male line of the founder, all migrants from the Wolof state of Djoloff. These families of Wolof origin, ruling primarily Wolof populations, intermarried with the *guelowar* chiefs of central Saloum. The combination of Wolof succession rules in the east and Serer rules in the west gave great power to those who inherited prestige and important resources in both areas. Not surprisingly, more than half of the Bours came from these powerful eastern Saloum families. The Wolof–Serer alliance raised Saloum to great power in the eighteenth century, when it collected tribute from many of its neighbours, and was an important slave mart; but by the middle of the nineteenth century, Saloum's power had declined and the increasing Islamization of the Wolof created a source of conflict that split Saloum in half.

Both Sine and Saloum participated in a Wolof-Serer state system which displayed a high degree of stability over a long period of time. The states of 1455 described by Cadamosto (1937: 54) were still in existence in 1850 and still occupied approximately the same area. It was only in the second half of the nineteenth century that the existence of this state system was threatened—and the first threat came not from the French but from a Muslim community that had long coexisted with and accepted the authority of the traditional political hierarchy. In 1861, a Tijani marabout, Ma Bâ, inspired by the example of Al Hajj 'Umar Tall, raised the flag of revolt in Rip, a Mandinka state just south of Saloum.[2] He speedily destroyed the traditional ruling class in Rip and probably would have done the same in Saloum if not for French intervention. At the peak of Ma Bâ's power in 1865, he dominated an area from the Gambia to the Senegal river; but by his death two years later, his state had been largely limited to an area between the Gambia and the Saloum.

[1] Oral sources. A study of Djilor traditions confirms what analysis of the state political structure suggests, that Djilor was a rival state that was conquered but managed to preserve some of its autonomy (see Sarr, 1949: 832–7; Le Mire, 1964: 55–63).

[2] Rip is the Wolof name for the Mandinka state of Badibu. While most of his forces were Wolof, Ma Ba had many Mandinka and Tukulor in his ranks; and the wars must be seen as a religious, not an ethnic conflict. I have dealt with the background to this conflict (1968). See also Bâ (1957: 564–91) and Gray (1940: Ch. 28, 30).

Ma Bâ's state never made the transition from charisma to a more stable bureaucratic structure. It was tied together by shared ideals and the fact of success, but there were no stable institutional ties between Nioro, the capital, and the lesser centres of power. Every area was dominated by one or more marabout chiefs, teachers of the Koran who had taken up the sword to further their faith, and in the process had become political leaders. Each appointed his own cadi and each supported his own military force. They owed allegiance to Nioro, but Nioro does not seem to have received much of the tax revenue or booty; nor is it clear how much control Nioro had over succession or the assignment of conquered lands. The most substantial checks on fragmentation were the charisma of Ma Bâ, his military successes, and a consensus among the major marabout chiefs about goals. With time, this consensus broke down and Ma Bâ's successors were unable to prevent conflict. By the middle eighties the marabout chiefs were divided into three camps. Early in 1887, the most powerful of these, led by Ma Bâ's son, Saër Maty Bâ, posted a series of successes against Saloum; and France decided to send troops into the area, ostensibly in answer to pleas from the Bour for help. The Franco-Saloum alliance quickly destroyed the marabout power, and a protectorate treaty was imposed on those marabout chiefs who did not flee to the Gambia (Coronnat, 1890; *Journal Officiel du Sénégal et Dépendances*, 1890).

The establishment of French authority (1887–98)

Departing French troops left behind a fifty-man garrison and military authority in Nioro, a civilian administrator in Sine–Saloum. The division of the region between civil and military authorities caused constant conflicts, with each authority identifying with and defending the interests of its chiefs. The religious wars of the earlier generation thus were perpetuated in countless petty bureaucratic conflicts. The chief reason for the separation was French insecurity in the face of militant Islam. These fears may have been exaggerated because the Muslim chiefs clearly recognized the superiority of French military power and accepted the defeat of 1887 as definitive. An astute group, which had risen to power by their own talents during a fluid period in Senegambian history, they controlled their own society and effectively carried out French directives. While they often manipulated the French, they were never openly disloyal. One combative old chief was removed

in 1888, but his removal seems to have resulted from a rival's getting
the ear of the lieutenant administering the area rather than from any
positive act of rebellion.[1] The conquest merely completed the break-up
of Ma Bâ's state into smaller units and altered the nature of conflict
from military confrontations to a manœuvring for political position.

The French tried to use the abler Muslim chiefs in the nearby *cercle*
of Niani-Ouli, but here the imposition of alien chiefs produced constant
conflict and complaints of pillaging. The problem was that the Muslim
jihad had not won a clear victory in Niani-Ouli. Therefore the population was divided between two groups, neither of which could accept
the authority of the other. An alien chief with little support in the area
could only establish his authority by frequent use of force. Several
French administrators could not understand how a chief could seem
competent in one area and produce nothing but a succession of complaints in the next one. The problem resulted from their failure to come
to grips with the nature of chiefship. They did, however, restrict the
commands of the Nioro chiefs to areas where their authority was
accepted.

In Sine-Saloum there had been a twelve-man garrison in Kaolack
from 1859 to 1887, but this garrison played only a secondary role during
this period, largely because it was commanded by sergeants who were
often barely literate. The instructions to these men generally denied
them the authority to do more than defend the post and explicitly
warned them not to make any promises to any traders or African rulers.
French domination of the area resulted more from its internal conflicts
than from French use of force. Locked in a bitter war with the Muslims,
Saloum could not afford to alienate French power, and frequently
sought French aid. Sine was less threatened by the jihad, but internal
conflicts operated to favour French interests. During the 1860s a strong
ruler with control of the political system tried to restrict peanut cultivation and therefore the presence of French commerce, but his successors
all faced internal opposition. France had invaded Sine in 1859 and 1861,
and the different contestants for the throne were all determined to
neutralize French power. Through most of this period France had no
desire to intervene, but those who sought power did not know this
and constantly acted to prevent France from supporting a rival. The

[1] The chief, Biram Cissé, had been an aggressive warrior. When a large gathering was
convened at his village, the lieutenant in Nioro ordered his leading rival to arrest him.
It is likely that the lieutenant got his information about this conclave from the rival,
who thereupon became chief.

Dakar archives contain many letters from these contestants assuring France of their loyalty and their intention of protecting commerce.

The civilian administrators who replaced the sergeants at Kaolack had the judgement and intellectual capacity necessary to collect and act on information. The position of the administrator, however, was still weak. His staff included at best one interpreter and one clerk. He did not know the languages of the area, and he had only a limited understanding of the societies he was trying to command. Equally important, he had no military force in the *cercle*. Of necessity, he operated through the traditional chiefs. Only small areas around the trading settlements of Fatick, Foundiougne, and Kaolack were taken over under agreements with the two Bours and placed under direct administration. The administrator was able to force the removal of the more turbulent chiefs and to get compensation for traders whose goods had been stolen; but until 1898 no effort was made to influence the selection of chiefs. The administration, in fact, had little information on which to base such a selection.

The French did become the arbiters of existing conflicts. In Sine the administration stopped a bitter civil war which had seen five Bours in five years when it confirmed in power the existing Bour, M'Baké N'Diaye, and won from him a promise not to eliminate his rival. M'Baké was not strong enough to destroy his challenger, but he did successfully use French recognition to win over some of the challenger's men. The French hoped, at first, to use conflict to maximize their control; but the challenger, finding his position weaker, was forced to raid to find resources to support his entourage. In doing so, he became a hindrance to commercial development and alienated the French. Finally, in 1891, a new French administrator, interested in resolving the conflict, threatened to arrest any warrior participating in these raids (*ARS*, 1891*d*). The resulting flight of the challenger left M'Baké's position undisputed. From this time on, the traditional political structure in Sine showed a strength that surprised the French but proved useful to them. Throughout the crisis, the primary French interest was the protection of commerce, but in acting to safeguard commerce the administration stabilized the traditional political system and made it something different from what it had been. Conflict was intrinsic to the operation of that system. Though these conflicts made it easier for France to extend its control, they were incompatible with commercial development and had to be stopped.

Between 1887 and 1898, the administration worked slowly at bringing the traditional political structure under control. In order to do this,
the government had to control the revenues of the chiefs and to provide
funds for a French bureaucracy. A decree of 1891 set up a head-tax
and regional budgets in Senegal, with three-fourths of the revenue
staying in the *cercle* to pay for clerks, guards, schools, and roads
(*Bulletin Administratif du Sénégal et Dépendances*, 1891). When the
administration in St Louis suggested a fifty-centime tax, Administrator
Ernest Noirot proposed raising it to one franc, with half for the chiefs
(*ARS*, 1892a).[1] The decision to give the chiefs an interest in carrying
out a French policy proved a wise one, for though there was resistance
to the new taxes, it came from the peasants, not from the chiefs. The
very act of collecting the taxes altered the relationship between the
chiefs and the administration. The French had been checking the use
of force by the chiefs, since this often involved the harassment of
traders; but when peasant villagers refused to pay taxes, the governor's
instructions were clear:

Let the Bour engage in whatever repression he judges necessary...but you
will not accompany the Bour to Diohine when he goes there to punish his
subjects (*ARS*, 1892c).

This policy represented a reversal of the French attitude toward the
chiefs. The conquest had been justified by a myth that the *tiédo* were an
oppressive class and the conquest really a liberation of the unfortunate
peasantry. The French had little awareness that the Serer state, though
often oppressive, was a stable political unit based on time-tested relationships and generally accepted by its people. The French considered
the *tiédo* chiefs to be nothing but dissolute thieves. However, with the
imposition of the head-tax, the administration suddenly found itself
dependent on these chiefs for the collection of the tax. French attitudes
did not immediately change and the liberation myth still appeared
intermittently in bureaucratic correspondence,[2] but after 1891 the

[1] The 50 centimes was divided as follows: 25 to the Bour, 10 to the subchief, 15 to the
village chief.
[2] Thus, in 1896 an administrator described the Bour's entourage as parasites 'who only
live off the generosity of the Bours, the collection of taxes, and excesses committed
on their *administrés*' (*ARS*, 1896d). In advising an administrator to supervise a particular
chief, another high official wrote, 'In every Wolof there is a *tiédo*, who if given too
much liberty, will profit from it to live too much at the expense of those he has a
mission to protect' (*ARS*, 1893b). The term *tiédo* is being used here in a very general

administrators were more likely to look the other way when officially recognized chiefs used force to resolve conflicts and repress rebellious groups. With time, the French even expected the chiefs to use force on their own in carrying out policies. Thus, in 1896 the Bour Saloum was told: 'Your colleagues are not so weak towards their subjects as you; either that will change or the kingdom of Saloum will change' (*ARS*, 1896*b*).

In sanctioning the use of force by chiefs, the French were reinforcing the chief's ability to use force to assert his own prerogatives. Traditionally, the most important check on chiefly power was insecurity. Now, the chief had substantial freedom of action in moving against traditional rivals and against those of his own people who gave him trouble. There is a certain paradox that the head-tax forced the French to lean more heavily on traditional authority and on traditional methods and therefore to strengthen the chiefs, at the same time as it gave the administration funds to move towards its enunciated goal of bureaucratizing and controlling the chiefs. With the increase in funds, the number of personnel present in the *cercle* to supervise the chiefs steadily and rapidly increased. In 1892 Noirot had one clerk and one interpreter. In 1897, there was a payroll of fourteen, in 1902, twenty-nine (*Annuaire du Sénégal et Dépendances*).

The head-tax was part of a general tax reform that involved also the suppression of an export tax traditionally collected in the Serer states and the reduction of the tax on the *navetanes*, the migrant farmers. The reforms bucked vigorous opposition because both taxes had traditionally been farmed out to powerful members of the Bour's entourage. In 1859 the export tax had been set by treaty at three per cent—after the beginnings of the peanut trade—but had given rise to frequent demands for gifts and was passionately opposed by commercial houses.[1] It was replaced by a fifty-franc patent payable once each year to the Bour (*Journal Officiel du Sénégal et Dépendances*, 1892). The tax on the migrant farmers had been set at twenty francs, a prohibitive sum that severely limited the growth of a labour migration

---

sense, as it was by most nineteenth-century French writers. In fact, the term referred to the warriors, not to the chiefs themselves. In twentieth-century Senegal the term has also come to mean 'pagan', since this class was the most refractory to Islam.

[1] The peanut trade had already reached significant proportions—5,000 tons exported from Sine-Saloum in 1890. After several years in which a depressed world market limited expansion of the crop, exports shot up to a peak of 100,000 tons in 1914. See Brocard (1918).

that French commercial interests wanted to encourage. It took two years to overcome *tiédo* opposition, but Noirot finally induced the Bour Saloum to reduce the tax to five francs and introduced a registration system that permitted the administrator to check the tendency of the *tiédo* to take advantage of the strangers (*ARS*, 1895 *b*). These new revenues went directly into the Bour's coffers without being handled by the *tiédo*. This made the Bour less dependent on his entourage, while the revenues of the *tiédo* and their power to act independently in their own interests were substantially reduced.

There were a number of other changes during this transitional decade. First, the traditional social order was somewhat undermined by French willingness to free any slave who set foot on territory of direct administration—this included Kaolack, Fatick and Foundiougne. The law was that French soil freed. No large migration took place and the French were able to persuade the chiefs to sign a convention abolishing the slave-trade. The chiefs seem to have minimized their losses from this convention. If a slave caravan was stopped, or a slave freed because of the cruelty of his master, it was usually one of the chiefs who gave the freed slave land. The freed slave, who remained a slave in the eyes of local society, became a dependent of the chief. The Bour Sine even complained that absence of slave trade routes in Sine deprived him of freed slaves (*ARS*, 1893 *a*; *ARS*, Series K).

Second, there was a minimal amount of judicial reform. Most important, Noirot devoted himself to persuading the chiefs to replace the ordeal—the passing of a hot blade over the tongue—by an oath on a fetish. In Saloum, this reform was accepted only when the Bour died in 1894 and his successor sought to use French support to head off a possible challenge (*ARS*, 1895 *a*). In this case—as in so many others during the early period—the French found that change was accepted only under two circumstances. Either the chief received some compensation for whatever he lost in making the change, or the change was resisted until internal conflict made the chief dependent on the French. The Bour thus accepted the abolition of trial by ordeal because he needed French support to head off a succession crisis. In general, innovations proposed by the administration were resisted, and the administrator often found it wise to postpone a show-down. The force available to the administrator was limited, and the African élites did not accept the French right to dictate basic changes in law, custom and political structure.

Third, the administration made clear its interest in controlling the succession. In 1894 they merely accepted the newly-elected Bour Saloum—and in doing so, blocked a civil war. However, the same year, when the Boumi of Sine, the heir apparent, died, Noirot announced that no successor would be chosen until there was a candidate who spoke French. Neither candidate went to school for more than two weeks. It was easier to control the succession than to get a Serer noble to sit behind a desk with young boys.

Fourth, there was an insistence on the symbolic acceptance of French authority. Most important was the payment of taxes, which was for the French, as it had been earlier for the African states, the most important symbol of submission to alien sovereignty. In addition, the African rulers were forced to violate certain taboos, to adapt to French modes of behaviour, and to take part in such rituals as the annual Bastille Day affirmation of loyalty to the colonial power. In 1891 Noirot insisted that the Bour Saloum board a boat to greet the governor, a demand that was refused and led to a pained letter in which Bour Saloum Guédel M'Bodj tried to explain the taboos surrounding his office: 'The two things that I fear in life are first, to offend the governor, and second, to board a boat' (*ARS*, 1891*b*). On the governor's next trip, Guédel yielded and boarded the boat. During the same year, both Bours visited St Louis. The idea was M'Baké's, but the French insisted that both he and Guédel reduce their travelling parties from 500 men to ten. Though both Bours signed treaties in St Louis, these treaties were less important than the act of coming to the governor, and they were soon violated by their French authors (*AMFOS*, III 104*c*).[1]

Toward direct administration

By 1898, several plans for the creation of a more rational administrative structure had been discussed. The opportunity for a major reform was suddenly presented by the unexpected death of M'Baké N'Diaye in Sine. The Serer nobility, well aware that changes were on the way, chose Coumba N'Doffène Diouf as Bour before notifying the administrator of the old Bour's death. The administrator immediately announced that he did not accept the choice, and five weeks later he and the governor-general met the major chiefs of Sine to impose a more

[1] The treaties included commitments to the ruling families that the administration had no intention of honouring.

streamlined political structure. In spite of passionate protestations that the Sine-Sine wanted Coumba N'Doffène, the governor announced that henceforth Sine would be divided into two provinces, one under Coumba N'Doffène, the other under his rival, Coumba Djimbi N'Diaye. Each province was, in turn, divided into five cantons, each under a chief approved by the administration. A resident was assigned to Sine and a new judicial system was set up. All cases were to be decided by the canton chiefs subject to appeal to a council of notables and then to the administrator. A record was to be kept of all decisions, and the judges, like the canton and provincial chiefs, were to receive salaries (*AMFOS*, 1898*a*; *Journal Officiel de l'AOF*, 1898).

This, in effect, was the imposition of direct rule, a manifestation of France's *esprit cartésien*. Sine and Saloum were being divided into neat logical cantons and provinces just as the French Revolution had divided tradition-bound provinces into rationally conceived *départements*. The *chef de canton* was to be a salaried bureaucrat, an official of the state just like his counterpart in rural France, the chief difference being the absence of any representative institutions that could check the authoritarianism implicit in the structure. The chief was no longer even to be known by his traditional title. Furthermore, the administrator now had control over the courts. To be sure, the law applied was Koranic law for the Muslims, customary law for the pagans; but the administrator was in a position to check the chief's use of his judicial office.

While the governor-general was in Sine, the Bour Saloum also died suddenly. As in Sine, the Saloum chiefs chose a new Bour before notifying the administrator. This was of little avail, for an organization identical to that in Sine was immediately imposed (*AMFOS*, 1898*b*). The new structure soon ran into trouble, especially in Sine; and before a year was over, Sine and Saloum had begun to evolve in different directions.

In eastern Sine, Coumba N'Doffène's authority was accepted and taxes were collected without difficulty; but in Coumba Djimbi's province, many villages refused to pay. The French resident was chased from one village and a cavalry squadron was called in to make a show of force (*ARS*, 1899). When Coumba N'Doffène offered to collect in the dissident areas, he was charged provisionally with the second province. Coumba Djimbi, who objected strenuously, was deported. The expectation was that the second province would be given to a French-speaking chief as soon as the schools could produce one.

However, when St Louis suggested a candidate of low social status, Administrator Lefilliâtre pointed out the difficulties that would ensue and defended Coumba N'Doffène's performance.

Sine, at the head of which we have an intelligent chief, loved by his subjects and very devoted to the French cause, could not be more calm. . . .The man of Sine does not like to see his country divided. . .He will accept another chief only with a great deal of difficulty; I believe that I can say that without force, we cannot obtain such results in any other way (ARS, 1901 b).

Lefilliâtre had earlier been hostile to the idea of continuing reliance on hereditary chiefs, but experience had changed his mind.

The system in Sine was a form of indirect rule. Coumba N'Doffène's title was *chef de province*, but he was still the Bour and was referred to as such by several administrators. After 1901 there is surprisingly little correspondence in the archives about Sine, largely because Coumba N'Doffène and his chiefs did what was asked of them and in return were left alone. The resident continued to live in Fatick, some distance from the capital of Sine; and at the request of the Bour, Catholic missionaries were kept out (ARS, 1901 a). By co-operating with the French, Coumba N'Doffène was able to protect both his personal power and the autonomy of Sine. Sine is still known as a very traditionalist community; and Coumba N'Doffène's successor, though technically only a retired chief, is today one of the few traditional chiefs who wields great influence in Senegal.

The situation in Saloum was very different. The conquest of Rip had returned to the Bour Saloum Muslim Wolof areas hostile to the *tiédo*, which persistently refused to pay taxes. The separation of Saloum into two provinces, one Muslim and Wolof, the other predominantly Serer and pagan, was successful and consequently permanent. Equally striking in Saloum was the rapid decline in the traditional power structure, which had displayed apparent vitality in the 1880s and 1890s. None of the rulers of Saloum after 1898 had Coumba N'Doffène's prestige or influence. In 1911 Coumba N'Doffène's salary was 12,000 francs a year, while the provincial chief of western Saloum was paid only 3,000, little more than a canton chief. Increasingly the administration corresponded directly with the canton chiefs, and in both eastern and western Saloum, the provincial chief, heir to the Bour, became extraneous.

The reasons for the decline of the Saloum state are not hard to find.

First, there is the greater instability of the Saloum political structure, which incorporated a series of powerful semi-independent chiefships approximately the size of a canton. Second, there is possibly an element of chance in that Sine found able leadership and Saloum perhaps did not. Third, though Sine regularly produced bumper crops of peanuts, Saloum saw greater social change. In Sine the peanut moved into the crop cycle without causing any radical change in the peasant's way of life. He still grew enough millet to feed his family, and indebtedness was rare. In Saloum, the ports of Kaolack and Foundiougne and the railroad, which reached Kaolack in 1912, involved the creation of new communities whose loyalty was not primarily to the traditional political system.[1]

Fourth and most important was Islamization. A dissident wing of the Saloum nobility had been exposed to Islam in Ma Bâ's camp, and some became serious Muslims after the French conquest ended the religious wars. About 1890 Bour Saloum Guédel M'Bodj, a bitter rival of Islam on the field of battle, converted, probably in the hope of conciliating his Muslim subjects in eastern Saloum. While his successor was pagan, the Muslim faith made steady progress. The Serer areas of central Saloum, less than ten per cent Muslim in 1891, were over forty per cent Muslim when the First World War began (Marty, 1917: 308).[2] The maraboutic form taken by Senegalese Islam has meant the replacement of the chief by the marabout in the eyes of the believer. In Sine a concerted effort was made by Mouride marabouts to convert the Bour Sine, but Coumba N'Doffène resisted their blandishments, realizing that his power depended in part on his ritual position. Sine remained largely pagan until after World War II.

The 1898 administrative reforms were not definitive. The number of cantons was subsequently reduced, the borders were somewhat changed and the grouping into provinces was several times altered. Every administrator felt impelled to make some structural changes; but the basic organization, and outside Sine, the reliance on the canton chief, remained constant. The new régime did not weaken the chief. In fact, it strengthened his power while it limited the areas in which he was

[1] The railroad crossed the north-east corner of Sine; but Mourides, members of a Muslim religious fraternity, moved into the area near the station and it was eventually removed from the authority of the Bour Sine.
[2] Some of the increase in the Muslim population can be explained by the movement of Wolof into sparsely settled areas, but only large-scale conversion can explain the magnitude of the increase.

free to act. The chief's power was greatest in enforcing within African society his own rights and prerogatives. Most important, the new system reversed the relationship between the chief and his entourage. In the traditional system, the chief was dependent on his followers—the Bours had a force of over 500 men—and he was strongly influenced by their interests. Under the colonial régime, the number of chiefs supporting an entourage was reduced and the remaining group became completely dependent on the chief. The entourage did, however, remain important, and, in fact, was absolutely essential if the chief was to carry out the administration's decisions. The collection of taxes was strongly resisted in many areas and often required the use of force. Similarly, when systematic recruitment was begun in 1912, it met vigorous resistance and caused a significant emigration to the Gambia. One chief resigned rather than brave the hostility of his own people. Most of the others, however, carried out orders, either by using force or by exploiting traditional prestige.

The colonial system also radically reduced the number of chiefs. The traditional state had an extensive title system, where every title carried certain privileges and generally, certain revenues. The diffusion of privilege and to a lesser degree, of power, was an important stabilizing factor in the traditional state, for it gave many families a stake in the established order. The French focused both power and privilege in the hands of a small group of men.

Chiefs and administrators

The new model of chiefship was that of the salaried bureaucrat, but he still remained in many ways the traditional chief. Though the canton was not always identical with traditional political units, it was usually similar in area, and the canton chiefs were chosen from among those with traditional claims to authority. These claims remained the basis of the chief's power. The chief's salary was the only legitimate source of income, but it was not adequate to support an entourage. The chief received gifts and his fields were worked—though no governor issued decrees recognizing these as prerogatives of the chiefs. Some administrators were disturbed by these exactions, but in general, they seem to have realized the necessity of other sources of income and only in rare cases of excess did they check their underlings.

The chiefs were able to protect themselves against the demands of the administration because of their control of the administration's access to information. The first administrators were totally ignorant of the people they ruled. Their clerks, guards and interpreters were also foreign to the areas to which they were posted. Thus, they were often totally dependent on the chiefs. The most striking case of manipulation of French authority by an African chief was in Nioro. The lieutenants commanding the Nioro post in the early nineties were changed frequently, often every six months, and had explicit orders never to go outside the post. The garrison was made up of Senegalese *tirailleurs*, many of whom married locally and were loyal as much to the chief as to the commandant. The chief used his position to control access to the commandant. The invisible wall he constructed was discovered only by accident. A peasant with a problem had been trying to get in to see the commandant. Turned away by the Senegalese guards time after time, he went to Sine-Saloum and presented his complaint to Noirot, who gave him a note and told him to hand it to the lieutenant when he went out on a walk. When the peasant did so, the lieutenant, who either did not understand or did not want to understand, told the man to come see him in his office. The man never arrived. Apparently, he had been persuaded to return to his village (Obissier).

Many French officials were well aware of this problem. In 1896, the director of political affairs wrote about the problem of the administrator on tour:

He is almost always accompanied by local chiefs escorted by a troop of horsemen and foot soldiers who naturally live on the country. A good guard is kept around him; only those who have the consent of the chief can approach him. Those who would do without this formality will pay dearly for their audacity... The chiefs and their entourage even profit from his presence to inflict, on the least pretext, fines and penalties which are often considerable; thus they ruin populations they are charged with administering. All that is done, of course, in the name of Europeans, who become, as a result, an object of terror in the mind of the Negroes (*ARS*, 1896 a).

The success of the chiefs in manipulating French administrators did not mean that the chiefs were in a position to confront or to deny French power. The colonial administration, for example, broke down the capacity of the African communities to take any kind of united economic action. As early as the 1860s, the Bour Sine sought to prohibit peanut cultivation in the hope that the French would then go away. In the 1880s, when the world market price for peanuts was going down, it became a regular practice for both Bours to suspend the sale of peanuts until either a better price was arranged or they were given generous gifts. With the establishment of an administrator in Sine–Saloum, there was immediate pressure from the commercial houses to prevent these frequent hold-ups. In 1892, Noirot wrote the Bour Saloum:

Remember that as Bour Saloum you do not have the right to impede commerce and to stop the cultivators from selling their products. On the contrary, in your position as chief of Saloum, all of your efforts should tend to protect commerce, to aid it and to develop it. The purchase price is not your business, it is the business of the merchants and the cultivators...Raise the *laff* [boycott] immediately if you do not wish to see yourself replaced in Saloum (*ARS*, 1892 *b*).

Ironically, Noirot was also convinced that the commercial syndicate was pushing the price of peanuts unnecessarily low and was placing pressure on the commercial houses to pay more. At the same time, he was trying to destroy the limited capacity of the African community to take economic action in its own defence. After 1898, the type of confrontation that characterized the first decade ceased to take place. What was created, in effect, was a hierarchy of arbitrary authority. Both chief and administrator were restrained largely from above and by authorities that possessed limited information on which to act.

The community of clerks, interpreters and guards that surrounded the administration and was loyal to it should have provided both a check on the chiefs and an independent source of information, but they did not always do so. Noirot tried placing French-educated secretaries at the courts of the two Bours in the hope that these men would both influence the policies of the Serer rulers and provide the administration with information. The Bour Sine's secretary became a fawning courtier of the Bour, while the man assigned to the Bour Saloum met a solid wall of hostility and silence when he refused to play such a role. Internal conflict and the corrosive effect of time broke down some of the control the Bours had over their courts, especially in Saloum. At the same time, the opportunities for African staff to advance within the bureaucracy were increasingly blocked, giving these valuable aides few incentives for more than perfunctory loyalty.[1]

[1] The community from which these secretaries was chosen had substantial grievances, though it is not clear if this affected their performance or their loyalty. Up into

The second generation of administrators was not necessarily more knowledgeable than the first. In fact, Noirot (1890–6) knew the area better than did his successors. He was virtually alone, spent a great deal of time on tour and with Africans, and had to grope with the difficult problems of bringing the traditional states into the French administrative system. Increasingly, his successors were surrounded by underlings and lived in a small insulated Kaolack French community. They saw the local communities not from the saddle of a horse, but from behind a desk.

Limits on arbitrariness

The most significant real check on the arbitrariness of both chief and administration came not from within the administration but from an outside community, the citizens of the Four Communes. The Four Communes intruded themselves into Sine–Saloum in two ways. The first was the letter-writers, men literate in French who could frame a peasant's claims in good French and direct these claims to the proper authority. After 1905, the administration received these letters in increasing numbers. Second, political ties were extended from the Four Communes into the protectorates. As early as 1892, the Governor complained:

the natives do not correspond any more either with the Governor or with the administrators of their *cercles*; they no longer obey orders coming from functionaries who have the right and the duty to give them; but they address themselves uniquely to diverse members of the local assembly and to certain influential persons from St Louis, with whose opinion alone they comply (*ARS*, 1891 c).

Only after 1900 did the process become significant within Sine–Saloum; and then it was primarily through isolated incidents in which the actions of chief or administrator were brought to the attention of their superiors. For example, in 1912 a peasant in Sine complained that the Resident had camped in his fields and destroyed his crops. The Resident protested that the village chief had chosen the campsite. It is quite probable that in doing so, the village chief was striking out at

the 1890s they frequently had important political responsibilities, but by 1900 a crew of administrators and assistant administrators took over all political tasks and the abler Africans found themselves confined in routine tasks with few opportunities for advancement.

a man who had given him trouble. The peasant's case received a hearing largely because it was presented by Galandou Diouf, then a shopkeeper in a nearby village and a member of the *conseil général* of the Four Communes and later a member of the French Chamber of Deputies (*ARS*, 1912). The willingness of men like Diouf to use their influence to represent the unrepresented provided a significant check on the abuse of authority in rural Senegal and probably made French rule there less harsh than in other parts of France's African empire. This check, however, did not change the essentially arbitrary nature of both the chief's and the administrator's office.

By birth or training?

Many French officials wanted to go farther than they did in cutting loose from hereditary principles to make the chief an official completely dependent on French authority: 'The best way to have devoted and useful men at the head of provinces is to make them functionaries named by us, chosen from among the most intelligent and the most worthy regardless of family and heredity' (*ARS*, 1896c). They hoped to be able to reward soldiers, clerks and interpreters for faithful service. Many administrators, in fact, felt that such men, closely tied to the French, would be better chiefs. The opposite turned out to be true. Though there were exceptions, the administration discovered that its writ went farther when the chief had hereditary rights to command in his canton. This is nowhere clearer than in the case of Abdoulaye Diaw.

Diaw had been Noirot's clerk from 1891 to 1896, and had consistently received highest praise. He was acting administrator several times, and his reports showed intelligence and judgement. When eastern and western Saloum were separated in 1898, Diaw was placed in the east, first as resident, then as provincial chief. This post soon involved him in a struggle for power with several canton chiefs, in particular one former interpreter who, after becoming chief, had earned French gratitude by putting down a rebellion. Both men knew the psychology of the French and each instigated complaints against the other. The most important element of the battle was the struggle for the administrator's favour. N'Dao, the former interpreter, had hereditary rights to his command and had the resources of his family and its retainers behind him. Diaw, on the other hand, had to build up an entourage, support it by force if necessary, and place chiefs dependent on him in key positions. The effort to find the food and clothing for his entourage led to complaints about pillaging, and eventually to Diaw's replacement (*ARS*, 13 G, 334: 13 G, 335; 1903). Although he had been branded a thief, he returned to the bureaucracy, where he once again received high ratings for intelligence and integrity as a financial clerk in the Casamance (*ARS*, Dossier 1666). Diaw's problem was that the exercise of power required resources which he as a stranger did not have. The outsider chiefs seem to have worked out best in areas of direct administration. Here there were no traditional chiefs to buck, and the canton chief was close to the French authorities. Given a fluid situation, a new family could achieve legitimacy. In the 1870s, a respected Fulbe trader, Sega Poulo Sow, was chosen chief of Kaolack. The family held onto the position, and time gave the Sows a place in the local chiefly hierarchy.

The desirability of relying on hereditary chiefs was recognized by the men in the field before it was accepted by those who made the policy and theory, largely because it was the administrator who had to face the realities of diverse social and political systems. However, with time, policy caught up with reality; and in 1909 Governor-General William Ponty articulated his *politique des races*, which not only accepted the idea of relying on hereditary chiefs, but opposed the mixing, in political units, of separate ethnic groups, called *races*:

each population group should preserve its autonomy with regard to its neighbours...By letting each race evolve within its own particular mentality and conserving as much as possible the particularism of the tribe, we promote...individual effort, with each group free from the political or religious influence of its neighbour (*ARS*, 1909).

The problem was the tight-fistedness of the French parliament, which was willing to accept colonies but was not willing to provide financial support for the projects of colonial officials. An alliance with the hereditary rulers, they found, was cheaper than the creation of an entirely new power structure.

While the French reluctantly accepted the importance of legitimacy, they never seem to have realized that a French-speaking chief was not necessarily a better chief. This idea was most sorely tested in neighbouring Rip, where Insa Bâ, Ma Bâ's nephew, became chief in 1901. Bâ had been taken as a hostage in 1887 at about the age of twenty, and eight years later received his *bac* from a lycée in Algiers. Though very intelligent, he was a disappointing chief. Somewhat timid by nature, his

French education cut him off from his charges and made him dependent on several brothers the French considered too traditionalist, in particular Ousmane, a highly respected marabout. In order to free Insa from his influence, one administrator wanted to deport Ousmane. Instead, in 1907 Insa Bâ was removed and Ousmane became the chief. Ironically he turned out to be a very efficient instrument of French authority: 'He has a great deal of authority in his province, as much through his title of chief as through that of *tamsir*.[1] His reputation for probity permits him to be authoritarian without any complaints being formulated against him' (*ARS*, 1910; 1901–7; *ARS* Dossiers, 756, 3198, 3761).

The experience with Insa Bâ did not influence French policy towards the training of chiefs. There were no others who were so radically cut off from their society because no others in his generation or the succeeding one got to study in Algeria or in France. From the first, the French placed pressure on major chiefs to place their sons in French schools. These young men, especially those who graduated from the School for the Sons of Chiefs and Interpreters in St Louis, were generally placed in minor bureaucratic positions—as clerks or interpreters—until chiefships opened up. The army, 'the school of the regiment', also became an important training-ground for chiefs. When several chiefships became vacant during the Moroccan War, they were left open until the heir returned from Moroccan battlefields. Thus, service in both the army and the bureaucracy became an apprenticeship for the sons of chiefs. Almost all chiefs who inherited titles in the years just prior to the war had served this apprenticeship, were literate, and were ready to fit themselves to the new form of chiefship.

Conclusion

The existence of French-speaking chiefs meant that the administrator could correspond in French and no longer needed an Arabic interpreter, but the chief continued to exercise his authority through a combination of consent and the discreet use of force. He was stronger than before, because though limited in what he could do, he was secure as long as he kept his superiors happy. Politics remained important, but the chief's goal was not the support of his fellows but the favour of his superiors.

---

[1] *Tamsir* is a Fulbe word meaning 'one learned in the law'. It comes from the Arabic *tafsir*, meaning commentator, and has been borrowed by the Wolof. (See Trimingham, 1959: 247.)

Where power had been collegial, the French desire for simple and clearly articulated lines of authority made power both more personal and more absolute.

In doing so, the French may well have undermined the chief and prepared the way for changes they did not want. The chief was entrusted with the most unpopular tasks, collecting taxes and recruitment. As a result, he increasingly lost his standing with his own people and was unable to compete either with the marabouts or with the nationalist élites that sought power after World War II. The chief became a privileged instrument of the state's authority, but only in Sine did he continue to possess real power. By strengthening the chief, the French prepared the way for his downfall.

In discussing chiefship in Sine–Saloum, I have avoided most of the terms generally used in discussing the theory of French colonial rule: association, assimilation, and direct rule. In general, these terms add little to our understanding of the processes of political change. They are usually used to try to differentiate between French and British practice, but my own reading of such authors as M. G. Smith (1960: Ch. 6) and D. A. Low (1965: 1–56) leaves me convinced that the similarities are as important as the differences. Both colonial powers were faced with the same problem: controlling an alien society with limited resources and legislatures reluctant to subsidize the colonial enterprise. In order to survive, both adapted to the societies being ruled; and the variety of institutions and relationships, therefore, is such that the differences were greater within each system than between them.

The terms *association* or *assimilation* were the playthings of metropolitan theorists and do not describe the political relationships that existed in Sine–Saloum. Within the period and area studied the French administration was both pragmatic and adaptable, though an *esprit cartésien* was manifest in its official pronouncements and affected its ideals. During the early years the colonial administration had little choice but to make its authority felt through the traditional political systems. The often-made distinction between French direct rule and British indirect rule is more relevant, though we would be oversimplifying the realities of colonial policy if we considered the two approaches in direct contradiction to each other. Delavignette (1946: Ch. 5) and Deschamps,[1] two men whose attitudes are rooted in the

[1] Deschamps frequently uses the word 'indirect' to describe French methods (1956, 1953).

experience of administration, both stress in their works the indirect nature of French control and the administration's dependence on the chief. In Sine, where the political situation so dictated, a form of indirect rule evolved. Perhaps a more important distinction is to be found in the differences in metropolitan political ideals and in correspondingly different conceptions of the role of the chief. In Sine-Saloum, when I asked several retired chiefs what the job of the *chef de canton* consisted of, all mentioned taxes and recruitment first. I am sure they gave me the answer they would have given a French administrator. When I put the same question to two chiefs in the Gambia, both first mentioned their judicial responsibilities. The French thus saw the chief more as a local administrator, the British as a magistrate. A more complete understanding of the problem will depend on further research into the history of specific African societies during the colonial period.

BIBLIOGRAPHY

PRIMARY SOURCES

Archives de la Ministère d'Outremer, Sénégal (AMFOS). III, 104 c.
    (1898 a). Director of Native Affairs to Administrator Sine-Saloum, 25 January. IV, 128 c.
    (1898 b). Director of Native Affairs to Governor-General, 18 February. IV, 128 c.
Archives de la République du Sénégal (ARS). (1891 a). Census. Unclassified.
    (1891 b). Bour Saloum to Governor Senegal, received 20 March. Unclassified.
    (1891 c). Governor Senegal to Minister, 6 April. Unclassified.
    (1891 d). Noirot to Governor Senegal, 23 October. Unclassified.
    (1892 a). Noirot to Governor, 14 January. Unclassified.
    (1892 b). Administrator Sine-Saloum to Bour Saloum, 23 January. Unclassified.
    (1892 c). Governor to Administrator, 25 June. Unclassified.
    (1893 a). Administrator Sine-Saloum to Governor Senegal, 27 September. K 13. Extensive documentation on question of slavery, series K.
    (1893 b). Letter to Administrator, Noiro, 13 November. 13 G, 322.
    (1895 a). Noirot to Governor, 1 March.
    (1895 b). Decree of Bour Saloum, 21 June. Unclassified.
    (1896 a). Report on Boundary Commission, 2 February. 1 f, 19.
    (1896 b). Administrator Sine-Saloum to Bour Saloum, 6 March. 13 G, 326.

(1896 c). Administrator Sine-Saloum to Governor-General, 10 April. 13 G, 326.

(1896 d). Administrator to Governor-General, 10 November. 13 G, 327.

(1899). Resident to Administrator, 26 March and 6 April. Unclassified.

1901–7. Correspondence from Nioro. Unclassified.

(1901 a). Administrator to Director of Native Affairs, 8 March. Unclassified.

(1901 b). Administrator to Director of Native Affairs, 3 October. 13 G, 332.

(1903). Administrator of Secretary-General, 3 January. Unclassified.

For correspondence on N'Dao and Diaw, 13 G, 334 and 13 G, 335.

(1909). Circular to Lieutenant-Governors, 22 September. 13 G, 72.

(1910). Ousmane's personnel dossier, no. 1866, dated 9 June.

(1912). Resident for Sine to Lieutenant-Governor, 7 September. Unclassified.

Bâ's personnel dossier, nos. 756, 3198 and 3761.

Diaw's personnel dossier, no. 16666.

Obissier, Lt. Monograph on the *cercle* of Nioro du Rip. *Archives de la République du Sénégal.* 1 G, 217.

SECONDARY SOURCES

Annuaire du Sénégal et Dépendances.

Aujas, L. (1931). 'Les Sérères du Sénégal', *Bulletin du Comité d'Etudes Historiques et Scientifiques de l'A.O.F.*, **14**.

Bâ, Tamsir Ousman (1957). 'Essai historique sur le Rip', *Bulletin de l'Institut Français de l'Afrique Noire*, **19**.

Bourgeau, J. (1933). 'Notes sur la coûtume des Sérères du Sine et du Saloum', *Bulletin du Comité d'Etudes Historiques et Scientifiques de l'A.O.F.*, **16**.

Brocard, Paul (1918). *Note sur le développement de la culture de l'arachide au Sénégal.* Paris.

Bulletin Administratif du Sénégal et Dépendances (1891). Decree of 13 December.

Cadamosto, Alvise (1937). *The voyages of Cadamosto.* Tr. and ed. by G. R. Crone. London.

Coronnat, Col. (1890). *La guerre au Sénégal. La Colonne du Rip en 1887.* Paris.

Delavignette, Robert (1946). *Service africain.* Paris.

Deschamps, H. J. (1953). *Méthodes et doctrines coloniales de la France.* Paris. (1956). *The French Union.* Paris.

Diagne, Pathé (1967). *Pouvoir politique traditionnel en Afrique Occidentale.* Paris.

Gamble, David P. (1957). *The Wolof of Senegambia, Ethnographic Survey of Africa: Western Africa*, part XIV. London, International African Institute.

Gray, J. M. (1940). *A history of the Gambia.* Cambridge University Press.

Journal Officiel du Sénégal et Dépendances, 30 June 1890.

Bour's announcement, 4 June 1892.

Klein, Martin (1968). *Islam and imperialism in Senegal: Sine-Saloum, 1847–1914.* Stanford University Press.

(1969). 'The Moslem revolution in 19th century Senegambia', in *Western African history*, Daniel McCall, ed. New York. Vol. IV of Boston University Papers on Africa.

Le Mire, P. (1964). 'Petite Chronique du Djilor', *Bulletin de l'Institut Français de l'Afrique Noire*, **8**.

Lombard, Jacques (1967). *Autorités traditionelles et pouvoirs européens en Afrique Noire*. Paris.

Low, D. A. (1965). 'British East Africa: the establishment of British Rule, 1895–1912', in *A history of East Africa*, vol. II, Vincent Harlow and E. M. Chilver, eds. Oxford, Clarendon Press.

Marty, Paul (1917). *Etudes sur l'Islam au Sénégal*, I. Paris.

Obissier, Lt. *See* Primary Sources, above.

Sarr, A. (1949). 'Histoire du Sine-Saloum', *Présence Africaine*, **5**.

Smith, M. G. (1960). *Government in Zazzau, 1800–1950*. London, Oxford University Press.

Trimingham, J. S. (1959). *Islam in West Africa*. Oxford, Clarendon Press.

CHAPTER 3

FROM EMPIRE TO COLONY: BORNU IN THE NINETEENTH AND TWENTIETH CENTURIES

by

RONALD COHEN

Bornu in the nineteenth century

Detailed records on African political systems in the pre-colonial period are hard to obtain. Hence, many misconceptions have arisen concerning the way in which independent African states were incorporated into European colonies whose boundaries did not correspond to those of older states. This essay attempts to document the changeover as it occurred in Bornu, Nigeria. It tries to answer certain questions concerning the nature and effects of structural changes brought about by colonialism—changes that had profound effects on life in Bornu.[1]

The details of nineteenth-century Bornu history have been described

[1] Data for this paper were obtained during field-work in Bornu Province, Nigeria, during 1956–7, under the sponsorship of the Ford Foundation Area Training Fellowship Program. Besides the published literature, which is scattered, a number of primary sources have been utilized. The basic materials come from the author's own field notes collected from interviews conducted in Magumeri and Maiduguri. In a few places I have used materials collected by Professor A. Rosman, who was in Bornu during the same period; and I am grateful to Professor Rosman for permission to use these data. The then Resident Officer of Bornu Province, Thomas A. Letchworth, granted permission to my wife and me to use some of the early records of colonial rule in Bornu. I am grateful to have had this opportunity and fully acknowledge my debt to Mr Letchworth, as well as to all of the other officials of the Bornu Provincial Government and the Native Administration of Bornu Emirate for the help and guidance they gave during the field trip.

I should like to thank Professors John Middleton and H. F. C. Smith for critical comments and suggestions. A previous draft of this paper was discussed at Harvard University in March 1965, under the sponsorship of the Boston University Seminar in African History. I should like to thank also the members of the seminar, especially Professor Jeffrey Butler and Dr Louis Brenner of Boston University, for their many interesting comments and criticisms. Since the first writing of this essay, Dr Brenner's 'The Shehus of Kukawa: a history of the Al-Kanemi dynasty of Bornu' (Ph.D. thesis, Columbia University, 1967) has been completed and has forced a number of revisions which are cited in the text. See also Cohen and Brenner (1969).

74

elsewhere (Cohen, 1967; Brenner, 1967; Cohen and Brenner, 1969) and need only be summarized here. The most important event of the century was occasioned by the onslaught of the Fulani jihad to the west of Bornu. This was experienced in Bornu as a series of uprisings by the local Fulani, who were encouraged by the leader of these wars, 'Uthman dan Fodio of Sokoto. In order to withstand these attacks, it became necessary for the monarchy of Bornu to rely on a Kanembu Sheikh, Al Kanemi (remembered locally as Shehu Laminu). This man, a religious leader, became more and more successfully involved in the defence of Bornu, so that by about 1820 he was in fact the single most powerful person in the state.

In the ten to twelve years preceding 1820 the Bornu traditional rulers had been forced several times by Fulani attacks to abandon their ancient capital of Birni Gazargamu, and finally left it for good to take up residence closer to Lake Chad. In this same period, Al Kanemi founded the town of Kukawa, which was to become the nineteenth-century capital of the kingdom. The story of his rise to power is a fascinating but complex one (Brenner, 1967; Cohen and Brenner, 1969) which, by approximately 1820, had resulted in a situation in which Bornu had in effect two rulers—first, the ancient royal family who owed their tenure to Al Kanemi's support, and second, the authority and power of Al Kanemi himself.

This double regency continued well after Al Kanemi's death in 1837 into the reign of his son Umar. However, in 1846, because of some abortive attempts by the original rulers, the ancient Magumi Sefuwa dynasty was decimated and its leading royal heirs killed. This left Umar as the only ruler of Bornu and established the royal legitimacy of the Kanembu dynasty. Until this time the court of the Kanembu rulers had been less formal and ritualized than that of the Magumi Sefuwa rulers. There were fewer titled officials in the Kanembu court, even though it was by far the wealthier and more powerful of the two.

After 1846, the titles of the ancient Bornu monarchy and much, though not all, of the pomp and ceremony were taken over by the second dynasty. The monarch was now called Shehu instead of Mai, and he did not appear in a wooden cage as had the Mais before him. Also, his courtiers were not dressed in many robes and large turbans in order to make themselves look larger than the ordinary people.

Brenner (1967: Ch. 4) makes the interesting observation that within Bornu after 1846 the major modes of political competition changed.

75

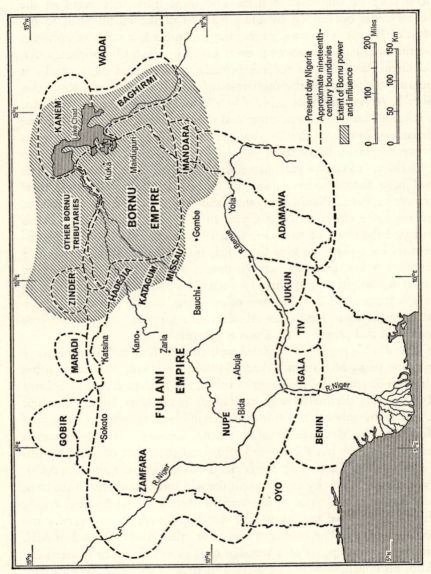

Figure 2. The empire of Bornu in the nineteenth century.

Present day Nigeria

Approximate nineteenth-century bornu boundaries

Extent of Bornu power and influence

From the time of Al Kanemi's rise to power, until the final demise of the former monarchy in 1846, there was constant tension between the two courts. The ancient rulers plotted with neighbouring kingdoms for a restoration of their power, and the Kanembu monarchs (Al Kanemi and Umar) had to be constantly on guard against such intrigue. Furthermore, they also had to pacify and gain control of areas of the kingdom which did not accede readily to the imposition of a new dynastic power at the centre of the state. As a result, the Kanembu court was not so dependent upon Kanuri support—using instead fellow Kanembu and even Shuwa as supporters. This, says Brenner (1967: Ch. 4), created solidarity within the Kanembu court. However, after 1846, the threat of a resurgence of Magumi Sefuwa power was over, and factionalism within the Kanembu court was able to surface—causing instability in the central government in the latter half of the nineteenth century.

The first serious indication of this occurred in 1853–4, when Shehu Umar's younger brother Abdurrahman usurped the throne for a short period. Along with most of the leading courtiers, Abdurrahman disliked the power that his brother's chief minister Haj Bashir had obtained—a power so great that it threatened the influence of the nobility. Finally the brother revolted and was able to grasp the throne away from Umar. However, Abdurrahman proved to be a much more arrogant and irresponsible ruler than his brother Umar. Within a year of the deposition, Umar was able to recoup enough support to challenge his younger brother and regain the throne. In the process, Haj Bashir lost his life, and this was followed soon after by the execution of Abdurrahman. Later, a chief follower of Bashir's (Laminu Njitiya) was to rise up and gain enormous power in Bornu during the rest of Shehu Umar's reign.

Umar ruled until his death in 1880. After his death, his son Bukar took the throne. Bukar had been a strong military leader during his father's reign, quelling rebellious tributary states and making many successful slave-raiding expeditions. There is a tradition that he was away on a campaign at the time of his father's death and was called back by his mother, who feared that he might not be made Shehu if he were away from the capital at the time. Landeroin (1911: 372) carries this story farther, and tells how Bukar refused at first to hear the proclamation of his regency because there were too few witnesses; and quickly called together a large company including his son Kiyari in order that the announcement might be made more public. In the third year of his reign he was unable to mount a campaign against pagans to the south because the people, tired of incessant wars, are supposed to have left unheeded his calls for troops, with the result that instead 'some sent only a slave, others a son, and still others, no one at all' (p. 373).[1] In response, Bukar is supposed to have levied a tax on one-half of all belongings in the state, which increased his unpopularity and made the palace storehouses richer than they had been under any other Shehu (p. 373). He died later in the following year—1884—just four years after taking office.

Brenner (1967: Ch. 4) gives this tax a different interpretation. He suggests that the entire region of the western Sudan was at this time experiencing an economic recession resulting from the decline of the trans-Saharan slave-trade. In order to maintain the state revenues, which were becoming sorely depleted, Bukar had to allow for a tax that came close to being plunder. Since this 'tax' had a special name (*Kumoreti*: literally, half the calabash, i.e., half of all grain in storage or half of all possessions), it is conceivable that it was in fact used prior to such times by monarchs and other leaders who were in financial difficulties, although this point is not clear.

It seems to have been agreed upon by all nobles and officials that Abba Masta, a son of Shehu Laminu, i.e., paternal uncle to the dead monarch, would succeed Bukar. Urvoy reports that 'after having been designated king by the palace nobility, he was then replaced by Ibrahim the next day (probably because his succession gifts were too paltry)' (Urvoy, 1949: 113). Another version of the same incident, given by a titled Kanuri whose own ancestors had taken part in the proceedings, is more detailed. Evidently, everyone believed that Abba Masta would become Shehu on the death of Bukar, and all concerned with the choice are supposed to have sworn on the Koran that they would, in fact, choose Abba Masta. However, that night the mother of Ibrahim (a son of Shehu Umar, and younger brother of Bukar) went to the houses of all those concerned in the choice and paid them large sums of *Gursu* (Maria Theresa dollars). The following day Abba Masta sat in his house waiting to receive those who would announce his regency; but Ibrahim was proclaimed Shehu instead, and all the royal household and titled nobles went off to Ibrahim's house to swear

[1] The Kanuri word for son (*tada*), translated as *fils* by Landeroin, is a generic term for client, which includes the kinship term 'son' as one of its meanings. It seems quite likely that the original connotation here was that of client or follower rather than son.

allegiance to the new monarch—all, that is, except Abba Masta, who refused and accused the entire court of being pagans, since they had sworn on the Koran that he and not Ibrahim was to be made Shehu (Rosman). True or not, the story indicates the kind of intrigue generally believed by informants to be part of the politics of royal succession.

After reigning for less than a year, Shehu Ibrahim died in 1885. His uncle, Abba Masta, had refused at first to acknowledge him and had fled the capital. The Shehu sent messengers to him promising his safety if he returned to Kukawa, which he did; but despite these assurances Abba Masta is supposed to have been assassinated by the Shehu's command soon after he returned. Ibrahim was succeeded (in 1885) by Hashimi, or Ashimi, his younger brother, who ruled until his death by assassination in 1893—a year that was to bring tragedy to Bornu.

It is necessary to consider events to the east of Bornu which were to bring war and defeat to the kingdom. In the Darfur region of what is now the Sudan, Suliman, son of Zubeir Pasha—an almost legendary slave-raider—had been defeated by Gessi Pasha, one of General Gordon's subordinates in 1879 (Urvoy, 1949: 126). Rabeh, one of Zubeir's lieutenants, tried to dissuade Suliman from surrender, and after failing declared himself independent. He was joined by a section of Suliman's army and the group moved westward, pursued by Gordon's forces. By degrees, Rabeh subdued and pillaged almost all of the area to the west of Darfur except Wadai, with whom he made a truce. He then went around Wadai to the south and defeated the Baghirmi army at the south end of Lake Chad. He was now on the south-eastern borders of Bornu, and in 1893 crossed the Shari river into south-east Bornu. He defeated the first Bornu army sent against him and put the commander to death. He then marched on the capital, Kukawa, and defeated Shehu Hashimi, who fled westward. Hashimi was killed by his own nephew, Kiyari, son of Shehu Bukar (1880–4), who took over the leadership of Bornu and reorganized a successful resistance against Rabeh's invasion. However, Rabeh checked his own army in flight and squashed the plunder-seeking Kanuri, who had rushed into the enemy camp unprepared for another battle. The power of the Kanembu Shehus was for the moment at an end. Rabeh tried several times to obtain a pledge of allegiance from Kiyari but was refused, and finally Kiyari was executed. Kukawa was sacked and burnt, and a large number of the Bornu royal family along with their followers fled to former vassal states to the north and west of Bornu.

Rabeh toured Bornu, pillaging as he went, and finally returned to present-day Dikwa in south-east Bornu, where he set up a walled citadel for his new kingdom. He kept a strong standing army estimated at 20,000 (Benton, 1913: 32; Urvoy, 1949: 127), uniformed and armed with guns, to whom he paid salaries. Many of his followers became fief-holders, although former Bornu nobles who swore allegiance to the new ruler were also retained. Rabeh's ostentatious monarchy and his standing army required heavy taxation, a quality of his rule which is still remembered in Bornu by contemporary informants. He also married his daughter Hauwa to a son of the Emir of Sokoto, and the son-in-law came to Dikwa to live for a time in Rabeh's court. This indicates that Rabeh was in contact with his powerful neighbours to the west and made some kind of treaty with them, which was in part made firm by a marriage between the families of the two rulers. He also maintained the judicial system of the nineteenth century and continued the practice of having the head of the state run the highest court of the land. Although his rule is remembered today as the most difficult and tragic period of Bornu history, it is very likely that had he not been interrupted by European expansion into the area, Rabeh would have founded the third Bornu dynasty. Intermarriage and general acculturative tendencies in Bornu that had affected the Kanembu at the beginning of the century would, given the time, probably have turned his intrusiveness into a more Kanuri-like cultural context in the long run, just as the Fulani at the beginning of the century had become more Hausa-like after their conquest of the Hausa states.

However, the Chad basin was already a matter of European as well as African political concern—England, France and Germany were all vitally interested in the area. Early in the 1890s the French worried lest the English get very far inland too quickly; consequently they started pushing up towards Lake Chad at that date. By 1897 Gentil was able to get a small force down the Shari river towards Chad and a French trader-explorer, de Behagle, visited Rabeh at Dikwa (Landeroin, 1911: 376). This French presence acted to increase the forces of disunity: the leaders of Baghirmi, a tributary of Rabeh's, asked the French for help. Rabeh, hearing of it, burnt a number of Baghirmi villages and put the French trader de Behagle to death (p. 376). In 1899 Rabeh fought at least two battles with the French, winning both but suffering many losses on his own part. Finally, in April 1900, the French under Major Lamy engaged Rabeh decisively, killing him and defeating his forces.

Those remaining fled back to Dikwa, which soon fell to the French. After this, only a small remnant under Rabeh's sons, especially Fadel Allah, held out against the Europeans, who by this time had obtained the support of many of the native Kanuri (see pp. 376–8 for a fuller description).

The French placed one of the Kanembu royal family, Umar Sanda, on the throne at Dikwa, but he was soon deposed for intriguing against his French supporters. (He later became the first District Head of Magumeri in British Bornu.) A brother of Sanda named Garbai was then given the throne at Dikwa, and later (1901), on coming to British Bornu, became the first Shehu of the colonial period.[1] The French lost not only the Shehu; they lost also Dikwa, which became, according to international agreement, a centre for the German Cameroons.

But the transition to colonial status was not so smoothly established as summary accounts sometimes lead us to believe. Fadel Allah at first set up a stronghold south of Dikwa on the Yedseram river. During the early part of 1901 he even managed to reconquer his father's capital at Dikwa, defeating Garbai, who then had to ask the French for help in order to keep himself in power. This was because Fadel Allah was not only raiding but provoking the Kotoko and the Shuwa Arabs to revolt against French overlordship and the French puppet Garbai. When the French finally moved against Fadel Allah, he retreated to British territory and positioned himself at Gujba in British Bornu, where he was finally vanquished by a French force later in 1901 (Landeroin, 1911: 378). There has been some speculation that the British may have helped or encouraged Fadel Allah in hopes of combating the French presence in the area; but there seems to be no evidence that such encouragement was, indeed, part of British policy, although local officials befriended Fadel Allah and gave him a few gifts.[2]

POLITICAL ORGANIZATION IN NINETEENTH-CENTURY BORNU. In the early part of the century, Bornu political life was complicated by a

---

[1] As is suggested by local informants, there may have been several contenders put on the throne by the Germans and/or the British for very short periods in 1901–2. But the point is unclear.

[2] Personal communication from Mrs B. A. Ballard, who has conducted research on this point in the French archives. I am grateful to Mrs Ballard for telling me of an article on Rabeh in the *Pall Mall Gazette*, 12 July 1899, by 'E.D.M.' (E. D. Morel?). The writer in the *Gazette* felt that it would be wise if Rabeh and the British could come to terms with one another, since Rabeh was an able leader and now in control of a great and ancient African kingdom.

fiction. The ancient Sefuwa rulers were still holding court, although it was the political organization of the Kanembu Shehus that effectively maintained control of the state. Al Kanemi came to Bornu with five close followers: Mallam Tarab, Ibrahim Wadaima, Mallam Ahmed Gwonimi, Haj Sudani and Mallam Tatali. These men were to become the five most powerful men of his administration whose households remained important centres of power throughout Al Kanemi's reign. Despite their power they did not acquire traditional Kanuri titles. Most of these were kept by the followers of the Sefuwa Mai in his elaborate but effete court. The Shehu made war, collected taxes and kept the peace; but even during the double regency, the common people still said 'my master' in referring to the Mai, while only slaves spoke of the Shehu in this way. Despite these difficulties, indeed because of them, the Kanembu Shehus built up a system of government very similar in cultural content to that of the Sefuwa Mais, although several organizational changes were developed because of the double regency.

After 1846 the sole ruler at the centre of the state was the Shehu. By the 1880s his office had become enmeshed in ritualism and pomp, incorporating some of the practices of the first dynasty, different to some extent, still regal as would befit the ruler of a powerful state, but including new elements of its own. Thus, as already noted, the Shehu did not meet his court in a *fanadir* (an enclosed cage), as had been the custom of the Mai,[1] although he did meet his court every morning in the palace at Kukawa as the Mai had done. Drums, pipes and horns announced the meeting, and all gathered in the royal presence, having taken off their shoes beforehand as a mark of respect. They would then seat themselves in a squat position to make sure they were beneath the Shehu, who sat in his royal seat or couch. As he appeared, all those in his presence simulated the throwing of earth on their heads and greeted the king with cries of 'long life, long life', to which he replied 'welcome' or 'peace', answered again by the court with 'ushe, ushe' (we are grateful) (Nachtigal, 1879: II, 709).

The Shehu's household consisted of his own family, his wives, female slaves, his mother (*Magira*) if she were still alive, and his unmarried agnatic sisters. Of these, his mother and senior wife (*Gumsu*) held titles and fiefs. If his mother were dead, the title of Magira went to his eldest living sister. There was a title for the eldest sister (*Mogorom*),

---

[1] From early times, it was probably a widespread practice in the Sudan for the monarch to remain veiled or hidden.

but this seems to have fallen out of use or to have been used by the Shehu for the head of the divorced women of the capital. It is reported by a few contemporary informants, but not by observers like Barth or Nachtigal, that on state occasions, such as annual religious festivals or a royal succession, the titled women of the palace, accompanied by their own slaves, appeared in public in men's clothing. It should be noted that wives whose sons became monarchs could take the title of Magira or king's mother, along with its attendant privileges. This obviously led to intrigue in which the mother plotted for the succession to fall to her own son, rather than to those of her co-wives. It is not clear whether or not sons born to the king of slave mothers could be legally included in this category. All records of succession for which maternal data are available indicate that royal heirs were sons of wives; but any man can free a female slave by marrying her.

The Shehu also had as part of his household organization a small armed force of cavalry not exceeding fifty to a hundred men as a personal bodyguard. This force followed him into battle for the purpose of protecting his person from harm and was under the command of a *Grema*, described as a second-rank or a low-ranking slave with military duties. The basic administrative tasks of the household were carried out by the *Sugurum*. These were servants (*waladi* or *tada*), slaves (*karliya*), or slave eunuchs (*adim*)—mostly the latter—a number of whom held important titles. Some of these titles were taken over from the pre-nineteenth century, and after the demise of the Sefuwa dynasty were re-issued, so to speak, to the Sugurum. The four highest ranking of these in descending order were the *Yuroma*, *Mastrema*, *Shettima*, and *Mala Agadi*. The first two of these had been associated with important administrative posts held by eunuchs in the government organization of the pre-nineteenth-century period when the state was divided up into four quadrants for purposes of royal taxation and administration. In the nineteenth century they were taken over by the Shehu and given to household or palace eunuchs. Because of their infertility, the incumbents to these four offices succeeded each other sequentially. Thus if the Yuroma died, his title was taken over by the Mastrema, and the Shettima became the Mastrema. All other non-titled eunuchs were called *abagana*, the kin-term used for father's younger brother.

The Shehu's court (*Nokena*) was made up of a number of categories of persons who varied in eligibility as a result of birth, occupational specialization and achievement. Members of the royal family—

especially first-generation male descendants of monarchs—were called *Maina*, although this term was used also to describe sons of nobles not of slave origin. The term can be translated roughly as prince. For royal prince the term *Abba* is used, too. A selected group of royal Maina sat behind the Shehu in a semi-circle facing his back and the rest of the assembled court. First-generation female descendants of monarchs were called *Mairam* and were not members of the Nokena, although their male children (*tada Mairambe*) were persons from whose ranks Bornu consuls who resided in vassal states as representatives of the Bornu government were often chosen. *Maidugu*, the term for a monarch's grandchildren, was reserved for agnatic male descendants of a monarch who were potentially Maina or Abba through their fathers and who therefore might one day be kings. Of all these royal family members, including the titled women of the royal household, only the royal Maina sat in the Shehu's court.

The rest of the court was made up of free men and slaves who sat in (and then behind) two straight parallel lines going out from the throne facing one another, with the exception of the *Galidima*, or lord of the north-western part of Bornu. When he was in court, that worthy gentleman sat in the middle of the lines in front of the throne facing the same way as the Shehu. This was to symbolize his separate, almost monarch-like, status as a territorial ruler within the Bornu state. The free men of the court were titled nobles who had descended from royalty or from close followers of Al Kanemi and representatives, often titled as well, of all the various occupational and some ethnic groups of the kingdom. If these free men were descendants of royalty or close associates of royalty, it was they to whom the term Maina was often extended in contradistinction to appointed client followers (*koguna*) and those who represented the various groups in the state. Another group of loyal followers of the throne—the *Kachella* or military leaders—was of slave origin. Kachella may have been the title of one or more slaves connected to military activity during the pre-nineteenth-century period. This point is not clear, but during the nineteenth century this office became an extremely important one in the organization of the state.

In pre-nineteenth-century Bornu, the head judge cum religious leader of the state, the *Talba*, was considered to be the *Mai Kanandi*, second to the ruler, or the second most powerful man in the state. When Al Kanemi rose to power, this title was presumably held by someone else

in the court of the Mai. Shehu Laminu acted as his own chief religious
and legal adviser. His royal court was also a high court of the realm.
There was also a mosque in Kuka that probably had judicial functions,
and the political hierarchy itself was an appellate court system. Muslim
scholars who were associated with the households of political office-
holders helped in the adjudication of cases. However, after the inception
of the Kanembu dynasty and the fall of the Magumi Sefuwa, the strict
designation of the Talba as the chief judiciary figure of the realm was
discontinued. It should be remembered in this regard that Al Kanemi
considered himself, and was considered by others, to be first and
foremost an Islamic scholar and teacher. Therefore his claim to
judicial competence was well taken and is certainly remembered as
legitimate.

The law itself seems to have been quite harsh, at least in the higher
courts. Adultery on a Muslim holy day could bring 400 lashes to a man
and 200 to a woman. It was believed that the judges in the capital of
Kukawa actually set spies upon the populace to search out such delicts.
Murder was punishable by death. Repeated apprehension as a thief
brought the loss of a hand, or torture by exposure of the head above
ground—buttered or honeyed to attract insects. Unpaid debts, if
proven in court, led to confiscation of property and a fine to the court.
However, the debtor had to give his consent, which was obtained from
him while he was pinned to the ground by court officials. If the debtor
clearly could not pay his debts because of lack of any property, the
judge was supposed to say, 'God send you the means' (Denham and
Clapperton, 1826: II, 150). The Shehu's court served as a final court of
appeal and could be used by even the lowest-status persons in the state,
although most civil cases involving non-office-holders generally
remained with lower courts. The following passage from Denham
and Clapperton (p. 150) describes the adjudication procedures of the
monarch, which were probably similar to those of the lower courts:

His [the Shehu's] court is simple, though numerously attended. On certain
days in the week, until the hour of midday prayer, he sits in the courtyard,
outside his private apartment, and all his subjects have access to his presence,
at liberty to state their grievances. The governors of the different provinces
sit immediately before him, and introduce the case of their people to his
notice in their own language: he listens to the different witnesses without
speaking, and decides promptly, and with judgment: a wave of the hand
passes for a sentence of death, which is instantly executed; and a whisper

---

decides a question of property which is, the moment after, placed in the possession of him who has the verdict in his favour.

Whether or not other religious leaders of the state sat in the royal court is not quite clear. Several informants claim they did, although the bulk of the reports on the court either do not mention them or suggest that the imam sat in the court on holy days. Indeed, the entire question of who had a right of membership in the royal court is somewhat vague. Perhaps this is due to the fact that by the end of the century the court did not have much power. Although Nachtigal speaks of titles, nobles, free men and slaves—some of whom had a vote and some of whom did not—he also observed that the Shehu's court had very little real political power (Nachtigal, 1879: II, 713):

The entire *Nokena* is merely a shadow of the former aristocratic constitution and has at present very little meaning. The institution comes from the time when the reigning families were still aware of their northern origin and when the king suffered the powerful aristocrats as rightful advisers, as is customary with all dwellers of the desert, be they Arabs, Berbers, or Tubu. Now only the word of the ruler and the influence of the favourites counts. The free Koguna naturally feel their origin to be superior to that of the Shehu's slaves. However, the Shehu considers the status of birth to be unimportant, and the freeborn have to vow before a slave if the latter stands in greater favour with the ruler.

Furthermore, like all offices in Bornu, membership in the Nokena must not be thought of as the undisputed right of this or that set of persons occupying a strictly delimited set number of roles. In the same passage as that quoted above, Nachtigal reported on the activities of Mohammed el Titiwi, who came every morning to the Nokena, even though he had no proper right to sit there. This man had great power and influence and had begun to replace a nobleman in the latter's rights and obligations. He could do this by making large gifts to the Shehu and by having a large band of armed followers supported by himself who could fight for the state. An even better example is that of Laminu Njitiya (Brenner, 1967; Cohen and Brenner, 1969). This man began, say the traditions, as a highway robber and rose through proper client relations to become the trusted aide of Haj Bashir, Waziri to Shehu Umar. After Bashir's death he finally became the right-hand man of the Shehu. Such meteoric rises were rare, but they kept alive the dream of upward mobility in a society that was highly stratified and dedicated to the values of inherited status as well.

The operation of political forces within the state at a level below that of the monarch can best be seen in the succession to office of a new Shehu. Since the death of the monarch removed the central power of the state, other political forces usually less visible came into view. According to one version, the new Shehu was chosen by a group of nine persons. These included the Yuroma, the Mastrema, the Shettima (all household slaves and eunuchs as well), the Kaigama (i.e., the chief Kachella or military commander, who was a slave in the nineteenth century), the Yerima, the Shettima Kanuribe, the Mallam Tirab, the Ibrahim Wadaima, and the Mallam Ahmed Gwonimi (all free and titled). When the Shettima heard of the death of the Shehu, he told the other eight in secret. He heard of it first because as his personal attendant he was closest to the Shehu. In secret these nine chose the new Shehu, informed him that he was the new Shehu and then let the world know that the old Shehu had died. If the secret of the royal death was not kept until a successor was chosen, then it was believed civil war, rioting and general disorder would inevitably follow. If there were two equally good successors, the nine men were supposed to have taken two threads, one white and one black, each representing a candidate, rolled these into balls, placed sand on them and thrown them into water. The ball that came to the surface first represented the next Shehu. They might also throw the two balls and ask a child to go and retrieve one, and the one chosen in this fashion decided who was to be the next ruler (Rosman).

Another version of this succession story suggests that these methods were indeed used, but that the *Digma* (slave-title) was a member of the group, while the Shettima and the Kaigama were not. This same version also includes information that the Digma was sent by the group to inform the new Shehu of his succession. On the other hand, Landeroin states that at the death of Shehu Umar in 1881, only three eunuchs—the *Mala Kerim*, the *Irama* (Yuroma?) and the Mastrema—made the decision regarding the royal succession. The Mala Kerim's views were the dominant ones because 'he commanded the largest numbers of soldiers' (Landeroin, 1911: 372). He then chose Bukar, son of Umar, and took Umar's ring, prayer beads and skull cap to Bukar's house, where he is reported to have said, 'Your father is dead, here are the symbols of power' (Landeroin, 1911: 372).

The difficulty with such attempts at reconstruction is that they cannot take into account the fact that the group choosing the new Shehu probably changed in accordance with the power structure of the state. Again, it does not take into account the attempts by interested persons to sway the opinions of the electors and to commit them to a particular choice, which, as we have seen, actually happened in the 1880s (Cohen, 1966 a). Also, before his death a powerful monarch like Al Kanemi could influence through his own edict the choice concerning the succession. In this case he named his own son, who in fact did succeed him. Again, there is the role of the dead king's wives. Each one wanted her son, or her favourite son, to take over the throne rather than a son of one of her co-wives. There are several stories extant of a dead king's wife who heard secretly that the king was dead and sent word to a son— who was off fighting a military campaign—to hurry back to the capital or he would not have a chance of obtaining the succession. Fact or fiction, the stories point to a possible kind of intrigue. As we have pointed out, the king's wife can only maintain her royal status by becoming a king's mother—which obviously serves as a structural stimulus for king's wives with sons to participate in the succession rivalry.

THE STRUCTURE OF ADMINISTRATION. All titled officials, or even untitled royal followers, could be given fiefs or rights of revenue collection for their own support in one or more settlements spread throughout the state. The rights to revenue collection were granted by the Shehu, nominal owner of all land within the political boundaries of Bornu, in return for services rendered to the throne. Such rights were hereditary, but the Shehu could diminish or expand the holdings of one fief-holder at the expense of another; and a new monarch was expected to patronize his own favourites. Brenner (1967: Ch. 5) notes that the successor to his father's office among free followers of the monarch had the right to inherit one-third of the fiefs and property acquired by their deceased father. The remaining two-thirds was equally divided between the Shehu and the remaining heirs of the deceased noble. In the case of slaves, all property and fiefs reverted to the monarch. Obviously this kept a constant flow of property and privileges flowing through the hands of the monarch for redistribution. However, it should be noted that although this may have been a rule, in practice slave nobles did inherit the statuses of their fathers, and in a number of notable cases, free nobles were stripped at death of their prerogatives. These were then redistributed by the monarch to favourites at the court. Thus, if necessary, the monarch had the power to abrogate such prerogatives among his subordinates no matter what the general rule. On the other hand, the very existence of such patterns meant that a monarch overturned them only when necessary, unless he wished to lose the support of his courtiers, who might, in extreme circumstances, plot with royal rivals for his deposition.

As shown in Fig. 3 A, page 110, a fief-holder was called a *Chima Kura* and there were two types of fiefs, *Chidibe* (territorial) and *Jilibe* (ethnic or clan-based). The fief-holder remained in the capital and administered his various holdings—spread out in various-sized lots throughout the kingdom—through his subordinates the *Chima Gana*. The Chima Gana lived in the fief. If it were a large one, there might be two or even three men with this office in the various sectors of the holdings. He was the highest authority in the fief and from him one could appeal to the Shehu, being presented to the Shehu by representatives of the Chima Gana and his superior, the Chima Kura.

The local organization into which this centralized structure articulated was based ideally on agnatic descent, although the real basis of organization was residential. A town head belonged to the agnatic line of the founders of the settlement. He was called the *Bullama*. On taking office he paid a *kafela*, or gift of succession, to the office of Chima Gana; and if his administration were not to the liking of the Chima Gana, or if the people under him complained, he could be deposed by the Chima Gana and another agnate from the same family chosen to replace him. Indeed, records from various Bornu district notebooks (Borsari, Nganzei and Geidam) indicate that the Chima Gana could shift the office to other family lines if he wished. As settlements grew in size, sons, clients and even slaves of the original town head would hive off and form small settlements or satellite communities under the overall jurisdiction of the original town head and the local leadership of the satellite founder. The heads of these new villages were called *Mbarma*. Thus a fief could expand in size, and successful Chima Kura and their Chima Gana tried to create conditions for such expansion by not being too expensive in their demands on the peasants and by protecting them from raiders and other forms of depredation. A Chima Kura was a permanent resident of the capital whose political success depended in part on wealth and on the ability to recruit followers for military purposes.[1] Thus it was to his own best interest to govern well, or to see to it that his subordinates were not unjust or tyrannical. Continual complaints could lead to the granting of fief rights inside the original fief to another Chima Kura, or in extreme cases to the transferring of the entire fief to another titled person.

An extremely successful town head, i.e., the head of a large and flourishing settlement with many satellite communities, could be rewarded for his increase in stature by being brought to Kukawa by the Shehu and given the title of *Lawan*. For this title he paid a *kafela* to the Shehu and not to the Chima Gana. There were at least two exceptions to this rule, both of these located in northern Bornu where the Chima Gana were empowered to bestow the title of Lawan. In both these instances the localities were border areas where the Chima Gana had much military work to do in order to contain Tuareg and Tubu raiders who made depredations into the settlements and molested caravans. Powerful Bullama and Lawan whose family connections to a particular village were old might find that the headship of a town carried with it a local title. Thus there was a *Gujima* (title) of Guji (the town), and a *Dapchima* (title) of Dapchi (the town). These titles were locally conferred by the Chima Gana to the person succeeding to the office of town head. The title of Lawan, when passed on, required that the new incumbent be 'turbaned' (entitled) by going to the capital, paying his kafela to the Shehu and then returning to his district. Only through this validation at the centre was the office made fully legitimate.

Local leaders carried on adjudication of disputes, and the political hierarchy of Mbarma–Bullama–Chima Gana served as an appeal court system. However, the Chima Gana, perhaps also the Bullama in cases where he was powerful, had Koranic mallams in their households who helped adjudicate cases, referring serious ones such as homicide to the capital in Kukawa. The only information available (Borsari District Notebook) suggests that the fines from local courts belonged to the Chima Gana; thus the local judge was an administrative subordinate of the Chima Gana.

The other type of Chima was the *Chima Jilibe*. *Jili* refers to a variety or kind. People speak of this or that *jili* of soil, or tree, or person. In

---

[1] Political success depended also upon the success or failure of those with whom he was allied in the state, and upon his ability to maintain and/or create subordination to the winning side at the top of the emirate.

using it to refer to a person, they cite his territorial or settlement background, or ethnic group, or (in the nineteenth century) his clan grouping, if this differed from territorial identification.[1] *Jili* were represented in the monarch's court by *Chima Kura Jilibe* who could appoint Chima Gana as their representatives among their groups if the people were nomadic. Some informants claim that the Chima Kura Jilibe was the 'big man' of the group by hereditary right, and that the monarch chose this man from the agnates of one family. A few others, plus several reports in District Notebooks, suggest that the Shehu could appoint one of his followers as the Chima Kura of *jili*—much as he would make the same appointment for a territorial grouping. In all likelihood both of these versions are correct and both systems obtained. The system afforded the Bornu government a means of maintaining political authority over non-localized groups and over localized ones that might be suddenly broken up.

The extent of such groups is a little puzzling because of their variety. Large named subsections of Fulani or Shuwa nomads or small segments of new ethnic groups might be lumped together. Thus in one report (Borsari District Notebook) the Kwoyam were divided up into three main subgroups named after the three sons (Ayindi Kur, Magandi and Wagaji) of the original founder (Birchiri). Each of these groups was divided in turn into four segments, making twelve minor segments in all. The Chima Jilibe could be head of all Kwoyam, of one of the three main segments, or of one or more of the minor segments.

Documentation is available for other named groups in the Bornu state with a similar organization, such as the Ngau, the Budduwai, and the Bedde groups of western Bornu. It is important to note, however, that many of these peoples—like the Kwoyam—are now dispersed all over Bornu. Thus many of the persons in five of the Kwoyam minor segments came to the vicinity of contemporary Magumeri in the early nineteenth century, while the remainder stayed in northern Bornu.

Although conclusive evidence on this point is lacking at present, it is plausible and conducive to further research to suggest that a number of important processes were in operation here to produce this double system of Chima-ship. First of all, there was the power of the Shehu

[1] Today all Kanuri know their clan, or sub-ethnic classification, and know that they are supposed to receive this identification patrilineally, although there are no functioning clan groups in existence. The exact nature of Kanuri clans and their relationship to territorial units and ethnic identity is a complex subject that will be discussed in more detail in a future publication.

himself. If the monarch wished to make a fief larger or smaller, he could easily do so. He could unite parts of a *jili* under one man, or split it up under several men, probably using agnation, or agnation plus territorial unity if the groups were widely dispersed, as the principle of division. Secondly, the political stability or instability of the state as a whole, as well as economic prosperity or famines, would tend either to keep groups in one place or to disperse them over the entire state. Dispersed groups, such as those which broke up after the Fulani wars at the beginning of the century, would tend to maintain some identity, and this could be institutionalized in the Chima Jilibe system. Thirdly and most importantly, it should be realized that Bornu local residence patterning was conducive to the formation of clans, based on an original settlement under the Bullama and the satellite hamlets related by agnation under Mbarma. Over time, political, economic and perhaps other factors tended to disperse this localized group of settlements. Under such circumstances, especially if they occurred very rapidly, the head of such an organization could legitimately claim some degree of political authority over his dispersed group; or conversely, the group could be viewed by the monarch as having some form or organizational identity over which he could place a Chima Jilibe. If this reconstruction is correct, it would be expected that the Chima Jilibe would be important political leaders during times of political and social upheaval, and less important during periods of long peaceful settlement when local residential ties created the basis for the most important political units. What information we have seems to support this notion. When Denham visited Bornu in the 1820s only a decade after the Fulani invasions, he saw the army reviewed; and large numbers of troops passed by, each under their *Jilima* or head of their *jili* (Denham and Clapperton, 1826: 1, 265). At the same time he also mentions seeing many large Bornu towns that had been abandoned because of the Fulani wars (p. 211). Later in the century, during the time of Nachtigal (1880s), when the population had been stable for a long time, such an organization as that of the *jili* with a Chima Jilibe or Jilima at its head is not mentioned as part of the military establishment of the state.

Complicating the simple settlement patterns and their accompanying political structure were several factors. A Chima Kura might give permission to some group to set up a village in one of his fief territories. In this case, the new group was directly related to the Chima Kura through its own local representatives—not to the local leaders such as the Mbarma and the Bullama—and might one day become a separate fief. The Chima Kura also might settle some of his own slaves in a fief territory and obtain the same structural arrangement. Even more complicated was the possibility that a high official of state might ask a Chima Kura in the capital for permission to settle some of his own slaves in one or more of that Chima's fiefs. If permission were granted, then the slaves would farm and/or practise some craft speciality and deliver produce to their owner, who would send gifts of the produce to the fief-holder. It was also possible for the monarch, the Chima Kura, or someone to whom he granted this privilege, to settle Koranic scholars throughout the countryside in priest settlements. Since such settlements were usually tax-free, permission of the proper person was usually sought and granted.

THE TAXATION SYSTEM. Taxation varied with the type of fief and the territorial and population size of the fief holding. For the territorially-based fiefs there were two annual state taxes and innumerable smaller ones, as well as an implicit right of the monarch to tax as he saw fit. The two state taxes reflected the structure of the central government. One was collected by the fief-holder, the other by the monarch.

On the basis of information coming from the fief during any one year, the Chima Kura, or fief-holder living in the capital, decided on the amount of taxation. During the cold season (Binəm) he sent a trusted messenger known as the *kingam* to his subordinate in the fief—the Chima Gana—to collect the *binəmram* tax on the harvest. The Chima Gana and the kingam called together all the headmen in the fief and announced the tax. This announcement meeting was in itself a small tax, since a tribute known as the *kingaram* was brought for the kingam. The main tax was then collected by the headman of the fief, who kept some surpluses if possible and passed on the rest to the kingam through the Chima Gana, who also took some for himself. After all collections were completed, another small tax or tribute called the *salaamaram* was given to the kingam. On receipt of his tax (the binəmram), the fief-holder in the capital—Chima Kura—passed on a token gift to the Shehu; but the greatest portion of this tax went to maintain the following of the fief-holder (Chima Kura) and the Kukawa household. In practice the Chima Kura were almost continuously delivering to the royal household gifts obtained from their fiefs. These were presented at times of religious festivals and *rites de passage* held in the palace, as well as on other state occasions.

Once a year—in the winter season, but close to harvest time for any particular year—the Shehu collected his *sadaga* or royal tithe.[1] It is not clear whether this tax followed or preceded the binɔmram or if there were any rule at all in this matter. The towns and villages near Kukawa sent in the Shehu's sadaga themselves, but other means were used for areas farther away from the capital. The peasants were supposed to bury one-tenth of their crop and to take this grain to the capital if it were sent for. If not, they were supposed to sell this royal portion in the local market and give the proceeds to the monarch's tax-collector. By right, this tax-collector was not the fief-holder. Any courtier could ask the king for permission, or be requested by him to collect sadaga anywhere in the state. After being granted the privilege, the courtier sent out his own kingam (tax messenger) and the same procedures were followed as with the binɔmram tax; but this time this was done in the name of the Shehu.

Besides these two main taxes, peasant householders, or perhaps just household heads (this point is not clear), paid small fees called *kaskaram* to their local headman Bullama or Mbarma, a portion of which was passed up the hierarchy to the Chima Gana, and to Lawan—if these were present in the local hierarchy. Each year, before farm plots were cleared for replanting, this tax—plus an additional fee of one straw mat paid to the local headman (shared with the Chima Gana)—was paid by those clearing new land. After the harvest, another small tax (the *kassasi*) was delivered in kind to the local headman; and through him part of this was also given to the Chima Gana. Taxes in kind were also collected from craftsmen, from people with irrigated farms, indeed from anyone with specialized economic pursuits.

Complicating the taxation system was the organization of administrative units by *jili* or ethnic and clan organizations, rather than by localized territorial organizations based on settled town life. Ethnic units were assessed, usually in cattle; and the two taxes—one through the Chima Kura (fief-holder) and one from the Shehu—collected in a manner similar to that described above for the binɔmram and sadaga.

---

[1] Sadaga is the Kanuri word for religious charity, which is set at one-tenth of a man's produce per year. The royal tithe is thus a recognition of the congruence of church and state in the emirate where the monarch is the commander of the faithful. See Boahen (1964: 249), who accepts H. F. C. Smith's position on the lack of distinction between church and state in Islamic government.

This latter tax, for the nomads, was in the form of one head of cattle taken from every ten and was often referred to as *jangali* (Brenner, 1967: Ch. 6). However, as we have already mentioned, some of these nomad groups, or members of previously unified ethnic and/or territorial groups, could be dispersed by migration, warfare, droughts, disease or other natural disasters. For some time after this dispersal they still paid small tributes to the heads of their former organizations. Thus an immigrant group in the settled organization of a fief would pay the usual taxes as members of the fief, plus some small tributes to heads of organizations to which they had previously belonged. Even a large settlement, broken up into migrating units and absorbed into other territorial units, could look upon the head of its former territorial organization as if it were a *jili* or sub-ethnic unit.

Several oppressive taxes are remembered that indicate the lengths to which the central government could occasionally go if it chose to do so. We have already mentioned kumoreti, or 'half the calabash', supposedly instituted by Shehu Bukar (1880–4) to help him keep up government revenues during a period of recession. This simply involved collecting half the possessions of the populace through court agents. Another such tax is referred to in Kanuri as 'rolling up the mats'. On occasion, the monarch could grant special rights of tax collection to a favourite—often one of his own sons who wished to start off in life with some capital. The person receiving this privilege could then go to stipulated villages and collect whatever he wanted, using force and 'rolling' the possessions of the people up in mats for transport to his own household in the capital. Such actions can also be interpreted to be a means by which punishments could be inflicted on an area by the throne, although clear evidence for such a statement is not available.

Tax exemptions or reductions were granted to religious leaders and settlements made up of such groups; to groups that may have settled in a fief through some agreements made between leaders of the group and officials in the capital; and to groups that had suffered some economic or social catastrophe such as a flood, famine, epidemic, or a series of very mad incursions from desert raiders.

It is in the military organization of the state that the nineteenth-century tendencies towards centralization in Bornu political development are most easily seen. Although the Sefuwa Mai of the pre-nineteenth-century periods had standing troops, what records remain indicate that the army was primarily a body of common peasants called by the monarch through their local leaders to meet at some rendezvous and to set out on a campaign. However, by the mid-nineteenth century there were large standing armies observed by Barth, and later by Nachtigal, under the command of *Kachellawa*, or military leaders, who were slaves of the Shehu. Nachtigal (1879: II, 725–7) reported 1,432 cavalry soldiers under fourteen Kachellawa (plural of Kachella) and 532 riflemen under thirteen Kachellawa. The Shehu was estimated to own another 500 fire-arms. Two other Kachellawa had approximately 200 archers under them and another single Kachellawa led a force of 500 spearmen with shields. Besides this force, which can be estimated at about 3,000, the Shehu could command the armed following of various nobles and courtiers, some of whom had fairly large militia. In the 1870s this amounted to approximately 4,000 soldiers under arms. Add to this the men who could be coaxed and conscripted if necessary from fief holdings, and it is easy to imagine the Shehu of Bornu fielding an army of 10,000 or more soldiers.

In his own household the Shehu kept only a small force of about fifty armed cavalry. All other militia were the economic concern of the Kachella or other titled nobles who were their leaders. Their numbers varied with the power of the particular leader. Thus the leading Kachella might have a force as high as 225 cavalry—outfitted in horses and arms, and sustained economically by the leader—while a very weak Kachella is recorded as heading up a force of only five cavalry. The same is true of the titled nobles, whose forces ranged from 1,000 cavalry to as low as fifteen (Nachtigal, 1879: 725–7).

The wealth and power of a military leader, free noble or slave Kachella, was determined by the success of his fiefs, from the extent of his booty in war, and from the degree of favour granted to him by the monarch, who had much to say in both the granting of fiefs and the disposal of booty from war campaigns. The Shehu could grant a man new fiefs if he were a successful and loyal client, and a leader could obtain power from hereditary rights to a large following and many fiefs. In other words, from a combination of achieved and ascribed rights and obligations, a leader in the Bornu state could have a variable number of armed military followers. It should also be noted that although the Shehu had a very large body of militia under his power through his slave military leaders, the Kachellawa, there was still a large military force available to the title nobles, some of whom were his rival heirs to the throne. This fact underlies events such as those of the 1850s, when a group of nobles under the Shehu's brother tried to take over the throne.

Perhaps the most significant distinction in nineteenth-century Bornu political organization was that made between an office and a title. Although the Kanuri did not completely differentiate these two categories of political role, they certainly viewed them as potentially different things. An office was a position in the government giving the incumbent rights, duties and obligations. The incumbent might already have a title or obtain one after assuming office. Both offices and titles could be conferred or inherited, although it was much more common to obtain an office through the use of agnatic descent ties as one of the criteria for selection. Offices could vary independently of titles or—and this confuses the picture—they may, as in the case of the Shehu himself, become permanently associated with an office. However, even at this level, the title of Shehu for the monarch began only in the nineteenth century, while prior to that the ruler was entitled Mai. Titles, however, are not offices; they are emblems adding honorific qualities to the person doing those jobs associated with his office. Much of the confusion concerning Bornu political organization in the pre-colonial period results from attempts to reconstruct pre-colonial political structure using offices and titles interchangeably and not keeping them separate in the analysis.

The nineteenth-century state had a great many titles, only some of which are known; but there were only a limited number of offices in the political organization. To summarize and recapitulate the political organization, these offices are given below.

The *monarch* or king—he was head of state, commander of the faithful, nominal owner of all the land, primary legislator in the government. His titles were Mai (pre-nineteenth century) and Shehu (nineteenth century up to the present).

The *king's mother*—with its own special title (Magira).

The *king's senior wife*—with its own special title (Gumsu).

Both of these offices give their female incumbents rights to fief holdings.

Household slave to the royal palace (Sugurum)—these positions, many of them held by eunuchs, gave the incumbents access to the royal presence and control over the access. Titles most often associated with the most influential of these offices were Yuroma, Mastrema, Shettima, and Mala Agadi (see discussion above).

Councillor to the monarch—these were divided into the free nobles and princes, who had hereditary rights to their positions, and the *koguna* or followers, who were divided in turn into the freemen, who represented ethnic groups and occupations in the state, and the Kachellawa or military leaders, who were slaves. Titles varied here a great deal, although that of Galidima, the noble head of a consolidated fief in north-west Bornu, was always the same.

Religious leaders, or Mallams—these men sat as advisers to political leaders at all levels of the hierarchy. They were diversely schooled in Islamic learning, made charms and could perform divination. They also served as teachers to the young in religious matters. In the political system they served as scribes and legal advisers to the administration.

All of the above with the exception of the king also held, as an associated right to their special office or offices, the office of Chima Kura. That is to say, they were holders of rights of taxation over some group or groups within the state. This office involved a separate hierarchy of offices because the Chima Kura had to remain in the capital. Under him was the Chima Gana, who lived in the fief. In the case of a nomad group it could be a local man chosen for his loyalty to the Chima Kura.

Headman of a local settlement, Bullama—he could have other titles associated with the name of his settlement, or conferred on him by the Shehu in the capital (e.g., Lawan).

Head of a satellite settlement, under the jurisdiction of the Bullama—Mbarma.

These offices could be repeated in the household organization of powerful men in the state. Thus a titled noble could have his own Sugurum (household slaves), his own religious advisers or Mallams, his own military leaders—although this position was referred to as that of a Grema rather than Kachella—and his own Koguna or followers, both slave and free. Brenner (1967, Ch. 5) suggests that followers of Koguna, at least royal Koguna, who had been given horses, were called *furma* (literally horse [*fur*] man [*ma*]) to distinguish them from those without horses. I have heard this word used to describe any client follower of a 'big man' who has been given a horse, including Koguna.

What has confused a number of writers on this subject has been the tendency for some of the Bornu titles to be strongly associated with offices while others were only weakly so. Those offices most strongly associated with titles are given in the summary above. However, other titles such as that of Kaigama, which for centuries had been tied to a high military office, lost the association in the nineteenth century when they were held by persons attached to the old dynasty, while the functions of the office shifted to someone in the administration of the new dynasty. The title came back to life in the latter half of the century after it had been used for some time. People began applying it to Kachella Bilal, the most powerful military slave (Kachella) of Shehu Umar (Nachtigal, 1879: 714). In the same reference to titles Nachtigal also notes that the title of Digma was of very little consequence in the pre-nineteenth-century period, but was picked up and given to a powerful slave by the first Shehu, Laminu. By the mid-nineteenth century the title was held by a very powerful person who had a number of important offices in the royal palace. Finally, by the 1880s it had again become inconsequential (p. 714). In the mid-nineteenth century the Digma controlled all the correspondence of the monarch, had something to do with the succession to office of Shehu, and controlled to a large extent all personal audiences with the king. By the 1870s all of these offices were filled by other persons, and the Digma at that time had fewer fiefs and moved as an equal or inferior among courtiers who would have paid the previous title-holder much respect (p. 714). The implication in this remark is that both the offices and the title have shifted in personnel and not in association with one another, so that a few of the offices have remained with the title but others have gone to other persons.

Finally, one other quality of titles should be made clear. They could come into existence and go out of use over time. The title of *Fufuma*, or headman of Birni Gazargamo, was dropped during the nineteenth century. On the other hand, the names of the five close followers of the first Shehu became important titles in Bornu and were passed down in the agnatic lines of the founders of these households for most of the century. To understand Kanuri political organization it is therefore necessary to concentrate not on titles, which are embellishments of the important political roles, but on the political offices themselves and on how they operate vis-à-vis one another and the state as a whole. Among the courtiers, especially in the latter half of the nineteenth century, there was constant competition for royal favours (Brenner, 1967: Ch. 4). Those few courtiers who obtained the trust and confidence of the ruler formed his working executive body, no matter what their particular titles or status. The leading member of such a group, and therefore the Shehu's closest subordinate, was referred to as *Waziri* or chief minister.

This was not a conferred title but a functional one that described the office of a man who served as the chief minister to the throne at any particular time.

ECONOMIC ORGANIZATION IN THE NINETEENTH CENTURY. The internal economy of Bornu in the nineteenth century was that of a semi-specialized productive system that required market transactions by all producers in order for them to obtain the full range of consumer goods and services required by the ordinary household. Almost all households had access to and worked some land, of which there seems to have been no shortage. Clearing new land was tantamount to establishing ownership, and the most common crop was millet.[1] Land ownership was not simply based on the usufruct right. Freehold rights, or the right of transfer, could be obtained through inheritance of the land or after a period of use right. If a man and/or his relatives and subordinates continued to use a piece of land, they not only had the right to its produce but to its dispensation, which could involve the giving of use rights to others, i.e., the right of transfer, since those to whom they gave the right could do the same thing in their turn.

This conception of land tenure—which is a type of freehold rather than usufruct property right—is an important mechanism in the political growth of communities. Under this system a satellite group hiving off from a parent village could, through its leaders, eventually establish rights of transfer over lands without referring the matter higher up the hierarchy, thus enhancing the political authority of its nascent leadership.

Larger towns in Bornu carried out some irrigated production, particularly of beans, onions and tomatoes. Domesticated animals included dogs, chickens, sheep, goats, cows, oxen, donkeys and, more rarely, camels and horses. Bornu herds seem to have diminished throughout the century (Benton, 1913: 124). Denham and Clapperton described 'herds beyond all calculation' (1826: II, 146) near Lake Chad and even more down near the Shari river, which was associated mostly with the Shuwa peoples. Barth (1857: II, 310) often speaks of herds of a hundred, not often of more, and in 1913 Benton (p. 124) felt that in Bornu fifty cattle constituted a large herd. Wild game was hunted and the produce—as well as roasted and boiled bees—was sold in the

[1] See Denham and Clapperton (1926: I, 251: 'a planter takes possession of any spot that has not been planted the preceding year, and then it becomes exclusively his property ').

markets. Barth describes the people as essentially vegetarian except for the rich who could afford meat (1857: II, 310). The most ubiquitous tool was the African hoe.

The list of specializations is extensive. There were blacksmiths, dyers, weavers, butchers, tanners, snake charmers, leather goods makers, tailors, sandal makers, calabash carvers, traders of various kinds, brokers who took a commission for selling cattle, sheep and goats in the markets, fishermen, hunters, musician-entertainers, medicine sellers, barbers and many others. Men helped to some extent at agricultural labour, but the main load of such work was carried by women and often by female slaves. Occupations were organized under local heads who benefited economically by their positions and tried to keep the office in their own agnatic descent group.

Distribution of goods was carried on in the local markets, each of which was held weekly, while a group of locally connected ones were held on different days of the week. There were daily markets in the large towns where quantities of goods were smaller, prices higher, and the diversity of items available much restricted. Each market was under the jurisdiction of a headman who settled disputes and exacted fines under the authority of the town head. Markets were divided into sections, each having its own products, and were attended at the heat of the day by very large numbers of people. Barth describes in detail the products for sale in mid-century. The list is long but ordinary enough that it becomes obvious that market buying and selling were part of the everyday needs of the average family (1857: 306–16).

As far as can be ascertained, the items that were used as currency and trade by means of barter covered a wide range. It is likely, but not completely demonstrable, that reliance on some form of currency became steadily more widespread throughout the century. Doubt is cast upon this generalization because of the supposed use of a standard copper currency in the pre-nineteenth century era, which is not ever directly referred to before the nineteenth century. Barth is quite clear on this point and says that it is hard to trade in the markets because the old standard, 'the pound of copper, has long since fallen into disuse, although the name *rotl* still remains' (p. 310). In the 1820s Denham and Clapperton observed that 'most of the trade carried out in Bornu was done in the local markets through the use of barter' (1826: I, 95). Beads, coral, amber and coarse rolls of cotton (*gabaga*) were used as standardized exchange measures, especially cotton—which could be purchased for ten *rotl* to the dollar (Maria Theresa dollars). There were three to four *gabaga* per *rotl* throughout the entire first half of the century. Generally speaking, a *gabaga* was three inches wide by one yard long. The dollar was either Spanish, Arabic or Austrian—with the Austrian being preferred. Cowries were not used in the early part of the century, and Clapperton had to change over to their use on his way from Bornu to Hausa territory (II, 220). In other parts of the country, as in the southeast or in the area south of Chad, iron boomerang-shaped bars, wrapped up in packages of ten or twelve, were used as a standard of exchange. Three parcels could usually be traded for one dollar. In other markets the authors report bullocks (p. 146) or even slaves (p. 36) were used as a medium of exchange.

By the 1850s Barth was able to use cowries in the major markets, but he is very clear in his opinion that rural farmers coming into the markets would not trade for cowries or dollars, but only for robes or clothes (II, 312). Barth reports the use of *gabaga*, slaves, iron bars, dollars, and cowries. The price of cowries was eight to the *gabaga* or thirty-two to the *rotl* (p. 311). The *rotl* had, however, fallen in price since the 1820s. Instead of ten to the dollar it was now somewhere between fifty and one hundred, depending upon how many cowries were being collected by the political leaders and thrown on the market (p. 311). On the other hand, the earliest British reports of the area tell of taxes being collected in the form of dollars in late nineteenth-century Bornu, and the British went to some effort to abolish the use of cowries as currency. We may therefore infer that currency was in more general use by the end of the century. Looking at the century as a whole, however, we find a lack of overall consensus on any one particular item and a number of more limited-purpose currencies used for specialized purposes. Certainly one thing is clear. Despite the lack of standardized currency, which Barth felt was a fatiguing quality of Bornu life, it cannot be said that such a lack inhibited the marketing of goods or the enormous amount of trade that is described as having taken place in some of the large centres (Cohen, 1965: 353–69).

The other major kind of internal distribution took place within the socio-political structure of the state and reached no mean proportions. Denham and Clapperton describe how such things were done on religious holidays. 'Garments, according to the estimation in which the giver holds the receiver, are distributed by all great people to their followers: the sheikh (Al Kanemi) gave away upwards of a thousand robes (men's robes), and as many bullocks and sheep' (1926: 1, 261). Later, at a slave wrestling match, the same authors watched clothing being thrown at the victor by the crowd. The owner would divest himself of one of his own articles of clothing and give it to the victorious slave whose life he had just threatened if defeated (p. 261). In innumerable ways goods continually moved back down the political and social hierarchy or even randomly through it. Superiors were enjoined by custom to distribute goods to subordinates at all holidays, *rites de passage*, and after successful war campaigns. In a more random way, the performances of entertainers, wrestling matches and other public events brought gift-giving by the public at large to otherwise unrelated persons. Thus there was a constant and considerable flow of goods through the society which was not part of the market system, if that system is meant to refer to the physical market-place and the trading which occurred there (Cohen, 1965: 353–69).

FOREIGN TRADE. Foreign trade in the nineteenth century declined steadily as it shifted to Kano away from the Chad–Tripoli route, although it never stopped completely (Boahen, 1962: 349–59). This may be attributed to several historical events hitherto unmentioned. After the death of Al Kanemi in the late 1830s, a period of east–west struggles, which had smouldered earlier, broke out between Bornu, Wadai, and Baghirmi to the east of Bornu (Denham and Clapperton, 1826: 1, 307). This antagonism finally resulted in almost continual warfare in the region. Complicating the events of the 1830s, the arrival of the Turks in North Africa led in the first place to a weakening of political control in the northern Saharan part of the Chad–Tripoli route, and in the second to the mass migration of the Walid Sliman to the Kanem area, where they became professional raiders and pillagers at the vital south end of the trade route. Brenner (1957: Ch. 4) mentions as well the decline of the slave-trade and depressive economic conditions in Europe in the 1870s and 1880s, which cut back on the trade in ostrich plumes and ivory coming out of Bornu. This resulted in a movement of trade towards the west to the Ghadames–Air–Kano route, plus an overall decline in trans-Saharan trade across the entire Sudan.

Commodities imported into the area included calicoes, cotton prints, fine silk, linens, beads, sword blades, writing paper, looking glasses, needles, razors, snuff boxes, scissors, knives and cheap jewelry—

as well as ammunition and guns from Europe. Burnouses, shawls, red caps and sashes, trousers, long striped carpets, coarse silk, religious books, spices, perfumes and cowries were shipped in from their points of origin in North Africa. Tobacco, wheat, barley, wild rice, salt, natron, camels, medicines and most especially *drupa* (a herb believed to produce female fertility) came in from the desert. In return, cloth, hides, leather work, leather water-skin buckets, sandals, feathers, ivory, gum, wax, Korans written by Bornu scholars, slaves, and kola nuts were sent out to North Africa (Boahen, 1962: 351).

Compared to the trans-Atlantic slave-trade, this traffic in slaves seems paltry. Boahen (p. 357) estimates that it never exceeded 9,500 per annum, of whom about twenty per cent were sent to Asia Minor and as far north as Albania.

Because of the dangers of the Bornu–Tripoli trade in the nineteenth century, trade caravans were large on this route and usually annual affairs. Both Denham and Clapperton in the 1820s, and Barth in the 1850s, crossed over the desert with large parties of several hundred. Prices were high at the south end of the trade. One copper kettle from North Africa could fetch a good male slave (Denham and Clapperton, 1826: II, 156). In general, a camel-load worth 150 dollars in Murzuk (the southernmost Maghrebian entrepôt) would bring 500 dollars in profit in Bornu after the expenses of the trip had been deducted, i.e., in net profit. In order to build up a caravan, traders at both ends would send two or three camels along with the caravan and give the man who took them on the trip one-third of the profit. Traders' quarters existed in all major Bornu towns, but especially in the capital city of Kukawa. In Al Kanemi's time, caravans were not allowed to enter the city of Kuka without his consent; and if he were not in the capital, the traders had to remain outside the city walls until he returned.

The importance of this foreign trade to local life is indicated in the fact that no well-dressed man in nineteenth-century Bornu felt fully resplendent unless he was wearing some article of foreign (usually trans-Saharan) manufacture. The Kanuri leaders needed weapons and other manufactured goods of North Africa and Europe to maintain their influence and power. Foreign cloth was prized; and when the Shehu gave out robes as presents, foreign cloth was considered a better gift than cloth of local manufacture. How much all this affected the life of the ordinary people is somewhat more difficult to say. *Drupa*, paper, cottons, kola nuts, iron, and other import commodities were on sale at most markets throughout the country. Traders and high government officials distributed imported products to local markets and to subordinates within their own organization. Thus in all likelihood the entire population shared in the use of the import goods and helped keep the demand and price high enough so that the trade, evenly distributed by warfare as it was in the nineteenth century, was still profitable enough to continue.

The colonial period and the founding of the modern emirate

POLITICAL CHANGE. As we noted earlier, the French killed Rabeh and later his son, and then set Sanda Kura up at Dikwa as Shehu. He was quickly replaced by his younger brother Garbai. The French allowed the Shehu to organize the political structure in the traditional way and to pay them 80,000 Maria Theresa dollars per year as a tribute. In 1902 Lugard sent Captain Morland to Bornu. It is reported that the Captain 'sent for Garbai, and formally installed him as the Shehu of British Bornu' (Bornu Annual Report, 1909). Data on how this was accomplished were not available in the public records of Bornu. Boyd Alexander claims that an associate of Morland's, a Captain Murrough, 'by a brilliant *coup de main* enticed him [the Shehu] out of his alien palace one night before the people were aware that anything irregular was afoot, and brought him on horseback back over the border to Maifoni [i.e., Maiduguri], where he was made Sultan of Bornu' (Alexander, 1907: 287). What enticed the Shehu to come to Bornu is not known. Perhaps it was because he disliked the French, or because he wished to return to Kukawa—the city of his ruling forebears—or because the mass of the Kanuri were in Bornu, or for all of these and other reasons. At any rate, Garbai's return to Bornu marks the beginning of the modern twentieth-century version of the ancient Kanuri kingdom. The Shehu went to the Kukawa area to supervise the rebuilding of the Kanembu family palace and set up his court in the traditional manner. The British officers decided at first to set up their headquarters at Magumeri, some distance to the west. In 1907 the British persuaded the Shehu to come southward and set up his court at Maiduguri, where they had moved, because of poor water supply at Kukawa, and perhaps because of the difficulties inherent in separation between the two administrations. This town then became the capital of Bornu Emirate and of the Province of Bornu.

RONALD COHEN

At first (1902) the British did very little except establish residence in the area. The Shehu was allowed to reconstitute the pre-Rabeh fiefdoms from amongst his followers and to carry on former nineteenth-century political life. During that first year enfeoffed nobles remained at the Shehu's court and must have ruled their holdings through Chima Gana. In 1903 one of the quarterly reports from Bornu to Lugard put forward the opinion that the extortion and inefficiency in the local system would stop when the 'headmen reside in their districts' (Bornu Provincial Report, 1904), and the districts become compact units instead of being scattered all over. He opined that the country would settle down as soon as it was partitioned into larger districts, and later that year this scheme was carried out. The fief-holders were ordered to give up all rights they might have in any particular area and the Shehu was asked to choose twenty-seven of his best leaders to take over these areas (Bornu Provincial Report, 1905).[1] By the middle of 1905 the resident, W. P. Hewby (1905), was able to report that with three exceptions there were no fief-holders left in Kukawa. Some had gone to their districts, and the rest had remained in court with the Shehu, but with no powers of taxation or rule. Although there is no information available on the details of this change, it is radical enough for us to assume that at least at the outset it must have caused some little confusion.

There seems to have been some difficulty in obtaining agreements over the appointments of village heads to the sub-units of the districts. At first, the village areas were set up by a group of Kanuri, who are referred to in early reports as the 'Land Board' and were appointed by the Shehu. This group is reported to have divided up districts into village areas so that the areas represented a close approximation to the pre-Rabeh fiefs of Shehu Hashimi (Magumeri and Borsari District Notebooks). However, the British were reluctant to sanction the appointments of village heads and to agree summarily to the village areas that were being delineated. Instead they conducted investigations throughout Bornu and tried to obtain lists of agnatic descendants of prior headmen who they felt had a right to the office. This resulted in some extensive accounts of pre-1900 Bornu that are still extant in the district notebooks. An early summary by G. C. Whitely (1909) in the Magumeri District Notebook will serve to illustrate the above process:

[1] The Shehu objected strenuously to the British suggestion that five of his brothers be made district heads. Presumably he would rather have loyal followers who were non-kinsmen in these important offices.

106

On the establishment of British Bornu, the creation of districts under resident district headmen was inaugurated...the next step was performed in Bornu by the Land Board. It is difficult to perceive the principle of division they adopted. They rarely if ever followed the path indicated by history...it seems to have been their habit rather to pass over the applicants with historical claims in favour of slaves, mallams, influential strangers, or friends of important men.

Later on in the same report Whitely recommended that seven village units near the town of Magumeri all be united into one village area under the jurisdiction of the headman of Magumeri town, whose family had an historical claim to all of these villages. The district headman of the area had pre-1900 claims on the fief and the village head of Magumeri town was his slave, whilst the headmen of the other six surroundings villages were new to the area—put there through the consent of earlier British administrative officers on the advice of the Land Board. Whitely's recommendation was not acted upon, presumably because of decisions taken by his superiors, and/or because of the wishes of the Shehu. Data are lacking on this point. In other districts, however, Land Board claims were not honoured. In Borsari District the Land Board set up forty-three village areas in 1903-4, which were reduced to fourteen in 1907; and seventy-three such units were reduced to thirty-one in Geidam District during this same period (Palmer, 1907).

What resulted was a formal hierarchy of offices that was not necessarily hierarchical in traditional terms. When the district head arrived in his district with his retinue of supporters, he found that the local village area heads might be of several different kinds. They might be persons who had been his own subordinates because of his previous connections to a fief in the area; or they could be traditionally subordinate to other pre-1900 fief-holders who were either district heads elsewhere in Bornu, or simply living in the capital. Finally, they might be persons proposed and appointed at the instigation of the British on the basis of some historical claim to the office by that person's agnatic antecedents. In effect this was an inevitable consequence when it is recalled that the districts were much larger than the pre-1900 fiefs, and as such included a number of what were originally independent political segments of the state.

Informants in the field state that the district head could respond to this situation in several ways. He could try to win the loyalty of the local village heads to himself or, conversely, some village heads, sensing danger in the new situation, might come to the district head and ask to be 'his man'. However, there were obstacles to this simple method of rapprochement. If the village head already had a strong functioning relationship to some other 'big man' in the Kanuri state who was a powerful person in the post-1900 administration, or if the district head was anxious to reward his own supporters with lucrative and prestigious offices, then this method was not too successful. In such an event two methods seem to have been developed. First, the district head could try to obtain the dismissal of a truculent village head by complaining to the British officers that this man was unsuitable, and then have the vacant office filled by one of his followers. Thus, in 1919 a British district officer visiting Magumeri District was told by Abba Kiyari, the district head, that two of the village heads in his district were inefficient and should be deposed. He felt that the two villages in question were close enough together so that they could be joined into one unit; and he offered one of his own followers as the logical candidate for the new office (Whitely, 1909).

A second method was to send out followers whom they dubbed Chima Gana to all the villages of the district over which the district head had no previous administrative control. In some cases they seem to have worked very much like the nineteenth-century Chima Gana, only at the district level with the senior man being the district head. Chima Gana administered tax collections jointly with the local head-man, held judicial hearings and levied fines. In 1906 a man in a northern district was flogged to death for telling the people in his town that they could complain of this system to the British (Bornu Provincial Report, 1906). This event and other complaints made by touring officers finally led to an order by the resident of Bornu in 1910 to the effect that no district head could station his men in any of the towns of his district with the exception of his own headquarters. However, provincial records indicate that the Chima Gana problem plagued the British administration for many years afterwards.

Several other pre-colonial forms of organization had to be coped with and absorbed into the new district and village area system. Members of former slave towns, and towns reserved for religious practitioners, initially refused to have anything to do with the new territorial divisions. Their requests were honoured at first by the Land Board and the British. These villagers maintained that their allegiances lay elsewhere. Religious practitioners produced papers (*Mahrams*) showing that they were exempt from all levies except prayers for the Shehu; and slave villages claimed through their own headmen that their first responsibilities were to their owners and not to the local territorial organization. However, by 1910 the territorially arranged hierarchy was the dominant organizational goal of the British, who abolished these special relationships with the result that the religious practitioners and slaves alike had to come formally under the jurisdiction of their local headmen and district head.

In a few isolated cases Kanuri leaders still regarded village areas as potentially separate political entities, i.e., as if they were nineteenth-century fiefs. Thus, as late as 1930 in Mobber District a younger brother of the Shehu was reported as having taken over complete control of one village which now seemed to be outside the jurisdiction of the district head (Mobber District Notebook). Another interesting report in this regard which indicates that other nineteenth-century practices continued for some time is the complaint made in 1921 by a British official that people were still paying tributes to their jilima (head of ethnic, clan, or previous organization) on a completely non-territorial basis. By the 1950s all of these older practices were gone, with the possible exception of isolated instances of the Chima Gana system.

From the beginning of the British reorganization, the title given to the district head was that of *Ajia*. This may be a new title in Bornu, or an older one refurbished for this new role; the point is unclear. The village area heads were called Bullama for the first few years, but the title was later changed to that of *Lawan*. Both titles reflect the Kanuri attitude to these offices in light of the pre-colonial political organization discussed above. It will be recalled that in nineteenth-century Bornu a Lawan was a highly successful territorial leader within the fief who received his title from the Shehu. In changing to the British system the Kanuri recognized the territorially-based political organization being instituted, with its new emphasis on the fact that the official must reside in the territory of his jurisdiction. They did this by giving the office a title that was related to these same functions, namely residence in a large unit of administration. The district head (Ajia) was the superior of the Lawan, and both were appointed by the Shehu in a ceremony at the capital. Again, these attributes fit into the territorial organization of the nineteenth century. The novelty in the new situation lay in the fact that the Shehu–Ajia–Lawan hierarchy was not part

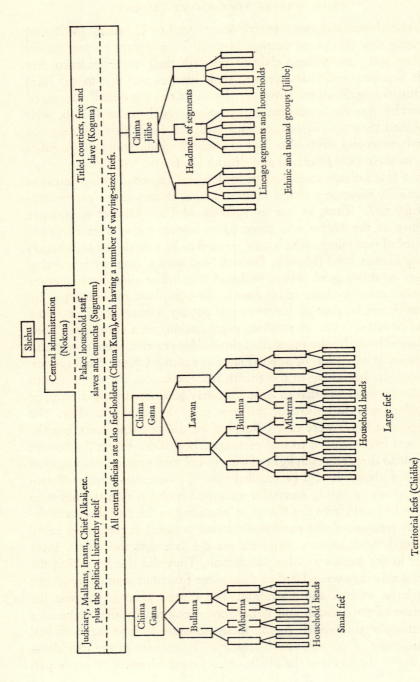

Figure 3A. Bornu political structures, nineteenth century.

Shechu

Central administration (Nokena)

Palace household staff, slaves and eunuchs (Sugurun)

Titled courtiers, free and slave (Koguna)

Judiciary, Mallams, Imam, Chief Alkali, etc. plus the political hierarchy itself

All central officials are also fief-holders (Chima Kura), each having a number of varying-sized fiefs.

Chima Jilibe

Headmen of segments

Lineage segments and households

Ethnic and nomad groups (Jilibe)

Chima Gana

Lawan

Bullama

Mbarma

Household heads

Large fief

Territorial fiefs (Chidibe)

Chima Gana

Bullama

Mbarma

Household heads

Small fief

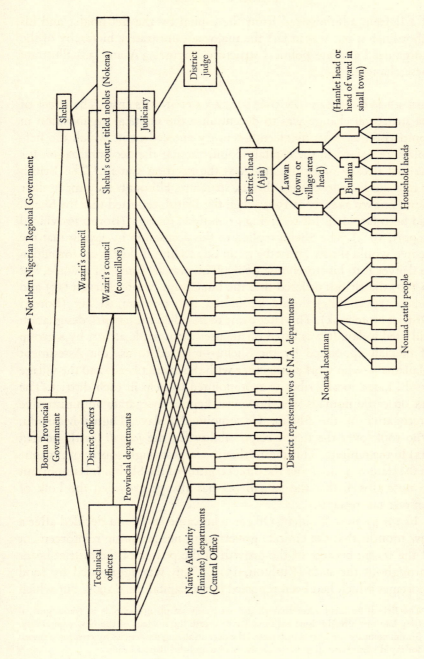

Figure 3B. Bornu political structures, twentieth century (1914 to founding of new states, 1968).

of a fiefship administered from the capital by the fief-holder and his subordinates, but was in fact the major administrative hierarchy of the reorganized emirate political structure. Figures 3 A and 3 B illustrate these changes.

THE REORGANIZATION OF THE TAXATION SYSTEM. The effect of the structural change was to decentralize the political organization in comparison with its nineteenth-century antecedent in which the fief-holder remained in the capital. Counteracting the decentralization for the first decade of British rule was the taxation system.[1] The British at first did little to change the tax structure, although they made their views known as early as 1903 when the British reported that the Shehu had been 'scolded' for receiving grain tithes (sadaga) (Bornu Provincial Report, 1903). The Shehu replied to this accusation by saying that the people would throw away the grain due to him if they were forbidden to deliver it to his storehouse (*ibid.*). This was accepted for a while, but in 1907 the British ordered that the binamram (winter harvest tax) and sadaga (royal tithe) should be united into one annual tax (Borsari District Notebook). This later came to be called the *haraji*, a designation still used today. It was based on an assessment made at first by a group of officials appointed by the Shehu—referred to as 'the Assessment Mallams'—who worked together with the district heads and the village heads. Later, local scribes were appointed to help in each district. The tax on cattle nomads was, however, kept as a separate administrative prerogative of the Shehu. He appointed a slave, Digma Momadu, who took over the major responsibility for the *jangali* (cattle nomad tax) in the emirate. This meant that the largest single source of revenue in the state was still under the direct control of the Shehu. It is important to note as well that the jangali tax has always provided the bulk of emirate tax receipts.

In 1914 a new Resident Officer who came to Bornu decided after a few months that the emirate government needed some reinforcement at the centre because of the growth in the power of the district heads throughout the state (Rushton, 1914). This was aggravated by food shortages which had been reported in the capital since 1908, but which

[1] The British Resident asked that all district heads set up households in Maiduguri, if they had not already done so, in order to create the nucleus of the new capital city. Simultaneously this also counteracted the decentralizing tendencies by creating a means for rapid communication between the Shehu and the district heads.

became serious in 1914 because of a very poor crop in Bornu. It will be remembered that since 1907–8 the Shehu had not been officially collecting a separate grain tithe. In 1914 the scarcity of grain became so serious that troops had to be sent to the district surrounding the capital in order to force them to take turns supplying 800 *sa* (about twenty tons) of grain to Maiduguri market each week.

The Resident resolved to organize for the Shehu a working council which could develop eventually into a working cabinet of a centralized native administration. At first the council was composed of the Shehu and the Imam or Liman (chief religious-legal adviser). A third member was added shortly after in the person of Sanda Kura, the older brother of the Shehu, who was brought in to take care of taxation matters and the Native Authority Treasury. Up to this point, Sanda Kura had been district head of Gujba. He was replaced in that post by Digma Momadu, the slave of the Shehu who had been collecting jangali, the cattle nomad tax, for the entire emirate of Bornu. However, the British decided to place the cattle tax under the jurisdiction of the Shehu and his council, to be handled by each district head within his own district along with the haraji tax (tax on settled population). At the same time Rushton, the Resident, reported that henceforth no British official would issue instructions directly to any district head, but that all such communications would be through the Shehu and his council down the hierarchy (Rushton, 1914).

THE SHEHU AFTER 1914. In its rough organizational outlines the post-1914 organization is the one that has survived to the present day. The district head is a direct formal subordinate of the Shehu-in-Council. He collects all official taxes in his district through the organization and passes on the receipt to the Native Authority Treasury. Starting with its original two members, the Native Authority Council has grown steadily in the size and scope of its activities. By the late 1940s it did resemble a sort of local cabinet with a Waziri, or chief minister, as its head under the titular headship of the Shehu, and with each member having at least one portfolio. The Shehu's Nokena, or court, still operated; the nobles still took their places in long parallel lines going out from the throne; and the Galidima, whose ancient district was now called Nguru, after its chief town, still sat in the middle of the two rows facing the same way as the Shehu. This court continued to operate as a decision-making and adjudicating body in important matters dealing with the political organization and the administration of the emirate. The members of the Waziri's Council, with the Waziri as its chairman, all sat, as they presently do, in the Shehu's court; but slowly, especially since World War II, the power has shifted to the Waziri's Council, where it resided until the death in December 1967 of Shehu Sanda (Cohen, 1970). Nevertheless, 1914 was the watershed. The present organization of the emirate has not changed in any radical sense since that time, when Resident Rushton instituted his tax reforms and set up the council.

From the overview given to us by the passage of time, it is interesting to evaluate the changes made by the British around 1914 and to ask whether or not they did in fact strengthen the central control of the Shehu—a tendency which had reached its greatest strength compared to previous periods during the nineteenth century. Taking away the jangali (cattle nomad tax) from the administrative control of the Shehu's slave and moving its collection into the new territorial structure of the districts could be construed as a development that led to the weakening of the Shehu's power.

In political terms this result depends upon the degree of control that the Shehu could exert over the district heads. Certainly it must have strengthened the new government organization of the emirate by adding to the responsibilities of the Shehu/district head/village head hierarchy. Qualifying this ambiguous development is the fact that Rushton clearly separated the emirate government from that of the British colonial administration, except through contact at the top. This meant that the Shehu could stand between the two systems and, if necessary, carry on informally many practices that the British would not have sanctioned if all dealings between the hierarchical levels of the emirate had to obtain British legitimation. As we shall see, British officials still had much to say about the day-to-day administration of the emirate; and through their ultimate power to depose chiefs at all levels of the hierarchy they could enforce conformity whenever they wished (Cohen, 1964: 495–521). However, the formal separation of the colonial and emirate political structures meant that much power was left to the Shehu even though the organization he headed had changed considerably, progressing from the pre-British era structure towards a decentralized one.

ECONOMIC CHANGE. In the economic sphere the political organization of the emirate had almost immediate effects on patterns of distribution in the area. After 1907, when the plans to rebuild the nineteenth-century capital of Kukawa were abandoned, this formerly great centre dwindled in size and importance and soon became just another rural village. On the other hand, the capital of Maiduguri emerged as the central marketing location of the kingdom. However, the lack of recognized fief-holders at the capital and the accompanying changes that occurred in revenue collections left this town very short of food supplies; and, as we have seen, it was necessary in 1914 to actually force peasants to bring crops to the Maiduguri market. The lumping of all taxes into one officially recognized tax after the inception of the colonial period could not be so easily buffered, since this practice was traditionally associated by the large stores with the pre-1900 taxation system. Consequently, any curtailment of market selling produced a more serious shortage in the city than would have been the case in the nineteenth century. Furthermore, the official reaction was completely different. Traditionally a food shortage in the capital would have been allayed by pressures placed on the revenue collection system, with a resulting levy on the fiefs and distribution of the receipts through household and client relations. After 1907 the market-place and its distributive system were emphasized, even though the older distributive system through clients did not necessarily cease to operate.

In a similar but less spectacular manner, each district capital became the headquarters of an expanded market town when the district heads, bringing with them their retinues and specialized needs, came out to these towns to set up their residences. Thus an economic change was inadvertently instituted along with the political changes brought about by the British. The consumption needs of the large upper class that moved to Maiduguri, as well as the smaller enclaves of this same class that were forced to move out to the districts, had to be satisfied. In other words, new nuclei of consumption were created in the Kanuri state while others were abandoned or shrunk. Distributive channels developed in response to these changes in the settlement of the non-productive upper class, and roads were built connecting the new emirate capital at Maiduguri to the district capitals.

In other realms of economic activity, the British strenuously put down the slave-trade and promoted a growth of trade towards the west (Kano).[1] This soon brought the Bornu–Tripoli trade to a sad end, and

[1] An ex-slave-trader in Bornu claimed that his last raid was conducted circa 1921–2. He gave up the trade because of the strong opposition from European authorities

Bornu's new trading relations with the outside world emerged from its position in Nigeria and the west coast of Africa. In this sense it is important to remember that Bornu is in a remote corner of West Africa. Even though it had been a major terminus for the trans-Saharan trade from the inception of colonial rule onwards, it was still an outpost—indeed, the farthest corner of Nigeria—from the point of view of the exporter in Lagos.

At first, gum arabic and skins formed the major export items, while cloth was the largest import. However, from the middle twenties onwards, ground-nuts increased in importance as an export crop. The government introduced a sterling coin currency that gradually replaced the Maria Theresa dollar as the most generally accepted medium of exchange. In the Bornu Annual Report of 1915 there was a complaint by the Resident of Bornu that the European trading companies had not paid currency for purchases from the natives, but were instead paying for goods with cloth. The natives were in their turn selling the cloth in the markets, sometimes at a loss, in order to obtain English currency. This seems to indicate that by 1915 English currency was in fairly high demand, at least amongst those who traded with the commercial companies.

After some pressure by the government, the European traders dropped their practice of paying in cloth and began to use the present system of cash credit. The companies advanced credit to a limited number of middlemen, who then bought company goods for resale at local markets, and/or used the money to purchase export goods for sale to the credit-advancing company. Obviously this was also a way of spreading the use and acceptance of Western money. At first the African traders dealing with the companies were few and their volume not impressive; also, as noted below, barriers to their development in terms of direct access to credit soon emerged.

Reports from this early period indicate that the British political officials did not wholly approve of the trading methods of the companies, not only because of the modes of exchange, but for reasons of price as well. In the Bornu Annual Report of 1909, Major A. McClintock suggested that trade with the natives of Bornu would increase at a much greater rate if prices were somewhat more attractive.

Thus he quoted the price given to natives for gum arabic as 3s. 6d.

which made the enterprise both more lucrative and progressively more dangerous during the first few decades of the colonial period.

per hundredweight, while the United Kingdom price at the same time was 30s. to 50s. Later, in the Bornu Annual Report of 1911, Sciortina complained that the Royal Niger Company's prices at Nafada had discouraged trade.

In order to increase volume and price, companies were encouraged to set up branches in Maiduguri; and by 1915 there were five European firms in the capital. In addition to the desire of the Europeans to expand trading volume, the willingness and ability of Levantine traders to take and pay back credit soon encouraged a small but very active minority of Arabic-speaking traders—from North Africa, the Near East, and the Sudan—to enter Bornu. Traders from these groups acted as middlemen between the European companies and the more numerous African traders. The result was that a small group of Arabic-speaking traders was established in Maiduguri, thus absorbing a large portion of the available credit from the European companies and filtering it, second-hand as it were, into the economy of Bornu.

The European trade in Bornu, like that of many parts of West Africa, developed a distinctive quality that arose primarily as a result of the dearth of available excess capital at the local level. For this reason local trade involved, as it currently does, a strong competition in the financing of traders in the more usual aspects of commerce, such as price, quality and sole distributorships. Also, the major competition between the Europeans for Arabic-speaking traders served as a stimulus in expanding the number of traders in the native population.

THE PROCESS OF ADJUSTMENT. The outside influences coming into Bornu after 1903 were thus of a two-pronged variety, and these in turn set up various responses in the political and economic activities within the emirate. Up to the Second World War the main concern of the colonial official was that of making the policies of indirect rule applicable to the local scene, while always pressing for a more comprehensive understanding and conformity to the general values and standards of English culture. The theme for all annual reports running from about 1915 to 1944 can best be expressed in the oft-repeated phrase 'steady progress'. Each year tax collections were a little better; a few more students attended the provincial schools; a few more roads were built or improved, and once in a while extended; local European trading companies reported 'steady progress' in business volume; living conditions in the province for European staff 'steadily improved', medical facilities 'steadily expanded', and so on. Certainly there always seemed to be a rather high turnover in chiefs, but this came to be an expected part of everyday life in Bornu.

In effect, what occurred was an adjustment. The British administration had set up the organization of indirect rule, and the task of each new Resident Officer in Bornu was to implement the Lugard policies to the best of his abilities. The general methods of resistance to the English administration were fairly well known to both the British and the Kanuri; and very few jarring outside influences entered the scene to upset the gentlemanly tug-of-war that characterized the colonial contacts as a game in which everyone knew the rules and the conditions of play, while the overall techniques of the players did not change much through time.

How the game was played at the political level can best be seen in the following example of the deposition of the district head of Mobber in the late 1920s.[1] Mobber district is in the extreme north-west portion of Bornu Emirate on the border between Nigeria and Niger. Its relative isolation from British surveillance contributed to the maintenance of officially prohibited practices well into the late 1920s.

During 1929, a British official reported that there were indications of widespread 'extortion' of the peasants of Mobber district by the district head and his Chima Ganas. In May of 1930, Reed, an Assistant District Officer, was sent up to Mobber to investigate the situation. He reported that the district head had stationed his Chima in many of the towns of the district. These Chima were conducting judicial proceedings, administering whippings, and raising levies for themselves and the district head. The district head, when questioned, admitted that he was using Chima, but complained that the Lawan (village area heads) were for the most part hostile to his jurisdiction in the district. Reed told the district head to abolish the Chima system and tour around the district himself, with his followers accompanying him, in order to maintain the peace. The district head replied that touring would be insufficient and that in order to keep the peace he had to maintain men in the more distant towns of the district. Reed agreed to this compromise and said he would return in about a month's time to see if the agreed-upon reforms had been carried out. On Reed's return it was noted that nothing at all had been done to change the administration of the

[1] This account is taken from various notes and memoranda in the Mobber District File, Provincial Office, Bornu Province.

district. Reed arrested five of the most complained-of Chima and took them to Maiduguri for hearings on the matter.[1]

On 7 July 1930, the Shehu, during an interview with the Resident, mentioned that the district head of Mobber had requested the removal of the district judge of Mobber on the grounds of ignorance and inefficiency. Upon investigating the situation, the Shehu advanced the opinion that this request might be due to bad feelings between the district head and the judge (Alkali). In his turn, the Resident opined that it might more particularly be the case that the judge disapproved of the district head's illegal use of Chima and his raising of personal tax levies through these illegal officers. The Shehu was much closer to the actual politics of the situation, both practically and in his analysis. If a district head and his district judge do not get on well together, each finds his duties more difficult to perform. This is especially true of adjudication, which both men carry out. The Resident was, of course, projecting his own British standards of political propriety onto the judge, who in all likelihood would have seen nothing wrong in the use of Chima by the district head.

In another meeting between the Shehu and the Resident later that month, when the Mobber matter was brought up again, the Shehu agreed that things did not seem to be going well in Mobber. On the fourteenth of August when the Mobber misdemeanours were mentioned, the Shehu suggested to the Resident that the Mobber peasants were an extremely difficult group to manage and that possibly Chima might be required for the proper administration of the district. In so doing, he was trying to persuade the British to leave the political behaviour of Bornu to its practitioners who were more familiar with the real requirements of the system. The ideological demands of 'indirect rule' dictated that the Resident should not move to enforce his wishes immediately, even though he disagreed with the activities being carried out.

At the end of August the Shehu requested of the Resident that the five men who had been arrested by Reed be sent back to Mobber. The Resident agreed in principle but felt that the one who had beaten a villager very badly should be kept in Maiduguri a little longer. He added that the men could be sent back to their homes only if the Shehu would take upon himself full responsibility for any further trouble in the Mobber area.

[1] The complaints were gathered from villagers and *Lawan* (village area heads) of the towns in which *chima* were stationed.

In September, and again in October of 1930, Reed was sent up to check on the situation in Mobber district. The Chima were operating as before and the district head was reported as having been 'not respectful' to the British officer on tour. Only one change had occurred. An entire village area appeared to have been relinquished by the district head and was now under the control of a new head, a man who proved to be a younger brother of the Shehu, appointed to the job evidently by the Waziri of Bornu. In other words, the Shehu was trying through his Waziri to shield his political subordinate from the demands of the British. He had been partially successful up to this point and thus felt he could place his younger brother in the district on the replica of a nineteenth-century fief, giving this brother local autonomy and thereby undercutting the district system of territorial units and resuscitating, or maintaining, the pre-colonial system of political organization.

Several months later, in February 1931, the district head of Mobber appeared in Maiduguri for an annual meeting and was warned by the Resident that 'unless considerable improvement was shown he would be dismissed' (Mobber District File). From this point on, there were few new items reported in the files. One short item tells of a rumour picked up by a junior officer to the effect that the district head of Mobber was a favourite of the Shehu and was married to a daughter of the Waziri. By the end of 1931 the matter began to congeal. The British district officer of Bornu Emirate wrote a memorandum to the Resident claiming that the time had come to dispose of the district head of Mobber, since it was now obvious that this man would not reform. Several names were offered as replacements. In early 1932 the matter was mentioned briefly in a report from the Resident of Bornu to the Secretary of the Northern Provinces of Nigeria. It stated that 'the Shehu-in-Council have found it necessary to depose the district head of Mobber' (Mobber District File). The names put up by the British were matched against those put up by the council, and a council nominee was given the job as the new district head of Mobber.

The British administrators had tried for two years to persuade the district head of Mobber to stop using his own system of political organization and to work through the village area heads (Lawan) of his district. They had even compromised in this position for a while. The complete disregard of British administrative goals finally brought about the district head's removal. However, the entire push and pull of the deposition did not materially disturb relations between the British and the political leaders of Bornu. The case certainly hints at a well organized political system operating independently of the one formally recognized by the British. However, it also illustrates the formalized and balanced relationship between the Shehu and the Resident. The Resident patiently tried to press forward with his own conception of government, while the Shehu was at the same time attempting to mollify English demands in order that emirate political organization could be maintained unmolested. The unsettling feature of the relations between the colonial and the emirate government was the touring British officer who might, by coming into contact with local complaints, discover a necessity for reform that could bring British power into play.

Conclusion

The nineteenth-century Kanuri emirate of Bornu may now be seen more clearly in its relationship to its own internal dynamics and to the changes it experienced as it was incorporated into the colonial organization of Northern Nigeria. Al Kanemi, the founder of the second dynasty of Kanem-Bornu, developed a system of government involving slave military leaders and a highly centralized governmental structure. The state was administered through a complicated system of innumerable and unconsolidated fiefships which articulated the central government into a flexible set of offices at the local level that also took care of nomadic and migrant members of the population. The economy was semi-self-sufficient, with foreign trade playing an important part in state affairs.

With the loss of independence the system was reorganized and consolidated into larger holdings, or districts, which brought a selected group of fief-holders out to the bush (rural) areas. At the top of the society a colonial régime articulated with the local one and maintained some contact with all sectors of the administration through the touring colonial official. The economy was directed southward, and Bornu entered into the political and economic relations which have made it a part of the modern Nigerian nation.

How much change, or how drastic a change, did colonialism exert eventually over the ancient Bornu kingdom? Elsewhere (Cohen, 1964) I have described in detail how the district heads of Bornu have been able to accommodate to both Kanuri and to Western-oriented values and standards of political behaviour, so that both systems do in fact operate together within one social field. The main point to remember in this regard is the fact that the British left day-to-day political relations alone, with the result that superiors and subordinates in the Kanuri political system dealt with one another using traditional values and standards together with British standards. The British standards became limiting conditions within which traditional modes of behaviour have operated, and these were used as sanctions by both Kanuri and British officials to enforce discipline. In this sense there was, and is, continuity; and the only change was the realization on the part of everyone that another set of standards, which on occasion could be utilized by both Kanuri and British officials, was available. As I have also noted elsewhere (Cohen, 1964), this has made political life hazardous but not impossible—as long as a subordinate in the system is in a position to learn ahead of time what demands and what standards are to be enforced at any given moment.

In the present essay I have been concerned with isolating and describing the nature of structural changes brought on by the inception of colonialism. This has involved the presentation of detailed material on the nineteenth-century system so that a full appraisal of the structural realignment can be made.

The first point to note is that regarding Bornu's own pre-colonial social change. The nineteenth-century political system was founded on continuity with the past, plus the usurpation of power by the Kanembu Shehus. In order to grasp and maintain authority they were forced to create a standing military force under a set of Kachella or slave military leaders. They changed the site of the capital city, and redistributed the fiefs as well as the leading offices of the state. Change and adaptation then were not sudden and shocking occurrences to the people of Bornu and their leaders. Indeed colonialism came just as Rabeh was establishing his hold over the kingdom and beginning the foundation of a third dynasty. In this sense the colonial conquerors were also liberators, and many older Bornu informants took just this attitude in describing the coming of the British.

Given the underlying fact that Bornu was accustomed to change, and that it welcomed the British as liberators, there were still some basic changes made in the structure of the society. The nineteenth-century political structure was essentially a centralized government that articulated with local government through the person of the Chima Gana or the fief-holder's trusted and loyal follower, who lived in the fief. Fiefs themselves could expand or contract and be cut up or transferred at the pleasure of the monarch. Furthermore, the fief system included an organizational technique for incorporating nomads or groups that had suddenly become dispersed and displaced throughout the kingdom until they again settled and could be administered territorially. This very flexible system was changed into a system based totally on a single hierarchy—from monarch through district head, to village area head, to hamlet head, to compound head. Each level of the hierarchy was identified with a delineated set of territorial boundaries and correlated to an expanding scale of jurisdictional responsibility. There was no room in such a system for articulating ethnic groups, or clans or dispersed groups into the state unless they were identified with one of the stabilized territorial units of the state such as a district. Even though territoriality had been of some importance in the nineteenth century, the relationship of groups to one another had been the major criterion for relating segments of the political system. A man was a member of such and such a group, and therefore owed his subordination to a known set of superiors. In the twentieth century, this tradition persists, and peasants still speak of themselves as the peasant of such and such a village area head. But the structure of the state is now based on land and the way boundaries are drawn on it, whether or not the groups on it are nomads, or related to one another in traditional political terms. In this system the pivotal political role is that of the district head, for he articulates the local communities into the central government. It is interesting to note here that the district heads tried at first to integrate the towns under their control by using chima, i.e., people related to them, rather than trusting to local headmen. In summary, then, the political structure has changed from one in which segments were defined by the relationships existing between groups and their leaders to one in which the relations between groups depend upon the locality and its size (hamlet, town, district and emirate).

The development of a specialized council under the chairmanship of the Waziri has produced changes and potential change that is revolutionizing Bornu. The Shehu and his court still exist, but, as the council develops more and more into a cabinet with growing civil service departments under it, this body becomes more and more the dominant political authority in the state, while the Shehu becomes more and more a constitutional monarch. In this sense Bornu under colonialism, and now after independence, has become a bureaucratic state run by

5-2

RONALD COHEN

appointed officials who more and more are operating the government with a set of professional colleagues and subordinates. Parenthetically, in such a system the political party has been a subordinate and ancillary wing of the ruling bureaucracy, rather than vice versa.

In the economic sphere there has been much less change compared with that in the political sphere. A hierarchy of trading organization has been set up to handle the export-import movement of commodities in and out of Bornu through Nigerian ports, and cash cropping has made generalized currency universally valued—in the Western sense. However, it should be noted that taxation in cash has also stimulated this particular innovation to a considerable extent. On the other hand, the local markets still resemble descriptions made of them a hundred years ago and earlier by European explorers. Farming techniques and the general run of subsistence crops are the same as they were before colonialism, and they are harvested and marketed in the same time-honoured ways. Indeed, what changes have occurred, such as the recent digging of deep wells all over Bornu, or the inception of a ground-nut mill and meat-processing plant in Maiduguri, have all been brought about by the Waziri's Council in co-operation with other Northern Nigerian governmental bodies. Thus the origins of significant economic change can be found in the political sector, and will most likely come from there in the future.

In conclusion, Bornu may be viewed as a complex interaction between continuity and change. Like all that is human, there are no really sharp breaks. There is instead accommodation by a people and their leaders whose past has witnessed many successful adaptations. Furthermore, today they are accommodating to the conditions of a contemporary world that has challenged them to continue utilizing this adaptability to move forward with the confidence that their past may share in, and has something to contribute to, their future.

BIBLIOGRAPHY

PRIMARY SOURCES

Besides the few pieces of information from the Rosman field notes and the one reference to the *Pall Mall Gazette* of 12 July 1899, the bulk of the primary material comes from oral history accounts and from three types of documentary material in the Provincial Office at Maiduguri, Bornu Province.

By far the most useful of these materials are the district notebooks. These contain reports on the district made by early touring officers, memos concerning affairs of the district during the colonial period, and very often some attempts at an account of the nineteenth-century organization of that particular district. The two other sources are more official; these are the Bornu Annual Reports by the Resident to his superiors in the Northern Region Government, and the Bornu Provincial Reports, which for the period from 1903 to approximately 1914 were written quarterly by the Resident. The latter are more useful, since they deal in some detail with day-to-day problems of the colonial administration.

Bornu Province, Annual Report, 1909.
1911.
1915.
Bornu Province, Provincial Report, 1903. No. 5.
1904. No. 9.
1905. No. 26.
1906. No. 32. Borsari, Geidam, Nganzei, Magumeri and Mobber. Provincial Office, Maiduguri.
E.D.M. (1899). *Pall Mall Gazette*, 12 July.
Hewby, W. P. (1905). Bornu Province, Provincial Report, No. 26. Mobber District File.
Palmer, H. R. (1907). Borsari District Notebook.
Rosman, A. (1957). Unpublished field notes.
Rushton, A. R. (1914). Bornu Province, Provincial Report, September.
Whitely, G. C. (1909). 'Report on Magumeri District', in Magumeri District Notebook.

SECONDARY SOURCES

Alexander, B. (1907). *From the Niger to the Nile*. 2 vols. London.
Arkell, A. J. (1951). 'History of Darfur', *Sudan Notes and Records*, **32**, no. 2.
Barth, H. (1857). *Travels and discoveries in northern and central Africa*. 5 vols. London.
Benton, P. A. (1913). *The Sultanate of Bornu, translated from the German of Dr A. Schultze with additions and appendices*. London.
Boahen, A. Adu (1962). 'The caravan trade in the nineteenth century', *Journal of African History*, **3**, no. 2.
(1964). *Britain, the Sahara and the western Sudan, 1788–1861*. London, Oxford University Press.
Brenner, L. (1967). 'The Shehus of Kukawa: a history of the Al-Kanemi dynasty of Bornu.' Ph.D. thesis, Columbia University.

Cohen, R. (1964). 'Conflict and change in a Northern Nigerian emirate', in *Explorations in social change*, G. Zollschan and W. Hirsch, eds. Boston.

(1965). 'Some aspects of institutionalized exchange: a Kanuri example', *Cahiers d'Etudes Africaines*, **19**.

(1966a). 'The dynamics of feudalism in Bornu', in *Boston University Papers in African History*, II.

(1966b). 'The Bornu king lists', in *Boston University Papers in African History*, II.

(1967). *The Kanuri of Bornu*. New York.

(1970). 'The kingship in Bornu', in *West African chiefs*, M. Crowder and A. L. Ajayi, eds. London.

(with L. Brenner) (1969). 'Bornu in the nineteenth century', in *History of West Africa*, J. F. Ade Ajayi and M. Crowder, eds. Oxford.

Denham (Major) and Clapperton (Captain) (1826). *Travels and discoveries in Northern and Central Africa*. 3 vols. London.

Landeroin (Capitaine) (1911). 'Du Tchad au Niger: notes historiques', in M. Tilho, *Documents scientifiques de la mission Tilho (1906–1909)*. Paris, Ministère de la Marine et des Colonies.

Nachtigal, G. (1879). *Sahara und Sudan*. Berlin.

Palmer, H. R. (1936). *The Bornu, Sahara, and Sudan*. London.

Urvoy, Y. (1949). *Histoire de l'Empire du Bornou*. Mémoires de l'Institut Français d'Afrique Noire (IFAN), VII.

CHAPTER 4

TRIBALISM, RURALISM AND URBANISM IN SOUTH AND CENTRAL AFRICA

by

MAX GLUCKMAN

The present essay sets forth my overall view of certain developments in the history of Africa, from before colonial occupation, through that occupation, and into independence. I make some predictions, or guesses, about future developments. My subject is a highly emotive one. Hence some of the interpretations of facts which I propound in the present study may lead to varying allegations about my political attitudes and motives. I therefore affirm these at the start. I have been, in feeling and in action, on the side of the Africans in their struggle against apartheid in South Africa and in their striving for independence elsewhere in Africa. Nevertheless I insist that the facts we have to try to comprehend in our analyses show that over a fair run of time the Republic of South Africa is likely to manifest considerable internal stability (in the common-sense meaning of the word), and the sharp divisions between its colour-groups are unlikely to lead to revolution unless there is international intervention. On the other hand, independent African states are unlikely to show that stability, but are liable to be more subject to internal coups and crowd violence. I come to these conclusions despite my political wishes.

South Africa seems to be marked principally by divisions and opposition, with a large section of the population kept in submission by brutal force under harsh legislation. Without question, these operate to keep Africans and other coloured groups, as well as their white supporters, from attempting to alter the system. But it is essential to remember that there are large areas of collaboration between these opponents of the policy of apartheid and those who support that policy and enforce its regulations. My own research was in one of the tribal areas in the 1930s, and I found there a high degree of what I shall call 'social cohesion' rooted in an interdependence of interests between whites and Africans; and an excellent study by L. Kuper of *An African bourgeoisie* (1965) in the towns has demonstrated that a parallel inter-dependence of interests exists there. These interests create divisions in the ranks of both whites and Africans, linking some members of each group with members of other groups, despite apartheid, so as to create a situation from which all draw some profit. Out of these relationships fresh conflicts have been (and are) emerging in a continual process by which, as new conflicts emerged, so too new forms of collaboration have developed, to lead in turn to new conflicts, and so on. My main contention is an oft-stated one:[1] 'even if ultimately the whites maintain power by their superior force, there is a considerable degree of cohesion in the system from the development of economic and other forms of interdependence within regions, within special institutions like factories and farms, and within various sets of small-scale relationships; and this interdependence within parts is communicated to the whole within which some overall cohesion also exists. This is so despite the continual development of the dominant cleavage between whites and coloured' (Gluckman, 1958).

I have to explain what I mean by 'cohesion' and the other terms I use. The types of problems I am discussing, as well as others, have been often obscured, in my opinion, by the failure to develop a sufficiently elaborate vocabulary. We can only develop an appropriate vocabulary by stipulating that we will use certain words to refer to a limited set of phenomena or analytically derived institutions and processes, even if we allow some terms, like 'structure', to retain their original flexibility. (I take 'structure' to mean any ordered arrangement of parts within a postulated whole.) In advancing the following stipulations of how I shall use words, I consider I have taken into account earlier attempts to specialize them.

Terminology for analysis

We need a series of words to refer both to the observable interactions of persons in their varied roles and of groups, and also to refer to ranges and levels of societal interdependence. English has a fair number of words that we can employ thus. I propose to stipulate that I shall specialize different words for different purposes. Immediately, I note

[1] It is central to the Marxist thesis of the struggle between classes, to Durkheim's organic solidarity, to Weber, and to many other sociologists and economists. For my own formulations see Gluckman, 1940*a*; 1940*b*; 1958; 1955*a*, Ch. VI; 1960*a*. See also Kuper, 1965, *passim*, for parallel formulations of the basis of interdependence of whites and Africans in South Africa. It is vividly brought out in a novel by Gillon (1952).

that in English there are many more words to describe clashes between persons than to describe collaboration between them. We can use, therefore, 'work with', 'help (aid, assist, succour)', 'depend on', to describe observable interaction, with 'co-operate' as a general word to describe them all. Against forms of co-operation stand 'disturb', 'argue', 'dispute', 'quarrel', 'fight', 'contend', 'compete', 'riot', 'strike', 'war', all covered by the general word 'strife'. I shall use these words to cover observable action and presumed associated motivation. On the descriptive level of ideology we can generally speak of 'agree' and 'disagree'. Dr Martin Southwold has urged on me that when we move to first-order abstractions from observable reality we must distinguish between the ideas which people have about what is occurring in their relationships, and the relations that we as social scientists abstract from our observations. I shall use *consensus* and *dissensus* as polar types to refer to agreement or disagreement between particular persons on a goal or value or closely associated set of goals or values. *Coherence* and the neologism *discoherence* are polar types to cover whether all goals and values, and held views of what the society is like, are considered to be compatible with one another.

When we come to look at the patterns of relations which we as analysts abstract from our observations, we need first to distinguish between *motivation* and *social interest*. I shall speak of whites and Africans having 'common interests' in peace and in production, in the way that managers and workers have a common interest in a factory or mine continuing to work and produce. One colleague has argued that it is specious to say that workers have this common interest. He said that workers go to work to earn wages. I consider that this criticism is, in sociological or social-anthropological analysis, to commit the error of 'psychologism'. The motives which induce people to do certain things are not the same as the complex of social interests which their actions serve: this is clear from social-anthropological or sociological analysis of, e.g., rules of exogamy, or of ritual. Nevertheless, I believe that a common or shared social interest must be demonstrated in the action of persons. The interest of English workers in factory and mine had developed when outbursts of Luddism ceased, and when striking workers did not damage the machines or plant on which the productive process depended. The manner in which, for example, striking miners keep essential services going expresses their common interest with mine-owners and managers in the mine. It is significant that though the

Zambian (formerly Northern Rhodesian) Copperbelt mines were opened in the late twenties, and some closed down in the depression of 1931 before reopening in 1933, even in 1935 and 1940 the plant and machinery were not attacked by striking African miners who concentrated their assaults on personnel offices. Apparently in 1935 essential services were kept going. In the 1940 strike, at three mines on the first day 'the smelter staff were called to work to prevent damage to the furnaces through their going out'; but on the next day the smelter shifts were threatened by other workers and they were no longer called out. (Note that in 1926 British steelworkers did not join in the General Strike because if the furnaces went out it would take months to repair them.) Clearly, then, by 1940 African miners at all mines did not appreciate the consequences of not keeping the smelting furnaces working, for, according to the District Commissioner's description (Epstein, 1958: 95) of the first day of a strike at a mine in 1952, 'no one came to work except a handful of essential service workers'. Yet though the maintenance of essential services was written into an agreement with the African Mineworkers Union, when a more militant leadership of underground workers was elected at one mine in 1954, it called 'a strike of all African employees, including essential service men, which lasted nearly a week' (Epstein, 1958: 141, fn. 1). Recognition of common interest was demonstrated in these events, but not always observed, since miners were aware of these interests in varying degrees. Yet Epstein in his masterly analysis in *Politics in an urban African community* (1958: 132–3) of Copperbelt history was able to write: In 1935 and 1940,

conceivably, the Africans might have taken to smashing machinery as an expression of resentment against the new system, just as the Luddites had done at a corresponding period of the Industrial Revolution of England.

Significantly, they did not do this. By their behaviour on these occasions they showed that they were not protesting against an industrial system as such; they were complaining of the position accorded to them within the system.

He then points out that there was, however, an important historical difference. In England production was being moved from cottages into factories; in Central Africa workers from a traditional subsistence economy were moving into highly developed industry which gave them new wealth.

Acceptance of the industrial system thus involves recognition of an interest in the system. Kuper, in his *An African bourgeoisie* (1965–6), writes in terms similar to mine: 'Social relationships extend across racial barriers, weaving complex and varied patterns of interracial contact and creating common interests transcending those of race.' The objector to the use of 'common interests' was prepared to allow 'convergent interests': and I would be prepared to accept this, if 'common interests' causes confusion. But I feel that one must speak of 'common interests' because this emphasizes the high degree of fairly long-term collaboration that establishes systematic interdependence in the economic sphere. 'Convergent' seems to me to imply that there is a temporary coming together of interested parties, as among allies like the Soviet Union and the Western powers during the Second World War. African interest in the industrial system of South Africa is not temporary: it is permanent. But out of the common interest between them and whites arise new clashes, as the citation from Epstein above clearly shows.

We therefore need a number of descriptive words for forms of *co-operation*, etc., involving common interest in a system of *collaboration*. At further levels of abstraction we may see collaboration as arising out of solidarities and/or the exercise of authority with force at its command. Against this we need a number of descriptive words for forms of strife, leading to clashes within that collaboration. These clashes may arise from straightforward competition between different persons for the same thing. Or they may manifest periodic irruptions of strife out of permanent *struggles* between types of persons, groups or categories on different sides of a dominant cleavage or subsidiary cleavage in the total system or in one of its parts. Struggles may arise out of what I call *conflict* (Gluckman, 1955a; 1965a) of interest or loyalty or allegiance or value in the system, whenever these conflicts can be resolved by a return to something like the original pattern of social relationships. I am trying here to specialize *struggle* and *conflict* as concepts used as we move more deeply into our analysis of the social system. Both can be used, and have been used, to describe surface interaction: but there are many other words for description, and only struggle and conflict can be given these wider connotations. If the clashes arising out of struggles cannot be resolved by anything like a return to the preceding patterns of social relations, I shall speak of *contradiction* in interests, values, loyalties and allegiances. When a cleavage involves a contradiction, it must develop through more forms of struggle. In this convention, conflicts can be resolved in the pattern of the system; contradictions cannot, but lead steadily to radical changes of pattern (see Gluckman, 1958:46f.).

Despite the development of the dominant cleavage (Gluckman, 1942; 1958) between whites and Africans in South Africa, affecting all social developments, the various parts of the polity are linked together in a relatively high interdependence. We may then speak of South Africa as highly articulated. *Articulated* and *unarticulated* are two polar concepts to define the extent to which parts of a system are linked, or not linked, together. (Unarticulated is a neologism, since 'disarticulated' strictly describes not the state of not being linked together, but 'undoing the articulation of', 'separating'.) If parts of a system are highly articulated, I shall speak of that part as having 'cohesion'. Some scholars consider that 'cohesion' implies moral approbation. I find no such implication in the dictionary's 'tendency to remain united', 'force with which molecules cohere'; but 'cohesiveness' is a possible substitute.

The crucial purpose of my terminology is to emphasize that it is essential to distinguish between 'consensus', as agreement on values and goals, and structural 'cohesion', as defining the extent to which the structure of a particular social field is maintained in something like continuous pattern. This pattern may be maintained by a variety of factors, such as outright force, and/or interdependence, and/or agreement of all the people involved on ultimate goals and their readiness to sacrifice for those goals, and/or the cross-linking of individuals within the total field in terms of a variety of associations and values which prevent most persons from becoming wholeheartedly loyal to one bond and hostile to all other bonds (Gluckman, 1955; 1965a).

Consensus and cohesion are therefore to some extent independent of each other. The distinction can be made most explicitly by emphasizing that one can have, in regard to certain ultimate goals, a very high degree of consensus among the actors in a social field, while the degree of structural cohesion is very low. This seems to be the position in many newly-independent African states: the goals of independence, of Pan–Africanism, of some kind of welfare policy, etc., may be accepted by most of the population and emphasized through a one-party organization. Yet these goals are not realized by consensus: some of them can only be achieved through industrial and agricultural development leading to what Durkheim called organic interdependence between the segments of new states. This would produce cohesion. On the other hand, there may be in South Africa radical disagreement between various ethnic groups and within them about the goals and values ultimately to be aimed at, so that at *national and provincial, and perhaps city or district levels,* there is little overall consensus, but structural cohesion may be relatively great, since it emerges at least both from determined use of force by the white government and from the relatively great development of the industrial sector and the farming-for-markets sector. Cohesion arises from high articulation of the parts of a system or sub-system. If cohesion exists in a system where there is also a high degree of consensus, we may speak perhaps of a society with a high degree of integration. Integration is lacking where there is cohesion but relatively little consensus, or the consensus exists only within restricted groups.

I am here, I repeat, trying to stipulate that I will use these words in this particular way. I do so because I cannot think of any other suitable words. But I consider that my proposals do not clash with the use of these words in sociology and social anthropology in general.

I set these varied terms out in a chart to aid readers. Please note that a spatial representation oversimplifies the complexity of reality. I have to show separately, and apparently as opposed, co-operation and strife, when in fact co-operation itself is the source of strife and certain forms of strife can lead to co-operation. The chart is only a listing of terms, not a substitute for analysis.

Terminology for analysing social consensus and cohesion

Co-operation (work with, help, etc.) tending to produce *common interests in system of collaboration*	*Strife* (dispute, fight, etc.) leading to *clashes* based on *struggles*
which produces	some of which arise out of
either or	*conflicts* or *contradictions*
solidarities *forceful*	present in leading to
maintenance	stable or quantitative
(or both)	slowly shifts in more
	changing rapidly chang-
	states of ing temporary
	stasis[1] stasis until
	radical change[1]
	(or both)

[1] Gluckman, 1968. Cf. G. and M. Wilson, 1945: Ch. v.

The above terms are used to describe elements in a system marked in the following ways:

1. *ideologically*: by various degrees of participants' agreement or disagreement: (*a*) degrees of consensus to dissensus on single or sets of values and goals; (*b*) degrees of coherence to discoherence in all values and goals.

2. *analytically*: by (*a*) degrees of cohesion to discohesion in parts of the total system; (*b*) degrees of articulation to unarticulation in the relation of parts within the whole system.

3. *analytically and ideologically*: by degrees of consistency and inconsistency in the relation of consensus ↔ dissensus and cohesion ↔ discohesion. High consensus and high articulation produce high consistency and high integration. Low and high consensus with, respectively, high or low cohesion, produce inconsistency and little integration.

I speak therefore of ideological consensus and structural cohesion in parts of the total system. Clearly, then, consensus and cohesion occur in different areas or in different domains of relationships, and they are present for varying periods of time. We may speak of consensus and cohesion at different levels and for varying runs of time. These remarks apply also to dissensus and lack of cohesion. Above all, consensus between Africans and whites might be mobilized for specific limited purposes in particular situations, while dissensus was manifested in other segregated situations (Gluckman, 1958). There were enough, and sufficiently varied, situations of consensus, occurring in the articulation of economic and administrative interdependence, to produce for my observation a fair degree of consistency and integration in Zululand as a whole. Meanwhile the dominance of the potential force which whites could exercise prevented the Zulu from taking action on the basis of their dissensus from whites. White force was a persistent essential in the cohesiveness of Zululand society.

The colonial plural society

Since Furnivall applied the phrase 'plural society' to Burma and India, it has become established as the appropriate introduction to an analysis of the so-called colonial societies, with their population of whites and darker-skinned groups of different origin (see Kuper and Smith, 1969; Smith, 1965). This use of 'pluralism' emphasizes that there is domination of the society, militarily, administratively and economically, by an alien minority group which controls major resources and elements of power. There is a concentration of control of the society in the hands of a few. Hence 'pluralism' of this kind differs markedly from the kind of pluralism covered by the term used in political science to describe a system with many centres of power, as in Britain there are political parties, economic interest groups (firms, organizations of employers, trade unions, co-operatives), newspapers, churches, universities, etc. In 'colonial pluralism' there is domination by foreign conquerors who are separated by a big gap, culturally and economically, from the mass of the population, and have protected privileges in jobs, education, residence and so forth; these privileges are protected against competition so that social mobility upwards is barred; and social intercourse is restricted, often to the point of segregation in statute and convention, save in the economic sphere. As Mitchell saw Furnivall's analysis, it emphasized three characteristics.[1] First, 'there is a medley of peoples...Each group holds by its religion, its own culture and language, and its own ideas and ways'. Second, in a plural society the different groups, largely defined by ethnic criteria, live side by side, but as separate communities within the same major political unit. Third, and this Furnivall emphasized strongly, the members of these ethnic groups meet as individuals but only when buying and selling in the market-place. Furnivall goes on to argue that the people comprising such a society are so broken up into groupings of isolated individuals that they show a lack of agreement about common action, or, in his own words, 'a disintegration of social will'. This is reflected in a corresponding disorganization of 'social demand'—i.e., moral and ethical considerations play little part in the relationship between the individuals of different ethnic groups. In short, there are no commonly accepted norms and values in terms of which members of different ethnic groups may interact.

I have taken Mitchell's admirable summary of Furnivall's complex argument from his Inaugural Lecture on *Tribalism and the plural society* (1960), in order to emphasize Mitchell's comment:

Sociologically [Furnivall's]...characteristics are related. The social distance between the different ethnic groups is related to their differences in custom, language, religion, moral codes, and so on, and it is a fairly well-established sociological principle that relationships across social distances become

[1] Mitchell, 1960: 25f.

categorized. In other words, in situations where groups are socially separated, an individual of one group is treated primarily as a representative of the group and seldom in any other capacity.[1] Presumably this is what Furnivall takes to be 'atomization'.

The sort of data I [Mitchell] have been presenting...suggests that Furnivall's formulation of the problem is incomplete and the weakness seems to lie in the assumption that categorical relationships imply 'individualization'. The evidence we have is that even in the situations where we could expect more of what Furnivall calls 'atomization'—in the industrial towns—the African population [of the Rhodesias] is linked and cross-linked by ties of many sorts. Their bonds with their own tribesmen are counterbalanced by innumerable ties which they create with other tribesfolk through common membership in church congregations, through sharing a common position on a scale of social prestige, through having been classmates at the same school, through belonging to the same cultural associations, through taking part in the same political movements, through playing games with one another, through marriage, through neighbourliness, through working together in the same factory or gang, and perhaps most important of all, through being all of one race in a society where racial cleavages are paramount. Categorization implies anonymity and categorical relationships between tribes give a false semblance of tribalism among Africans in towns. As the various cross-cutting ties of the sort I [Mitchell] have mentioned come into being so the anonymity disappears. The sort of close, intense, personal social relationships characteristic of tribal communities may not exist in industrial towns but other different sorts of relationships ensure that there is no social 'atomization'. Furnivall's picture, then, of plural societies as collectivities of foreign people acting towards each other as depersonalized 'economic men' gives way to one in which people stand opposed to one another in one situation and in doing so operate in terms of a common set of norms and values, and stand divided in another, separated by different customs and beliefs.[2]

If there is not atomization within the African urban population, it may nevertheless exist in relationships of Africans vis-à-vis settler populations—or have existed in the past. Mitchell himself chooses the relative lack of counterbalancing cleavages across the component ethnic groups as one of the significant features of the plural society. The cultural

[1] Mitchell here cites his own important study of *The Kalela dance* (1956) on the Northern Rhodesian Copperbelt, which established this point as clearly and graphically as it has been done for the several criteria defining categories of persons in Central Africa. Cf. the title of Hilda Kuper's book on White-Swazi relationships: *The uniform of colour* (1947).

[2] Mitchell then cites my own study of a rural area in South Africa (Gluckman, 1940; 1942; 1958) and my general treatment of this theme (Gluckman, 1955a).

and ethnic differences by themselves are of no account. There are linguistic, religious, and social differences and divergences of custom amongst the inhabitants of the United Kingdom, but this does not mean that the United Kingdom is a plural society (Mitchell 1960: 28–9).

I myself have phrased it: 'The tribalism in African towns is in sharper form the tribalism of all towns' (Gluckman, 1960), since cities like London, Paris, New York, Manchester, are inhabited by many ethnic groups. But in these modern cities the significant groups, politically, are largely, though not entirely, functional groups—trade unions, employers and trade associations, educational interests, religious sects, political parties, and the like. Mitchell adds that maybe it would be appropriate to regard England at the time when Disraeli spoke of two nations as a 'plural society' in Furnivall's sense, presumably because he feels that there was then a relative lack of counterbalancing cleavages. It is this possible comparison of earlier phases of English history with the societies of modern Africa that I wish to consider in this essay.

Furnivall and other writers on colonial plural societies (see essays in Kuper and Smith, editors, 1969) remark that cross-links between the ethnic sections of such a society are tenuous and rare. I propose to consider the problem starting from the position of the rural segments— often tribal—of these societies and to speculate on the kind of consensus and dissensus, collaboration and conflicts and cohesion and contradictions, that will develop in them after independence. These tribal and rural areas are of great importance, because the population of African territories is often proportionately heavily rural. My central theme is: while it was useful to classify certain territorial states as 'plural' when they were dominated by foreign settlers of quite different culture, who possessed more powerful industrial and military technologies, in order to analyse a certain range of problems by emphasizing the foreign origin of dominant power in those states, it may now be more useful to look at other criteria for classification of plurality. I stress at once that I do not deny the crucial importance of foreign domination.

Traditional tribal societies

All societies contain what I have called 'conflicts' of social principle, as well as conflicts of interest between individuals and groups; and a great deal of research has been focused on demonstrating how these conflicts, by dividing on the basis of one interest or value persons who

Table 2. *Dominant characteristics of tribal society*

social aspects	Material bases			
	Production	Consumption	Communications	Weapons
social units and linkages	simple tools self-subsistent settlements	simple goods egalitarian standards of living	poor and limited quasi-status barter	simple self-equipped warriors
formal organization	'independent' feuding units (or) semi-autonomous counties in states	kin-idiom between segments with reciprocity	non-organic trade well developed	private troops for leaders
political power	strong local basis of support for subordinate leaders to whom also 'delegation' in régime of authority	wealth for distribution is part of authority; wealth produces authority	weakened at centre, strengthened locally	armed support for local authorities and for royal contenders
political processes	potential independence of segments	redistribution of goods in kin and affinal relationships (plus) in states, collection and redistribution of tribute: competition for dependents	relatively easy escape in groups out of structure	intrigue and endemic civil war producing rebellion and not revolution (or) breaks out of structure
type of solidarity and integration	greater ease for men to move to food, than to move food to men	close identification of leaders and led; small material insignia of magnified importance; ceremonial and ritual feasts crucial	high importance of ceremonial objects, easily transported, with much symbolic accretion, in trade	established leaders and unit (e.g., royal family) have occult attributes validating authority against arms of upstarts

are united in terms of another principle or value, during disputes drive wedges into whole-hearted solidarities within one group, by establishing cross-linkages into other groups. Thus a wider cohesion is established. In these terms, I propose to look at the historical development of tribalism, ruralism and urbanism in order to consider their significance in African societies.

Traditional tribal societies, as I have shown in Table 2, were characterized by their simple tools used in simple methods of husbandry, simple consumption goods, undeveloped systems of communication, and simple weapons. Simple tools and husbandry meant that workers could produce little more than was necessary to support themselves; hence, though slaves are found in the tribal world, their lot was very different from that of slaves in systems with better methods of production and with a richer variety of consumption goods. As long as all consumption goods are simple, the rich and powerful cannot develop a standard of living markedly higher than that of the poor and weak; there is a limit to what an individual can consume. When all weapons are simple, every man can be a self-equipped warrior. The rich and powerful, therefore, in the interests of their own struggles for power, expend their wealth and power on attracting dependents who then form their private armies, and support them in their struggles for position, prestige and greater power. Generosity is the marked attribute of the rich and powerful in all tribal societies, as studies of Eskimo, Bushmen, Cheyennes, Solomon Islanders, Zulu, Bemba, and many other tribes, testify. There are even built-in mechanisms in many of these societies that compel the wealthy to distribute their wealth, from the lynching of a miser among the Western Alaskan Eskimo, to the sumptuary *potlatches* of Kwakiutl chiefs and funerary feasts of Ifugao, and to the great feasts staged by a Zulu king, or the way the Barotse king redistributed to his subjects the tribute they paid to him. Basic within these systems, is that people live in small settlements, even when the population is relatively dense, as among Tallensi of Ghana or Bantu Kavirondo of Kenya; and for many purposes these settlements are self-subsistent and independent. Trade by barter is limited and covers a relatively small proportion of the total economy, since methods of transport are poor. The law of commercial contracts is barely developed.[1]

---

[1] This generalization about tribal societies has been criticized by Pospisil (1967) in reviewing my elaboration of the point in *Politics, law and ritual in tribal society* (1965a), where again I summarize a full argument in my *The ideas in Barotse jurisprudence* (1965b). Pospisil contends that the Kapauka Papuans he studied (Pospisil, 1954, 1958)

We may therefore think of the settlements in these situations as to a considerable extent isolated cells, divided vertically from one another. But a striking feature of human societies (including hunters and collectors like the Eskimo and Bushmen, and particularly the Australian Aborigines) is the extent to which links between those cells are established by conflicts of social principles and custom. In certain New Guinea societies a man cannot eat, under pain of severe illness, a pig which he himself, or one of his close kin, has bred. Therefore men in different groups take in one another's pigs. In this way extensive chains of interlinking through pig-exchanges (which economically are quite unnecessary) are set up between otherwise independent, and potentially hostile, groups. Furthermore, an important man is one who can organize a big pig-feast, on behalf of his group, in which he seeks to outdo another, and possibly foreign, group. To achieve this, he has to build up credits in pigs among his own people, so that he can assemble plenty for a big feast to which the foreigners can be invited. It follows therefore that each man aspiring to social bigness in these tribes must ensure that there is enough peace between his group and neighbours for him to invite the latter to a feast which will enhance his internal prestige and power. Anthropologists will immediately be reminded of the role of Kwakiutl chiefs in the *potlatch*; and of the manner in which the whole yam crop of the Trobriand Islands is picked up after harvest and transported around the island, since men feed not their wives and children who dwell with them, but their sisters who under taboo may not be near their brothers but live in turn with their husbands and children. Ceremonial trade of the New Guinea pig-exchange or *kula* type provides protection for some trade in useful objects; but it means that utilitarian trade is restricted to exchanges between linked partners—i.e., it operates only in established status or quasi-status relationships.

are capitalists who are involved in commercial contracts continually. But in my opinion his analysis of their contracts in *Kapauku Papuans and their law* (1958, 121 f., 208 f.) demonstrates that Kapauka law of contract contains all the characteristics which I have argued in my analysis of African law (1965 b: Ch. VI) to be typical of undeveloped contract law. It is still dominated by ideas appropriate to a legal system where the ethos of status and quasi-status influences transactions: high warranties, the rule *caveat vendor* rather than *caveat emptor*, high particularity, and so forth. His so-called Kapauku capitalists are typical Melanesian 'big-men', building up their prestige and influence through credits and debts in fixed sets of quasi-status relationships (see my discussion immediately below). To call them 'capitalists' is, I consider, to make that term meaningless in sociological and economic analysis.

In short—and this applies also to tribes as poor as Eskimo and Bushmen—in these tribal societies there is what I (Gluckman, 1965: Ch. IV) have called (following Roscoe Pound's phrasing) a 'social interest' in accelerating and increasing the circulation of goods in ways that are not necessary from a utilitarian point of view. This social interest appears in many customs, such as feasts, joking partnerships, gift exchanges, systems of inheritance in which movables are distributed among different kinsfolk from those who inherit land, systems of payment for marriages to women, and so forth. These circulations of goods accompany rules of exogamy which force men and women in most tribes to marry out of the close kin-group, and establish links of sentiment into other similar groups, links marked by the circulating of goods to which I have referred. These links are also validated by occult beliefs: e.g., among the agnatic Nuer it is significant that the most powerful curse against a man, a curse to make him fail to have children and cause his cattle to die, resides in the power of his maternal uncle, not of his father. Conversely, the most powerful spirits influencing a family among the matrilineal Tonga are those of the father's, and not of the mother's, side. Marriage itself, in which different groups meet in their interests in spouses and children, is given exaggerated complementariness by taboos which emphasize the femininity of women and the masculinity of men beyond their physiological differentiation. Tonga men must be married if they are to be ritually complete: a man can offer to his own matrilineal spirits only beer brewed by his own wife. It is taboo for a man to cook in the village: to be independent he needs a wife.

I have sketched out analyses I have made elsewhere more fully (Gluckman, 1955a; 1965a) in order to emphasize that in tribal societies many, if not most, cross-linkages between independent units are established by custom and validated by occult belief. These customs and beliefs can produce extremely complicated social systems which, to use a geometrical analogy, establish horizontal linkages between the otherwise vertically divided cells of the society, the virtually self-subsistent settlements of people who regard themselves as closely related to one another. Because of the simplicity of weapons, each settlement has an independent 'army'. We are here looking at what Durkheim called 'mechanical solidarity', but it is a more complicated solidarity than he envisaged. For he saw each of the vertically isolated cells as capable of growing into a complete society, if cut off;

141

and this is almost possible. But the cross-links are of a more complicated pattern than he could know. This is strikingly shown in his argument in his *De la division du travail social* (1893), where he asserts that in tribal society men and women are much more alike, when in fact taboos, conventions, and occult belief exaggerate the differences between the sexes much more than do the customs and practices of industrial society.

Societies of this type have obviously endured for many centuries, if not millennia, in a relatively limited pattern of social relationships and with a persisting culture; and one important achievement of modern social anthropological research has been to examine the mechanisms by which this has been possible in the absence of instituted authority of a clear, forceful, governmental type, with officers backed by police to settle disputes and to maintain codes of law and morals so that men and women can continue to deal with one another in terms of reasonable expectation that obligations will be met. Important among these mechanisms, securing conformity with morality and law, including customary observances, are the conflicts (in my sense of the word) set up between the allegiances of men and women to various groups and in various sets of relationships. Hence in any dispute between groups, whether these be local settlements or dispersed vengeance groups, there are some parties on each side who owe some allegiance to the enemy. Then there are persons related to the two sets of opponents who can act as mediators in various ways. Or there may be ritual mediators, empowered with occult curses by which they can compel the obdurate to come to terms, or at least enable the proud to give way ostensibly on threat of the effects of the curse. These ritual mediators may represent the general need for some peace, over a local area, to secure prosperity and success. This is symbolized by the fact that their curse is often connected with the powers of the Earth. It is important to note that beliefs such as that a homicide contaminates the earth with the blood he has shed, and threatens danger if he and his kin eat with the kin of his victim, compel admission of guilt in order to get purification. This may apply, as among Nuer, to admission of adultery. Again, customary beliefs, rather than direct utilitarian interdependence, establish here cross-links across vertical divisions.

In some tribal societies the vertically divided cells constitute segments in permanent feuding relationships with one another. This means that there can never be a final settlement of their tale of debts of blood and

TRIBALISM, RURALISM AND URBANISM

injury: temporary peace is established by customary horizontal ties operating to produce conflicts of loyalty within each group, and then temporary war succeeds temporary peace.

This kind of vertical division continues to be dominant in early forms of states—those which Southall has characterized as 'segmentary states'. Among the Zulu, for example, the different counties of the nation were not bound together in mutual economic interdependence. Firstly, they were associated within the nation by allegiance to the highly valued kingship, and their attachment to princes of the royal family. Secondly, they mobilized under the king in regiments formed by conscripting men of the same age-grade, and housing them for part of the year in royal barracks. Thirdly, they presented tribute to the king which—since he could not consume all—he returned to the givers in feasts enhancing his prestige and power. But, as I have shown in a whole series of analyses (1940*b*; 1955*a*; 1965*a*; 1965*b*), the vertical divisions remained dominant: civil war was endemic in the nation. It involved men in fighting for their county chiefs, and beyond these for their royal princes, in an attempt to secure the kingship for their own royal leader, to whom they were attached already. Characteristic of this type of state were frequent break-ups arising from civil war and dissidence, or the hiving off of segments, or a constant struggle of segments to put their own prince on the throne. If the polity persisted, it did so with civil war. Logically, within this kind of system there are rules of succession to the chieftainship which produce a number of claimants who have valid claims, or there is choice of heir. Men have mediated allegiance to the king through intermediate lords, as well as direct allegiance. They are under duty to support their intermediate lords, who, in law, have the right to rebel if the king does not fulfil his duties to them or oppresses them. And there can be dispute about fulfilment and oppression. After a revolt, those who have supported their intermediate lord are not guilty of treason, since they had fulfilled their duty in fighting for the lord: they might be slain in battle or executed, but were not tried at law. The simple weapons meant that every lord, competing for power in these terms, had his private army to support him, just as in feuding societies each segment consisted of armed men.

In short, as feud marked the vertical divisions of segmentary society, so rebellious civil war marked the states where horizontal cross-linking was based on force at the centre and forms of custom-enforced interdependence, without adequate development of economic interdependence. If we arrange states in a morphological developmental series, this form of civil strife remains dominant late into the series. It characterizes the polity of Barotseland, where already radical ecological differences between the homeland of the dominant Lozi tribe and the homes of their subject peoples linked the provinces into the centre in complementary exchange of products. In the Zulu and Bemba type of polities, the king collected tribute, which he distributed to his people in feasts and help. In Barotseland this redistribution of tribute supplemented barter in achieving a profitable exchange of different goods. Rebellions to replace kings on the throne by other princes continued; but intrigue at the palace and in the capital became more important.

As other forms of differentiation emerge in yet other African states, additional political processes complicate the system. In Ruanda, where Tutsi overlords formed a status grade superior to Hutu cultivators, for the first time we find a kind of millenarian cult among a category of subjects, the poorer Hutu cultivators; but the movement is still in attachment to the spirit of a member—a queen—of the royal family. In the economically more developed West African emirates, we find mercenary generals and mercenary troops; and there is one report of a peasant revolt against the ruling status grade, living in 'luxury' in a city, where there were artisan guilds, and where the city mob of the unemployed and underemployed (Hobsbawn, 1959: Ch. VII) appeared as in classical and mediaeval cities of Europe. Here there were slaves, and also wider and more complicated trade. The horizontal cross-linking binding the segments was more than customary, and produced occasional civil strife across the horizontal lines. But vertical divisions still dominated, and most civil strife was still rebellious around the throne. Civil strife was often concentrated in palace intrigues; and sections of the ruling élite played for support of the mob.

Comparisons with European society

In these respects African history shows startlingly similar developments to those in Europe and Asia. In Europe, the dominance of strife between vertical divisions continues to an astonishing late stage of history (as witness the Wars of the Roses), despite the development of cities, trade with money as a free currency, great variation in standards of living, and the making of more complex weapons. That the right to rebel existed, and that constant rebellions occurred (as in Africa), appears graphically in Magna Carta. In Chapter 61 of the version of Magna Carta signed by King John,[1] he created a committee of barons whom he empowered in the event that he or his officers had committed any excess, to

distress and harass us by all the ways in which they are able; that is to say, by the taking of our castles, lands and possessions, and by any other means in their power, until the excess shall have been redressed, according to their verdict, saving harmless our persons and the persons of our Queen and children.

John further first stated he would allow any man to swear to follow the barons, then gave leave to all men to do so, and in climax *ordered* all men so to join in harassing him. Magna Carta thus entrenched the right to revolt against alleged oppression, which was so important an element in mediaeval law. As part of that law, while it was treason to conspire or imagine the death of the king, it was not treason to wage war against him. Leaders in such wars were prosecuted not so much in law, as by bills of attainder; and their followers were virtuous in supporting their lords, and not guilty of treason against the king.

In 1352 a statute of Edward III first made it treason to levy war on the king. Yet when, after the Battle of Shrewsbury in 1403, the Earl of Northumberland was arrested while marching against Henry IV at the head of his troops, and tried by his peers under this statute, he was acquitted of treason and held guilty only of trespass. The statute clearly was not directed against rebellious feudal lords, and thus did not simply reflect the birth of a new idea that made the state immune against civil attack, as some constitutional historians and lawyers have asserted. It appears to me that it must be aimed elsewhere; and I find its quarry in the lower classes. The date of the statute is surely significant. It followed in the year after the Statute of Labourers, which was a more or less abortive attempt to cope with the better bargaining power of serfs and town artisans after the Black Death had so reduced their numbers that men became again much more valuable than land. According to Trevelyan (1942: 11, 38, and *passim*), there was now a quarrel between two classes of peasants—the small farmer and the landless labourer— with the small farmers, formerly serfs, becoming yeomen. The great landlords, now reduced to a few families with very substantial landholdings, backed the yeomen because high wages endangered the

---

[1] The following analysis is summarized from Gluckman (1965b: Ch. II).

payment of rent by their tenants. There was a 'gradual change from a society based on local customs of personal service to a money-economy that was nation wide'. Meanwhile 'the journeyman in the shop felt the same movement of aspiration and unrest as the labourer in the field. He too struck for higher wages when the Black Death made labour scarce.' Trade was expanding and 'the harmony of the mediaeval City Guilds was being disturbed by social and economic cleavages between master and man'. The Statute of Labourers was abortive because masters and farmers themselves broke its regulations to get labour.

All this disturbance followed on struggles between landed magnates and city burghers. Sporadic unrest culminated in the great Peasant's Revolt of 1381, and immediately by a new statute 'it was made treason to begin a riot'. This remained a treason—in sharp contrast with an enactment in the same reign that it should be a treason 'not only to encompass the king's death, but also his deposition or the rendering up by anyone of his liege homage; and that anyone who procured or counselled the repeal of the statutes in that Parliament should be guilty of treason'. Henry IV was compelled by the barons to repeal this statute.

I have elsewhere pursued this argument more fully (Gluckman, 1965 b). Here I summarily emphasize that at a time when England, like the rest of Europe, was disturbed by peasant revolts and journey-men's and apprentices' riots to indicate the emergence of horizontal cleavages based on economic roles, there remained a core of political struggles arising from the continuing importance of vertical divisions, cutting the country into segments under feudal lords who maintained their right to engage, inside the law, in civil war against the king and one another. The pattern of warfare altered in the religious wars between Catholics and Protestants, and in the wars between Cavaliers and Roundheads. But it was only in the reign of Queen Anne that it was made treasonable in law to hinder the succession to the Crown of the person entitled thereto under the Act of Settlement of 1688, or to maintain in writing the invalidity of the line of succession to the Crown established by the Act of Settlement. That is to say, only at this politico-economic stage, with production increasing and trade further developed, did it cease to be possible for English contenders for political power to mobilize behind a claimant for the throne, a mobilization made possible by the existence of several claimants asserting title on varying grounds of law plus suitability of character. Moreover, this change in the law of treason occurred during several centuries which saw major developments of commercial law, and the separation of the law of tort from the law of contract; the appearance in sale of the rule *caveat emptor* as against *caveat vendor*; and changes in personal relationships manifested in the law banning accusations of witchcraft (Gluckman, 1965 b). All these elements seem to mark a development in the political system towards a linking together of the vertically divided segments of a nation in an organic economic interdependence, to use Durkheim's phrase.

In short, I have been arguing that the kind of civil war which marked mediaeval European history was logically associated with particular kinds of rules of succession to the throne and particular kinds of laws of treason. They seem to mark the structure of kingdoms in which the territorial segments are not bound into the centre and to one another by the development of a diversified economic system, so that various parts depend on one another for their subsistence and welfare. The early periods are characterized by the fact that those who command military forces are the main contenders for political power, a fact shown even earlier by the role of generals, including mercenary generals, in ancient Rome and Greece. In states where civil wars were rebellions rather than revolutions, interdependence of this kind was relatively tenuous: much of the horizontal interlinking of segments was customary in form. Men were moved by self-interest, both to gain goods and resources and to gain power, but they acted within the bounds set by customary linkages: it is striking, as many historians have commented, that no English feudal lord tried to assert his independence of the Crown (though feudal lords on the continent of Europe did so, without claiming the crown). It was really only with the burgeoning of trade to a considerable extent, and then with the first beginnings of factory production, that organic interlinking appeared; and at this period the principle of the one legitimate heir to the throne was established and it became treasonable to be even a minor follower in a revolt. Wat Tyler, with his followers, believed a change of royal advisers would ameliorate their lot; when he was slain, his followers could be enticed by the boy king's promise to lead them. There was still largely destructive rebellion in the peasants' jacquerie and the riots of city mobs, though some had Utopian programmes. Only with the first stages of organic horizontal interdependence did revolution to change the structure of the system begin to threaten. Yet even then vertical divisions persisted. The city mob could be raised in London in the 1830s. From then on, a new police force was able to control the potential mob until its members were absorbed in the developing economy. The enclosure acts of the eighteenth and early nineteenth centuries were brought in piecemeal to cover particular parcels of land, and the first combination acts against organization of labour in agriculture and industry were directed to protect particular localized employers. Only in 1871 did England have full legal recognition of trade unions. Since then there has been a greater and greater proliferation of secondary and tertiary associations in industrial and political life to link 'the two nations' of Disraeli together and to stress their mutuality of interests in an interdependent national economy; and their struggles for shares in that economy are controlled by this elaborate structure. Schism occurs at the lower levels of the system, without erupting to destroy organization at higher levels. Government is by someone in the centre of the political spectrum. A multiplicity of persons of different religion, ethnic origin, culture, and tradition can be accommodated in the society, since there are multiple series of agreements and cross-cutting ties based on organic interdependence. Domains of domestic, religious, recreational, etc., life can be diverse because they are isolated from one another, while common employment and membership in functional groups are central to the system. A constantly expanding economy, with a high degree of upward mobility, moves the able into positions of greater reward and prestige in the multiple élites with greater life-chances for their children. The system allows a considerable degree of dissidence within wide limits, even a lack of consensus, since it has a very high degree of cohesion arising from utilitarian organic interdependence. The open use of force to maintain cohesion is reduced.

Developments in colonial Africa and South Africa

I consider that it may be profitable to look at the so-called 'plural societies' of Africa in the light of this categorization of political systems. For I would say that what characterized most colonial societies before the full establishment of a modern industrial economy, with marketing from some agricultural areas to the cities, is that these societies consisted of a number of areas of relationships, some of which were linked together by horizontal organic exchanges, while others were not thus linked. These other areas were isolated from the organic system of utilitarian economic interdependence, or only very partially involved in it through the sale of crops from a 'windfall' surplus above subsistence requirements in good seasons (Allan, 1965), or through the sale of the labour of men and women, largely as migrant workers. Some of the South and Central African cities in which organic cross-linkages were focused were now mostly very different from the European cities of the feudal and following periods, which were later to be the principal centres for the development of industrialism.

Some African cities are newly established and mark the abrupt introduction of fully developed mining, and later industrial, production involved in nation-wide and even international trade. On the other hand, some produce only the primary products of mining for a long period, before secondary industries develop. Tropical and sub-tropical agricultural products are marketed into the international system. Hence commercial centres emerge, sometimes superadded to indigenous proto-cities, where in many respects the level of economic output of many inhabitants is very low. Since large parts of the rural population are substantially poorer than even the meanest workers in the industrial cities, there is a constant drift of people from countryside to town, where, owing to the surplus of labour, there may begin to emerge a city mob of unemployed and partially employed with all this implies for processes of political struggle. The city mob can be reduced in numbers only by draconian measures of a determined government. In ancient Buganda, according to Dr Southwold, it is possible that the king prevented such a mob's emerging to threaten his position, since his executioners prowled the capital with powers to execute all peasants who could not validate their presence by exhibiting a pass from their country chiefs (quoted Gluckman, 1965 a: 153). Since 1938, the South African government has prevented, as far as it could, the emergence of a mob of unemployed and unemployable by requiring migrants from the rural areas to have similar passes guaranteeing that they have a job. Periodically, also, it has deported from the cities those whom it regarded as redundant for industrial purposes.[1] This control it could enforce

[1] On 27 April 1967 the Deputy Minister of Bantu [African] development, in a speech opening a white agricultural show, announced a plan to register every African worker in the reserves. He said a scheme was being worked out to decentralize labour bureaux from his department to tribal and regional authorities to ensure the maximum use of available labour. Every African must register as a 'work-seeker'—and be 'allotted to specific labour categories according to his abilities and qualifications'. Observers

because weapons are now highly complex; and the government, having access to the most complex and destructive weapons, is able to dominate subjects. On the whole, the days of the barricades are past. Machine-guns and tanks, the aeroplane, radio communications, etc., put the revolting mob in a weak position which is only slightly redressed by the plastic bomb. Guerrilla war can be waged in certain favourable conditions; but it is less effective against a government which is heavily armed and determined. It was divisions over policy towards colonial peoples in Britain, France, Belgium and Holland that helped the Indian, African and Indonesian independence movements to succeed. Portugal and Spain, where there are no effective divisions to disrupt determination to rule, though these countries as states are themselves very much weaker than the other European powers, are maintaining their colonial positions. The Rhodesian and South African governments, who have only a small proportion of their enfranchised electors hostile to their policy, rule harshly but most effectively.

They rule effectively partly because they are determined and ruthless. Force maintains power. As Mitchell (1960) says:

where there is no overall system of values and there are no counterbalancing cleavages [across the colour-groups], the hostilities...must be suppressed by legislation or ultimately by force if the body politic is to be maintained intact. Hence constraint rather than consensus would seem to be the basis of cohesion in plural societies.

In South Africa, force is increasingly applied, through harsher repressive legislation, greater fire-power and more effective communications, as well as more informers if not actual numbers of uniformed police. Nevertheless, while there may not be overall consensus by all people of all groups about goals and values, there is at least within the industrial system, and radiating from it, an overall system of interdependent interests between whites and Africans (L. Kuper, 1965). Where the Africans are involved in the industrial economy, or are dependent on goods coming from that economy, their interaction with whites pro-

saw the proposed measure as another step in the government's attempts to control the influx of African workers to white areas. On the same day, the Transport Minister warned that insults by Afrikaner cultural leaders against Roman Catholic worker immigrants (from Portugal and Italy) made in fear lest they swamp Afrikaner traditions and endanger the Afrikaans language, were damaging to South Africa's cause (*The Times*, London, 28 April 1967). As noted below, immigrants are essential to make up for the relatively low fertility rates of whites. Here is a further contradiction in South African white society and culture.

duces an organic, utilitarian cross-linking between the two races which may be more effective in establishing cohesion than the kind of non-utilitarian, non-organic cross-linking between vertically divided segments that marked the earlier kinds of polities from which I started my analysis, and also more effective than a high national consensus following a revolution.

In this view, the increasing induction of Africans into the South African economy, until some forty per cent of the African population is permanently urban-dwelling, is the main means of achieving some stability, in the commonsense meaning of the word, in the colonial plural society, which I take to be an inappropriate combination of a vertically segmented society with partial organic, horizontal interdependence. The England of Disraeli, 'the two nations', therefore was a plural society, with many impoverished rural persons moving into towns in too great numbers for the growing industrial system. As they moved into the towns, they formed a potential city mob, which could have exercised some power in political life. Rapid industrial development absorbed most of them. With that development came the increasing organization of economic and political struggle across the horizontal cleavage, rather than through vertically divided segments. The recognition of common interests in terms of struggle for shares in industrial rewards united both employers and workers against one another. It later became clear that their common interests in peace to produce goods required reciprocal organization. National legislation achieved this; and now many bargains are struck at national level.

I must interpolate here that following Hobsbawn (1959) I restrict my use of the 'city mob' to the unemployed and partially employed who may be drawn into 'rioting'. This does not mean that all disturbances and riots, so-called by those in power, are by the city mob. Certain militant, if not violent, protests are by people gainfully employed at various levels of the economy, both to achieve political liberation and economic betterment, as at Peterloo, and in many strikes, as at Sharpeville. I ask readers to bear in mind this limitation of definition of the city mob in the discussion that follows.

The same common interests that emerged in England between Disraeli's 'two nations' are also present in South Africa between the two major 'colour-groups' (L. Kuper, 1965). What is forbidden is the right of African workers to organize to defend their common economic interest or political aspirations; and they are further forbidden from organizing with workers of different race, as those of different race have been increasingly prevented from trying to organize African workers. The South African government might be wiser in its own interests if it allowed Africans to organize in trade unions and to strike to defend their position. This would emphasize their commitment to the industrial system. Since the whites have a relatively low fertility rate, they are unable to staff the jobs and posts regarded as appropriately reserved for whites, even with the help of immigration. In other industrial countries this staffing is managed by advancing able persons from the working classes into 'higher' occupational grades through education. The colour bar prevents this in South Africa; but more and more Africans are moved into the lower grades of skilled and technical work by necessity. The contradictions between an expanding economy and the policy of apartheid are great. Nevertheless, in this situation permanently industrialized African urban workers come to have interests in conflict with those of the poorer Africans from the rural areas trying to press into the industrial economy; and these conflicts are similar to those which existed between urban workers and peasants in Russia, in China and elsewhere.

Hence we have to examine the industrial system of South Africa in terms of several sub-systems. In the sheer process of gaining a living, for whites and Africans, there is cohesion within a common productive system. What distinguishes South Africa from other industrial countries is that African workers cannot organize to defend their interests when these clash with those of their employers. Yet they riot rarely, and there is no indication (despite Sharpeville) that rioting of this kind can dominate the course of struggles of power in South Africa. Most Africans in town work; and as workers they are involved in the cohesion as a workless city mob are not. There is cohesion without political or cultural consensus.

This cohesion is partly possible because of conflicts obstructing the allegiance of most Africans to some ideal of African independence, which might otherwise draw them into concerted action for its attainment, even allowing that the ruthless use of force by the South African government dominates the situation. Many Africans have vested interest in the system. Some are servants of the government and assist in implementing its policy. Others make their living out of apartheid. Like all industrial workers, Africans in employment are dependent on work for themselves and their families to survive, and again, under a ruthless government which would possibly let them starve, cannot manage without the working of the system that moves food, water, etc., to them.

I turn now to the tribal areas. My own experience in the rural areas of South Africa and Zululand leads me to disagree profoundly with a statement by Basil Davidson in an essay on the history of Zambia in Kuper and Smith, eds. (1969), *Pluralism in Africa*, that 'nothing appears to have tied these two groupings [of Africans and settlers] together except a mutual hateful contiguity from which neither could escape'. I agree with him that their interdependence was 'in the highest common factor...economic', but for the rest his view is much too simple. In the rural areas there did develop a considerable degree of common interests, and a consensus on values, *at certain levels*, between tribesmen and those whites allowed into their territories—government officials, technical aides, and missionaries. This statement has been validated by considerable research both in South and in Central Africa. For example, the Zulu may occasionally have regretfully looked back on the days when as raiding warriors they terrorized other tribes: they remembered, too, the terror and uncertainty of life, and valued the peace brought by white government. So did the Barotse. Even more strongly, raided tribes like the Tonga, though full of grievances against the whites over serious matters such as the loss of their land, felt grateful at least to government officials because they had brought peace and other valued things. In each tribe there were specific groups and persons who turned increasingly for what they valued to white culture and to relationships with white patrons. Monica Hunter (1936) in Pondoland, and Mayer in his study of *Townsmen or tribesmen* (1960), showed how decisions to be Christianized taken 150 years before had largely cut off the schooled people from their pagan neighbours, and had linked them to whites. I found in Zululand that the division was less marked: Christian and pagan kin still dealt with one another, and Christian kin were the means by which many white influences were introduced to the pagans. Above all, both Hilda Kuper among the Swazi, and I among the Zulu, found that to understand how the system worked, it was quite inadequate to think in terms of overall attitudes such as hatred and rejection: one had to break interaction and separation of whites and tribesmen into several domains or sub-systems, in which inconsistent and often contradictory attitudes could be manifested by the same people in different types of situations. By different types of values and aims they shifted their allegiances from white officials or missionaries to chiefs and other traditional personages; or in towns might find attachment to a potential labour organizer important. Conflicts in terms of varied values, varied goals, and varied types of association among Zulu prevented their manifesting, save in very rare situations, wholehearted resentment against the dominant whites. Similar conflicts operated on some of the whites, particularly on government officials concerned with the welfare of the tribes they administered, and on missionaries. Officials tried to push their districts' interests against the stated policy of central government (Gluckman, 1968).

Considerable research in South Africa and Central Africa (summarized in Gluckman, 1960a) has demonstrated how this system of tribal organization, locked horizontally into the industrial sector by the movement of men to labour there, was maintained by the whole economic situation, as well as by tradition and the support of the white government. The production of crops by rural Africans for subsistence was a large section of the national income in territories like Northern Rhodesia and Nyasaland (Deane, 1953), Southern Rhodesia and South Africa; and there was some production of cash-crops. But these rural areas were for the most part relatively poor, and men had to work in industry to get the goods they wanted. They resented low wages. These wages were indeed subsidized by subsistence production so that, in reporting on the national income of Northern Rhodesia (Zambia) and Nyasaland (Malawi), Deane could speak of the poorest but largest sector of the economy—subsistence agriculture—subsidizing the richest—mining. But the rural Africans regarded work at these wages as essential, and competed for it. In this movement of 'migrant labourers' men looked to the tribal areas for security against the uncertainties of industrial employment and for ultimate retirement, when they could aim for prestige and status and general satisfaction within the tribal system. They paid part of the money they earned into the tribal system to retain their stake in it. Loss of land to whites, and increasing population, made some tribal areas incapable of adequately fulfilling this role: but tribal organization survived, vertically isolated from the industrial sector, and it has operated in most cases to give some satisfaction in many ways save where land degradation has removed the agricultural base and made impossible the continuance of traditional relationships with chief and kin. Researches on this problem have shown how fundamentally different this tribal organization is from the categorization of fellow-Africans by tribal affiliation which helped Africans order their relationships in the towns (Mitchell, 1956; 1960). But for my present purpose I want to stress that tribal organization in the rural areas provided an ordered system within which men and women could lead, often, some kind of satisfying life (Gluckman, 1960).

In order to analyse, it is necessary to distort. My distortion is that I am trying to correct the factually false image of the relationships between whites and Africans presented by some writers (e.g., Davidson, as cited above, in Kuper and Smith, eds., 1969). I have so far selected processes of interaction showing how the overall system of South Africa and Northern Rhodesia (Zambia) worked, so that people could move about the country, accommodating to persons of the same race and of the opposite race, with some degree of satisfaction. Davidson distorts by concentrating on such actions as John Cilembwe's rising in Nyasaland (Malawi) during the First World War, and the rise of the Watchtower movement, leading on to the nationalist movements. There were plenty of hostilities; but they did not continually affect the daily life of Africans; and the picture of Africans in constant and unceasing antagonism to whites is false for the rural areas, and probably for the urban areas. A relatively small proportion of the African population was involved in persistent struggle against the system, possibly as small a proportion as that of whites who did not approve of the system and tried to combat it. Periodically there would come outbreaks of large-scale protest: and, as at Sharpeville, or Nkata Bay, or on the Copperbelt, these would move to riots as they must when there is no adequate development of secondary associations in which rulers and ruled are associated as allies, or can at least negotiate, instead of meeting only as enemies. In British colonies such riots, investigated by judicial committees or Royal Commissions, usually produced changes favourable to Africans. But, as I have shown in an examination of Zulu history (1940b; 1958), the Zulu attempted 'Luddism' resistance to oust the whites for virtually the last time in the 1906 Bambata revolt. Thereafter they tended to seek good in the new system, till for the educated that search was blocked by the colour bar and a few of them sought a return to Zuluhood, while others hoped for revolution to alter the system radically. Most did not move that far: in seeking good in the system, they committed themselves to its cohesion. They resented restrictions, police raids, etc.; but they have in the past struggled mostly against difficulties in their positions as consumers. Resentment was always there, and therefore the potentiality of riot and revolt. It was kept within bounds because in the rural areas there was an organized system of life; and the government had prevented the emergence of a foot-loose, uncommitted mob in the cities to dominate the political situation.

I have quoted Mitchell on how networks of relationships, categorical and others, bring order into the life of very many urban Africans. This order does not stretch across into the other group; and the cleavage into whites and Africans dominates other developments, as is shown by the increasing polarization of ideologies and political leaders. White voters in South Africa and Rhodesia have steadily put into power those who stand most clearly for separation of the races in all but industry, and for white dominance, by force. In reaction African opponents move to a policy of violence as the only way of achieving betterment and freedom from oppression for their people (see L. Kuper in Kuper and Smith, eds., 1969).

South Africa is the most heavily industrialized nation of the continent. However little consensus there be in some ultimate sense, South Africa has the kind of cohesion that arises from a developed industrial sector which links many of its major segments together in organic interdependence. The white farming areas mostly link into the industrial sector. Force keeps the system going in its whole and in its parts. But within a whole series of parts (factories, trade) there is a series of agreements between Africans and whites within the contracts of the industrial sector. There are agreements in African Reserves between some Africans and some whites. These in turn produce sufficient conflicts among Africans, while they are getting satisfactions from the system, to prevent their uniting solidly and continually. So long as associations linking Africans with members of other races are prevented from developing, a wider consensus covering all races cannot develop, if I use the word 'consensus' correctly. But this is a different matter from social cohesion. Africans will continue to struggle for political rights and for the rights to bargain for their interests in industry which link them to, and align them against, whites. But, though criminal gangs operate in white and African areas, the unemployed mass which constitutes a core for a mob dominating a city cannot emerge, since a ruthless government prevents this. In my opinion, the rural areas are more likely to be the source of widespread rioting against the government, as most of them become less capable of providing adequate basic subsistence[1] and as they are prevented from sending men to the cities. In addition, deterioration of the land must strike at the fundamental attributes of the tribal system, which has provided an arena for cultural organization and prestigious goals both for those who remain in the reserves and for those who leave them periodically for the towns. Between permanent town-dwelling Africans and rural Africans there are fundamental ultimate clashes of interest. Even if urbanized, educated Africans provide the leadership for peasant as well as for urban protests, those who thus lead are a very small proportion of the total urban African population. In most revolts, leadership has come from such élites. Therefore I consider that South Africa, like China in the past and perhaps in the future, and other similar countries, is more likely to see risings from the rural areas (see Mbeki, 1964) than in the industrial towns, particularly as the breakdown of tribal organization creates a mass of peasantry, landless or short of land. Few places in South Africa are suitable for guerrilla warfare; and with its ruthless and efficient use of force, the South African government can hold the situation for some time. It seems to me that only external international action can shake its control in the near future unless there is a major slump to shatter the stabilizing urban economy. Yet for stability an agricultural revolution seems as necessary as an industrial revolution; in South Africa this has been achieved by large white landowners, while so-called poor whites have moved mainly into industrial employment. Despite relatively poor soils and unsuitable conditions, large capital investments by individuals and government have done much for white agriculture. African agriculture has not had this investment or a major revolution.

Developments in independent Africa

Looked at from this point of view, the newly independent, formerly colonial, territories remain plural societies, in my reading, in that they have only partial development of organic interdependence through industrial and economic development. The limited development of the industrial sector creates a situation in which there is a more restricted domain of horizontal cross-linking of a utilitarian sort than in South Africa, and large areas of the rural hinterland may be excluded from this domain. There may be much consensus arising from the national

[1] There are plans to develop agricultural production in these areas, but it is uncertain how far they will succeed—or be implemented.

157

struggle for independence, despite tribal divisions. But there is relatively little cohesion. Cohesion varies from a higher development in Zambia, to a much lower development in the less industrialized countries. It is difficult for African governments to be as ruthless as is the South African government in forbidding the movement of their own people from the more impoverished rural areas into the cities.[1] Large-city mobs are already emerging in many territories; and already there are signs that it is necessary to woo the mob, or bow to it, in order to maintain or achieve power in national politics. From all we know of crowds, we would expect that these mobs, mobilized around different slogans, can shift their allegiances. Like the apprentices in mediaeval times, students—often only schoolboys—provide leadership. The drive for education produces large numbers of those who are unemployable in terms of their skills because of the slow development of the economy. The political system is likely to be not well articulated, therefore, with a crust of élites—sometimes ethnically homogeneous, sometimes ethnically heterogeneous, within the African population—taking power partly on the basis of their control of armed force, partly by securing the support of the crowd. These shifts will be related to current world, as well as intra-national, cleavages; but their roots are involved in the unarticulated structure of the society arising from its unarticulated economic development.[2]

My discussion of the movement of people from relatively poorer rural areas into the towns has made me begin my discussion from the possible emergence of a city mob. But clearly the main focus of power is in those who control armed forces, now armed with the more complex weapons of repeating rifles, machine-guns, armoured vehicles, aeroplanes, wireless, etc. When we look at the series of military coups in Africa, or in Latin America, or in Asia, it is most important to remember, as I have described above, that in most societies through

---

[1] The *San Francisco Chronicle* reported on 29 August 1967 that 'there was going to be a back-to-the-land roundup of unemployed in Dar es Salaam'.

[2] I wrote this chapter in 1966, when student protests in the USA were just beginning and before the student 'revolt' in Europe. On my analysis, as stated, I had expected student 'power' to influence strongly politics in the developing countries, and had not anticipated even an essay by students to do this in the highly industrialized countries. Here I can only insert a late (July 1969) interpolation, that in my opinion the ability of highly industrialized countries to sustain, in some cases, major disturbances, fits with my main thesis: similar disturbances in a country with little articulation would be likely to shake its governmental and municipal organizations. I dare suggest that the USA will even manage to contain the black 'revolt'.

human history those who led armed men, including kings, were the main contenders for central and regional powers. This was true of tribal states and of mediaeval Europe, of Ancient Rome and of Greece, of Mogul and of Mongol and of Chinese empires. The opposite situation, in which men in command of troops were not likely to try to seize political control, is much rarer, and on the whole fairly recent, in Europe and North America. In states in those continents in recent centuries the military have had important influence on policy; but among industrialized countries only in Germany, and in France over Algeria, have we seen anything like essays at military coups.[1] (Earlier in France, Napoleon I's coming to power is a clear illustration.) In the United States, the President, by mobilizing the local militia in Southern states under federal command, has been able to get Southerners to 'enforce' policies of which they disapprove. This is a striking contrast to situations where local military power led to power in national affairs. It is not surprising, therefore, that African states, with their inadequate economic and political development on a national scale, are subject to military coups, and sometimes to a succession of these. The failure, inevitable in the circumstances, of civilian authorities to achieve the hoped-for national development and betterment, which became so high in aspiration during the struggle against foreign domination, and the risks of sectional cleavages, as well as perhaps individual desires for power, lead those who command armed force to take over. It is essential to realize that these commanders are not members of an 'exploiting' upper class, but are moved by dissatisfaction at failure to achieve goals of national stability and strength with social development and welfare at which they themselves aim. Yet as soon as commanders become responsible for organizing the state, they have to delegate command of troops to others, previously subordinate; and the risk of a new military coup is set in train. The national system is so unarticulated that attempts, perhaps temporarily successful, can be made by men with relatively small commands to seize some of the few key centres of power.[2]

This kind of situation did not threaten the colonial dominating powers, and does not threaten the South African and Rhodesian

---

[1] The exception is the recent military coup in relatively underdeveloped Greece (21 April 1967).

[2] A case in point is the unsuccessful attempt at a coup by a small commander in Ghana, who was able to seize the national radio station (May 1967).

governments. In these latter situations the military forces, in so far as they were and are staffed by and composed of whites, are prevented from turning on the civilian governments by their situation as members of the white 'élite' sharply distinguished from the Africans. (Indeed, as Algeria shows, they are likely to turn only where the civilian government is ready to give away power to the subordinated people.) And it is important to note that many Africans in the past, and nowadays in South Africa and Rhodesia, assist the armed forces of the white minorities. There have been mutinies, particularly in the Belgian Congo, where a serious mutiny at transfer of power broke that country's first essay at unity. But mutineers in the past were suppressed by metropolitan or white-officered troops.

Other dangers accentuate this tendency to coups and disturbances. The struggle for, and move to, independence raised high aspirations, and also high hopes of the better world that would follow on the end of colonial domination. With these aspirations and hopes, and the dreams of national unity, temporarily achieved to some extent in the independence struggle, a demand for high consensus emerged. With a demand for high consensus, when so many factors prevent its achievement, any deviation tends to be regarded as criminal: we would expect this from Durkheim's discussion of crime in *Les Règles de la méthode sociologique* (1895), where he shows that as the 'collective conscience' becomes more sensitive, acts previously regarded as venial will be treated as crimes. Dissidence is more likely to be reproved and regarded as renegadism, treachery and even heresy; and as Simmel has shown, renegade, traitor and heretic are more hated and more savagely treated than foreign enemies. A similar process has occurred in South Africa as the government has enforced more strictly the segregation of colour-groups: dissidence previously allowed is now forbidden and ruthlessly punished (Gluckman, 1968).

The divisions between ethnic groups, tribes and religious sects, which in a developed modern country are controlled in the articulation of economic and political secondary and tertiary associations, in a newly-independent country threaten constant schism. Even in Britain a prime minister must take account of these factors in selecting his cabinet. Representation of sections is sought for in many other situations. Special areas have to be cared for out of national wealth. But in new countries this representation has to be arranged more delicately, and it may lead to dispute, particularly with differential regional development, with wealth not adequately channelled into and distributed from national centres, and with a bigger gap existing between the very poor and the industrially and bureaucratically powerful. So-called 'tribal' strife always threatens. In some ways, the division of Africa into French-speaking and English-speaking territories particularly, has advantages, in that a common language and to some extent common culture especially for the educated, may create a national unity as against neighbouring territories which came under a different colonial power.

The staffing of cadres by those who happen to be available at independence, and who may not be very able but are likely to be young, blocks access to position and power for many years for those who follow. This may stimulate a special kind of revolt, as abler and better-trained younger people aspire to positions of importance.

Future developments in the rural areas are more uncertain. New élites are likely to regard traditional tribal authorities as potential competitors for power, because both draw support from the people, in ways that the white District Officers or *chefs de territoires*, whose bases of authority lay in the European countries and with fellow-whites, did not. Tribal systems of organization may survive and even in some places become foci of submerged opposition to a national government, or replace in some territories the inability of the central government to rule effectively. In other areas, the fragility of tribal organization will cause them to weaken at least for a time before the high demand for consensus at an ideological level. Attachment to them will be denigrated. If this happens, and there is no substitute development of secondary associations, the social, cultural and political life of the rural areas will be impoverished. The knitting together of vertical sections within the tribe will be weakened; and there will be left a large number of peasants with a minimum development of cross-links between them. The situation may become akin to that of the peasantry of southern Italy and Sicily. This may, from experience elsewhere, lead to the emergence of banditry and of political racketeers, as well as to a proliferation of millenarian cults and other forms of dissident religious groupings. A populist people's party is another possible development. The major political party organization of each territory is likely to be based on the industrialized sector and on the managers and workers who get their living and other rewards from industry, from which the great mass of the population is perforce excluded. Representatives of the national party in rural areas, even of rural origin, because of the demand for consensus may represent the ostensible interests of this élite sector, and not the interests of the rural population. It is possible that such representatives may move (as District Officers of colonial régimes did) into being, as far as they can, representatives of the interests of the rural sections they administer, even trying to operate against major policy directives from the centre. But the pressure of the party organization, with its ideology of high consensus, is quite likely to prevent this development. Disorder is likely also to arise in the rural areas, as in South Africa.

Developments in states will vary with many factors. Most strikingly, the small state of Swaziland, occupied by one historic 'nation' under a king and now economically developed with mining, some secondary industry, and major agricultural improvement, is showing high cohesion and consensus within its articulation, both social and cultural. The king's party has swept the elections—and we have the paradox of a modern developed small country adhering in many ways to traditional culture.

Conclusion

I come out of this analysis, working it out in detail as my argument has advanced, with gloomy conclusions against my own political predilections and hopes, but not against my anticipations. I may add as a personal postscript that when I discussed this analysis with an American colleague, he asked why no liberal sociologist, backing African independence, was able to predict what has happened. In fact I did so, in evidence to the Monckton Commission on Central African Federation in 1960; and I published an analysis of my anticipations in that year (Gluckman, 1960b) in a Sydney journal. He then asked why I supported the African demands for independence. I did so because gloomy as my anticipations were, I felt that any foreign domination is immoral and Africans were entitled to their freedom. The problems raised by European domination were insoluble: Africans have a right to solve their own problems, and with time and help they will do so. The tragedy was that the European powers were driven out of their colonies always both too early and too late.

Of course, I hope that I am wrong. Even if I am, I consider the theoretical implications of my analysis indicate that with the passing of colonialism we need to abandon the view that in these kinds of colonial societies the principal social factor was the forceful domination of self-interested alien minorities. These minorities produced and produce special kinds of social systems, but their extrusion leaves many underlying problems which persist in the same form. The colonial situation involved many kinds of countervailing principles. We need to look at various sectors and domains of interaction, to work out differences between categorical alignments and allegiances as against group alignments and allegiances, to map and analyse social networks as these focus on different types of individuals. Solidarity and cohesion, consensus and lack of consensus, agreement and disagreement, as against dispute and struggle, conflict and contradiction, are present in varying degrees in different domains of life and at different levels in each domain. Problems of articulation and unarticulation are not solved by consensus. Individuals are moved, even more than in temporarily stabilized societies, by independent, discrepant, and inconsistent, and even contradictory, interests and values. To some extent, they may solve the resulting difficulties by situational selection.

Domestic life, organized by a particular set of traditional values and customs, can be insulated to some extent from major changes in economic and political life. But so long as utilitarian, organic interdependence between the segments of the nation is weak, many of the characteristics of the plural society will remain, despite the disappearance of the hegemony of colonial settlers backed by metropolitan authority. For the dominant characteristic of these societies is a mass of peasantry, possibly with their traditional culture more violently disturbed than in the past, dominated by the small industrial sector in cities containing large proportions of unemployed, or underemployed and underpaid, peasants, and many unemployable literati. Secondary associations will be underdeveloped in the insistence on high consensus. The absence of these associations will allow dispute, when it arises, to spread and proliferate upwards. The type of force in the form of complex weapons in the hands of the government, and the government's willingness to use it, may be the main determinant of degree of stability. Otherwise there is likely to be a shifting of personnel due to armed coups, as in a rebellious structure, through vaguely defined authority positions, unless a highly doctrinated party seizes power. But not even such a party may be able to stop the working of the forces I have outlined. Economic development and political stability are thus dependent on each other.

Since I began from the number of potential legitimate heirs to power and the law of treason, I conclude with a brief word about them. The first man to power will be endowed with high charisma, and all thought of a successor will be ruled out. This will be backed by the demand for high consensus. As secondary associations are little developed, modern forms of election cannot be carried out. Success in the effort to institute new leadership will depend successively therefore on ability to control force and to use the mob in the city or the underprivileged peasants. Dissidence will be increasingly regarded as treasonable. Though a plural society is in fact largely divided vertically into relatively independent segments, these are not regarded as legitimate centres of authority as against central authority. This was the position under colonial régimes which tended to look askance at all dissidence. And this position is not likely to change substantially if the central power is sufficiently strong.

BIBLIOGRAPHY

Allan, W. (1965). *The African husbandman*. Edinburgh.

Barnes, J. A., J. C. Mitchell and M. Gluckman (1949). 'The village headman in British Central Africa', *Africa*, **19**, no. 2. Repub. in M. Gluckman, *Order and rebellion in tribal Africa*. London, Eng., and Glencoe, Ill.

Deane, P. (1953). *Colonial social accounting*. Cambridge University Press.

Durkheim, E. (1933). *De la division du travail social*. Paris, 1893. Trans. as *The division of labour* by G. Simpson. Glencoe, Ill.

(1938). *Les règles de la méthode sociologique*. Paris, 1895. Trans. as *The rules of sociological method* by S. A. Soloway and H. J. Mueller. Glencoe, Ill.

Epstein, A. L. (1958). *Politics in an urban African community*. Manchester University Press for the Rhodes–Livingstone Institute.

Fortes, M., and E. E. Evans-Pritchard (1940). *African political systems*. London, Oxford University Press for the International African Institute.

Furnivall, J. S. (1948). *Colonial policy and practice*. Cambridge University Press.

Gillon, P. (1952). *Frail barrier* [novel]. New York.

Gluckman, M. (1940a). 'The kingdom of the Zulu of South Africa', in *African political systems*, M. Fortes and E. E. Evans-Pritchard, eds. London, Oxford University Press for the International African Institute.

(1940b). 'Analysis of a social situation in modern Zululand', *Bantu Studies*, **14**, nos. 1 and 2. Repub. in Gluckman, 1958.

(1942). 'Some processes of social change illustrated with Zululand data', *African Studies*, **1**, no. 4.

(1955a). *Custom and conflict in Africa*. Oxford, England, and Glencoe, Ill.

Gluckman, M. (1958). *Analysis of a social situation in modern Zululand*, Rhodes-Livingstone Paper, no. 28. (Repub. of Gluckman, 1940*b* and 1942.)

(1960*a*). 'Tribalism in modern British Central Africa', *Cahiers d'études africaines*, **1**. Repub. in *Africa: social problems of change and conflict*, R. L. Van den Berghe, ed. (San Francisco, 1965); and in *Social change: the colonial situation*, I. Wallerstein, ed. London and New York, 1966.

(1960*b*). 'From town to tribe', *Nation* (Sydney, Australia), **53**.

(1965*a*). *Law, politics and ritual in tribal society*. Oxford, Chicago, and New York.

(1965*b*). *The ideas in Barotse jurisprudence*. New Haven, Yale University Press.

(1968*a*). 'Inter-hierarchical roles: professional and party ethics in the tribal areas in South and Central Africa', in *Local-level politics*, M. Swartz, ed. Chicago.

(1968*b*). 'The utility of the equilibrium model in the study of social change', *American Anthropologist*, **70**, no. 2, April.

(1969). 'The tribal areas in South and Central Africa', in *Pluralism in Africa*, L. Kuper and M. G. Smith, eds. Berkeley, University of California Press.

Hobsbawn, E. J. (1959). *Primitive rebels*. Manchester University Press.

Hunter, M. (1961). *Reaction to conquest*. London, Oxford University Press for the International African Institute (first publ. 1936).

Kuper, H. (1947). *The uniform of colour: a study of white-black relationships in Swaziland*. Johannesburg, Witwatersrand University Press.

Kuper, L. (1965). *An African bourgeoisie: race, class and politics in South Africa*. New Haven, Yale University Press.

and M. G. Smith, eds. (1968). *Pluralism in Africa*. Berkeley, University of California Press.

Laslett, P. (1965). *The world we have lost*. London.

Mayer, P. (1960). *Townsmen or tribesmen: conservatism and the process of urbanization in a South African city*. Cape Town, Oxford University Press.

(1966). 'The tribal élite and the Transkeian elections of 1963', in *The new élites of Tropical Africa*, P. C. Lloyd, ed. London, Oxford University Press for the International African Institute.

Mbeki, G. (1964). *South Africa: the peasants' revolt*. Harmondsworth, Middlesex.

Mitchell, J. C. (1956). *The Kalela dance*, Rhodes-Livingstone Paper, no. 27.

(1960). *Tribalism and the plural society*. London, Oxford University Press.

Pospisil, L. (1958). *Kapauka Papuans and their law*. Yale University Publications in Anthropology, No. 54.

(1963). *Kapauka Papuan economy*. Yale University Publications in Anthropology, No. 67.

Pospisil, L. (1966). Review of M. Gluckman's *Politics, law and ritual in tribal society* in *American Anthropologist*, **68**, no. 6.

Smith, M. G. (1965). *The plural society in the West Indies*. Berkeley and Los Angeles, University of California Press.

Swartz, M., ed. (1968). *Local-level politics*. Chicago.

Trevelyan, G. M. (1942). *English social history: a survey of six centuries, Chaucer to Queen Victoria*. New York.

Watson, W. (1958). *Tribal cohesion in a money economy*. Manchester University Press for the Rhodes–Livingstone Institute.

(1960). 'The impact of federation on Africans: the social background', in *A new deal in Central Africa*, C. Leys and C. Pratt, eds. London.

Wilson, G., and M. Wilson (1945). *The analysis of social change*. Cambridge University Press.

Worsley, P. M. (1964). *The third world*. London.

CHAPTER 5

NEW ELITES IN EAST AND WEST AFRICA

by

LUCY MAIR

Authority in pre-colonial Africa might be ascribed on the basis of lineage membership; it might be partly achieved, in the sense that one of several members of a ruling lineage could be selected to hold office, or that armed contests for the succession were part of the recognized procedure; it might be wholly achieved in the absence of any lineage claim. In the many cases where succession was not automatic the person selected was ostensibly chosen for the qualities that were thought to be desirable in a leader, and in practice was also generally one who already had a following. A following can be built up and maintained only by the ability to reward and protect, and this is a matter of the possession, or control, of wealth. It may be that this generally counted for more than personal qualities. Nevertheless, these formed part of the image of a ruler, an image that includes as an essential the ability to settle disputes to the satisfaction of the disputants and in accordance with recognized principles. Possibly this can be thought of as the possession of a special skill. Some ethnographic accounts tell how a future chief would be prepared for his responsibilities by listening to the proceedings of his father's council. It is a skill, however, that is not acquired through any deliberate process of instruction. Headmasters might classify it as pertaining to wisdom rather than knowledge, and it was commonly thought of in Africa as an attribute of age.

Where there was no hereditary rule, leadership commonly fell by general consensus, or, in systems of organization by age, by the judgement of seniors, to individuals with 'leadership qualities'— courage and the ability to persuade and reconcile, to 'speak' and to be listened to. In the West African conciliar systems, where the entry into superior councils was gained by the payment of fees, wealth was the dominant criterion of fitness.

New élites before colonial rule

There are instances on record of changes in the source of recruitment of the political élite before the establishment of colonial rule. It could indeed be argued that if the ancestors of the pastoral aristocrats in the interlacustrine states were egalitarian Nilotes, they must at some time have developed a new élite; but this is a process that we are never likely to be able to trace. But we have historical evidence for the effects of the Fulani conquest of Zazzau (now Zaria) as analysed by Smith (1950), in which an existing set of political offices was taken over (with some modifications) by invaders, and the incumbents replaced by nominees of the conquerors, some of them outsiders, some Fulani already living there.

This replacement of one set of office-holders by another is less interesting to students of social change than the emergence of a new élite which follows the opening of new avenues of social mobility. It is a truism that this has been one of the effects of colonial rule, but there is at any rate one example of it which belongs to an earlier period. This is the story of the 'canoe houses' of the Niger Delta as they developed in the early nineteenth century as a result of competition between the coastal settlements for control of the waterways to the interior, and through this of the trade first in slaves and then in palm-oil. Although the slave-trade had been going on from the fifteenth century, it was only in its final stages that this competition became intense. This occurred when fire-arms began to be imported in large numbers, increasing the scale on which wars of conquest were practicable—though Jones believes that competition for control of the inland waterways stimulated the import of fire-arms in the first place.[1] In any case, the need to make effective use of them led to the recruitment of the political élite from new sources and on new principles.

Ibo society at the earliest times of which we know, and in the inland country right up to the colonial period, was based on descent. Lineages, or 'houses', were corporate groups with a common patrimony and a common head chosen by the male members, usually on the principle of seniority. The basic 'house' was a group of full brothers with wives and dependents. The patrimony of a house included slaves; but, as in so many parts of Africa, the relationship of the slave to his master was hardly distinguishable from that of a client or dependent kinsman, and it was only recently acquired slaves whose alien origin was con-

[1] Jones, 1963: 48.

spicuous. On the one hand, slaves could acquire property; on the other, full members of the lineage could be sold out of it. It was essentially his alien origin that distinguished the slave, and, in Ibo as in many other African societies, debarred him from hereditary office. In the organization of the 'canoe houses' founded in the late eighteenth and early nineteenth centuries, whose traditions Jones has collected, this distinction disappeared.

A canoe house consisted, in essence, of a body of persons with adequate resources to man, equip and maintain a war canoe, under the authority of a single leader. The status of 'canoe chief' was ritually recognized by the lineage heads who constituted the ultimate political authority of the community. It was gained by success in building up a following, with one's own lineage kin and dependents as a nucleus, but eventually extending beyond them. A man who showed the capacity to do this would be recognized as leader within the lineage group whatever his seniority. Once a canoe house was established, it was very common for a slave to succeed to the position of chief. Lip-service was given to the principle of heredity by describing such men as 'adopted sons'; but, except in ritual matters, the distinction between slave and free birth had now been obliterated. The canoe chiefs became the *de facto* political authorities, and their position was consolidated by the practice of the European traders (the 'supercargoes') of treating them as the spokesmen of their communities. Hereditary lineage heads were described by the derogatory term 'Parliament gentlemen'.

Keen traders such as these were alive to the value of technical skills; unlike the missionaries who taught it, they regarded literacy in English as a technical skill. Some had already acquired it. The diary of the Efik Antera Duke, recently edited by Forde,[1] dates from 1767; and when Hope Waddell arrived in the Efik town of Calabar, he found that King Eyo's son, who kept his father's accounts, was better at writing and arithmetic than the schoolmaster Waddell had brought with him. The Ibo chiefs of Bonny, when they tried to get a trading firm to find missionaries for them, wrote: 'We expect that those gentlemen to be sent us shall be capable of instructing our young people in the English language.'[2]

At that time the African chiefs did not see, though the missionaries did, that literacy in English would become the criterion for recruitment of an élite almost wholly independent of ascribed status.

[1] Forde, ed., 1957.   [2] Ajayi, 1965: 65.

In East Africa it has been said of the kingdom of Buganda that status was as much a matter of achievement before as after the introduction of Western techniques. Office was the reward for loyal service to superiors. Hereditary claims, except those to the monarchy itself and to three very old-established chiefships, had ceased to be valid. This was also true of the major offices in the Nigerian emirates. As Smith has reconstructed the history of Zazzau,[1] these offices were filled under Habe rule by an elaborate promotion system in which the existing office-holders had a say. Under the Fulani, the rulers, who were supplied alternately by two lineages, nominated the office-holders, each appointing his own kinsmen or clients in a simple spoils system.

Contemporary élites

Today's new élite derives its prestige not from literacy alone, but from the various statuses for which literacy is a prerequisite. It would be a gross oversimplification to describe it purely in terms of opposition to the traditional élite. At certain times there was a clear opposition of interests, but at others they have been united in the pursuit of common aims, and in one or two places the position of the traditional élite has barely been challenged. Moreover, as has already been indicated, the members of the traditional élite have not turned their backs on literacy, or on the Western mode of life attainable by an income above the average.

One can see a typical pattern. First, men appear who are qualified by their literacy and specialist training to occupy positions not accessible to the older élite. They do not seek to displace the latter from the offices they hold, no doubt in part because in most countries the most important activities of the new élite lie ouside the scope of this authority. They see themselves, along with or instead of the traditional élite, as spokesmen for the population in general vis-à-vis the colonial authorities, but they do not necessarily find this incompatible with the maintenance of the colonial régime, of which they are in some ways beneficiaries. Later, political leaders appear who may or may not have the same specialist qualifications, but who rely for their support on a section of the people with some, but much less, education. It is they who have demanded and secured independence, often at the same time demanding the abolition of the traditional élite, though when their

[1] Smith, 1950.

power is secure they have often accorded some degree of recognition to the latter. There may now be appearing a third generation, again claiming superiority on the grounds of educational attainments acquired in universities in Africa or abroad.

But advanced education is not the only criterion of élite status. It can also be attained, as in the past, by wealth—nowadays wealth acquired in new ways, through participation in the world economy. Some members of the élite of wealth have reached their position with a minimum of schooling. Another road, significant in the period when the new élite have been demanding, and have secured, the independence of their countries, has been that of leadership in the organization of labour, again a role which initially called for the minimum of schooling.

Morgenthau's study of political parties in Francophone West Africa illustrates the development of an élite based on commercial success rather than on educational attainment. Such an élite exists, of course, in the Anglophone countries, too; they are the members of Nigerian party executives who describe themselves as 'businessmen'. Azikiwe is their most conspicuous example. Some may have derived from cocoa farms the capital with which they started their enterprises; but in Senegal and the Ivory Coast it seems that there is an élite of wealth based directly on farming. Thus, Ibrahim Seydou N'Daw, who was president of the territorial assembly of Senegal, was head of an association of ground-nut growers and buyers and was locally called the 'Chief' of the Kaolack region.[1] Houphouët-Boigny, though he could certainly qualify for élite status as a graduate of the William Ponty School and possibly also as a member of a traditional chief's family, was also a successful coffee planter and first won a following as a champion of the interests of African planters against French settlers.

Some of the women traders in Nigeria could qualify for élite membership in terms of the magnitude of their operations. Their professional associations with their own heads have been recognized from pre-colonial times, and these head women had traditionally a seat in the councils of some Yoruba towns. But in the field of modern politics, though the market women as a body are a force to be reckoned with, individual women do not take a prominent part; indeed this is hardly to be expected.

The representation of labour, too, has rarely led to the attainment of political power at the highest level. More often labour unions have been

[1] Morgenthau, 1964: 143.

thought of as the adjuncts of political parties in much the same way as farmers' unions or women's unions or youth organizations, and their leaders have been put in their place as soon as they opposed the policies of independent governments in the interests of their members. Nevertheless, there are several whose names are known outside their own countries—Anthony Woode and Tettegah in Ghana for example, and two still holding high office, Sékou Touré in Guinea and Rashidi Kawawa in Tanzania. A third was Tom Mboya, who was thought of as a possible successor to the President of Kenya until his assassination in 1969.

Trade union organizers are not necessarily wage-labourers, a fact that was often held against them in the early days of African unions. But they need not have a high standard of education; indeed a position as union organizer has been the entrée into politics for one or two well-known characters who could qualify for élite membership neither by diplomas nor by wealth.

Sékou Touré had only elementary schooling. While a post office clerk he was one of the first members of the communist study groups. Later he became secretary-general of the West African branch of the French Confédération Générale du Travail (CGT), which he developed into an autonomous organization. As its head he was one of the élite figures for the whole of French West Africa, and he continued to hold this post after he became President of Guinea. Tom Mboya went farther in his schooling, but for want of money was disappointed of his highest ambitions. He was trained as a sanitary inspector and, within a year of his first employment with the Nairobi City Council, was elected secretary of the African Staff Association. Within another twelve months he had organized a union of local government workers for all Kenya. Just as the graduates of Fourah Bay or of the William Ponty School in Senegal form an 'old boy' network, so Mboya was able to call on the co-operation of a number of men who had been trained along with him. Two years later he became general secretary of the Kenya Federation of Labour (KFL). Whereas Touré's Parti Démocratique de Guinée developed out of a trade union organization, Mboya's KFL became the substitute for a nationalist party during the time when country-wide parties were banned in Kenya, lest they should become instruments of Mau Mau. Like Touré's, his first foreign journeys were made to attend trade union conferences (non-communist in his case), but unlike Touré he had a year at Ruskin College, Oxford, before returning to take part in politics.

Access to Western education

GHANA. The first European school that we know of in sub-Saharan Africa was opened by the Dutch at Elmina, on the Gold Coast, in 1644. An Ashanti chief sent fourteen children there.[1] The Danes followed in 1722 with a school at Christiansborg (Accra), and in 1827 took the historically significant step of inviting members of the Basel Mission to do the teaching. When in 1843 members of the mission moved to the healthier climate of Akropong, they created the first inland centre for the teaching of literacy and made the first experiments with possible commercial crops, including cocoa. A school was opened in Cape Coast in 1752, and was held in the castle with an African headmaster, Philip Quaque, from 1776. This school may be seen as the first step in the development that made Cape Coast the leading centre of secondary education in the country. Schooling was not established in Ashanti until early in the present century. According to Busia,[2] by 1905 the Basel Mission had ten schools there and the Wesleyans seven. A government school for boys was opened at Kumasi in 1909. All these were attended mainly by pupils from the southern part of Ashanti whose families had contacts with educated Africans from the coastal area.

The concentration of secondary schools in limited areas has affected the geographical sources from which the new élites are drawn. It is natural for secondary education to flourish in larger towns where there is a considerable primary educated population to draw on, and Cape Coast and Accra have never lost their initial lead. Studies made in 1963 and later refer to Mfantsipim in Cape Coast and to Achimota in Accra as 'élite schools' as in England one would talk of 'major public schools'.[3] Their pupils, who are predominantly city-born and the children of educated parents in stable employment, have their choice of jobs; and this fact introduces a hereditary element into the composition of today's professional élite. Access to universities, at which practically all students are maintained by scholarships or grants, is limited by the fact that secondary education is not free. A recent study of undergraduates at the University of Legon (Accra) indicates, however, that the proportion of students whose parents were farmers is increasing. There is also some increase in the number, small as it still is, who come from Ashanti.[4]

[1] Wise, 1956: 1.
[2] Busia, 1951.
[3] 'Public' being the equivalent of 'private' in America.
[4] Peil, 1965: 19–28.

The pupils in the early Gold Coast schools were the children either of foreign traders and African mothers or of African merchants. Some parents in both these categories sent their sons to England, and some to Sierra Leone, to the school opened there in 1792. The education of these students consisted largely of book-learning, but it was not, as is so often argued today, deliberately designed with no wider aim than to produce the clerks required by traders and government; it was what educators of those days thought appropriate for any school. Although some missions in Africa gave instruction in crafts, it was a century and a half before people began to talk about education specially designed for African needs, and this in its turn has been found inadequate as the new rulers have come to believe that what is wanted is education in a wider range of Western techniques.

In any case, it was not to make craftsmen of their sons that parents sent them to school, and they judged rightly, since it was book-learning and not new manual skills that equipped them for positions of authority and for professions that had not previously existed in their society.

NIGERIA. On the coast of what was later Nigeria, missionaries opened schools at Badagri in 1845 and at Calabar in 1848. Members of the mission at Badagri moved to its hinterland ally, Abeokuta, in 1846. These towns were not selected for their political importance. They welcomed missionaries as an earnest of British protection against dangerous neighbours. The Church Missionary Society moved from Badagri to Lagos as soon as a chief friendly to Britain had been installed there (1852). For thirty years only Lagos and its immediate hinterland were under British control; this made it inevitable that it should continue to be the seat of government when British authority was extended inland and that secondary education (started in 1859) should be concentrated there.

Lugard's refusal to support missionary activity in the Muslim north, except where the emirs expressly asked for it, is commonly cited as the principal reason why the percentage of literates in the population is so small to this day. The percentage in Mali, where the French administration showed no such tenderness towards Muslim susceptibilities, is nearly as small, but the reasons were primarily financial. British control in Northern Nigeria was imposed only in 1900, and two emirs, of Bida and of Zaria, invited missions to open schools in their territories in 1903 and 1905 respectively. But these were islands in the great ocean of what impatient modernizers have called the 'frozen north'. Mission schools were allowed to operate in the pagan areas of the Northern Region, now called the Middle Belt. But developments there have little bearing on the question of the tenacity of the traditional élite.

Cape Coast merchants and doctors from Sierra Leone were pressing claims on the government of the Gold Coast at a time when Nigeria as a British dependency did not exist. For the emergence of a modern-educated élite in Nigeria we have to look fifty years later. Coleman shows from census records that in 1920–5 there were in all Nigeria 15 barristers and 12 physicians. Of those, 20 were Yoruba and the remainder 'native foreigners' (from Sierra Leone and the Gold Coast, presumably). Thirty years later there were 150 barristers. Physicians numbered 160—76 Yoruba, 49 Ibo, *one* Hausa or Fulani (i.e., a Northerner) and 34 'others'. After the creation in 1934 of Yaba Higher College, on the outskirts of Lagos, a number of other professions were opened to Nigerians who had not left their country. The purpose of the college was to train Nigerians for employment in the technical departments of government. There would have been little demand outside government service for the specialists whom it produced, but its students, in addition to being expected to enter this service, were not allowed to choose their subject.[1] Yaba turned out medical, agricultural and forestry officers, engineers and surveyors.

By the time of the Second World War Nigerians were following the example of the Gold Coast and were going overseas for study. Not all of these were the sons of wealthy parents. Some were financed by local or tribal 'improvement unions', and some managed to save money to pay for themselves. The autobiography of Obafemi Awolowo shows what straits an African who seeks to enter the élite may be in even in his own country, while the autobiographies of Azikiwe and Nkrumah describe their hard times as students in America.

Of the twenty Nigerian students on the books of American universities before 1938, Azikiwe was the only Ibo, though there were others from the Eastern Region. The numbers have risen steadily since the end of the war, thanks partly to the offer of scholarships from American foundations and partly to the efforts of improvement unions and individual Nigerians in raising funds; and Ibo students have consistently accounted for more than half. This is a striking manifestation of the late but determined entry of the Ibo into the new

[1] Coleman, 1958: 123, 142.

élite. One attraction of American universities is the lower entrance qualifications and what Azikiwe regards as their more practical orientation. But the rapid expansion of secondary education in the east made it possible in the post-war period for its scholars to enter British universities in equally striking numbers.

FRENCH WEST AFRICA. In considering European education as the seed-bed of the new élite, we must treat the eight French-speaking West African states together, since under French administration they formed part of a single unit with its capital at Dakar. The early establishment of schools at the first point where French control was effective, and the concentration of advanced education at the same point, have had consequences not only for Senegal, the country to which Dakar now belongs, but for all the other seven.

The first school was opened at St Louis, north of Dakar, in 1816. Education at this time was entrusted to missionaries and so was looked at askance by Muslims. Faidherbe in 1854 introduced non-religious schools, and Gallieni set up schools in the Sudan (now Mali) as an essential element in the establishment of French authority. Lay schools were opened at Conakry in 1878 and at Grand Bassam (Ivory Coast) in 1893.

When a systematic educational policy was worked out, it followed the principle that most pupils should receive an education appropriate for peasant farmers and only the select few should proceed to further studies (*Instruire la masse et dégager l'élite*). Whatever could be said about this system, nobody could complain that it sought only to give Africans the skills that made them useful to Europeans; but one may wonder whether it would have had much appeal for those who complain of the literary bias of education in British colonies.

A school for chiefs' sons—originally a 'school for hostages'—was opened at St Louis in 1856 with the declared aim of producing 'a native élite to help us in our civilizing work'. Three others in different parts of the country followed. They were later entitled 'schools for the sons of chiefs and interpreters', a description that implied the intention of creating a better qualified second-generation bureaucracy.

The Ecole William Ponty, first at Dakar and then at St Louis, was founded in 1912 for the training of teachers; and a medical school was attached to it in 1919. By 1945 it was estimated to have produced 2,000 graduates, about a third of them medical assistants. A lycée opened in 1920 for the education of French boys also took African pupils. Some of these went on to universities in France, notably Lamine Guèye, who qualified in law and became a judge in Martinique, and Sédar Senghor, who became the first African *agrégé* of the Ecole Normale Supérieure, served as an officer in the Second World War, and taught in French lycées as well as at the Ecole Nationale de la France d'Outremer, where Frenchmen were trained for the colonial service. In the few years between 1956 and the accession of the French territories to independence, some Africans were admitted to the latter school.

A source of adult education, particularly for trade unionists, which became available under the Popular Front government in 1936, was the communist study-groups set up in the principal towns. The Communist Party also provided opportunities, particularly after 1945, for Africans to attend conferences in France and elsewhere. These are, of course, open to Africans from all over the continent, but French West Africa alone experienced this intensive indoctrination. (It should not be assumed from this that its present leaders, despite their Marxist vocabulary, see their practical problems in Marxist terms, still less that they are politically committed to Russia or China.)

From 1946 the overseas territories were represented in the two houses of the French parliament and in a consultative body called the Assembly of the French Union. At the maximum there were 67 representatives from French West Africa in these three bodies, where they learned one way of playing the Western political game, three or four of them as ministers. Some became thoroughly disillusioned with it and made their disillusion an argument in favour of the one-party state. Some set themselves to study while they were in Paris, notably Mamadou Dia from Senegal, whose work bore fruit in a number of treatises on economics.

Although Dakar now has its university, the flow of Africans to France, assisted by government grants, has greatly increased. In Morgenthau's view this has produced a situation somewhat similar to that in Ghana, though for different reasons. The existing political élite are men of much lower academic attainment than the returned graduates, who have seen their education as giving them a claim to leadership, but find themselves relegated to subordinate posts in the civil service. Of course this intellectual difference between civil servants and politicians is not peculiar to Africa; but in the older countries the civil servants have learned to take it for granted. More difficult may be the situation, bound to develop in the new countries, in which well-educated bureaucrats are subordinate to less well-educated men who were appointed in the first rush of Africanization.

European education, then, has been available to Africans in and near Dakar for a generation longer than it has in the other French-speaking states. But the fact that men from all the other states have had to go to Dakar for any kind of advanced education has created an inter-territorial élite with close personal ties.[1] The closest parallel to this in the history of the English-speaking states is the intellectual dominance of Sierra Leone in the days when it had in Fourah Bay College the only institution of university status in West Africa. But Fourah Bay lost its pre-eminence as the other British territories set up their own colleges, while Ponty graduates were a close-knit élite right up to the end of French colonial rule.

The influence of Fourah Bay, again, was not solely a matter of intellectual prestige. The colony of Sierra Leone was originally created as a place of refuge for liberated slaves. After the slave-trade was declared illegal, slave-ships could be captured at sea and the slaves landed at Freetown. Many of them were anxious to return to homes from which they had only recently been taken. Perhaps the most famous is the Yoruba Samuel Crowther, who after a few years in Freetown returned as a missionary and later became a bishop. It was not, then, only the demand for skills not obtainable in the Gold Coast and Nigeria that led to the appearance of an élite educated at Fourah Bay. But on the other hand, students from the Gold Coast and from Lagos did go to Fourah Bay for university education. Intermarriage between their families led them to keep in contact; and this common background made possible the foundation of the West African Congress, which put forward the claim of all West Africans for political representation as early as the First World War.

BUGANDA. In Central and Eastern Africa, too, the accidents of history gave certain areas and peoples a head start over their neighbours. Literacy in Swahili came to Buganda with the Arab trader Ahmed ben Ibrahim in 1854, literacy in English with the missionary Mackay in 1877. Buganda had a literate bureaucracy before British over-rule was established there. In contrast, the Kikuyu of Kenya, who later gained

[1] Morgenthau, 1964: 19–21.

the educational lead in that country, only became interested in school-ing in about 1909 when they saw it as the road to better-paid employ-ment on European farms.

Buganda stands, vis-à-vis Uganda as a whole, in a relationship some-what similar to that of Freetown with the rest of Sierra Leone. The Ganda see themselves collectively as the élite among the peoples making up Uganda, a claim which they base in part on their greater achievements in literacy and economic development and in part on their traditions of superiority in the past. Like the Creoles of Freetown they are a minority in the total population of the country, though a much larger minority—about one-fifth. They have not in recent years claimed to dominate the majority, only not to be dominated by them. But unlike the Creoles, they represent, in the eyes of the political parties drawing support from outside Buganda, an oligarchical system, in which political power depends largely on nomination from above, that is an anachronism in modern times. Within Buganda there are critics of this system, but it would hardly be appropriate to call these an élite.

The East African Institute of Economic and Social Research has carried out a very detailed study of the modern Ganda élite, which is published under the editorship of Fallers.[1] While showing that it is nothing new in Buganda for élite positions to be attained by achieve-ment, the contributors also show how the type of achievement demanded has changed.

Mission teaching, both Islamic and Christian, had been at work in Buganda for a generation before the protectorate was proclaimed in 1900. Converts were, interestingly enough, called 'readers', and by this date adherence to a monotheistic religion and the culture associated with it was, as Fallers puts it, a 'new élite idiom'. In simpler terms, chiefs were expected by 1900 to be both Christian and literate. The British administration even planted them out as a foreign governing élite among those other peoples of Uganda who did not have their own centralized political institutions.

The Uganda Agreement, allotting land in freehold to individuals who could show that they held chiefly offices in 1900, created a heredi-tary landlord class, which within a generation was distinct from the class of political office-holders, but who constituted an élite of wealth, and still exercise political authority over tenants on their land. The

[1] Fallers, ed., 1964: 144.

original 'one thousand chiefs and private landowners'—actually rather more—have now increased greatly in number through the sale of portions of the grants made after 1900; and though every Ganda aspires to be a landowner, it could not be said that every landowner is a member of the élite. It has been calculated that in 1956 there were 20,000–25,000 persons owning land on a scale that justifies the name of landlord. Only a minority of these—for whom figures are not available —could be called 'relatively large-scale, profit-minded cultivators'. These appear to be mainly men who did not inherit land but bought it after some experience of commercial activity or life on European plantations. There were also twenty-eight all-African business firms.

Among the professions, teaching predominates, and in its upper reaches, at Makerere University or in the élite boarding schools, one Protestant, one Catholic, it confers élite status. African medical assistants began to be trained in 1913, but full medical training was not given until Makerere became a university college in 1945. In 1956 there were 48 Ganda doctors, of whom 30 were employed in central government service outside Buganda. Although as early as 1944 the report of an inquiry into native courts in Kenya recommended that training in law should be given at Makerere,[1] the authorities continued to take the view that the legal profession should not be encouraged; and up to the time of Uganda's independence the country's small number of lawyers were men who had studied overseas.

A study made in 1957–8 of the educational level and social origins of a sample of 298 members of the Ganda élite[2] throws light on the question whether by that date recruitment had become more open than it had been earlier. The persons questioned included the Kabaka's 6 ministers, 66 of the 90 members of his legislature (Lukiiko), 73 servants of the Ganda and 15 of the protectorate governments, 66 ministers of religion (Christian and Muslim), and smaller numbers of doctors, lawyers, editors, officials of political parties, large landowners and traders, and retired civil servants. Five-sixths of the total had had secondary education. But whereas it has sometimes been assumed, since secondary education is not free, that this must tend to become a monopoly of the higher income groups, the figures show at any rate that the class created by the land allocation of 1900 by no means engrosses the élite positions. The majority of those questioned were not descended from beneficiaries of the allocation; and even among the

---

[1] Phillips, 1945. [2] Fallers, ed., 1964: 194–204.

university-educated, only about a third had this advantage. Slightly over half attended schools other than the two recognized as élite. More than a third described themselves as the sons of peasants. Nearly half of the number with only primary education were elected members of the Lukiiko. Here we see a parallel with the rise of the underprivileged and less well educated to political leadership in other new African states: popular choice falls on representatives of 'the common man'.

The Lukiiko at the time of Fallers's study included a majority of members elected by popular vote. But Ganda solidarity in resisting attempts from outside to diminish the pre-eminence of the country within Uganda had up to that time been expressed through defence of the Kabaka's privileges, including that of appointment to ministerial and civil service posts, in relation to which he by no means modelled himself on a constitutional monarch. Since his chiefs were in fact chosen for a combination of educational qualifications, experience and loyalty to himself, they were not open to the kind of criticism levelled against chiefs in West Africa. They were already bureaucrats, and it was recognized that Buganda must have bureaucrats; there was nothing in democratic ideology which called for their rejection as a class. The main ground of opposition to the mode of their selection was one that stemmed from the unique history of Buganda: the monopoly by Protestants of official posts in the areas—two-thirds of the country— that were allotted to the Protestants after the nineteenth-century religious wars. Today Catholics outnumber Protestants, and Catholic dissatisfaction has accounted for such support as has been given in Buganda to political parties that draw their main strength from other parts of Uganda.

Old and new élites

If the élite are to be thought of as the limited section of a population members of which compete for political control, there can be none in the strict sense in countries where political power is in the hands of aliens. But the alien rulers have usually found it necessary to make up their minds on the subject of whom they would treat as accredited spokesmen for the generality of the population. A large part of the story of African nationalism is also the story of the claims of a new class of person—the new élite in this sense—to perform this role.

The accredited representatives of independent African peoples could have been none other than their rulers and their envoys. At that time the office-holders, many of whom were hereditary, were the undisputed élite. But once alien over-rule had been established, it was for the new overlords to decide whom they should treat as the appropriate channels of communication. British policy was in general to maintain the status of the traditional élite, the 'natural rulers' as they were called and liked to call themselves, in contrast to that of the French, who appointed as their African agents of local administration 'chiefs' selected without regard to traditional claims. But at the coastal trading posts of West Africa an urban merchant population had already grown up before British authority was extended inland; and it is there that the 'new men' were first taken seriously. It was assumed, however, that they spoke only for their own class, and should not be treated as representatives of the mass of the population.

In the early days of the Gold Coast Colony it was the practice to nominate members of the merchant community as magistrates; Africans and mulattoes were not in principle excluded, and some were promoted to higher posts. In 1850 a mulatto held the post of acting governor and three of his sons were commandants of towns (what would now be district commissioners). Other positions held by Africans were those of justice of the peace, chief clerk to the treasury and chief collector of customs. But as it became easier to recruit officials from Britain, the arguments against the employment of Africans prevailed.

In 1857–8, again, elected town councils were set up in Accra and Cape Coast, to form 'a kind of Government, which should not directly supersede, but incorporate within itself, the authority of the chiefs'.[1] But these bodies were abolished almost at once, and the attitude of most governors towards the 'semi-educated' was as hostile as the epithet suggests, while in the Colonial Office the 'scholars' were described as 'the curse of the West Coast'.[2]

More permanent was the effect of the entry of Africans into professions requiring literacy. The first African minister was ordained in the Wesleyan church in 1852. A few Africans, though not holding legal qualifications that would be recognized in Britain, were licensed as 'attorneys' from 1864. The first qualified lawyer began practice in 1883, the first of wholly African descent in 1887. Within a few years they were earning the highest incomes in the country, partly for their services in drawing up concession agreements during the 'gold rush' of the nineties. Journalism was at first a part-time occupation for

[1] Kimble, 1963: 185.   [2] Kimble, 1963: 91.

churchmen writing for papers printed and financed by the missions. But by 1861 one of the three commandants mentioned above was editing his own newspaper. Only men who could go to Britain were able to qualify as doctors.

It would be an oversimplification to see everywhere the clear-cut battle which we are sometimes asked to picture, between 'natural rulers' acquiescing in government policy as the price of their main-tenance in office and 'new men' heroically battling for democracy; as it would be an oversimplification to suppose that no 'natural rulers' ever entered the ranks of the educated. At the time when African nationalism came to full flower and successfully asserted itself, this was how they and their sympathizers pictured the situation, and sometimes with a good deal of truth. But this was the culmination of a long process. At first the 'scholars' were allies, supporters, perhaps even employees of the chiefs, as was the Joseph Martin whom King Aggrey of Cape Coast appointed as magistrate when he sought to assert his independent jurisdiction outside the walls of the fort.

It is of some interest that the first association of Western-educated men had the conservative aim of resisting the 'encroachments into their nationality' of demoralizing European influences—cultural rather than political, if the latter word is taken to be restricted to contests for power.

But they soon found themselves allied with the chiefs on the strictly political issue of the chiefs' right to administer land, and accordingly, in 1897 they transformed their association into the Aborigines' Rights Protection Society (ARPS), to protest against a bill which would have authorized the government to dispose of unoccupied land. They were the people who could read and analyse the bill, and question whether it violated earlier agreements made with the chiefs. In one town the Wesleyan minister held a meeting of the literate inhabitants and formed a committee to 'educate' the neighbouring chiefs about the changes that threatened them. The first announcement by the ARPS declared that, since government proposals were now published in the *Gazette* instead of being discussed, as in the past, with meetings of chiefs, the society, consisting, it was implied, of people who could not only read but understand legal language, had been formed to supply the need for public discussion.[1] A year later it sent a deputation to London. Its members described themselves as emissaries of the chiefs.

[1] Kimble, 1963: 341–2.

Kimble thinks this was done primarily to make sure of a hearing from the Secretary of State; in any case, they did not at that stage repudiate the chiefs. Indeed, twenty-six head chiefs, all from the western part of the colony, were said to have been foundation members of the society.

During the next few years governors wavered between refusing to discuss petitions from the society and consulting them on proposed bills and on details of native custom. As Kimble points out, they were indispensable as a medium for the expression of the chiefs' opinions. Only a commoner who had the confidence of all of them could do this; any chief who sought to speak for his fellows would be claiming a paramountcy to which he had no right. The ARPS at this stage (1907) was committed to constitutional action and loyalty to the Crown.[1] The primacy of Cape Coast as an educational centre was reflected in the fact that it remained throughout its existence essentially a Cape Coast organization.

When Guggisberg introduced the first constitution providing for the election of unofficial members, the inevitable conflict arose as to who should speak for the people. The British asserted, in the standard manner, that the educated were alienated from the masses, and that the chiefs should speak for the common people. (As independence approached, this was everywhere the slogan of the last-ditchers.) Guggisberg's constitution—for the colony only—gave the franchise to rate-payers in the three principal towns, and set up a council of chiefs in each of the three provinces, each of these councils having the power to elect from among its members two representatives for the legislature. The support given to this proposal by J. B. Danquah, himself the son of a chief, is an illustration of the overlap between the intelligentsia and the traditional aristocracy. But Danquah had supposed that it would be possible for chiefs to elect educated men from outside their number; this was allowed only from 1940.

But the ARPS never sought directly to reduce the political power of the 'natural rulers'. It did not regard them as an obstacle to its aims, and even its successor, the United Gold Coast Convention (UGCC), founded by Danquah in 1947 to demand self-government, thought of the chiefs as allies. Indeed, Austin sees the Gold Coast élite, as it was on the eve of Nkrumah's return in 1947, as a fairly homogeneous combination of chiefs, intellectuals, and the few recently appointed administrative officials.[2] Chiefs and intellectuals had together discussed the

[1] Kimble, 1963: 362. [2] Austin, 1964: Ch. II.

plans for constitutional reform that led to the representative constitution of 1946.

In Austin's view the rise of Nkrumah to leadership marked both the conscious resentment of commoners against hereditary authority and the appearance of a newer élite, literate of course, but not professional, and relying for its influence on the support of the illiterate masses.

The first president of the UGCC was a timber merchant. All its other prominent members were lawyers except William Ofori Atta, who was a graduate and a school-teacher. When Nkrumah broke away from it in 1949 he founded the Convention People's Party (CPP) with a central committee of nine, of whom two, including himself, were university graduates, three had secondary and four only elementary schooling. According to Austin, secondary-school leavers could get employment as 'primary-school teachers, clerks in offices, petty traders, storekeepers, local constructors, not very successful business men with a one-lorry transport enterprise or [in] small import-export trade'.[1] For those who failed to reach the leaving certificate, there were 'unskilled jobs as market-stall assistants, messengers in government offices, drivers' mates or apprentices to a master carpenter or motor-fitter who had his "workshop" under the trees of a vacant lot at the outskirts of the town'. This was the first recruiting ground of Ghana's modern élite. Prepared, if they could, to jostle existing office-holders out of the way, they were despised by the older professional men and regarded by the chiefs as an undisciplined mob. They in turn could dismiss the older élite as 'reactionary lackeys', or even, when they organized political opposition after the CPP was in power, as 'lawless elements'.

As the CPP, which in this respect has been the model for several other Anglophone African states, decided to replace career civil servants in the key posts of regional (or provincial) and district commissioners, a new avenue of social mobility was opened, in which entry to the élite was gained by party loyalty with a bare minimum of technical equipment. Membership of the political élite now carried with it a range of money incomes which at the upper end exceeded anything attainable in colonial days, and at all levels far exceeded what could be attained outside politics for equivalent qualifications.

In the same year (1922) that Guggisberg created the Provincial Councils of Chiefs in the Gold Coast, Nigeria introduced a constitution

---

[1] Austin, 1964: 16.

which gave Africans a membership in the Legislative Council of ten, four elected by rate-payers in Lagos and Calabar and the remainder nominated by the governor to represent divisions of the territory. At that time only the southern regions were represented. According to Wheare, about half of the twenty-seven men who sat in the Council in the twenty-three years that this constitution was in force were or had been members of some Native Authority.[1] It was the practice of the later governors to invite nominations from representative bodies; sometimes these were the improvement unions, the leaders of which were drawn from the new élites, and sometimes they were Native Authorities. Coleman[2] gives the professions of the elected members: five ministers of religion, six lawyers, a journalist, a merchant and—from the Cameroons—a chief. Wheare says of the nominated members that those who came from the Native Authorities were at one end of a wide range of sophistication extending to lawyers and clergy at the other.

The 1946 constitution took what is commonly thought of as a crucial first step towards the transfer of power: the creation of a legislature with a majority of non-official members. It also included members from the Northern Region. All the non-officials were elected from the membership of three regional assemblies, in each of which non-officials were in a majority of one over civil servants. But this majority was made up in large part of Native Authorities, who were seen by the government as the accredited spokesmen of the mass of the people. To the post-war élite they appeared, on the contrary, as the lowest order in the official hierarchy; and they treated the grant of an unofficial majority on these terms as a pure pretence.

The survival of the old élites

Both in Ghana and in Nigeria the new African leaders have agreed, and not unwillingly, that an appropriate place in the policy must be found for the 'natural rulers'. In Ghana the chiefs of each region form a House of Chiefs which decides disputed matters of customary law and succession to chiefly office; and the republican constitution required the President, on assuming office, to declare that he would preserve the chieftaincy. But dismissals of chiefs who supported opposition parties showed clearly where the limits of their freedom came, and in July

[1] Wheare, 1950: 76.   [2] Coleman, 1958: 153.

1965 it was announced that the institution was to be modified 'to bring it into line with the Socialist aspirations of the people'. The same theme is approached from another angle in Senghor's 'The maintenance of traditional chiefs is in conformity with the spirit of scientific socialism'.[1]

There was a House of Chiefs also in each of the regions of Nigeria; the east, which had been thought not to require one in view of its egalitarian social structure, demanded and obtained it by an amendment of the constitution in 1959. These bodies were thought of as analogous to the British House of Lords, and were endowed with similar power to delay legislation. In fact they differed from it in that their members had only one common interest, namely the maintenance of their own status.

Although it could now be said, both in Ghana and in the three southern regions of Nigeria, that the traditional élite had been displaced from any effective exercise of power, it should not be supposed that there is, even now, a clear-cut division or absence of social relations between members of the old and new élites. It has been indicated that the stereotype of the illiterate old man dominated by his clerk and the district commissioner does not correspond to reality. Chiefs were quite capable of appreciating the value of schooling. As Busia remarked of Ashanti, the chief's traditional councillors were illiterate and not interested in questions of social welfare and economic development, while the chiefs themselves had a very different outlook.

Lloyd has remarked that many Yoruba chiefs were wealthy businessmen before succeeding to the office.[2] The most conspicuous example is the Oni of Ife, the spiritual head of all Yoruba, who sat in the Legislative Council from 1946. The Oni was a staunch supporter of Awolowo from Awolowo's return from his law studies in London. He contributed to the finance of Awolowo's newspaper, and was appointed the first African governor of the Western Region. In July 1965 the traditional leaders in the region called a meeting under his chairmanship with the aim of inducing the opposed political parties to agree that the impending elections should be 'fair, free and peaceful'. Lloyd remarks also that in the days of local administration through Native Authorities it was the superior chief—for a long time designated Sole Native Authority—who dealt with the Resident Commissioner, and that the latter made it his business to 'train them as educated and intelligent chief executive officers of their kingdoms'.[3]

[1] Morgenthau, 1964: 149.   [2] Lloyd, 1964.   [3] Lloyd, 1964: 387.

The title of chief is still sought after in Yoruba and Ibo country, where many titles imply general eminence rather than specific office. Most politicians on attaining ministerial office considered it appropriate to have a chiefly title. In some cases they obtained these in virtue of a hereditary claim. More often 'honorary' titles, held for life only, were bestowed by chiefs on eminent citizens abroad, notably successful businessmen in Lagos, who paid them a fee for the honour. When it became clear that politicians welcomed such marks of distinction, some towns began to offer titles to other than 'native sons'. Thus Awolowo obtained seven titles during his first five years as Premier of the Western Region.[1]

It is at the level of national politics that the new élites have firmly established their claim. Within a chiefdom the position is not always so clear. Thus in Benin the Otu Edo, a political party supporting the Oba, in 1951 defeated the Taxpayers' Association, which had been formed in the late thirties with the aim of demanding elective representation on his council, and had achieved considerable power with the development of local government after 1945. A significant element in this situation was the fact that the Taxpayers' Association was largely supported by immigrant Yoruba; the Otu Edo drew its strength perhaps more from this than from a positive affection for the *ancien régime*. But the incident illustrates the fact that tribal patriotism still looks to the old élite as its symbol.

The Northern Region, having developed in the Native Administrations of the six great Muslim emirates a demand for clerks and technicians on a considerable scale, paradoxically had to call upon the products of southern schools to supply this demand. The majority of these Native Administration employees, as well as those of federal services such as the railway, or alien enterprises such as the banks, were Ibo, though there certainly were also a good many Yoruba. These men were critical of the conservatism of the emirates, and when they had the opportunity, they voted for southern-based political parties. But— aliens as they were in social theory though not in legal terms—they had no means by which they could replace the traditional élite.

But the north is not in fact 'frozen' beyond the possibility of movement. A thaw will come in time from the entry into the bureaucracy of commoners from the Muslim areas and of pupils of mission schools in the Middle Belt.[2] The most distinguished of these commoners was the

[1] Sklar, 1963: 234n.   [2] Lloyd, 1964: 402–3.

188

late Sir Abubakar Tafawa Balewa, former Federal Premier of Nigeria, who was one of a small number of teachers—four in each year—sent from 1945 onwards to take courses at the Institute of Education in London University, and who founded the Northern People's Congress (NPC). Another of these, Mallam Aminu Kano, was the founder of the radical Northern Elements Progressive Union.[1]

The former opened his career by a demand for the reform of the Native Authorities, but his party soon became the instrument of their interests, since only Native Administration staff were literate enough to supervise elections, and voters, rightly or wrongly, took this as an indication how they should vote. Most NPC members in the regional and federal assemblies were officials of Native Administrations, and many of them were members of ruling families. The striking characteristic of the Northern Region is that the goal of political ambition is still high office in an emirate and not in a representative assembly. The federal assembly and civil service were convenient places of temporary exile for critics of the status quo. But some regional ministers, who, even if they belonged to the ruling class, had attained their position by a different process of recruitment, showed signs of seeking to curtail the powers of the hereditary rulers.[2]

The striking contrast between this story and that of Mali (the former French Sudan) lies in the fact that Mali does have a French-trained élite, albeit a small one, but that many of these took the opportunity, when their country was part of a larger whole, to move to the coastal areas where they were not isolated from the company of other educated men.[3]

In Guinea, as in Ghana and southern Nigeria, hereditary status no longer gives any claim to administrative authority. But those to whom it still gives influence have sometimes been appointed to high office outside their own domains—as vice-president of the Assembly, or president of the Conseil Economique in the case of a chief who was also a leading trader. This is the same process, with the reverse effect, as that by which radicals from northern Nigeria were sponsored by the emirs for high office in Lagos.

In Senegal and Sierra Leone the rise of a new élite has been complicated by the fact that they were not asserting themselves primarily in opposition to leaders of traditionally accredited status. The population of the colony of Sierra Leone—descendants of the liberated slaves who

---

[1] Coleman, 1958: 356, 358.   [2] Lloyd, 1964: 400–3.
[3] Morgenthau, 1964: 270.

were settled there in the eighteenth and early nineteenth centuries, Westernized in culture, sometimes speaking English at home and with early access to education—claimed to provide the political élite for colony and protectorate alike. At the same time, a small number of persons from the hinterland tribes were obtaining university degrees at Fourah Bay and overseas. The battle for protectorate representation and that between old and new élites went on at the same time. The new protectorate élite won the day in that it now provides the political leadership of Sierra Leone; but the traditional rulers have secured a share in the legislature, constitutionally entrenched, which has not been accorded to their counterparts in any other African territory. The number of seats allotted to them is such that their agreement is necessary for any amendment of the constitution that would affect their position. It may be, of course, that Sierra Leone will in a few years give itself a wholly new constitution.

In Senegal the élite recognized by the French administration were those who qualified as 'citizens' by the acceptance of a Western mode of life, and this qualification exempted them from various disabilities imposed on the 'subject' population. Just as in Sierra Leone, where by no means all Creoles were in fact highly educated or even literate, so in Senegal a number of people—those born in the 'four communes' on the coast[1]—acquired citizenship automatically without being any more 'civilized' than the 'subjects' in the hinterland. All citizens—i.e., for practical purposes, the population of Dakar—were entitled to vote for 18 representatives in a deliberative council for the colony, in which the rest of Senegal was represented by 26 civil servant chiefs. Within this council citizens opposed chiefs in the same way that in a British Legislative Council the unofficials opposed the officials; these chiefs were in no sense an élite (except in the strictly political sense). Outside it the citizens themselves were objects of resentment to the rest of the population. When, after 1946, the status of 'subject' was abolished, the 'citizens' of long standing did not cease to regard themselves as the élite. In particular they dominated the only organized political party, the Section Française de l'Internationale Ouvrière (SFIO), and chose all candidates for election from among themselves. Senghor, the 'deputy of the bush', and Mamadou Dia—the latter never having applied for citizenship though clearly qualified—drew their main support from former 'subjects'.

[1] Dakar, Rufisque, St Louis and Gorée.

Whereas British officials in the period of the transfer of power did not conceal their preference for the Northern People's Congress over its more radical opponents, they did not seek to manipulate the elections in its favour. A cynic might say that the constitutional arrangements made this unnecessary. In corresponding French-speaking territory, however—that is, in the Sudanic region where traditional authority still continued to give influence—the administration openly intervened in elections on the side of the chiefs. Naturally, this intensified the resentment of the new élite against officially recognized authority. Whether traditional or not, French authorities did not, as the British did, make it a matter of principle to recognize as 'chiefs' only those who were entitled to the office. It seems from Morgenthau's account that to belong to a 'chiefly' family still enhances the prestige of a member of the new élite; but those who make this claim do not always indicate whether their fathers were 'traditional' or 'official' chiefs. Certainly glory may attach to descendants of those who were famous for their resistance to the French.

It seems then that in Africa, as in other parts of the world, the new élites often seek to take over from their predecessors the cultural symbols of élite status. The attachment of the mass of the population to the old élite is not merely a case of 'cultural lag'; it is in part an expression of the crucial political fact of the new African states, that, as Coleman and Rosberg (1964) have put it, it is only in the small ethnic groups, defined by the recognition of hereditary authority, that established political institutions actually exist.

BIBLIOGRAPHY

Ajayi, J. F. Ade (1965). *Christian missions in Nigeria, 1841–1891: the making of a new élite*. Evanston, Northwestern University Press.

Austin, Dennis G. (1964). *Politics in Ghana, 1946–1960*. London, Oxford University Press.

Busia, Kofi A. (1951). *The position of the chief in the modern political system of Ashanti*. London, Oxford University Press.

Coleman, James S. (1958). *Nigeria: background to nationalism*. Berkeley, University of California Press.

  and Carl Rosberg, eds. (1964). *Political parties and national integration in Tropical Africa*. Berkeley, University of California Press.

Fallers, Lloyd A., ed. (1964). *The king's men*. London, Oxford University Press.

Forde, Daryll, ed. (1957). *Efik traders of Old Calabar*. London, Oxford University Press.

Jones, Gwilym I. (1963). *The trading states of the Oil Rivers: a study of political development in Eastern Nigeria*. London, Oxford University Press.

Kimble, David (1963). *A political history of Ghana: the rise of Gold Coast nationalism, 1850–1928*. Oxford, Clarendon Press.

Lloyd, P. C. (1964). 'Traditional rulers', in *Political parties and national integration in Tropical Africa*, James Coleman and Carl Rosberg, eds. Berkeley, University of California Press.

Morgenthau, Ruth S. (1964). *Political parties in French-speaking West Africa*. Oxford, Clarendon Press.

Peil, M. (1965). 'Ghanaian university students: the broadening base', *British Journal of Sociology*, **16**.

Phillips, Arthur (1945). *Report on native tribunals*. Nairobi, Kenya Government.

Sklar, Richard (1963). *Nigerian political parties*. Princeton University Press.

Smith, Michael G. (1950). *Government in Zazzau*. London, Oxford University Press.

Wheare, Joan (1950). *The Nigerian legislative council*. London.

Wise, Colin G. (1956). *A history of education in British West Africa*. London.

CHAPTER 6

THE IMPACT OF THE COLONIAL PERIOD ON THE DEFINITION OF LAND RIGHTS

by

ELIZABETH COLSON

The end of the colonial era found the majority of Africans still rural people, dependent upon direct access to land for the bulk of their daily needs. Even so, their ties to the earth had been profoundly altered during the colonial years. New rights in land were being recognized by the people themselves, though the evolving legal systems of the colonial governments were usually reluctant to give these recognition. Old rights had fallen into abeyance or were being questioned. Given the importance of land as a subsistence base and a dwelling place, and the interrelationship of political and social institutions with land holding, radical change was to be expected in a time of rapid social and political change even if the colonial powers had been neutral to the development of new concepts of land ownership. They were not neutral, even when they thought to permit local peoples to develop along their own lines. The differing concepts held by rulers and ruled as to the nature of man's relationship to the earth he inhabits were always a factor. The various colonial territories recognized very different customary codes, even though they may have been dealing with people whose ideas about land holding had been much the same when the European officials arrived.[1]

It was inevitable that the colonial governments should impinge upon land rights even where they accepted an obligation to preserve existing rights and to recognize local custom. They created new centres of

---

[1] There is no dearth of information on African systems of land tenure. This is one aspect of African life which has seemed of vital importance to administrator, technical officer, lawyer and social scientist. All have written on the subject. In preparing this essay I have consulted the sources listed in the bibliography at the end of the chapter. In addition I have drawn on a general knowledge of the subject accumulated during twenty years of reading about African countries and of discussion with colleagues. Little or nothing here is original, though some points may be disputable. It would be difficult to pinpoint where particular ideas or arguments originated. Therefore I have not attempted to give a footnoted reference for every statement.

population that made new demands upon the land. They encouraged the growth of population by removing the old checks of war, epidemic and famine which had served to keep much of Africa sparsely settled. They encouraged population mobility by the establishment of control over wide territories and the provision of legal redress for wrongs done to the unprotected stranger, and by the creation of new methods of transportation and centres of employment. Even the most poverty-stricken of the colonial régimes encouraged a modicum of economic development which diverted some land to new uses and encouraged the emergence of new systems of tenure. Finally, they stimulated the desire for imported goods which could be met only by the exploitation of land in cash cropping.

By themselves such changes had an impact on local systems of land rights as men began to evaluate the land they used in new ways. They also led to an increasing number of legal battles over land; for men were encouraged to establish long-term rights in particular holdings either for immediate use or for subsequent gain. Some disputes—and these were essentially disputes over boundaries—arose because individuals or communities claimed the same rights in the same areas. Other disputes involved a much more fundamental clash, since they arose from claims based on different and conflicting principles inherent in most of the pre-colonial land systems whatever their superficial differences.

One was the principle that for the support of himself and his dependents each citizen should have the right of direct access to the resources of the territory controlled by the political unit to which he belonged. Gulliver (1961: 17), writing of agricultural communities in East Africa, refers to this as a basic dogma which holds that every man has a right to land for cultivation. Such a right, of course, could not be ceded or sold to another any more than the citizenship on which it rested. The second principle, probably equally ancient, recognized an individual's right to anything he had created, whether this be an office, a pot, a homestead, or a field. Such a right could be inherited according to the regular rules of inheritance of private property. Rights in improved land could thus become the particular rights of an individual or of a small family corporation which might also be a section of the political community if descent groups had a political function. The originator of such a right could transfer it during his lifetime to another person, either as a gift or for some consideration; but as long as land was plentiful and improvements minimal it was unlikely that anyone would be prepared to pay for what he could easily obtain by other means. In the absence of buyers, no one raised the question of the legality of sale or rent. A restraint upon the right of transfer did exist, though this may be interpreted as a practical obstacle rather than as a legal dictum—the recipient had to be someone acceptable to the local community, since he would need to be associated with its members to use the land in any fashion.[1]

So long as land was seen as plentiful, these two principles, of general rights based on citizenship and of particular rights based on creative pre-emption, did not clash. Furthermore, in pre-colonial Africa there was rarely any need to differentiate between the political and economic implications of the occupation of a region. A political community occupied a region and used its resources, and there was no need to distinguish rights of ownership from rights of sovereignty.[2]

Whenever land began to be thought of as being in short supply or when men began to wish to use it in different and mutually incompatible fashions or when land began to be seen as having potential and unpredictable value, then both communities and individuals were likely to obtain exclusive control of any available land for economic purposes and also to claim new rights in the land as they discovered new uses for it. This development proceeded most rapidly in sections of West Africa where some communities had made a clear distinction between sovereignty and land ownership long before they came under colonial rule. Here the existence of towns and cities, sizeable populations and market systems, and the cultivation of export crops had created the conditions which led to the development of clear definitions of various kinds of rights and the concept of a bounded land unit to which these rights could be referred. Elsewhere circumstances rarely favoured the maintenance of long-term claims to particular plots which could lead to the emergence of either individual or corporate group rights related to any given piece of land. Refuge areas where pressure on population might be extreme as people sought safety within them, or the few areas in East and Central Africa with highly fertile soils and stabilized agriculture, were exceptions to the general rule that land rights were rarely defined since they were rarely questioned.

[1] These principles are commonplaces of the study of African land systems. See the general introduction in Biebuyck (1963).
[2] This useful distinction is fully developed by Lloyd (1962) in his discussion of Yoruba land law.

The majority of African communities only began to come to grips with the concept of limited land during the colonial period. It was then that they became aware of the conflict between the old political obligation to maintain general access to adequate resources for all citizens, and the possibility of extracting an individual profit from areas pre-empted under the rule that a man might enjoy the fruits of his labour. Land claims then came to be tested in the courts, where adjudication encouraged the rapid development of fairly comprehensive bodies of customary, though untraditional, law which governed the allocation and use of land. This drive to formulate more precise rules reflected the local concern with land disputes. It occurred spontaneously as soon as men became aware of a clash of interests. But once the colonial period had begun, the resulting formulations rarely reflected only local decisions. Even customary courts were under the ultimate jurisdiction of colonial officials who expected the courts to enforce long-established custom rather than current opinion. Common official stereotypes about African customary land law thus came to be used by colonial officials in assessing the legality of current decisions, and so came to be incorporated in 'customary' systems of tenure.

Under the colonial régimes, both communities and individuals acquired new rights in land. The speed with which even apparently unoccupied land became subject to highly specific rights is one of the striking features of the period. This was due in part to the rapid growth of population and the intervention of colonial officials in land affairs. As representatives of their governments they had political power and could impose their views. They brought with them to the situation European concepts of legal tenure which they were prone to interpret as universal legal principles applicable everywhere; these became basic to the general land law of each territory. In particular they assumed that the full range of land rights covered by the concept of proprietary ownership must exist in Africa as in Europe. If no private person appeared to hold such rights over a given area, then they assumed that the rights must vest in the political unit whose members used the region. Failing this, they belonged to the newly created government which could then alienate the land on its own terms to commercial corporations or to European settlers.

Early colonial governments, intent on rapid economic development through European enterprise, tended to define African land rights as narrowly as possible and to recognize them only with reference to land under obvious occupation, thereby leaving large areas free for possible alienation to European companies and settlers. A closer acquaintance with local usage led to a vigorous reaction in favour of the recognition of very extensive rights as early twentieth-century officials adopted Delafosse's view that 'no land in West Africa is without an owner'.[1] This came to be used very generally in any African territory whether or not it might be locally applicable.

In the years between World War I and World War II, the principle of indirect rule through traditional authorities dominated the political scene in most British colonies and in the Belgian Congo. This principle led to the recognition of chiefs and rulers where none had existed in earlier periods. This had its parallel in the respect paid to supposed customary rules of land tenure. The theory that land must have an owner exercising rights comparable to proprietary rights encouraged the attribution of previously unclaimed privileges to village communities or to larger political bodies in regions where people had little reason to busy themselves with the definition of land rights, since the uses to which they put the land were limited and conflicts over land occurred only as conflicts between expanding political régimes. The official search for the owners of all land encouraged the confusion of sovereignty with proprietary ownership and the creation of systems of communal tenure which came into being with precisely defined rules. These rules now inhibited the development of individual rights in waste land because it was deemed that such rights encroached upon the ancient right of some community, lineage, or 'tribal' polity. The newly created system was described as resting on tradition and presumably derived its legitimacy from immemorial custom. The degree to which it was a reflection of the contemporary situation and the joint creation of colonial officials and African leaders, more especially of those holding political office, was unlikely to be recognized.

The development of communal tenure was taking place at the same time that economic developments encouraged the expenditure of individual effort upon the improvement and exploitation of particular plots of land, and so produced conditions leading to the rising demand for the recognition of individual tenure with full proprietary rights.

Throughout the continent, very similar experiences encouraged the various co-called customary land systems to develop on rather similar

[1] Quoted in Meek (1957: 114, n. 3). Meek notes the approval with which the statement was being used in Nigeria as early as 1912.

lines. It became important to distinguish between economic rights and political rights, and to define rights more rigidly as new uses for land developed and clashes about land became common. The territory of a people was progressively divided into holdings appropriated by persons or by corporations. Given the growing recognition of scarcity in land and the increase of land in value under plantation crops or improved farming methods or through proximity to towns, cultivators became more generally willing to deal in land as though it were a commodity which could be sold, leased, or pawned. Such transactions became common whether legally permissible by the law of the territory or not. The general trend may be described as one which converted territory or domain into economic holdings, and citizens into land-holders. In their last years the colonial governments had to cope with numerous demands, from both European officials and citizens, for the reform of customary codes to free land from restrictions created by the recognition of communal tenure. These prevented land from being negotiable and were seen as an impediment to further economic growth and to the unifying of the country. Provision for the legal registration and conveyancing of African land holdings was a popular demand in some territories among those aware of the economic advantages to be gained from such developments, though where European and Asian competition for land was feared, restrictions on sales to non-Africans were still considered desirable.[1]

Community and land

European and African conceptions of the essential relationship between people and land were fundamentally different in the nineteenth century even if the comparison is made between Europe and the most economically developed areas of Africa. Bohannan (1963) has gone so far as to query the propriety of the use of the term 'land tenure' in speaking of African systems of land use, on the grounds that the term is based on the European idea that land is something that can be measured, plotted, and subdivided into units which become 'things' in themselves and subject to rights assigned to holders. Such a view is common enough today among Africans in many parts of the continent, but in the pre-colonial period comparable views were found only in limited regions within West Africa and among a few other people such

[1] This is the burden of the *East Africa Royal Commission Report* (1955: 346–66).

as the Kikuyu of Kenya, who for some reason had introduced a system of private land holdings.

Elsewhere Africans were concerned to use land, not to hold it. They saw themselves as dealing with earth as a sacred entity which existed independently of men. A claim to control the earth itself might therefore very well amount to sacrilege. Earth in this sense was unbounded, though its qualities varied from one locality to another and different regions had different potentialities. Men had to deal with these potentialities, which included both those physical qualities which determined the practical purposes for which it could be used and also the mystical qualities which could affect men for good or evil. Knowledge of the physical qualities might be relatively easy to acquire and be applicable elsewhere. Knowledge of the mystical qualities was more difficult to acquire and less likely to be generally applicable. Those who had lived longest in a given area were most likely to know its physical qualities, but it was control over the techniques for dealing with the mystical qualities of the local earth that gave them a superior standing against newcomers. The first settler to transform unoccupied waste into human habitation and cultivation was assumed to have come to terms with the power of the earth. His heirs became the 'Earth Priests', who were the rightful intermediaries between other men and the earth of the new community. The priest either performed rituals at the local Earth Shrine or he approached the earth through the spirits of his ancestors who had also served the earth.

Earth Priests, representing the first settler and his alliance with the power of the earth, were found commonly throughout West Africa in the nineteenth century, both in highly developed states and among people who recognized no other form of community office. The importance and prevalence of the office no doubt reflected the localized nature of many West African communities in a region where agricultural settlements had existed for perhaps four thousand years and where systems of agriculture based on long-term fallow rotation were commonly practised. In much of the rest of Africa, agriculturalists were shifting cultivators who moved across the surface of the land. But wherever conditions permitted long-term association between a community and some limited area, Earth Priests were usually important ritual figures. They were, however, likely to share their duties with other priests who represented other aspects of the earth. Central African communities usually recognized a number of ritual offices which represented different uses made of the land. Earth was not only land to live upon and to farm under the office of the Earth Priest. It was land to be hunted upon, under a Priest of the Bush. It was land with lakes and rivers to be fished, under a Priest of the Waters. In East Africa, it was pasture land under a Priest of the Cattle. Given the close association between agriculture and rain, it was usually the Earth Priest who performed rain rituals when these were needed, though other priests might co-operate with him in the rituals.

Some observers have written as though the various priestly offices had particularized land rights. In some instances colonial officials sought to turn Earth Priests into landlords on the grounds that they were community leaders and therefore holders of the land rights of the community. Such an interpretation misrepresented the role of the priests. They were leaders of ritual and not allocators of land or rulers of men. Where newcomers had seized political control of a region inhabited by settled farmers, they were likely to leave control of the Earth rituals in the hands of the original priests and their descendants. In regions where expanding agriculturalists maintained a tradition of recent immigration, political rulers were more likely to claim ritual control of the earth as well. Anyone living in an area had to respect the local Earth Priest, or the ruler who had control of the rituals of the earth. This usually involved the presentation of first fruits. The community expected to provide helpers to assist the priest in his ritual task though not in his private labours. The residents had to observe the sanctity of the Earth Shrine, which usually involved care not to trespass on land surrounding the shrine. They observed other ritual taboos. For the rest, neither old residents nor newcomers approached a priest for the right to build a homestead or to obtain a field or for the right to hunt, fish or collect wild produce. They received these rights by virtue of entry into a community or social group which might well be headed by political officials. Acceptance into a community conferred rights of citizenship and at the same time membership in the ritual congregation that was coterminous with it. Only rarely were the rights conferred pinpointed in any way to particular sites. They referred to the land area exploited by the community.

Over most of Africa, during the pre-colonial period, men saw themselves linked to the land through membership in social groups. They were more concerned to maintain themselves in good standing in society than to obtain rights in land as such. The latter were assumed to follow the first and to be impossible without community support. Equally, of course, they were rights vested in the man or woman personally, as is citizenship, and could not be exercised by a deputy. Nor could the rights be subdivided. This fact has been obscured by writers who have assumed that Earth Priests or other authorities had the right to allocate land either to old residents or to newcomers and that the recipient then had the right of reallocation in the area given to him. A closer inspection of the evidence suggests that the claim to allocate land was rare indeed, and occurred only where demand ran close upon supply and where a real clash of interests could arise. Elsewhere elders or political rulers might accept, or reject, a petition for entry into the community and then point out areas in which no one was cultivating to guide an accepted newcomer in his choice of site. In doing so, they did not assign land but merely indicated a site suitable for farming or for building. Where shifting cultivation was practised, presumably on the next shift the newcomer took up land where he wished or received his share of the new village fields. By then he knew as much as the older residents about where he could and could not farm. Once a field had been cleared, a cultivator might permit another to make use of it, but this did not mean that he reallocated his land rights. He could still clear land elsewhere if he wished. He had the right to cultivate and to use land in other ways, not the right to a given piece of land or a given quantity of land.

As most nineteenth- and many twentieth-century African communities saw the matter, men ought to have fields since only thus could they support themselves and not be a burden to others. It was in the community's interest to see that every member had a plot from which to draw a subsistence and that he had the necessary assistance to raise a crop. In this sense it is possible to say that every member of the community had a right to a field. One might also say that every member had an obligation to work a field though we know little about the pressures that may have been used to force the lazy person to accept his obligation.

Wherever shifting cultivation was practised, cultivators did not differentiate agricultural land from other land. What was field today would be bush tomorrow. House sites and homestead sites became fields or bush through the course of the land-use cycle. The enduring thing was the social unit and its ritual relationship to the earth as an undivided entity. Cultivators under such systems resembled the pastoralist in their use of a territory, though the time for exploitation of particular sites might lengthen into months and even years, instead of the days and weeks of the pastoralist's occupancy. Among true pastoralists, such as the Turkana and Masai of Kenya or the pastoral Fulani of West Africa, foreigners might be excluded from grazing grounds or water-holes, but no herding group had a claim upon an area which could exclude other members of his community. Pastoralists had a range over which they travelled, rather than pastures in which they held exclusive rights. They used land; they did not hold it. They could foresee future needs to a limited extent, but conditions were such that they could not foresee which particular portion of a terrain would best meet these needs at a given time. To hold land against future needs was therefore meaningless.

In the same way the shifting cultivators of Central Africa moved to exploit a range of territory. Men usually lived in villages, which might also be the largest organized political groupings, but villages as such were not landed units. They were communities of men who moved across the country, clearing and then abandoning fields as they moved, and using the surrounding bush for hunting and for the collection of wild produce. Over the years one village might succeed another on the same general site without clash of interest or any concern to transfer ownership; for the villages did not claim land. They claimed men and assumed they could find land for the men to use. During a village's occupancy of an area, it might exclude strangers, but usually it was eager to welcome newcomers who might add to its strength. It was only when villages or other communities became anchored because some soils proved easier to work or permanently workable or where orchard crops became important or where defence was of paramount concern that a long-term concern with land as an economic asset appeared.

Even then, demand for land and a clash of interests were slow to develop, since technical considerations limited the acreage any sub-sistence cultivator could work efficiently. Agricultural specialists estimate that with traditional tools the subsistence cultivator farms most effectively when he limits himself to from one and a half to two acres per head of garden family, composed of those contributing to the cultivation and using its produce. The amount of land cultivated by any householder is therefore directly related to the labour force available and to the number of dependents to be fed. Over its lifetime, the family's need for land increases and then declines again. Given the prevailing condition of land abundance, men could cultivate large acreages only if they had control over the labour of a numerous following who looked to them for other reasons than their land holding. Social groups were therefore founded on other principles than the estate, which provided the basis of European society throughout the feudal period. In both continents, important political figures controlled the most land under cultivation, but this was for different reasons. In Africa the acreage a man claimed or cultivated depended directly on his control over others, and the ruler could call upon a larger number of men than the commoner. His acreage reflected his place in the social system; his place in the social system was not determined by the acreage he claimed.

Land holdings vaguely comparable to the estate occurred only sporadically in pre-colonial Africa: on the rich volcanic soils of the well-watered highlands of East Africa, in fertile Buganda, on the limited alluvial soils of the Upper Zambezi Plain in Central Africa, and most commonly in West Africa. Such estates apparently developed wherever men were encouraged to maintain long-term rights in cultivable land. The general right to cultivate a field became transformed into the right to hold particular fields, and this right became heritable according to the general rules for the inheritance of personal property.[1]

Such an estate was usually described as the creation of an ancestor who continued to be concerned with its fate just as the first settler supposedly retained his concern with the territory he had opened to human occupation. The land opened and improved by the first cultivator passed to his heirs, who usually formed a corporate descent group with common rights in the estate. Perhaps the most famous, and certainly the most quoted statement in the literature on African land tenure is that attributed to a Nigerian chief in the early twentieth century: 'I conceive that land belongs to a vast family of which many are dead, few are living and countless members are still unborn.'

This statement has been quoted, commented upon, and treated as though it were a legal maxim underlying all systems of land holding

[1] Harris (1964: 131–3) describes the existence of estates in the Taita Hills of Kenya; Mukwaya (1953) describes the early development of estates in Buganda; Gluckman (1941 and 1943) describes the complex system of land rights developed by the Lozi on the fertile Zambezi Plain; Meek (1957) describes the early development of estates in various parts of Nigeria.

in every part of Africa. It has influenced the development of African land law since it has been used to justify the recognition of communal non-transferable rights. Thus it has become imbedded in the law although originally it could have been no more than a statement about the ideal relationship that ought to exist between a group of men and the land on which they lived. Even then it applied to settled rather than to shifting communities. Even in Nigeria, descent groups which held estates allowed strangers to settle on their land, and members of land-holding lineages felt free to leave the ancestral estate to exploit unoccupied land or to beg land of others whenever this seemed to offer advantage despite the fact that this involved abandoning the graves of their ancestors. The continuity from first settler into the unborn future was but a potent fiction.

This fiction developed legal force as soon as men began to look at land in terms of economic gain. In West Africa much of the arable land in the most populated regions had been turned into estates controlled by descent groups before land values had become commercialized owing to the introduction of cash-crops or the appearance of other lucrative uses of land. This happened before the imposition of colonial rule or so early in the colonial period that lineage corporations had a powerful voice in the development of the new land systems. Where populations began to feel land pressures only after the imposition of colonial rule, the development of estates and the rules of tenure occurred simultaneously with the recognition of the commercial value of land. The colonial powers then determined the lines of future development by their particular policies for land development. Since most estates in these areas were still in the hands of the first cultivator and since hereditary estates were rare, the clash of interests that influenced the legal development was likely to lie between an individual claimant and the larger political unit to which he belonged rather than between lineages or lineages and the state.

While rights in arable land were becoming defined, the right to use other resources also became subject to litigation. It had always been possible to distinguish among the various uses to which land could be put, and even in communities with the most unrestricted access to resources some discrimination among uses was common. Apparently any man permitted to build a homestead and acquire a field also expected to use the land to pasture livestock, to hunt and fish, and to gather any products necessary for subsistence. Nonresidents might be permitted to hunt and fish without thereby gaining acceptance as settlers. Where transhumance was practised, as in Northern Nigeria and Northern Cameroons, or in the Kafue river plain of Zambia, cattle-owners pastured their cattle in districts where they did not expect to settle and where they did not accept the obligations of citizenship. Residents permitted the use of such resources by friendly strangers so long as they used these for their own immediate benefit. The visitors gave in return at best only a token in acknowledgement of the sovereignty of the resident communtiy; but as soon as it became apparent that they were exploiting the territory for a profit, the resident community began to demand its share. By the latter part of the nineteenth century travellers were usually charged passage fees for the privilege of crossing a district; hunters were expected to contribute a portion of their kill; and other uses of local resources were increasingly scrutinized as a possible source of revenue for local rulers or the local community. The extent to which mineral resources became subject to rights of ownership is a clear indication of how little people were inclined to claim property rights where marketing was not in question. Sundström (1965: 127, 218–20) has summarized the evidence for the control of mineral deposits before the colonial governments showed an interest in controlling their exploitation. Anyone, whether local resident or stranger, might work the mines. But as soon as mines became important producers of wealth, the interest of the local ruler was involved and he intervened 'to the point of claiming ownership'.

The introduction of new tools and agricultural techniques and the encouragement of a market for commodities focused attention on economic interests under the colonial régimes. This encouraged the development of land laws concerned with the exploitation of economic values. Earlier, the desire for security had encouraged the statement of land relationships in political terms; the new guarantees of the colonial governments allowed this concern to fall into abeyance.

The impact of colonial policy on land tenure

General trends in the development of different systems of tenure have been strikingly similar in various parts of the continent as similar economic opportunities had their impact on the rather similar views which had been held on the relationship of men with land. Yet the developments in each colonial territory had their unique quality dependent upon the particular policies of the colony and the recognition it gave to African interests. Policies varied between colonies, even between those belonging to the same imperial power. They reflected the nature of the resources available for exploitation, the power of Europeans settled in the colony and the degree to which Africans were able to influence decisions. Evidence from the Congo, Zambia, and Nigeria illustrates the extent to which policy decisions affected the developing systems of customary tenure.

Belgian officials in the Congo soon reacted against the wholesale disregard of African occupation characteristic of the Congo Free State with its drive to extract commercial profits from the region. During the Free State period, large-scale concessions were granted to European firms which permitted them to pre-empt large areas declared to be waste land. Much of the Congo was then sparsely populated. Most of its people were shifting cultivators, though in some areas hunting, fishing and gathering of wild produce were as important as agriculture and required access to extensive territories. Improvements on land were minimal. The end of the Free State and the beginnings of Belgian rule coincided with the growing acceptance of the view that Africans owned rights in land which were applicable not only to cultivated land. Administrators had learned that the kinds of agricultural systems practised in the region required large fallow areas in addition to the fields under actual cultivation. Officials of the new régime were still instructed that empty land for which no owner could be found must be treated as waste land available for state or private exploitation. But before lands could be certified as waste, there had to be an intensive official inquiry to make certain that neither person nor group had a claim upon it. Official inquiry usually found that even apparently uninhabited land still had its occasional visitors from the surrounding areas who made use of it for some purpose or another. A statement that people occasionally used the land was not enough to protect their interests even given the new dispensation with its emphasis upon African rights. Officials who wished to secure the land for African use or to obtain compensation for the users were tempted to give a precise legal definition to the vaguest claim and to extend these claims to their widest territorial extent. Use was converted to ownership, territories were assigned to users who became owners, boundaries were drawn to assign unclaimed land to different communities. The surface of the Congo became progressively laid out in estates that were assigned to owners. Given the existing systems of land use, it was rarely possible to allot an estate to an individual owner. Rather it was the political community which became the beneficiary of the official desire to assign land. It became axiomatic that only a community could own land: 'According to Congolese native law, individual land ownership does not exist; there is only collective ownership. The land belongs to the clan, a community made up of family groups consisting of all the descendants—living and dead—of a common ancestor, and in theory, all the generations to come' (Heldt, 1959: 204).

This is an echo of the old Nigerian ideal now cited as the customary law of a region which probably did not contain estates of land in the pre-colonial period.

It was policy that all owners of land should be found. It was also policy that declared that such owners must be protected against exploitation by being denied the right to dispose freely of their interests. It was still desirable for such lands to be used for the profit of the colony where this was commercially feasible. Landowners were therefore permitted to dispose of their rights to government either by sale or by lease. The government in turn offered it to corporations or to private persons. Had the government merely assigned the country to various local communities as proprietors, this presumably would have had little impact upon local evaluations of land rights. It was the possibility of profit from sale or lease that rapidly changed men's views of the nature of land. Communities sought to extend the boundaries of their holdings and sued one another over land that both had formerly ignored. Members of a community found themselves bound to their fellows in a new fashion, since they now had an hereditary interest in the cash to be derived from the land of the community. Those who moved to a new area had no legal claim to a share in its assets unless they belonged to the descent group to which the land had been assigned. Before the end of the Belgian Congo régime, local courts were overwhelmed with land suits as community sued community and private persons claimed the right to share in the profits realized from a communal estate.

The fact that the government was the sole purchaser and sole renter of African-owned land had further consequences. It supplied the incentive for a series of detailed official investigations into current land usage whereby a value could be assigned to the transaction. A law of 1934 declared that land might be ceded to government only after the most stringent inquiry into local use (Heldt, 1959: 208). The investigations provide a magnificent collection of detailed reports on Congolese land tenure systems unmatched for any other African territory. But they also gave a rigid definition of the rights of African users which became a matter of record, a basis for legal decisions, and a barrier to any further development of the land law of the colony save through some process of legislation. In the pre-colonial period Congolese communities had been able to alter their rules freely in accordance with new conditions. Now change became the prerogative of the central government. In its last days the Belgian Congo government found itself enmeshed in the web of legalities it had woven. The government-sponsored peasant farming schemes had recurrent problems because of the difficulties of extinguishing communal land rights, created by the earlier policy of finding an effective owner for all land within the Congo (Drachoussoff, 1965). Other enterprises had similar problems with communal tenure.

In Zambia, official land policy developed in a more casual fashion. After the early days of concession hunting when commercial companies signed agreements with any local dignitaries they could find, specific African rights in land aroused little interest. It was assumed that there was plenty of land and that Africans had only limited interests in land. If they were dispossessed for European settlement or for other reasons, they were expected to find alternative areas without difficulty. The British South Africa Company, which controlled the territory until 1923, assumed the right to make land grants throughout the country where and when it would except in Barotseland, where African rights were protected by treaty. In practice the bulk of the grants were made to settlers along the line of rail between Livingstone and Lusaka and in the Fort Jameson area to the east. On the railway line, Africans received a nominal compensation for their crops and homesteads. In the Fort Jameson area the authorities treated African land rights in a much more cavalier fashion. In 1924 the territory passed under the control of the British Colonial Office. The new authorities paid more attention to African land rights, but usually defined these according to current theory, which emphasized communal rather than individual rights as characteristic of African systems. The surface of the territory was also classified into three categories, each with a different legal status. Crown Land, which included those areas alienated to foreign settlers, was subject to the statute law of the territory which was based on English usage. Reserves and Native Trust lands were held for African use. Rights in land in these two categories were to be subject to customary law unless government specifically ruled otherwise.

The categorization of land had far-reaching effects upon the development of local tenure. Commercial, industrial and urban development was confined to Crown Land. Elsewhere on the continent the growth of towns and the consequent creation of new value for land often initiated changes in customary land systems. Gutkind has discussed the development of Baganda legal theory under the impact of the demand for land in and about Kampala and other towns (1963: 177–256). He noted that the expansion of towns and new improvements associated with the towns had led to land sales and land speculation. Lloyd (1962: 124) has reported a similar development in the Yoruba areas of Nigeria, where sales and speculation in town land became the rule, though agricultural land was still commonly given or loaned to one who asked for it. Communities on the outskirts of Congo cities looked forward to the sale of their lands as the city expanded. In Zambia, Africans had lost control of the area where the cities were to grow before they could explore the possibilities opened by the expanding town.

Reserve and Native Trust lands were assumed to be the permanent possession of African political communities, who in turn gave rights of occupation to their members. The government therefore refused to recognize the legality of transactions in land entered into by private persons using reserve or trust land. Neither did it envisage any opportunity for the political community to profit from the sale or lease of its communal holding, since commercial and industrial development was not scheduled for such regions, which were to be rather preserves of indigenous rural values. Before the colonial period, most of Zambia had been occupied by shifting cultivators who had little interest in acquiring permanent possession of any holding. This changed rapidly during the twentieth century. In the reserves near the railway line where commercial agriculture was profitable, pressure on the land resulted in individual pre-emption of most arable land by the early 1940s. Cultivators improved their fields, passed them to their heirs, and treated them as though in fact they were a form of private property. Rent and sale occurred occasionally, although the local courts refused to recognize the legality of such practices. Their stand was influenced by the view of colonial administrators that the land belonged to the rulers or to the 'tribe', whatever this meant, and therefore could not be sold. Periodically administrators invited the local African councils to discuss the possibility of recommending legislation to permit people to deal freely with their holdings without the restrictions of communal tenure. Periodically the local councils replied that they saw no reason to alter existing arrangements which prevented Europeans and Asians from acquiring land in the reserves. Given the Europeans' monopoly of political power and the Indians' hold on trade, the African determination to exclude them from the reserves was natural. African interest in changing land regulations centred on obtaining access to Crown Land from which Africans were largely excluded save as labourers on the land of others.

Given the fact that land dealings on any large scale were impossible, since government did not encourage or permit sale of communal land, communities showed little interest in extending their boundaries or in litigation over land. They made no attempt to transform themselves into estate owners as had lineages or local communities in the Congo or in Nigeria. The individual cultivator, however, staked a claim in such land as he had brought under cultivation.

The policy of indirect rule was probably carried farthest in Nigeria. It was also in Nigeria that the policy of the paramountcy of African interests received the greatest recognition. Very early in the history of the territory, the colonial government announced that European settlers would not be welcome and that land was not to be alienated to commercial corporations or to European settlers. Hence there was no need to define further African rights in land save as Africans themselves raised the question when they found themselves at odds with one another. Even the towns and cities were by and large regarded as African strongholds though European concerns tried to obtain security of tenure in sites they had taken under long-term leases, or in the earliest period claimed to have purchased from African landowners. The rapid commercialization of agriculture and the growth of towns provided the impetus for the development of more precise definition of rights. Colonial officials were prominent in the formulation of the new laws since they sat in courts and gave decisions based on what they thought was customary usage or on what they regarded as equity. But their freedom of pronouncement was restricted by the existence of powerful African political leaders who held traditional posts and whose views had to be considered. Officials were also early subject to the criticism of African lawyers trained in the metropolitan country who sought to give a greater precision to the laws of their own people.

By the end of the colonial period, Nigeria had been experimenting for decades with the problem of adjusting land rights to the changing economic scene. The right of the courts to reflect current opinion and thus to change the rules was generally recognized by colonial officials as well as by the local people. Descent groups were transforming themselves into economic corporations dealing in land. New estates were being created by pre-emption or by purchase. Dealings with both foreigners and local purchasers or renters were common. Despite the encouragement towards the development of communal holdings cumbered with restrictions supplied both by colonial officials and traditional authorities, general opinion in most areas seemed to favour the conversion of land to economic use wherever this was possible.

Conclusion

The colonial period was a time of rapid and drastic change, never more so than with respect to the use and view of land. European concepts of land tenure played a part in determining the nature of the changes. Equally important were other factors leading to rapid changes in the way in which men used the land; transport facilities improved, cities expanded, new industries sprang up, modern farming equipment was introduced, produce markets were developed and the population dependent upon the land increased. Together these phenomena altered men's relation to the earth and to one another. Today a man is likely to be a land holder and to think of his rights as relating to a specific piece of earth which he cultivates. These rights can be subdivided and disposed of independently of one another. Land may be held with long-term expectations that it will increase in value or convey some ultimate advantage. The new political régimes which emphasized property rights and sometimes valued these above social relationships also encouraged Africans to alter their values. They could acquire rights in land without also acquiring citizenship in a local community. They could uphold these rights in the courts against the attacks of their neighbours. They could convey their rights to a stranger who was not necessarily acceptable to the community. The work of missions, or of Muslim proselytizers, and the new values taught in school also worked together to destroy the old ritual congregation that had once existed wherever there was a community making use of the earth. Men could now cultivate without concern for the mystical dangers of the earth and without participation in the rituals which had once given them assurance of safety in the use of its resources. Prior settlement no longer differentiated the early settler from the newcomer. Where men were once concerned with the welfare of the community and the appropriate relationships with the earth, they were now free to acquire land as an economic good.

BIBLIOGRAPHY

Allan, William (1949). *Studies in African land usage in Northern Rhodesia*, Rhodes–Livingstone Paper, no. 15.

(1965). *The African husbandman*. Edinburgh.

M. Gluckman *et al.* (1948). *Land-holdings and land usage among the Plateau Tonga*, Rhodes–Livingstone Paper, no. 14.

Ardener, E. W. (1961). 'Social and demographic problems of the Southern Cameroons plantation area', in *Social change in modern Africa*, A. Southall, ed. London, Oxford University Press for the International African Institute.

Baldwin, K. (1963). 'Land-tenure problems in relation to agricultural development in the Northern Region of Nigeria', in *African agrarian systems*, D. Biebuyck, ed. London, Oxford University Press for the International African Institute.

Beckett, W. H. (1944). *Akokasa: a survey of a Gold Coast village*, London School of Economics monograph in social anthropology, no. 10.

Biebuyck, D., with the assistance of J. Dufour and Y. Kennes. *Bibliographie sur la tenure des terres et les problèmes fonciers*. Léopoldville, Commission pour l'étude du problème foncier.

ed. (1963). *African agrarian systems*. London, Oxford University Press for the International African Institute.

Bohannan, P. (1954). *Tiv farm and settlement*. London, H.M. Stationery Office.

(1963). '"Land", "tenure", and land-tenure', in *African agrarian systems*, D. Biebuyck, ed. London, Oxford University Press for the International African Institute.

Coker, G. B. A. (1958). *Family property among the Yorubas*. London.

Colson, E. (1966). 'Land law and land holdings among Valley Tonga of Zambia', *Southwestern Journal of Anthropology*, **22**.

Cory, H. (1953). *Sukuma law and custom*. London, Oxford University Press.

Cunnison, I. (1959). *The Luapula peoples of Northern Rhodesia*. Manchester University Press.

Dilly, Marjorie (1937). *British policy in Kenya Colony*. New York.

Douglas, Mary (1963). *The Lele of the Kasai*. London, Oxford University Press for the International African Institute.

Drachoussoff, V. (1965). *Agricultural change in the Belgian Congo: 1945–1960*. Stanford University, Food Research Institute.

Dufour, Jean (1963). 'Quelques aspects juridiques du problème foncier au Congo', in *African agrarian systems*, D. Biebuyck, ed. London, Oxford University Press for the International African Institute.

Elias, T. O. (1951). *Nigerian land law and custom*. London.

Fallers, L. (1956). *Bantu bureaucracy*. Cambridge, East African Institute of Social Research.

Forde, Daryll, ed. (1954). *African worlds*. London, Oxford University Press for the International African Institute.

Fortes, M. (1945). *The dynamics of clanship among the Tallensi*. London, Oxford University Press for the International African Institute.

Galletti, R., K. D. S. Baldwin, and I. O. Dina (1956). *An economic survey of Yoruba cocoa farming*. Oxford University Press.

Gluckman, M. (1941). *The economy of the central Barotse plain*, Rhodes-Livingstone Paper, no. 7.

(1943). *Essays on Lozi land and royal property*, Rhodes–Livingstone Paper, no. 10.

(1955). *The judicial process among the Barotse of Northern Rhodesia*. Manchester University Press.

Gray, Robert, and P. Gulliver, eds. (1964). *The family estate in Africa*. Boston University Press.

Great Britain (1950). *Bibliography of published sources relating to African land tenure*. C. O. 258. London, H.M. Stationery Office.

(1955). *East Africa Royal Commission 1953–1955 report*. Cmd. 9475. London, H.M. Stationery Office.

Green, M. (1947). *Ibo village affairs*. London.

Gulliver, P. (1955). *Family herds*. London.

(1958). *Land tenure and social change among the Nyakyusa*, East African Studies, no. 11.

(1961). 'Land shortage, social change, and social conflict in East Africa', *Journal of Conflict Resolution*, 5.

Gutkind, Peter (1963). *The royal capital of the Buganda*. The Hague.

Hailey, Lord (1957). *An African survey revised*. London, Oxford University Press.

Hancock, W. K. (1942). *Survey of British Commonwealth affairs*, vol. II. London, Oxford University Press.

Harris, A., and G. Harris (1964). 'Property and the cycle of domestic groups in Taita', in *The family estate in Africa*, R. Gray and P. Gulliver, eds. Boston University Press.

Haydon, E. S. (1960). *Law and justice in Buganda*. London.

Heldt, F. H., and C. Heldt, trans. (1959). *The Belgian Congo*, Vol. 1. Brussels, Belgian Congo and Ruanda–Urundi Information and Public Relations Office.

Herskovits, M. (1962). *The human factor in changing Africa*. New York.

Hill, Polly (1963). 'Three types of southern Ghana cocoa-farmer', in *African agrarian systems*, D. Biebuyck, ed. London, Oxford University Press for the International African Institute.

Homan, F. D. (1963). 'Land consolidation and redistribution of population in the Imenti sub-tribe of the Meru (Kenya)', in *African agrarian systems*, D. Biebuyck, ed. London, Oxford University Press for the International African Institute.

Howell, P. P. (1953). *A manual of Nuer law*. London, Oxford University Press for the International African Institute.

Kaberry, P. (1950). 'Land tenure among the Nsaw of the British Cameroons', *Africa*, **20**.

— (1952). *Women of the grassfields*. London, H.M. Stationery Office.

Kenyatta, Jomo (1963). *Facing Mount Kenya*. London.

Köbben, A. J. (1963). 'Land as an object of gain in a non-literate society: land-tenure among the Bete and Dida (Ivory Coast, West Africa)', in *African agrarian systems*, D. Biebuyck, ed. London, Oxford University Press for the International African Institute.

Kopytoff, I. (1964). 'Family and lineage among the Suku of the Congo', in *The family estate in Africa*, R. Gray and P. Gulliver, eds. Boston University Press.

Lambert, H. E. (1950). *The systems of land tenure in the Kikuyu land unit*, Communications from the School of African Studies, New Series, no. 22.

Lloyd, P. C. (1962). *Yoruba land law*. London, Oxford University Press.

Low, D. Anthony, and R. Cranford Pratt (1960). *Buganda and British overrule*. London, Oxford University Press.

Malcolm, D. (1953). *Sukumaland: an African people and their country*. London, Oxford University Press for the International African Institute.

Manners, R. (1962). 'Land use, trade, and the growth of market economy in Kipsigis country', in *Markets in Africa*, P. Bohannan and G. Dalton, eds. Evanston, Northwestern University Press.

Mayer, P., and I. Mayer (1965). 'Land law in the making', in *African law: adaptation and development*, Leo and Hilda Kuper, eds. Berkeley, University of California Press.

Meek, C. K. (1949). *Land law and custom in the colonies*. London, Oxford University Press.

— (1957). *Land tenure and land administration in Nigeria and the Cameroons*. London, H.M. Stationery Office.

Mitchell, Clyde (1956). *The Yao village*. Manchester University Press.

Mukwaya, A. B. (1953). *Land tenure in Buganda*, East African Studies, no. 1.

Obi, S. N. (1963). *The Ibo law of property*. London.

Peters, David (1950). *Land usage in Serenje District*, Rhodes–Livingstone Paper, no. 19.

Reining, Priscilla (1965). 'Land resources of the Haya', in *Ecology and economic development*, D. Brokensha, ed. Berkeley, University of California Press. (Research Series, no. 9, Institute of International Studies.)

Richards, A. I. (1939). *Land, labour, and diet in Northern Rhodesia*. London, Oxford University Press for the International African Institute.

(1963). 'Some effects of the introduction of individual freehold into Buganda', in *African agrarian systems*, D. Biebuyck, ed. London, Oxford University Press for the International African Institute.

ed. (1954). *Economic development and tribal change*. Cambridge.

ed. (1960). *East African chiefs*. London.

Schiller, A. A. (1965). 'Law', in *The African world*, R. Lystad, ed. New York.

Smith, M. G. (1955). *The economy of Hausa communities of Zaria*. London, H.M. Stationery Office.

Stenning, D. (1959). *Savannah nomads*. London, Oxford University Press for the International African Institute.

Sundström, Lars (1965). *The trade of Guinea*. Studia Ethnographica Upsaliensia, no. 24. Uppsala.

White, C. M. N. (n.d.). *Land tenure reports to the Northern Rhodesian government*. Lusaka, Mimeograph.

(1959). *A preliminary survey of Luvale rural economy*, Rhodes–Livingstone Paper, no. 29.

(1963). 'Factors determining the content of African land-tenure systems in Northern Rhodesia', in *African agrarian systems*, D. Biebuyck, ed. London, Oxford University Press for the International African Institute.

Wilson, G. (1938). *The land rights of individuals among the Nyakyusa*, Rhodes–Livingstone Paper, no. 1.

Wilson, Monica (1951). *Good company*. London, Oxford University Press for the International African Institute.

(1959). *Community rituals of the Nyakyusa*. London, Oxford University Press for the International African Institute.

(1963). 'Effects on the Xosa and Nyakyusa of scarcity of land', in *African agrarian systems*, D. Biebuyck, ed. London, Oxford University Press for the International African Institute.

Winans, E. V. (1962). *Shambala*. Berkeley, University of California Press.

Winter, E. H. (1955), *Bwamba economy*, East African Studies, no. 5.

Young, Crawford (1965). *Politics in the Congo*. Princeton University Press.

Young, Roland, and Henry Fosbrooke (1960). *Land and politics among the Luguru of Tanganyika*. London.

CHAPTER 7

THE IMPACT OF IMPERIALISM UPON URBAN DEVELOPMENT IN AFRICA

by

AIDAN SOUTHALL

It is usually assumed that African peoples south of the Sahara had no urban tradition worthy of the name, and hence that urban life and problems in contemporary Africa are essentially of external and European origin. There is no doubt that mid-twentieth century urban expansion is a world phenomenon, which began in the West and spread with many regional variations. It has also engulfed Africa in a way which leaves less and less trace of any continuity with the traditions of most indigenous African peoples. None the less, it is important to examine more closely the impact which the colonial empires had on African peoples in the context of urban development.

Nothing can possibly prevent this topic from being a delicate one which easily inflames passion and prejudice on either side. Any account that endeavours to consider the experiences of African peoples themselves is certain to be written off by white apologists as failing to give due credit to the good intentions of many Europeans which paved this particular path of history. Nor am I concerned to repeat the 'neutral' but potentially 'good' gifts of Europe to Africa, such as new food crops, elaborate technology, writing and Christianity. As a white writer I adopt the view, for present purposes, that the European nations are strong enough to stand a little criticism, that it is more important to present the experiences of multitudes of Africans than to devote all efforts to ensuring that no opportunity of giving credit to European good intentions is lost. I am appalled by the fact that so many Western scholars still seem unaware that the whole perspective of recent world history is quite different for Africans. The choice of the one perspective or the other cannot be made on the basis of any agreed criteria of right or wrong, of good or bad, of subjective or objective interpretations of events. The Western viewpoint is riddled with concealed unrealized assumptions. None the less, I am not prepared to capitulate to the one perspective or the other; I must meet my own relative standards of objectivity, which are bound to call forth criticism from either side.

The destructive impact of early imperialism

The Portuguese were the first imperial contenders to make contact with most of the coasts of tribal Africa, beginning from the west, extending to the south and up the east coast on their way to the Indies. There were hardly any indigenous settlements of real importance along the West African coastline during the early period of Portuguese exploration in the fifteenth and sixteenth centuries. But as soon as the Portugese attempted to establish channels of trade, they inevitably came in contact with the most powerful African states of the immediate hinterland, such as Benin near the Niger Delta, the kingdom of Kongo on the lower reaches of the Congo river and the Monomotapa kingdom just to the south of the Zambezi river.

Despite the ambiguities and inadequacies of contemporary accounts, it cannot be doubted that the capitals of the Benin, Kongo and Monomotapa kingdoms were settlements of considerable size and density, comprising many thousands of people. Although only marginally urban by some definitions, we may take them as representative of the nearest approach which the Negro peoples of tropical Africa had made to urbanization in the fifteenth and sixteenth centuries. None of these capitals was on the coast, or even on a navigable river; but all three were reasonably accessible to the Portuguese sailing along the coast near the mouths of the Niger, the Congo and the Zambezi.

The capital of the Kongo, at the first arrival of the Portuguese, seems to have been quite large but less complex than Benin. Winding paths led between the one-storey thatched straw houses and the wooden fenced enclosures of the nobles. But there was a definite orientation, with the royal enclosure towards the south containing the two separate sets of quarters of the king and queen, all surrounded by several concentric fences with guarded gates arranged like a labyrinth. The proximity to the royal enclosure of those of the nobles depended upon their relative rank (Cuvelier, 1946: 74-6). During the sixteenth century, churches, schools and other specialized buildings were constructed. A separate colonial settlement was made for the Portuguese, with its own encircling enclosure, for which stone began to be used, as also for that part of the royal enclosure which faced towards it (Balandier, 1965: 145). The population estimates for the sixteenth century range from one hundred thousand (Pigafetta, 1591, 1963: 74) down to thirty thousand (Balandier, 1965: 140–2). By the second half of the seventeenth century the kingdom was being torn to pieces by many conflicts and the capital had been largely abandoned and had fallen into ruin (Balandier, 1965: 65).

In all three cases, contact with European imperialists was in the long run disastrous. Benin survived the attentions of the Portuguese because the latter to some extent themselves lost interest. They found the way to the Indies, where much larger and more valuable trade was to be had with more highly organized economies. At the same time, they suffered more severe rivalry on the Benin coast from Dutch, Scandinavian, French and British traders. Added to this was the discouragingly unhealthy climate, which shifted their interests in more permanent settlement to Angola and Moçambique, where a less lethal climate was combined with greater freedom from European competition.

Benin survived as a great walled city, the head of a city state, until it was sacked by the British in 1897. Its traditional combination of political power, economic wealth and aesthetic achievement was unable to withstand the economic, political and military onslaught of industrialized European power. It still survived through the colonial period in a degenerate state, although it had become an economic backwater compared with its fifteenth-century prosperity. Today it may eventually achieve some urban and political recovery as capital of the new mid-western state of Federal Nigeria.

The influence of imperialism upon the capital cities of the Kongo and Monomotapa kingdoms was even more destructive than in the case of Benin. The early interaction between the Portuguese and the Kongo from the end of the fifteenth century was in certain respects most promising. The Portuguese brought to the capital craftsmen as well as missionaries and traders. The ruling family became both Christian and literate, so that the state might well seem set for peaceful and progressive incorporation of change and adaptation. Indeed, this first case of intensive, long-term interaction between a European power and a tropical African capital city is so important that it justifies some detail.[1]

[1] One of the most striking and disturbing features is the intertwining of emphasis on the Christian evangelical and civilizing mission with deeds of cruelty, violence and deceit which nullified it. The work of Cuvelier is particularly appropriate because, while broadly based on the original sources, the former Vicar Apostolic of Matadi is deeply concerned with the achievements of Christian missions in the Congo. On the other hand, Balandier's account is the most sophisticated and objective interpretation by a social scientist.

It is a tragic story, and many of its crucial features can be traced again and again in the subsequent dealings of Europeans with Africa. Its particular relevance here is that, as Balandier remarks (1965: 140), 'il y a une correlation entre le développement de l'organization politique kongo et la naissance d'une forme rudimentaire de civilisation urbaine'.

The story begins with trickery. Diogo Cao having discovered the Congo river and sent a party of missionaries inland three hundred kilometres to the capital of the king of Kongo, did not wait for news, or for their return, but falsely and without any evidence became suspicious of the king. So he tricked some local chiefs on board his ship for a visit to satisfy their curiosity and then made off with them to Lisbon (Cuvelier, 1946: 39). The king of Kongo had in fact received the envoys well; but when he heard of the trick, he banished them from the capital, to be put to death if the hostages did not return (Cuvelier, 1946: 40). They did return, with favourable accounts of their own reception by the king of Portugal. The king of Kongo was sufficiently impressed by the material goods, wealth and power of the king of Portugal to share his desire for a mutually advantageous relationship. It seems to have been as convenient for the king of Portugal to couch his dealings in terms of his ineluctable obligation, imposed by the Pope, to bring the heathen under the banner of Christ, as it was for the king of Kongo to phrase his demands in terms of aid in the development of the Kongo as a Christian state. Even his intelligent realization of the value of Portuguese carpenters and masons was officially related to the need for building churches rather than to any material needs of his people. It was the king of Kongo's governor on the Congo river who was most intensely affected by his direct contact with the Portuguese ships, their arms and provisions. He began to demand baptism for himself and put pressure on his overlord to do the same. In 1491 the king, queen and heir were all baptized. In order to receive this blessing the king had to carry on a vigorous campaign of burning fetishes and stamping out traditional religion wherever his authority permitted. This caused heavy opposition, which crystallized into a traditionalist faction and caused constant outbreaks of revolt and attempts to restore Kongo custom. As soon as the king's health failed, he turned back to the comfort of traditional beliefs and practices. The Portuguese backed his Christian son Affonso against him and intrigued on his behalf until opposition forced them to leave the capital and re-establish themselves in the son's province. Affonso threatened death to anyone found with fetishes and became estranged from his father, though continuing to send him the customary tribute of slaves. At his father's death in 1506, fighting broke out in the capital, but with Portuguese aid Affonso defeated the popular pagan candidate. He begged for arms from the Portuguese at São Tomé, saying significantly that he wanted to burn more fetishes but was convinced that if he did the people would revolt and try to kill him; therefore he had to assure himself of Portuguese aid (Cuvelier, 1946: 110). The constantly reiterated demands for fire-arms, both by Affonso and his successors, were always either ignored or refused, despite the sending of large consignments of slaves in payment. Affonso continued to put fetishists to death and actually made a pagan martyr of one of his classificatory mothers by burying her alive when she refused to abandon her traditional religion (Cuvelier, 1946: 120). The people were enraged and attempts were made on his life.

A complete stranglehold on the Kongo trade was maintained by the Portuguese of São Tomé. They consisted of deported Portuguese criminals and Jewish refugees from Spain, to each of whom the king of Portugal ordered a female slave to be given for the peopling of the island (Cuvelier, 1946: 137). The governor of São Tomé was a prominent courtier from the king of Portugal's entourage, but was referred to both as a pirate and as a chevalier of Christ. He intercepted the slaves and ivory which the king of Kongo sent with pathetic entreaties for aid and justice to the king of Portugal. For twenty-three years his crimes and exactions went unchecked until the king of Portugal finally replaced him. Affonso's loyal devotion to the king continued, but he informed him that greed for wealth was causing the destruction of the truth (Cuvelier, 1946: 136).

While São Tomé maintained its royally chartered trade monopoly from the Gold Coast to the Congo, the official interests of Portugal had passed on to the more attractive prizes of the Indies. Even on the coast of Africa, the newer Portuguese settlements in Angola began to detract from interest in the Kongo kingdom. The demand for slaves and ivory reverberated far inland, instigating the African peoples to continuous plundering of one another. At first, when the Kongo was their latest discovery, the Portuguese stimulus led to an expansion and strengthening of the Kongo kingdom; but as the Portuguese interest became diverted elsewhere, the Kongo rulers found it difficult to maintain control. The Ambundu people were already attacking the southern provinces of the Kongo kingdom and, as Angola became the major

Portuguese source of slaves for Brazil, the trade routes penetrated farther and farther inland, triggering intense chain reactions of rapacious plundering by one people of another, becoming ever fiercer as fire-arms spread and competition grew. The traditional structure of provincial administration in the Kongo was not designed to withstand this new kind of attack, unprecedentedly destructive in both its means and its end. In 1512 the king had to march to the rescue of the southern provinces, actually leaving the Portuguese ambassador to keep order in his capital, with authority to impose judgement and punishment on both white and black. Clearly this marked an important stage in the Kongo's loss of autonomy and increasing colonial dependence on the Portuguese. The king of Portugal instructed his ambassador that although Christ was their main objective, he must ensure that the king of Kongo send the Portuguese ships back full of slaves, ivory and copper (Cuvelier, 1946: 140). When the slaves revolted, the Kongo rulers joined forces with the Portuguese to suppress them. The king of Kongo actually took on a Portuguese legal adviser and planned to introduce Portuguese law, but the jurist fell out with the Portuguese ambassador, who stabbed him to death.

The Portuguese signalled disillusionment with their civilizing mission by refusing to receive any more Kongo students in Lisbon. The exploitation of Brazil demanded an intensification of the slave-trade. The Portuguese began to establish posts in the interior of the Kongo without reference to its king, who saw this as a direct threat to the state. He had always supported the institution of domestic slavery, but was opposed to the sale of domestic slaves to the overseas trade. He regarded war captives and criminals as legitimate objects of the latter, but was revolted by its cruelties and wished to prevent the indiscriminate plunder of human beings for it. Finally he reached the point of wanting to expel all the Portuguese traders. Lacking the power to achieve this, he proposed a system of inspection and licensing by his chiefs. Naturally the clamour of the local Portuguese against him increased, and they began to demand direct intervention. The king of Portugal sent a fully equipped mining engineer with orders to mine for gold. The king of Kongo was required to cede gold-mining rights (although no gold had been discovered) on pain of Portugal's declaring war upon him. Repeated attempts by the king of Kongo to send an embassy to the Pope were frustrated both by the local Portuguese of São Tomé and by the king in Lisbon. The Pope's concern was directed to providing for the baptism of slaves who died while being transported (Cuvelier, 1946: 233). Some four to five thousand slaves are said to have been embarking annually from the Kongo port of Mpinda, in addition to the large numbers dying on the way there, and while waiting for the ships. The Kongo Christians were in danger of falling back into paganism. Violence among the Portuguese as well as between them and the Kongo people was shaking the foundations of the state. In 1539 a party of Portuguese attempted to shoot the king as he knelt at the Easter Mass (Cuvelier, 1946: 243). Some were killed but the king escaped. He died a few years later, leaving the kingdom in chaos.

The next ruler reverted to traditional custom. Many short reigns followed. One king was assassinated by the Portuguese, who installed their own docile candidate, only to have him assassinated in turn by a popular xenophobic outburst. Another king died fighting the increasing irruptions of foreign tribes across the frontiers. In 1569 the invasion by the Yaka forced the king to abandon his capital completely, and the kingdom was only restored when eventually six hundred well trained Portuguese troops were sent to reinstate him, demonstrating his total submission to Portugal (Balandier, 1965: 57).

All positive features of the Portuguese Kongo experiment had come to an end. The subservient kingdom dragged on, dwindling but occasionally asserting itself. A hundred years later the Portuguese actually invaded the country, again on the pretext of a dispute over imaginary minerals, killing the king and then withdrawing. Only petty factions remained; and when the Bishop of Loanda visited the spot, he found that the capital city of the Kongo kingdom had become a haunt of wild animals.

While the historical details are unique, it is possible to extract from this very condensed account themes and sequences that are familiar in many other cases. The African ruler at first favours Christianity, bowled over by the displays of European fire-power and wealth; he alienates his people by insisting on their conversion, martyring those who refuse. He himself reverts to traditional beliefs and practices when times are bad, thus giving the foreigners a pretext to build up a faction against him in the name of true religion. Rule then oscillates between Westernizing and Christianizing attempts of Africans to participate in the apparent spoils of civilization, and reactionary traditionalist attempts to repair the damage done to the social fabric. The initial impact of European discovery stimulates and facilitates some strengthening and expansion of the African state. When the European interest wanes, the African ruler can neither maintain the new order towards which he had striven, nor return to the old one which he has undermined; the economic necessity of slavery and general exploitation cannot permit him to do so. The European state insists on its civilizing and even religious mission, but is unable to control the actions of its local representatives, even though it continues to recognize and profit by them. They are at one and the same time noble adventurers and Christian knights, pirates, thieves and murderers. The foreigners have to be granted extraterritorial rights and privileges because they claim that their standards are higher than those of the natives. They are strong enough to defend their privileges, but no one has the power to curb their offences; and the attempt to do so provides the ultimate pretext for direct intervention and defeat.

The fate of the capital of the Monomotapa was in general similar. In 1514 Duarte Barbosa had spoken of a large town called Zimbaoch (Zimbabwe), with houses of wood and straw, 'in which town the king of Benematapa frequently dwells, and from there to the city of Bene-matapa there are six days' journey...And in the said Benematapa, which is a very large town, the king is used to make his longest residence; and it is thence that the merchants bring to Sofala the gold which they sell to the Moors without weighing it, for coloured stuffs and beads from Cambay' (Duarte Barbosa, 1866: 5–8). In the same year Antonio Fernandes found the Monomotapa in a fort of stone without mortar (Axelson, 1949: 139).

The great metalliferous region of Central Africa had already enabled African societies to develop material cultures rich in iron, copper, gold and silver, controlled by powerful centralized kingdoms with extensive trading relations both inside Africa and leading to overseas outlets, notably through Sofala and with the Arabs, Persians, Indians and Chinese. The Arabs in particular had founded trading settlements all down the east coast from Mogadiscio in Somalia, down through Lamu, Manda and Pate, Malindi and Mombasa, Mafia and Kilwa, to Moçambique, Sofala and on to the Comoro Islands and the northern coasts of Madagascar.

It is not surprising that a number of African states competed, and fought, for the wealth of eastern Central Africa, and that different ethnic groups succeeded one another in dominance of different parts of the region. Nor is it surprising that traders were attracted from overseas. But there was a marked difference between the interaction of these African states with the Portuguese and with the other foreign traders who had preceded them, most particularly the Arabs. The latter were not strong enough and did not attempt interior conquest. They inter-married with coastal Africans, they spoke the Swahili language, which was indeed a symbol and product of the intermarriage and cultural assimilation of Arabs with Africans all down the coast. They provided sufficient outlet and stimulus to permit the gradual elaboration of political and economic institutions by the African states of the interior. Had this continued there is little doubt that their capitals would have become increasingly large, dense, urban settlements, with a progressive differentiation of political, economic and occupational roles.

It was far otherwise with the Portuguese. Their first contacts were violent, hostile and treacherous. Wherever they landed they kidnapped natives and bore them away to act as guides and interpreters. In their first contact with Moçambique they seized an Arab pilot from some boats and then fired on them. At Mombasa they tortured two Arab passengers in boiling oil, whom they had offered to take from Moçam-bique to Malindi. They captured an Arab dhow on the way to Malindi. At Malindi they seized the sheikh who came on board in good faith and threatened to drown him until he promised submission. Later they entered the town, after confessing and receiving absolution, pillaged it thoroughly (while the Franciscans proceeded through it with crosses, singing the *Te Deum*) and enslaved the inhabitants (Axelson, 1940: 13, 35–6, 41, 45–6, 57, 67, 84, 90, 99–100, 156).

It is tedious to recount the innumerable other incidents of this sort, but essential to note that this was the first impression made by Euro-peans on East Africans. It is all the more remarkable that these acts of infamy were recorded by the Portuguese themselves, along with important examples of Arab humanity, courtesy and magnanimity, as when they cared for the survivors of Portuguese shipwrecks, and when the rulers of Arab towns sent gifts and guarantees of peace to Portuguese ships, receiving in return bombardment and slaughter. As in the Kongo, the Portuguese officially claimed to be chevaliers of Christ while acting as ferocious pirates. Indeed, it was as though towards Muslims any kind of savagery was sanctified. The only superiority the Portuguese possessed was in their fire-arms. In other respects most European scholars have rated their cultural attainments far below those of the Arabs, even those in the far-flung outposts of East Africa in the sixteenth century.

The Portuguese were able to destroy much of the Arab urban culture of the east coast, as in the case of Sofala, Moçambique, Manda, Pate, Mombasa, Kilwa and Madagascar. However, the Arabs survived them on the northern part of the coast. Inland, events followed a similar tortuous course to that already described for the Kongo. The main differences were that gold and silver, rather than slaves, were the main object of gain, the Christian missionaries were less effective and the conversion of reigning Monomotapas more palpably utilitarian, with the conversion of Africans aimed mainly at the defeat and expulsion of the Arabs, for which the Portuguese were paid by the Pope's grant of ten per cent of his ecclesiastical revenues. Furthermore, the favourable climate of the interior highlands led to a kind of settlement which contributed to the enfeeblement and decay of the African kingdoms and of the whole Portuguese enterprise. There was no Portuguese strangle-hold of trade comparable to that of São Tomé, and Portuguese officials were never able to establish any effective commercial control. As else-where, they backed selected royal competitors in succession disputes, reduced them to dependence, insisted on recognition of Portuguese sovereignty, mineral concessions and acceptance of Christianity. They were eventually able to install their own puppet candidates on the thrones of the main rival kingdoms. In return for his allegiance the Monomotapa was granted a gift of 3,000 crusados of cloth from every captain of Sofala who took office. This was always in default, so that the Monomotapa each time tried in retaliation to expel all Portuguese traders from his kingdom, with inevitable Portuguese counterattacks resulting. The Portuguese were never able to secure enough settlers to man their stations, although they tried to round up criminals and prostitutes in Portugal for this purpose. It was the freelance traders who were granted estate concessions up-country who survived best. They established themselves like African chiefs, with private armies. They had absolute power, and there was no government or justice in their domains. Their barbarities caused a constant chain reaction of African uprisings and counter-reprisals. They diverted official Portuguese supplies and trade, robbing the Portuguese forts and towns of any chance of prosperity.

The Portuguese colonial system was further weakened by the appear-ance of new enemies. From one side the Dutch occupied Loanda in 1641 and established their station at the Cape in 1652. From the other, the Omani Arabs took Muscat from the Portuguese in 1650, appeared off Zanzibar in 1652, sacked Mombasa in 1661 and Moçambique itself in 1670. By the eighteenth century the Portuguese sway had been broken, and even Monomotapa and Changamire had banded together against them (Axelson, 1960: 194). The Portuguese had failed in their aims, but in the process they had also destroyed the earlier promise of the African states of the region.

Angola was a mere shambles, in which the criminal classes of Portugal were employed in inciting the native peoples to make war on each other in the interests of slave labor for Brazil. Mozambique based on gold rather than slaves was a shade less bloody but hardly less vicious. The effect of the two penetrations into the African mainland was almost wholly injurious to the African societies with which they came into direct contact (Oliver and Fage, 1962: 133–4).

As San Salvador had been abandoned by the early eighteenth century, so had Zimbabwe and the other stone structures of Zambezia.

It was somewhat paradoxical that the Portuguese influence on certain African peoples in the interior, farther away from direct contact with them, had a more positive and stimulating, less materially destructive and culturally demoralizing effect. The Portuguese demand for gold, copper, slaves and ivory stimulated the rise of the powerful Kuba, Lunda, Luba, Bemba, Kazembe and other Central African kingdoms (Gann and Duignan, 1962: 24; and Vansina, 1966: *passim*). All these peoples developed elaborate courts and capitals, which often came near to providing the basis for genuine urban culture. But while those nearer the Portuguese were destroyed by them, these remained too remote, without that cultural 'take-off' which only writing and other techniques of recording can bring.

Continuity and transformation of traditional urban developments in West and North Africa

On the west coast and in its hinterland there was the same phenomenon of indirect economic stimulus, with important political and cultural consequences deriving from the maritime trading influence of the European colonial powers. This influence was in conscious rivalry with, and a complementary stimulus to, the older commercial influence of Muslim North Africa mediated down the Sahara caravan routes. These re-inforcing exogenous influences eventually played upon a number of peoples (Hausa, Yoruba, Songhai, Ashanti, Bambara, Malinke and many more) who had already had direct or indirect access to a much older, more stable and more genuinely urban cultural tradition than anything available elsewhere in indigenous tropical or southern Africa. These traditions were themselves partly indigenous— to an extent which we cannot clearly know until more is known of such possible precursors as the prehistoric Nok culture of the Niger– Benue valley—and partly derived from early Berber immigration from the north and possibly from indirect and migratory contact with ancient Nubia.

Ancient Nubia was the channel through which influences from the urban civilization of Pharaonic Egypt were most likely to have been transmitted to the south, and more particularly to the south-west. Without falling prey to any exaggerated hypothesis of cultural deriva- tion from Egypt, it is impossible not to recognize the fact that the greatest urban civilization which Africa has ever known was located there and that for five or six millennia it retained a remarkable con- tinuity, absorbing successive waves of Nubians, Hittites, Semites, Greeks, Romans, Arabs, Turks and latter-day French and British conquerors. Nubia absorbed Pharaonic urban civilization not only through the constant Egyptian expeditions to Nubia during the third and second millennia B.C., but also through the Nubian conquest of Egypt in the middle of the first millennium B.C. As Egyptian culture became overlaid and transformed by Hellenistic Greek and Roman influence, the greatest continuity of Pharaonic urban civilization lay in the Nubian cities and kingdoms of Meroe, Napata and their derivatives. There was some cross-fertilization with the Axumitic kingdom of northern Ethiopia, whose rulers briefly conquered Meroe, and which must be regarded as the earliest experiment in urban civilization in the highland interior of north-eastern Africa.

However, after the Axumitic period, the Ethiopian capitals remained no more than mobile if elaborately organized military camps until the end of the nineteenth century. Later Muslim influence produced the mediaeval walled city of Harar, and the late feudal period produced the castles of Gondar; but otherwise the Emperor Menelik's foundation of Addis Ababa, at the end of the nineteenth century, produced the first Ethiopian city and capital to acquire importance as a modern urban settlement.

The influence of Meroe upon urban development was thus ineffective in Ethiopia. It reached southward to the mediaeval Fung kingdom of Sennar, of whose capital city little detail is available. Beyond there, apart from its possible influence on Shilluk kingship, it was largely barred by the swamps of the Upper Nile, which conferred upon its acephalous Nilotic peoples a relative impermeability until the present day. It was to the south-west that Meroitic influence must be assumed to have been most likely, although current archaeological opinion attaches little weight to it. It is the most economical hypothesis that at the final conquest and breakdown of Meroe its survivors may have passed to the south-west, where many traditions and the little explored remains of stone-built settlements in Darfur and the Central Sudan bear witness to such a probability. Here it must have converged eventually with the experience of urban civilization which passed across the Saharan caravan routes from Muslim North Africa to the Western Sudan. Even in earlier, pre-Islamic times, the movements of Berber peoples may have brought faint echoes of the ancient Mediterranean urban civilization of the North African coast across the desert to the savannah belt. Accumulating archaeological evidence suggests that the iron age in West Africa dates back at least to this epoch.

These are the possibilities that have to be weighed against the evidence for indigenous urban or at least proto-urban culture in West Africa. The Yoruba cities are of unknown age, but certainly go back for a millennium and perhaps considerably more. They are now speculatively linked with the Nok culture in the region of the Niger–Benue confluence, which appears to have been an original local development several centuries before the Christian era; but of its social organization and settlements nothing is known. It was already using iron, as well as producing its amazing works of art in terra cotta (Bascom, 1955: 449; and Lloyd, 1953: 30–44).

The Yoruba cities have become celebrated in comparative urban theory because they upset many accepted clichés. Those who think that agriculture is incompatible with urban life (having forgotten the part it played in most pre-industrial cities) call them agro-towns, because in many of them the majority of men were engaged in agriculture. They were city states, with hereditary rulers, composed of organized wards containing a number of localized kin groups each occupying its own compound. The kin groups corporately owned their urban compound and also their farmland outside the city. Farming was done by men, local trade and marketing by women, although men also controlled long-distance trade. Cowrie shells were used as money. At any one time many men, and families, would be outside the city on their farms. Some cities were surrounded by satellite towns, others by hundreds or even thousands of hamlets, which brought the farmers near to their land. But the central city was the dominant focus, the scene of most life-cycle rituals, the headquarters of all major institutions and the stage for public ceremonials. The southern Yoruba had a grid pattern, the northern Yoruba a radial design, with the king's palace and the great market at the centre. Buildings were not architecturally differentiated except in size. Women spun cotton, wove and dyed cloth, made pots and prepared foodstuffs for sale in the market. Men worked beads and leather, carved wood, ivory and calabashes, wrought iron and brass and made the royal regalia. The specialized crafts were hereditary in particular kin groups and organized in guilds. The cities were walled and gated and probably contained from twenty to fifty thousand inhabitants in the case of the larger capitals even in traditional times. They were certainly urban in size and density. Although they were largely homogeneous ethnically, they may properly be said to have been heterogeneous in the sense of having a much larger number of differentiated roles (political and ritual offices and titles, specialized crafts, in addition to age statuses and kinship roles) than were to be found in the African countryside. Although the Yoruba cities must have been indirectly involved in the European slave-trade along the coast, they never established direct contact. They were not certainly visited by Europeans until 1825, although they were mentioned by Portuguese and Dutch from the sixteenth century onward.

In the savannah of the Western Sudan there is no doubt that urban settlements were developing over a millennium ago, with some northern cultural influences and some immigration of northern peoples, but primarily as a result of the concentrations of trade and political power in the capitals of a series of sometimes quite extensive, yet frequently overlapping, empires and their satellite or successor states. The most celebrated of these were Ghana, Kanem, Bornu, Tekrur, Melle, Songhai and the numerous Hausa city states.

Perhaps the most important influence of European trading imperialism on the west coast from the fifteenth to the nineteenth century was that it reversed the direction of major economic attraction from the north to the south. This meant that the rain forest belt, with its heavy potential population-carrying capacity, even on the basis of subsistence agriculture, changed from being merely the remote end of long trans-desert trade routes to being in the forefront of the coastal trade. Benin and many of the Yoruba cities antedated this reversal; but none the less the Yoruba emphasis eventually shifted southwards because of it, just as the Sudanese horsemen pressing upon them from the north did so partly from the same change of economic orientation. From this stimulus arose the new state of Dahomey, in the seventeenth and eighteenth centuries, with its capital city at Abomey and its port city of Whydah. Oyo pressed, and was pushed, south, founding the city of New Oyo early in the nineteenth century and leading also to the founding of the city of Ibadan.

Yoruba involvement in the coast trade finally led to the growth of seaport towns like Badagry and Lagos. Ashanti, also, having consolidated to the north, developed contacts with the sea. All along the coast political brokerage developed between the European traders and the inland African suppliers. This political brokerage took the form of new trading city states, founded by Africans, for Africans and ruled by Africans, yet in direct response to the requirements of European trade. Such were Old Calabar, Bonny, Brass and Opobo, Porto Novo, Grand Popo, Grand Bassam and many more. In all these developments, of course, African states became as deeply involved as European nations in the transatlantic slave-trade, to the economic opportunities of which some owed their very origin and others much of their particular form. Some African peoples were enriched economically and strengthened politically; others were plundered and broken. But there can be no argument as to who were the authors and the main beneficiaries.

A slightly different variety of symbiosis gradually developed round the Gold Coast forts, whether under the Portuguese, the Danish, the Dutch or the British. Most had the same important implication of a gradual, permissive and hence culturally digestible introduction of literacy with new forms of commerce and urbanism, without necessary loss of political autonomy. Thus within the forts and 'factories' European influence was supreme, but extended very little beyond their walls, where a new type of settlement sprang up from which most of the modern coastal towns of Ghana have developed. In these essentially urban settlements Africans were dominant, even if sometimes as agents of the foreign traders; but they were also to some extent emancipated from their traditional political groups and allegiances. They also acquired literacy and much new technology, but to a large extent they were able to incorporate this new knowledge and source of power into their lives in their own way and in their own time, although certainly they themselves were considerably transformed in the process. Because the adaptation was gradual, they had no sense of losing their cultural identity or continuity, and this was fundamental. Despite extreme rivalry and instability between European groups themselves as well as between European and African, it was possible for relationships of mutual trust and respect, as well as material advantage, to develop between African and European. In token of this many Africans even took European names, which have survived to this day in African families of great contemporary importance. There was also inevitably a degree of interbreeding. The important fact was that in this context a new type of African urban man—and indeed woman—could appear, of lasting economic and political importance in his changing society, capable of dealing with Europeans on terms of dignity and equality, without losing cultural continuity and identity with the African past.

Very little of this story has been told, the best account being that of Priestley on the Brew family, descended from an Irish slave-trader who spent thirty years in the Fanti coastal towns during the eighteenth century (Priestley, 1966). One of his mulatto sons married into a Cape Coast family and contributed to the rise of an urban, coastal, educated élite which always claimed and was accorded African status and played a notable part in national politics up to and including the period of Ghana independence. Descendants were educated in mission schools or even trained as lawyers in England. Besides being respected as scholars and merchant princes, they became court clerks, judicial assessors, justices of the peace and administrative officers in the British system, while at the same time successfully claiming the status of Fanti chiefs and lineage elders. Such educated and intermarrying families of the coastal towns were able to bridge the gap between the two cultures because of the possibility of gradual acculturation and the degree of participation permitted in the European structure, until the more rigid colonialism of the late nineteenth century curtailed these possibilities. These men also had educated wives, some of chiefly families and some also traders in their own right. Despite the fame of the market 'mammy', the story has not yet been told of the African woman trader, who seems to have represented a positive and vital element in the evolution of West African urban culture from Senegal to Nigeria.

A culturally different variant within an otherwise similar context was that of the French communes on the coast of Senegal. Gorée and Rufisque were founded by the Dutch in the seventeenth century, as was St Louis by Dieppe. Despite capture and recapture, they became mainly French, and with their forts and satellite European and African settlements played a part similar to that of the Gold Coast forts and towns. French control extended little beyond them until the mid-nineteenth-century conquests of Faidherbe. As their political dominance became assured, they took the original step of granting full French citizenship to a very narrowly circumscribed African élite in St Louis, Rufisque, Gorée and Dakar, which began to supersede it. These French African communes were the first serious attempt at transference of European urban culture to Africans in its completeness. From it ensued the long and intimate association of the French West African urban élite with French urban culture, in particular that of Paris itself. It was, perhaps, only a temporary solution of the ubiquitous problem of African urban culture. Effective integration of a narrow élite to the metropolitan culture made a difficult contrast in intellectual and even spiritual orientation between them and the masses. The adjustment will probably await the second generation of independent African leaders.

Factors affecting the survival or suppression of African steps towards urbanization

There was a patchy yet widespread pre-industrial urban tradition in pre-colonial Africa. It was oldest and strongest in the west and in the Arab cities of the east coast, whereas in central and southern Africa the capitals of monarchical states, to judge from the inadequate historical record, are perhaps best described as proto-urban.

When British traders reached Durban (Port Natal) early in the nineteenth century, they soon came into contact with the Zulu monarch and his envoys—the most powerful political force in that whole region at the time. The Zulu king was eager for fire-arms and other technological improvements, so that a flourishing trade might very well have developed (had some miracle permitted the Zulu to retain their independence), causing the huge royal kraal headquarters, with its 12,000 inhabitants, mainly warriors, to develop into a true city. It was already large, dense and ethnically heterogeneous. However, the embroilment of Briton and Boer, with the rivalry of both in exploiting the country and gaining control of its resources the one before the other, left no chance for such a beneficial economic and urban development within the Zulu nation. The early embassies and trade contacts ceased and violent conflict ensued, so that subsequent urban development took place almost exclusively within the European economic sector of the new society and Africans lost all chance of incorporating and grafting urban culture onto their traditional life.

What effect did the colonial empires of the Portuguese, French and British have upon these pre-existing urban and proto-urban foundations? Everywhere they were eclipsed. Outside West Africa they were nearly all swamped and overwhelmed. Of all the many factors involved we come down to two which seem to be most consistently associated with the survival or collapse of pre-existing urban structures. These are the sheer size and density of the African urban population on the one hand, and the attractiveness or lack of appeal of the local climate to Europeans. With size and density of urban population are associated both the overall territorial density and the density of an interconnected network or system of cities. This inevitably also implies a certain political strength and elaboration. Indeed it appears that the larger, older and more stable a city was, and the more closely and intricately it was meshed in a wider economic, cultural and political system of cities, the greater its survival power and adaptability.

Thus, in West Africa, the two most notable clusters of traditional urbanization, the Hausa and the Yoruba, remain the most urbanized areas of West Africa today, with also the greatest continuity with the past. How far differing colonial policies have been relevant it is hard to say. Certainly Lugard's policy favoured this result, but it is doubtful that it was crucial.

Cities of older tradition also survived in the French West African Empire. The modern capitals of Bamako and Ouagadougou had traditional roots. Timbuctoo had already dwindled both as a result of the Moroccan conquest of the sixteenth century, with its unsuccessful aftermath, and from the radical change in the content and orientation of trade, due to the increasing pre-eminence of the west coast commerce over that of the ancient caravan routes from the north.

But the fact is that the area which became British Nigeria and the present Federal Republic has probably been by far the most populous area of tropical Africa for many centuries. The cities of the savannah conquered by the French were far less stable because dependent on a succession of far-flung empires based on mobile cavalry. The Nigerian

Hausa cities were also in the savannah, but had developed a much more integrated interurban economic system. In the forest areas conquered by the French there were no ancient cities of importance.

Many of the ancient cities of the Western Sudan dwindled, disappeared or changed their sites as they had many times before, in submission to new distributions of power or changed patterns of trade and communications. Hence the fluctuations of such cities as Timbuctoo, Gao, Djenne, Oualata, Audoghast, the ancient capitals of Mali and Ghana, and many more. All of these came within the French colonial empire.

On the other hand, in the case of the Hausa cities, while some old ones disappeared and a few new ones were founded, many like Kano, Zaria and Katsina had a remarkable continuity, and the complex as a whole was so dominant that the subsequent pattern of economic and technological change had to be grafted onto it rather than the other way about.

In modern Nigeria the development of railways, roads and airways and the siting of secondary industries has for the most part had to conform to the siting of the ancient cities. Since most of them were walled and diked, with densely congested settlement over much of the enclosed space, it was inevitable that overspills, reminiscent of the 'neustadts' and 'faubourgs' of ancient European cities, should develop adjacent to them. Colonial administrative and departmental offices and the residences of their incumbents; the shops, offices, factories and homes of European businessmen; the churches, schools, hospitals and homes of European missionaries; the small shops or market stalls of 'foreign' African traders and the dwellings of the masses of 'foreign' African workers, such as the Ibo in Northern Nigeria and the Hausa in Yorubaland—all these formed a large and sprawling adjunct which, with the frequent addition of a railway station, bus and lorry parks and hotels might rival or surpass the old city in size, population, wealth, volume of business and intensity of life, as well as tending to usurp the major urban function of focusing and disseminating change. With the end of political empire and the transfer of authority to Africans, this urban dichotomy is gradually transcended as Africans move into the offices and homes of the former colonial bureaucracies. But, as is well known, Africanization of the expatriate economy is proceeding much more slowly. The contrast becomes more blurred, less sharp and obvious, both as to the physical layout of cities and the separation of institutions and ethnic groups within them. But the old cities tend to remain as repositories of the local culture, its crafts, and its leaders in their more traditional form, while the new élites—political, economic and professional—as well as the clerks, skilled workers and migrants, are the heirs of the new city brought by colonial rule.

The same phenomenon appeared even in North African cities, whether in the case of the most ancient, such as Fez, or the more recent, such as Algiers. The same dichotomy appeared between the old city, retaining much of its traditional life and culture, and the new city, dominated during the colonial period by expatriate administration, commerce and residence, yet of equal importance after the attainment of independence when increasingly taken over by the new political élite. Many such changes of local emphasis have occurred in urban history, as in Cairo with the numerous switches from the Roman and pre-Roman fortress of Babylon and the Greco–Coptic city built within and upon it, to the originally tented camp of Al Fustat marking the initial Islamic conquest of the seventh century, to the great mediaeval city to the north and east with the Al Azhar centre of learning, the citadel of Saladin and the great bazaars, to the nineteenth-century city of modern commerce nearer the contemporary course of the Nile, and the concentration of élite European and cosmopolitan residence in Heliopolis and Zamalek. But the recent colonial dichotomy of most tropical African cities was, for its brief half or three-quarters of a century, a harsher ecological, cultural, social and economic division, still unhealed in most of east, central and southern Africa. It is less noticeable in the West, where the teeming populations of urban Africans are more firmly established and confident in themselves. Addis Ababa with its distinctive and independent history is also an exception to this spatial dichotomy. This was to be expected, since the relatively brief and late period of Italian conquest and imperialism in Ethiopia formed a break in the continuity of urban development rather than a part of it. It had a considerable influence upon architectural styles, language, and the direction of commerce, but not otherwise upon the structure or layout of the city.

In central, eastern and southern Africa there is hardly a single case in which a traditional urban settlement survived with sufficient strength to remain a significant element in a contemporary city. The most important African settlements that came in contact with colonial imperialism were, like the capitals of the Kongo and the Monomotapa, subjected to conditions that led to their disintegration and decline.

The only settlements of urban promise farther in the interior, the capitals of expansive states, still remained sufficiently below the demographic, technological and economic level of the Yoruba or Hausa that they were unable to achieve a comparable level of urbanization.

The Arab–Swahili cities of the east coast of Africa, northern Madagascar (Deschamps, 1965: 44–6) and the Comoros were based on far-flung maritime trading on the one hand and coastal plantation slave economies on the other. They suffered badly at the hands of the Portuguese as we have seen, although they survived on the northern part of the east coast, with the stimulus of new resources and energy from the Omani presence in Zanzibar. Most of them were unable to recapture their pre-Portuguese prosperity. The end of the slave-trade and the colonial partition of Africa deprived them of both political and economic freedom. Steamships made dhows obsolete on the sea, as roads and railways made the caravans obsolete by land. Kilwa, perhaps the greatest of them all, was already in ruins. So also was Gedi. Lamu has remained as an isolated Arab city in a state of deep depression. The remains of the coastal cities of north-west Madagascar have only recently been rediscovered.[1] Mombasa, with its outstanding harbour, was bound to be a factor in any coastal economy. It became for a short time capital of the East Africa Protectorate, the forerunner of Kenya, and remains Kenya's second city and East Africa's greatest port. But its real links with its past are tenuous, and its former Arab ruling élite succumbed not only to British imperialism but to the African nationalism which succeeded it. Dar es Salaam never was an independent Arab city, despite its name. Though chosen by the Sultan of Zanzibar, and temporarily settled on his behalf in the 1870s, its first stable urban settlement came with the German occupation of the 1880s.

Zanzibar City in a sense survived well, prosperous till the mid-twentieth century in its free port and its clove trade, remaining an Arab capital even under imperial protection, though ultimate power had passed to the British and economic dominance to the Indian traders and plantation owners. Eclipse came suddenly with the uprising against the Arabs and the sultanate, which quickly followed the granting of independence by the British. With the Tanzanian merger Zanzibar has become technically its second city; but despite the ousting and liquidation of many Arab families, Zanzibar probably still retains a stronger cultural continuity with its past in its present urban life than

[1] M. P. Vérin of the University of Madagascar has commenced excavation.

236

any other East African city. The capitals of the Comoro Islands are culturally similar, but little information is available on them. Moroni, the capital of Grande Comore, is reported to have 6,000 inhabitants, and Mutsamudu, capital of Anjouan, 3,000. Robineau gives Mutsamudu, Domoni (the ancient capital), Ouani and Moya as the four traditional towns of Anjouan, comprising only 12,000 inhabitants between them (Robineau, 1966: 20). During recent times there have in fact been more Comorians in Zanzibar City itself, as well as in the towns of Majunga and Diego Suarez in northern Madagascar. Mogadishu, as capital of Somalia, represents a convenient fusion between the Islamic culture of the ancient Arab city and the Islamic culture of the Somalis themselves, together now transcending the temporary intervention of half a century of Italian imperialism.

Marginal cases of significance

Between the survival power of the West African cities and the disintegration and decline of nearly all the indigenous settlements of central, eastern and southern Africa which showed the greatest potential for urban development in their traditional state, lies the unusual case of Kampala–Mengo in Uganda, which very adequately illustrates the intermediate range of the polarity. Given the definitive conditions of contact between the Ganda and the British—which are too well known to require repetition here (Fallers, 1964)—the Ganda capital of Mengo, which had never previously remained permanently in one place and was therefore only marginally urban, was able to develop into a truly African urban capital even during the period of imperial protection. It did so, however, as a twin city having as its politically and economically dominant partner the city of Kampala, by origin an expatriate European and Asian settlement (Southall and Gutkind, 1957; Southall, 1967), and now the African capital of independent Uganda.

The peculiarity of conditions that permitted the development of Kampala–Mengo is given further emphasis if one considers other cases which, had the circumstances been equally favourable, might have developed in the same way. We have already noted the relations of early Durban with the capital of the Zulu kings. In another instance, when Rhodes's bands of adventurers arrived to establish themselves in Rhodesia, they inevitably came to treat with Lobengula, the Ndebele

king, at the capital settlement of Gubulawayo founded by his pre-
decessor Mzilikazi. 'This kraal, Gubulawayo as it was always called
then, must have been more than half a mile in diameter, and was said
to have some fifteen or twenty thousand inhabitants. It was entirely
surrounded by a palisade or fence, with four big gates all made of
poles and reeds, laced tightly together and about three or four feet
thick' (Vaughan-Williams, 1947: 96).

The stage was set for the establishment of an expatriate town,
stimulating the parallel growth of an African capital into new urban
dimensions alongside it, as in the case of Kampala/Mengo. But given
the realistic mineral and farming interests of the Europeans and the
lack of effective restraint by themselves or control by any effective
imperial authority, encroachment on African rights, leading to armed
conflict, was the inevitable result. The traditional structure of Ndebele
society and its capital were rudely shattered; and urban growth was
exclusively dominated by European inspiration, with Africans as
lowly second-class participants on sufferance. Bulawayo developed
into an important industrial and communications centre, although
Salisbury became the national capital. The relationship of modern
Bulawayo to the traditional Gubulawayo, although an indisputable
historical fact, therefore means something quite different and much
less than that of Kampala to Mengo.

The same story was enacted with minor variations in many places.
Had the determining conditions more resembled those operative in the
Uganda case, European control of Zambia (Northern Rhodesia) might
have led to the healthy urban development of one of the Lozi capitals
such as Lialui, described in 1899 as 'a large native town of rather a
scattered character, the King's big house standing out from the surrounding huts' (J. P. R. Wallis, ed., *Barotseland journals of James
Stevenson-Hamilton, 1898–9*, London, 1923); whereas, with the diver-
gent mineral attractions of the Copperbelt and Broken Hill, together
with the European settlement and farming opportunities along the
railway line which led to these mining areas, Loziland (Barotseland)
was left as a backwater in respect of political, economic and urban
development.

To make a suggestion of this kind, in relation to a remote spot like
Lialui, in the inaccessible flood plain of the Zambezi, will seem to many
readers the height of unreason. But this only emphasizes the extent
to which we unwittingly concede inevitable primacy to European

interests. Of course, the mining areas east and north were bound to provide a strong base for urbanization, bound to attract railways, roads and airlines to them, bound to concentrate European efforts and investment upon them. This is really the whole point in a nutshell. Human interests could never prevail over economic profit. There were many virtuous government officials, missionaries and educators who certainly tried to do their best (often not very relevant); but where heavy mining interests were concerned, with all their long-term industrial and commercial implications, the human interests of the majority ceased to have much impact and were rarely heard. In the corridors of mineral power, the comfortable faith that European profit and African advancement went hand in hand has never been shaken. In the Barotse case, the kindly preservation of the traditional kingship could conveniently be presented as a local instance of the paramountcy of native interests, while in fact it was a useful pretext for leaving the country undeveloped, thus guaranteeing the Barotse cheap labour supply to the white-dominated mining agricultural economy. This was why little European colonial power was able to be devoted to those experiments in irrigated agriculture and improved cash-crops for Barotseland which could have led to economic growth from within and would have added new economic dimensions to the political capital, thus transforming it into a city. Such a development is only a fantasy, for the reasons stated. That is why we are bound to conclude that the imperial impact on specifically African forms and possibilities of urbanization was inevitably negative or destructive in most cases.

Modern capital cities are developing in newly independent Botswana (Bechuanaland), Lesotho (Basutoland) and Swaziland. Serowe (Ngwato), Kanye (Ngwaketse), Molepolote (Kwena), Mochudi (Kgatla), Ramontsa (Malete), Gaberones (Tlokwa) and Mafeking (Rolong) were remarkably large, dense settlements, concentrating permanent population in the climatically favourable eastern margin, while cattle were pastured over the vast, arid regions to the west. Serowe was largest, with a population of 40,000 (Stevens, 1967: 113), but, by an extraordinary anomaly, the colonial capital of Bechuanaland was Mafeking, actually beyond the frontier in South Africa. Independent Botswana chose Gaberones, smallest of the traditional capitals, but within the frontier, though doubtless favoured because of its situation on the railway, closely accessible to South Africa.

The Lesotho and Swazi capitals do not have this degree of continuity, though Maseru is mentioned as Moshoeshoe's royal palace (Stevens, 1967: 262). It was located at a convenient ford over the Caledon river frontier of South Africa, and became base for Moshoeshoe's British garrison in 1869. Mbabane was capital of British Swaziland, close to the South African border like Maseru and Gaberones; but independent Swaziland chose Lobamba, called after the traditional capital of King Sobhuza I (Kuper, 1970).

The exceptional Addis Ababa, already noted, is neither old nor colonial. Founded on the mountain tops by the Emperor Menelik at the end of the nineteenth century, in the style of the mobile military camps of Ethiopian rulers, and marking the successful southward extension of Amhara domination, it moved down to the more convenient slopes below when military considerations became less immediately pressing. Despite this move it remains the highest capital in Africa and one of its largest cities, with a present population estimated at more than half a million. Outside North Africa it is worth noting as probably the least colonial metropolis in structure and appearance. It must have had a highly dispersed plan from its early beginnings, with the older centres such as the main market and the Imperial Palace already far apart. It has remained ecologically diverse, covering a huge area at relatively low density and retaining many focal points such as the market, the palaces, the modern shopping areas, the city hall, the railway station and the headquarters of the Economic Commission for Africa and the Organization of African Unity, both widely separate from one another and none of them significantly dominant. Between these focal points are large pockets of dense and largely uncontrolled indigenous working-class settlement, not as usual relegated to the peripheries or to any sort of separate cité indigène. The lack of colonial dominance is further expressed in the diversity of European tongues that are prevalent, notably English, French and Italian, in addition to the local Amharic, Galla and other indigenous languages. This pattern of diversity is well capped by what might well be called a diplomatic economy, in which the presence of the United Nations African headquarters, with its considerable staff, and more recently the establishment of the Organization of African Unity, have brought in train the largest diplomatic representation of African countries anywhere in the continent. In countless ways, direct and indirect, this means a boom in building, construction and employment generally, causing a superficial commercial prosperity, which as yet spreads little beyond the city limits.

A final example of a city with indigenous roots, which strikingly illustrates the operation of factors already mentioned, is that of Tananarive, the capital of Madagascar, a city of 300,000 people. Situated in the middle of the island, it was already by the end of the eighteenth century the royal capital of the dominant ethnic group. It became the inevitable goal of foreign traders, missionaries and colonizers, just as the capital of Buganda did in the East African mainland. But the Merina of Tananarive had an even longer period for acquaintance with the impact of Western knowledge and technology before being deprived of their political independence. This factor is crucial. The Ganda had only the period from the 1830s, when the first Arabs reached them, until the declaration of the Protectorate in 1890 with the definitive Agreement following in 1900. But the effective period of assimilation did not begin until the 1870s with the frequent visits and continuous presence of Arabs and Europeans. This period was thus at the most thirty years, but was of vast importance. Tananarive was visited by Europeans as early as 1777, and the period of the continuous presence of Europeans (apart from a few periods of violent rejection) began in the 1820s. Definitive conquest by the French came in 1895, so that there was here a period of some seventy-five years for selective assimilation. The result was that, however great the colonial transformation, the initial period of adjustment occurred, and Tananarive became unquestionably a city while still directly under the authority of its indigenous rulers. By 1828 it is said to have had a population of about 30,000 with 38 schools started by Christian missionaries, including over 2,000 pupils. By the time of conquest the population is estimated to have reached 50,000. The result of this long independent development is that there is no distinct French or European quarter or reservation, no separate *cité indigène* and none of the familiar contours and landmarks of a colonial city. More remarkably, there developed a distinctive style of domestic architecture, which is a genuine hybrid, deriving both from traditional Malagasy and Mediterranean or Colonial Oceanian traditions, and which gives to Tananarive and other towns of the high plateau an original style of indigenous urban life. This reinforces the argument that, for indigenous societies possessing an adequately centralized authority, it was the time allowed for selective assimilation of Western urban culture in its post-industrial form that has been most crucial in permitting continuity and survival.

AIDAN SOUTHALL

The legacy of urbanization imposed upon Africa
by imperialism

Now that I have dealt at some length with the indigenous African urban potential and its treatment at the hands of imperialism, it is time to assess the essential qualities of the foreign urbanization bequeathed by imperialism to Africa.

There were some striking uniformities running through the cities and towns which were more direct creations of colonial imperialism. Despite the contrasts of colonial policy and the varying demands of different areas according to climate, disease and rainfall, or agricultural, pastoral, forestry or mineral resources, some of these uniformities transcended such factors to a surprising degree.

Most noticeable was the *de facto* segregation, in the purely objective sense of physical separation, between predominantly African and predominantly European areas. As is well known, in practice segregation never means separate but equal facilities. Urban segregation in Africa has always been accompanied by differences in the provision of material facilities, such as water and electricity, drainage and sewage, roads, social services and housing itself. Such differences inevitably tell against—and indeed in part create—the poorer areas and populations, which always contain the majority of Africans. For those familiar with the fact that any city shows a differentiation of functional zones and rich and poor areas, and that when markedly different ethnic groups are present they almost invariably show some clustering, this may seem patently obvious; but it has not on the whole been so regarded. In Rhodesia and South Africa it is naturally seen as the direct result of particular policies of racial inequality and discrimination culminating in apartheid. But even in relatively liberal Uganda the metropolis was planned in the first decades of this century to leave unoccupied zones between the areas occupied by Africans, Asians and Europeans, although such a policy of segregation was countermanded by the imperial government after the First World War. Thus, in central, eastern and southern Africa the European areas were established first (necessarily so, if European imperialists required an urban settlement where none was), and the native areas usually took a subordinate place on the outskirts. But in West Africa the process was frequently reversed, and the Europeans established their separate settlement on the outskirts of an older African city. This happened even in the case of a city like

Lagos, which, though essentially African, grew up in direct response to the stimulus of the European coastal trade. However, in all regions of Africa, and in Portuguese, French, British or Belgian-ruled territories alike, the same separation appeared. It is true that there were some differences of nature and degree, in the harshness and rigidity with which the dividing lines were drawn and the rigour with which they were enforced. Kampala–Mengo was again an intermediate case, in that Mengo was already there, as the capital of the Kabaka of Buganda, when the first settlement of Kampala was established on the next hill to it, although Kampala eventually outstripped Mengo in general density and wealth. We have noted Addis Ababa and Tananarive as special exceptions, and Cairo with its long history as much more complex.

Whichever way and within whatever policy the duality arose, it was equally inevitable that the manifestations of Western technology, which were for Africa also the symbols of progress and modernity (however ambivalently they were regarded), should be concentrated mainly in the European sector. This included the largest shops, banks and other businesses; hotels, restaurants and cinemas, the main government offices and the most luxurious residences—hence the vexing post-independence problem of making these concentrations of foreign buildings and institutions look and feel African, even when authority over the city itself is in African hands. As we have seen, Tananarive did succeed in evolving an original hybrid architectural style of its own. Some Yoruba cities have houses in the distinctive style brought by the freed slaves who returned from Brazil, but this is a minor element. The West African cities manifest their Africanness more in their teeming crowds and markets, their distinctive costumes, music and dancing.

A corollary of this duality was the tendency of colonial authorities to treat Africans as if they did not belong in urban areas. In West Africa, where there was already an African urban tradition, this factor did not apply either to the old towns or to the new towns that grew up within the same countries. It was most characteristic of the mine-based towns of southern Africa, where Africans from the rural areas were expected to stay in town only as long as they were employed. There was an implicit lack of tolerance and recognition for African self-employment in hawking, petty trading, repair work, arts and crafts and other minor yet from many points of view desirable forms of entrepreneurship. Likewise women had no right to be in town unless they could prove legitimate employment—usually domestic service to Europeans—or that they had husbands legitimately in town. Such systems applied, with varying strictness and efficacy, in South Africa, Southern and Northern Rhodesia, the Belgian Congo and Kenya. They formed the basis of attempts to control population movement, but where appreciable population pressure built up they never succeeded.

In countries like Uganda and Nyasaland (now Malawi) the urban needs of Africans were also officially ignored until after the Second World War. But this did not reflect any attempt to control population movement or to exclude Africans from urban life. Rather it reflected lack of foresight into the inevitable trend of development. In many territories lacking appreciable mining or other industries, with very low rates of urban African employment until well after the Second World War, there was a general feeling among colonial authorities that urban life was demoralizing to tribal Africans, who therefore should not be exposed to it unnecessarily. Up to a point, tribal kinship and family systems provided social insurance for the unemployed, the aged and the handicapped; for this no substitute was provided in the towns. There was more talk in colonial circles of detribalization as a process of dis-organization harmful to the Africans and troublesome to their European rulers, than of urbanization as a positive process, inevitable in the course of economic and social development.

The same general line of thinking also led to tortuous economic policies that had an important influence on the pattern of urban growth. Thus, in East Africa Asian traders were not usually permitted to establish shops in rural areas, but only in gazetted settlements. Many colonial administrators sincerely believed this to be for the protection of the African population from economic exploitation. The result was to delay the development of African trade and commerce altogether. In theory, Africans had something of a protected rural market. In practice, they came to rely on the nearest Indian trading centre. Trade was thus the more concentrated in foreign hands and in cities, which themselves became that much more inherently foreign. Where there was a strong indigenous trading tradition—owing some of its strength to the long period of adjustment to foreign trade before political subjection to colonial régimes—this polarization did not occur to the same extent, although certain foreign commercial interests were always bound to derive special advantages from the colonial system.

Paradoxically, the countries that were least oppressive and harassing to Africans in towns were also those who did least for them by way of providing housing or any other urban services. The claims so often made for South Africa, Rhodesia and the Belgian Congo that their urban Africans were better cared for than in other countries are whimsical. Where Africans were prohibited or effectively discouraged from owning urban land or property or building for themselves, the Europeans who demanded their labour had no alternative but to provide their accommodation. It is true that in the Belgian Congo relatively high standards of material provision for urban Africans were achieved by civic authorities and large enterprises. This reflected the belief that within reason a healthy, happy, labour force was good for all concerned. There was also a scarcely veiled recognition of participation in an appropriate level of material benefits as a substitute for participation in political power. Unfortunately, as soon as the momentum of rapid urban growth spread all over Africa in the 1950s, none of these countries that had saddled themselves with the obligation of almost total official provision of accommodation for urban Africans was able to fulfil it. They had some fine schemes and good designs but were never able nor willing to afford the quantity required. The overflow population, which they were unable to control, was forced to produce its own shanty-towns and *bidonvilles* in which to live as best it could.

The tendency to regard Africans as properly rural, and to control their presence in towns to that required by employment and labour indispensable to the Europeans themselves, naturally went along with the implicit assumption that all Africans constituted a fairly homogeneous mass, which in any overall status system would not spread beyond the level of peasant cultivators, unskilled workers and much smaller numbers of skilled artisans. This is in no way contradictory with the fact that in the Congo small numbers of Africans were trained to quite high levels of technical and mechanical skill with correspondingly high earnings. The point was that any intrusion of Africans into the urban élite of highly educated and professional persons was never seriously envisaged. No politician who dared to entertain it as more than a piece of verbal deception has survived in power.

It is a very safe generalization that the colonial experience, which has brought a new type of urbanization to African countries, has everywhere subjected the great majority of urban-dwelling Africans to highly unsatisfactory and shameful housing conditions. The economic difficulty of achieving any alternative is very great; hence the new

African nations, which have taken over the reins of government at a period of frighteningly rapid urban expansion, are very unlikely to be able to change these conditions for the majority in the foreseeable future.

The great mining areas, such as the South African Rand, the Copper-belt of Zambia and Katanga in the Congo, certainly could have done better, since housing and living conditions could very well have been made a first charge upon their production. Some mines have indeed produced some worthy housing; but since they are the magnets for vast secondary urbanization extending far beyond the mine compound, they have failed to make any appreciable impact on the whole.

New mining centres in countries that were, colonially speaking, liberal and that have now become independent, such as the diamond-mining town of Mwadui in Tanzania, or the iron-mining town of Lunsar in Sierra Leone, have perhaps been able to achieve most; but these are small by comparison with the older and larger mining areas previously mentioned, which have all become the focus of major urban networks.

The idea that Africans do not rightfully or desirably belong in towns is certainly a popularly held notion in southern Africa and also a reasonable deduction from the actual state of provision for urban Africans. The many official commissions that for more than half a century have sounded warning notes led only to delayed and minor palliative action.

Reader has documented the history of East London, which he says 'is almost certainly typical of the growth of locations in many major urban centers of the Union' (1961: 103-4). From 1928 to 1940 no municipal action was taken in the main African urban location, and efforts since then have only led to the building of a few hundred houses. In 1955 some 11,900 Africans were municipally housed, with an esti-mated 15,000 living on sufferance attached to their employers' premises and the main mass of 42,570 in shacks. Already in 1900 the town clerk of East London had said that 'it is undesirable to have Natives living in the town, as their presence invariably leads to the accumulation of filth and generation of disease, besides being in other respects a great nuisance to the white population' (Reader, 1961: 106). During the First World War the African population had reached 9,500 supplied with water through eleven stand-pipes.

In 1914 the Tuberculosis Commission stated that 'the majority of such locations are a menace to the health of the inhabitants...[It] is with the character of the dwellings that the greatest fault must be found. With few exceptions these are a disgrace, and the majority are quite unfit for human habitation' (Reader, 1961: 106). It seems that since then the situation has expanded rather than improved. 'Every survey of shack townships demonstrates overcrowding. However many houses it were practicable to build for years to come, they would be saturated beyond minimal housing standards, only gradually alleviating the gigantic problem of proper accommodation for the urban Bantu.' 'The implicit principle that the Bantu urban population was temporary, in town only to supply the needs of the whites, not in any way forming an integral part of the community, was central in the view of the authorities. To a certain extent it still is' (Reader, 1961: 12).

It must be noted that this ostrich policy has a further corollary. Decades of demand for skilled labour by whites, reinforced with ameliorative educational efforts by missionary bodies, have, despite all paramount policy to the contrary, produced a sizeable educated middle class, an 'African bourgeoisie' (Kuper, 1965). This bourgeoisie is in Western terms the most urbanized and the most sophisticated in Africa south of the Sahara. Though rejected by the ruling race, segregated and subjected to material deprivation, it includes economically successful individuals of comparative wealth. It has also shown distinctive signs of creativity in literature, music and the arts. The imperial impact must be credited with this unintended success.

The subjection of the majority of urban Africans to slum living in the same cities where whites enjoy one of the highest standards of living in the world is a disgrace, but also a poignant reminder of the intractability of slum conditions in the predominantly Negro areas of all the great cities of the United States. But slums and overcrowding are also a menace in Cairo, Nairobi, Lagos and Accra. In other words, slum living has been conferred upon Africa by the colonial experience and remains prevalent in all the great cities, whether under white or black government, although it seems a greater scandal in the wealthiest mining areas where finance was potentially available. 'In the wealthiest white cities of the South, the flotsam and jetsam of the African proletariat reaches a depth of social and physical degradation unknown elsewhere' (Reader, 1961: 120–2).

In the view of many, including the present writer, the only hope of relieving the housing shortage and indirectly reducing the slum problem in most African cities is by providing adequate quantities of land and harnessing to the task of construction the energies of African entrepreneurs and of the very people who need housing. However, under government encouragement and supervision, this is virtually impossible where Africans are precluded from rights to urban land and where their political influence is negligible. It is also perhaps impossible in the very greatest cities, where any land values within a tolerable distance may be prohibitive, unless past policy has already resulted in an enormously sprawling and relatively low density urban area, as seems to be the case with Addis Ababa and Kinshasa (Léopoldville). In 1960 the latter city already spread over an area of 100 square kilometres, and its present effective area is certainly very much greater. In 1960 density was 3,800 per sq. km. compared with the Lagos density of 5,600 per sq. km. (Comhaire, 1961). The government of the Belgian Congo made exceptional efforts in developing *cités africaines* outside Léopoldville (Kinshasa), but still could not keep pace with the flow of immigration. Already by 1945 the excess population had successfully begun to take over new areas for settlement by illegal squatting. The process has continued, swelling to vast proportions during the troubled period after independence. These huge squatter settlements call to mind the *barriadas* of Lima and the *favelas* of Rio de Janeiro.

Comhaire is able to sum up the housing situation in both Léopoldville and Lagos, despite their rather radical differences of origin, history and political context, by saying that 'the authorities seem to be incapable of providing sufficient, or, what is more important, cheap enough housing' (Comhaire, 1961).

The impact of the colonial empires has thus been, on the negative side, to develop in African cities most of the social evils characteristic of the poorer areas of Western cities during the industrial period. Not only were no answers found, but the independent successor governments are finding these problems equally insoluble.

An oft-noted legacy of imperialism is the fact that African countries that owed their creation to the expansionism of European powers were inevitably outward-looking, towards the metropole, rather than inward-looking, towards their hinterlands. The vast majority of countries that border the sea have coastal capitals, convenient for trade with the metropole, but often most inconveniently sited as national centres, with their hinterlands consequently remaining very isolated. Dahomey, Togo and Ghana are striking examples, but also Liberia,

Sierra Leone, Tanzania and Moçambique. Independent African countries have made great efforts to correct the economic emphasis in the direction of mobilizing their internal resources for the benefit of their inhabitants, but they are stuck with the capital cities that their colonizers developed; and these cities continue to grow at a rate disproportionate with that of the rest of their countries and of the other towns in them.[1] A further corollary is that international communications, which to a large extent are communications between capital cities, are still hampered by illogical gaps, detours and discontinuities resulting from the overriding past concern with metropolitan connections. New roads and air-routes have improved matters, but the general pattern of communication between the great cities of Africa remains irrational, at least in terms of the stated aspirations of the African countries themselves. The external trade, which is such an important aspect of the life of these great cities, also continues to follow metropolitan channels to an extraordinary degree, with most of the Francophone countries in particular seeming incapable of cutting this umbilical cord.

It is not possible to say much effectively about the smaller cities and towns, in their enormous number and variety, for very little has been published on them and our account has had to concentrate inordinately upon capital cities. However, despite the pre-colonial cities, especially in West Africa, the mining towns, the ports that are not capitals and the numerous other instances of specialized economic function, the vast majority of small African towns owe their origin to colonial administrative convenience and are solely derived from the regional, provincial and district headquarters of the colonial era. Though they were often chosen and sited by administrators with obvious practical considerations in mind, they have tended to determine the subsequent pattern of communications and economic development rather than the other way round.

We have considered the impact of imperialism upon urban development in Africa mainly in the context of two questions. What effect did imperialism have upon pre-existing cities or near approaches to cities? And what was the difference of impact upon Africans of the cities which imperialism itself brought? In a sense, urbanization in its modern form now appears to have been one of the most important and lasting aspects

---

[1] W. Hance, 1960: 136, 'considerable growth of inland cities may be expected as internal exchange, now relatively unimportant, increases, and as general economic growth proceeds'.

of the imperial impact. But in this general sense urbanization in Africa is far too vast a subject to be properly considered here. We must endeavour to concentrate on those aspects that seem most specifically linked to imperialism and most distinctive of Africa. We have given most attention to the impact of imperialism upon pre-existing cities and upon the progress of those tentative steps towards urban life that were being taken in many indigenous African societies, because this seems the most fundamentally important part of the question. The second question is much more involved with the general problem of urbanization in the modern world and the reactions of Africans to it.

As to the first question, we have suggested some broad variables which seem to be of general validity. Imperialism usually seems to have had a destructive effect on indigenous urbanization and steps towards it except where certain conditions were fulfilled. The survival of such indigenous forms depended upon the size and density, the age and permanence of the indigenous settlement, the scale of the society of which it was a part, and the extent of its centralized political power, and the period allowed for selective assimilation, during which Western technology was presented in its general aspects without immediately depriving the indigenous society of its political independence. These factors were closely interlocked. There were no indigenous settlements of any great size except in the framework of political centralization. Indeed they were almost invariably capitals, and in many notable instances city-states. The greater their size and power, the better their chance of dealing with imperial invaders on terms of near equality and the more likelihood of successful delaying tactics providing a period of selective assimilation and adjustment while retaining political independence. A fairly unhealthy climate from the European point of view, and absence of readily exploitable mineral resources were additional favourable factors. Where a combination of these various conditions permitted the survival, growth and transformation of an indigenous community, there was obviously greater continuity and integration, with less acute problems of culture and identity.

Conclusions

As has been shown with numerous examples, Western imperialism had a negative and destructive impact upon many of those lines of development in African society which could have led towards the foundation of urban living properly rooted in African culture. Its impact must be considered far more positive and beneficial in those fewer cases where indigenous forms had the strength, in terms of the factors indicated, to survive and adapt to the onslaught, selecting and incorporating new elements in a continuous process of transformation, without losing their roots in the general culture of the people.

We now come to the second question, that of the Western urban way of life which has been imposed from without upon millions of Africans without their having an effective choice in the matter. Intrinsically, this urbanization is that of the Western world in general and requires no further exploration here. We cannot properly speak of this as the imperial impact upon urban development in Africa. Rather it is the urban aspect of the imperial impact upon Africa. Certainly the social and physical conditions of Africa in confrontation with its imperial invaders have imposed distinctive characteristics upon Western urbanization in Africa, which recur widely despite regional variations. This, then, is the impact of Africa upon imperial or colonial urban development. The study of African urbanization is relatively recent and still patchy, but already sufficiently voluminous to make adequate treatment of its results impracticable here. Only the most salient features can be mentioned.

We have so far laid most emphasis on the notorious segregation and relative deprivation imposed upon Africans by this form of urbanization. The two other paramount factors are that these towns have been recruited by migration from very diverse ethnic groups. Vast complexities are involved in this simple statement: unequal sex ratios, preponderance of able-bodied men, relaxing of sexual, marital and family regulations, instability of urban residence and consequently of almost every other feature of urban life, ethnic diversity spelling linguistic confusion and lack of cultural integration. Many of these must be relatively transitory phenomena, though they weigh heavily during the period of their transience. Furthermore, most of the former characteristics, though not the latter two, marked early nineteenth-century industrialization in Western Europe; but the context and the outcome were both very different from those of the African situation. We must be careful. People communicate despite linguistic diversity. Many languages are impoverished and some may in the long run be enriched. Social life is not strictly speaking chaotic, for people manage to live and to create the organization necessary for their survival. But it is fair to say that the imposed urbanization of which we are speaking has inhibited the finer flowering of cultural originality. But even where conditions are adverse, they have sometimes been sufficiently stable to produce worth while and original expressions of culture out of the stimulus of adversity, as was suggested in the unusual case of the South African bourgeoisie.

The impact of imperialism and the experience of colonialism conferred on Africa the equivocal benefits of modern urbanization. These were particularly equivocal in Africa because they have not yet brought to Africans, except to a tiny minority, the wealth and amenities which they imply in developed countries. For most African peoples it meant a rather sudden transition from primeval subsistence living to participation, however marginal, in twentieth-century urban and industrial life. The less preparation permitted by the situation, in the way of selective assimilation over a protracted period, the more devastating this experience was bound to be.

It is difficult for the social historian to escape a feeling of inevitability. Given the conditions of the nineteenth-century world, it was inconceivable that the vast remaining portions of primeval Africa should have been left in isolation to work out over further centuries their slow accommodation with the outside world. It seems inevitable that modern urban living should have been transmitted to sub-Saharan Africa by foreigners. Whatever regret there may be that this was done by Europeans, whose obtrusive difference of race, culture and technological power made antagonism inevitable and rapid integration impossible, the facts of history have to be recognized. The nearest alternative which it is possible to imagine is that the process should have been carried out by the Arab and Muslim peoples of North Africa, Egypt and the east coast. It is useless to follow such an unreal hypothesis to its logical conclusions, but there can be little confidence that the results would have been any more beneficial in the long run. The Africans of the Southern Sudan are no happier with the northern Sudanese Muslims than the Africans of Moçambique or Rhodesia are with their European overlords.

For better or worse the imperial intervention created the new African nations, with their capital cities and their small towns, their ports, mines, industries, commerce and communications centres. The same is true in all major fields of activity: the new religion of the Christian missions, the schools and colleges, the legal and administrative systems, the literature and the whole basic technology. These great gifts were spoilt by being conferred willy-nilly, with some arguable exceptions (such as the Ganda people inviting in the missionaries through their Kabaka and Henry Stanley). But they were gifts that no African now wishes to forswear. There is no quick or complete intellectual answer to this major dilemma of our times, only the answer of human sympathy and of humbly facing the problems of a shrunken world in which Africa can neither be evaded nor escape. At the end of the Development Decade it can now be seen that the independent nations of tropical Africa show no sign of catching up on the affluence of the West or even of narrowing the gap. Their relatively affluent élites have increased in number, but there is no evidence that the average material well-being of the masses has risen. It is pointless to apportion blame for this depressing situation between unfavourable terms of trade, dwindling foreign aid, lack of necessary skills, unwillingness to control population growth, or any of the myriad other detailed factors. The African peoples have been drawn into an urban industrial civilization whose benefits may not decisively outweigh its costs for the majority of them, let alone compensate their sense of relative deprivation vis-à-vis the rich nations. In a technologically united world it may become as impossible for rich nations to evade the external demands of poor nations as the internal demands of poor citizens. In an age of nuclear proliferation the former demands may even be more dangerous, and may have to be satisfied by the rich nations simply as the price of survival, at which point the precise allocation of causes and responsibilities and praise or blame becomes irrelevant.

BIBLIOGRAPHY

Abu Lughod, J. (1967). 'Migrant adjustment to city life: the Egyptian case', *American Journal of Sociology*, **67**.

Arkell, A. J. (1955). *A history of the Sudan*. University of London.

Axelson, E. (1940). *South-East Africa, 1488–1530*. London.

(1960). *The Portuguese in South-East Africa, 1600–1700*. Johannesburg, Witwatersrand University Press.

Balandier, G. (1965). *La vie quotidienne au royaume de Kongo du XVIe au XVIIIe siècle*. Paris.

Bascom, W. (1955). 'Urbanization among the Yoruba', *American Journal of Sociology*, **60**.

Bradbury, R. (1957). *The Benin kingdom, Ethnographic survey of Africa, Western Africa*, part 13. London, International African Institute.

Comhaire, J. (1961). 'Leopoldville and Lagos', *Economic Bulletin of Africa*, **2**.

Cuvelier, J. (1946). *L'ancien royaume de Congo*. Bruges.

Deschamps, H. (1965). *Histoire de Madagascar*. Paris.

Duarte Barbosa (1866). *Description of the coasts of East Africa and Malabar*. Trans. by H. E. J. Stanley. London, Hakluyt Society.

Duffy, J. (1962). *Portugal in Africa*. Cambridge, Harvard University Press.

Fagan, B. (1966). *Southern Africa during the Iron Age*. New York.

Fage, J. D. (1955). *An introduction to the history of West Africa*. Cambridge University Press.

Fallers, L. A., ed. (1964). *The king's men*. London, Oxford University Press for the East African Institute of Social Research.

Gann, L. H., and P. Duignan (1962). *White settlers in tropical Africa*. Harmondsworth, Middlesex.

Gutkind, P. C. W. (1963). *The royal capital of Buganda*. The Hague.

Hance, W. (1960). 'The economic location and functions of tropical African cities', *Human Organization*, **19**.

Kuper, H. (1970). Personal communication.

Kuper, L. (1965). *An African bourgeoisie*. New Haven, Yale University Press.

Lloyd, P. C. (1953). 'Craft organization in Yoruba towns', *Africa*, **23**.
  (1965). 'The Yoruba', in *Peoples of Africa*, J. Gibbs, ed. New York.
  ed. (1966). *The new élites of tropical Africa*. Oxford University Press.

Low, D. A., and R. C. Pratt (1960). *Buganda and British overrule, 1900–1955*. London, Oxford University Press for the East African Institute of Social Research.

Meillasoux, C. (1965). 'The social structure of modern Bamako', *Africa*, **35**.

Mercier, Paul, L. Massé and A. Hauser (1954). 'Aspects de la société africaine dans l'agglomération dakaroise', *Etudes Sénégalaises*, **5**.

Miner, H. (1953). *The primitive city of Timbuctoo*. Princeton University Press for the American Philosophical Society.

Oliver, R., and J. D. Fage (1962). *A short history of Africa*. Harmondsworth, Middlesex.

Pigafetta, F. (1881). *A report of the kingdom of Congo and of the surrounding countries, drawn out of the writings of the Portuguese, Duarte Lopez*. Trans. by Marguerite Hutchinson. London (first publ. Rome, 1591).

Priestley, M. (1966). 'The emergence of an élite: a case study of a west coast family', in *The new élites of tropical Africa*, P. C. Lloyd, ed. Oxford University Press.

Reader, D. H. (1961). *The black man's portion*. Cape Town, Oxford University Press.

Robineau, C. (1966). *Société et économie d'Anjouan (Océan Indien)*. Paris, ORSTOM (Office de la Recherche Scientifique et Technique Outre-Mer).

Schapera, I. (1943). *Native land tenure in the Bechuanaland Protectorate*. Lovedale, South Africa.

— (1956). *Government and politics in tribal societies*. London.

Skinner, E. (1964). *The Mossi of the Upper Volta*. Stanford University Press.

Southall, A. W. (1967). 'Kampala-Mengo', in *The city in modern Africa*, H. Miner, ed. New York.

— ed. (1961). *Social change in modern Africa*. London, Oxford University Press.

Southall, A.W., and P. C. W. Gutkind (1957). *Townsmen in the making*. London. (East African Studies, no. 9.)

Stevens, R. P. (1967). *Lesotho, Botswana and Swaziland*. New York.

Tardits, C. (1958). *Porto Novo*. Paris.

UNESCO (1956). *Social implications of urbanization and industrialization in Africa south of the Sahara*.

Vansina, J. (1966). *Kingdoms of the savannah*. Madison, University of Wisconsin Press.

Vaughan-Williams, H. (1947). *A visit to Lobengula in 1889*. Pietermaritzburg.

Wallis, J. P. R., ed. (1923). *Barotseland journals of James Stevenson-Hamilton, 1898-9*. London.

CHAPTER 8

URBANIZATION AND THE COLOUR LINE IN AFRICA

by

MICHAEL BANTON

A sociological or social anthropological approach to race relations in Africa can profitably look for guidance to analyses of race relations in the United States. In the first place, the American studies include a series of outstanding monographs, deriving from the work of John Dollard, W. Lloyd Warner, Gunnar Myrdal and many others. Their books do not stand alone. They form part of a tradition of analysis which, subjected to criticism from varying standpoints, has developed considerable intellectual rigour and has been supplemented by the researches of historians, economists and scholars from outside the sociological field. In the second place, the American race relations scene is much simpler than the African. In the Southern states especially there are only two major groups interacting within a fairly coherent overall political order. In Africa, by contrast, race relations tend to be confounded with cultural, political, economic and other factors and the various groups do not interrelate within so integrated a social system. Consequently it is more difficult to detect significant patterns in the accounts of African race relations; and the observer is more inclined to conclude—wrongly, I believe—that the only intellectually satisfactory approach is the historical study of the development of race relations within particular territories.

Wishing to present a synoptic view of the structures of race relations in the towns of colonial Africa, I therefore propose to utilize what to the historian would seem an outrageously simple model of group relations borrowed from American social anthropology, and to see how closely the African evidence can be fitted around it. The use of this sort of simplification can be defended as providing the reader with a rough chart to help him plot partially-explored territory; it suggests which may be the more significant trends, and it poses questions for further investigation.

One fundamental assumption must be explained first of all. The general pattern which this essay envisages is one of acculturation. Europeans, Africans and other sociocultural groups are pictured as meeting, influencing one another, and then with economic development being drawn into an overarching political order based firstly upon a world market economy and secondly upon territorial political considerations. Initially separate groups have slowly interpenetrated one another. Settler governments have opposed this process; but industrialization and urbanization have tended, in the long run and with several qualifications, to produce a more integrated social system based upon social criteria inconsistent with racial discrimination. Patterns of race relations in colonial Africa were influenced appreciably by the contrary pulls of minority politics and industrialization. Ruling minorities sought to divide and to keep their societies pluralistic, while the economic tendencies promoted a unitary social order; the conflicts between the two were usually most apparent in the towns.

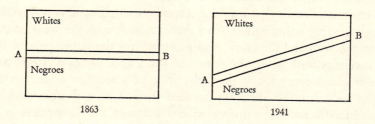

1863   1941

The simplest race relations structures are the two-category systems, such as that described for Mississippi. All members of the society are assigned, from the moment they enter it, to one of two categories. Skin colour or other racial features are used as signs of the individual's category; as his membership in one or the other category determines a man's rights and obligations in most of the social relationships open to him, it constitutes a basic role. However a man may think of himself, if he is assigned to one such category, there are very strong pressures upon him to play the appropriate role. The physical marks of race are thus used as role signs (Banton, 1965). Lloyd Warner represents this state of affairs with a diagram in which the line *AB* denotes what has been variously called the 'colour line', 'caste line' or 'status gap'. It expresses the practice whereby the lowest member of the upper group is ranked (for certain purposes at least) above the highest member of the lower group. Warner holds that at the end of the Civil War the colour line was in approximately a horizontal position and that subsequently it has moved round diagonally. In Natchez, Mississippi, in the late 1930s, while all Negroes were socially inferior and categorically subordinate to all whites in colour caste, a growing number were superordinate by social class criteria to many, if not most, whites (Davis and Gardner, 1941: 10; Warner, 1952: 17–19).

Which social systems in colonial Africa have resembled that of the Deep South? A short answer would be to name those territories where white settlers established themselves. A distinction between a 'tropical dependency' and a true colony or settler colony was, in fact, drawn at an early stage. Sir Harry Johnston, for example, believed that tropical Africa between the Zambezi and the Atlas must be ruled by whites, developed by Indians, and worked by blacks. In 1897 he held that in such regions where 'we merely impose our rule to secure a fair field and no favour for all races, and inferentially for our own trade, there the local government must depend directly on London'. This policy was contrasted with that for 'districts where...climatic considerations encourage true colonization, (for) there undoubtedly the weakest must go to the wall and the black man must pay for the unprogressive turn his ancestors took some thousands of years ago' (Mason, 1958: 214). In a tropical dependency the behaviour of European administrators might be relatively altruistic because there was a double division: between Africans and Europeans; and between the Europeans in the dependency and the officials in Whitehall. The administrators were employed in a colonial bureaucracy and, according to their success in implementing the policy formulated by their superiors, they might either be transferred to another territory on promotion or moved away from a district in which they had built up local ties and interests. Their primary allegiance was owing to the Crown, and they were not allowed to let other loyalties interfere. Paternalism was evident in legislation prohibiting aliens from acquiring permanent land rights and in preventing competition between Europeans and Africans (Hailey, 1938: 825–7). In the settler colony, however, the majority of Europeans could not anticipate any postings to other territories or any civil service pension. They had invested their capital in their farms, their enterprises and their homes; and without the power to defend their interests, they could lose everything. Political relations within the ruling minority therefore put local interests before imperial ones and minority interests before majority ones. In the early stages of the growth of some colonies the European minority was united by a stronger sense of opposition to the metropolitan power than by any conflict with the indigenous peoples (the Dutch at the Cape often exemplified this proposition). The colonists demanded liberty from rule by officials without envisaging any comparable liberty for the *indigènes*. When, under colonial rule, a settler community became numerous and well established, its outlook often influenced the views of the officials. The development of a two-category system can be discerned in the history of political alignment in the Republic of South Africa, where the white groups have been drawn together in an ever more solid alliance; though it has been in the interest of the whites to keep the subordinate racial groups divided, the white alliance has forced these other groups to move closer to one another in the direction of a single, homogeneous 'non-white' category. But a simpler and more immediate parallel to American experience may be found in the case of Rhodesia.

Characteristics of the colour line

Rhodesia provides the only clear example among the British African colonies of a society in which there was a definite colour line from the beginning. Some colonies, like Kenya and Zambia, seemed at times to be heading in the same direction but were drawn back by the tide of African nationalism. Yet other colonies, like Uganda and much of British West Africa, approximated to the idea of the tropical dependency; they were governed by officials, admitted very few people who could be counted as white settlers and, though they displayed varied forms of racial discrimination, never developed the two-category social system of the dominative order.

It is possible to speak of Southern Rhodesia (now Rhodesia) as a single society comprising both Europeans and Africans from the 1890s onwards. In 1893 Jameson entered Bulawayo at the head of a military force. In 1898 Her Majesty's government established a Legislative Council in Southern Rhodesia on which the European settlers were represented, serving with officials appointed by the Crown, but the territory was not directly subject to the Crown. It was under the control of the British South Africa Company, a private company operating under a royal charter of 1889, and did not become a colony until 1923 (when the whites voted against incorporation into the Union of South

Africa, and in favour of the ending of company rule in exchange for the status of a partially independent colony). At the birth of Southern Rhodesia as a distinctive society, the whites and the Africans were far apart. The status gap between them was not the result of social contrivance but a reflection of the greater military power of the whites and of their command of skills with a much higher market value.

In all the African territories there were from the earliest periods of contact changes which made for a filling in of the gap between the groups. Like nature, society abhors a vacuum. Some Africans adopted European ways. They were often encouraged to do so, for there was a pressing demand for interpreters, clerks, policemen, telegraphists, catechists, craftsmen and other trained personnel whose assistance might enable European skills to be more economically deployed (Gann, 1958: 39–40). Some Europeans took native wives or concubines. Some intermediate groups grew by immigration, like the Lebanese in West Africa, the Arabs on the east coast and the Indians in several territories that were at one time under British administration. In Rhodesia there was a demand for native auxiliaries and there was miscegenation; but the relative separateness of the white and African populations, the pattern of settlement, and the absence of any significant intermediate group meant that the gap was not rapidly filled in.

The maintenance of a colour line depends upon the transmission of status from one generation to another, so that a child remains in the category into which it is born. When a child's parents belong to different categories an anomalous situation arises: all such children need to be allocated unequivocally to one category or the other and, as analysis of racial status in the Deep South shows, the logic of domination favours their ascription to the lower category. In Rhodesia, though the children of white fathers and African mothers have received many privileges, their place has been on the African side of the colour line; and their very presence causes some Europeans to feel uneasy (Keatley, 1963: 259). Another possible threat to a pattern of inherited racial status is posed by an economic overlap. Commenting on Rhodesian politics before World War I, Philip Mason writes: 'This was one strand of argument in the continuous debate: "Preserve the gap—and to preserve it, make sure the native does not advance"'. He refers to a report from 1918 which describes white farmers' disapproval of the selling to Africans of European cattle as breeding stock; at a meeting it was pointed out that such sales were not in violation of the law—as if the farmers thought they should be (Mason, 1958: 253, 265). From the same standpoint, an educated African was also a social anomaly. In 1903 a Rhodesian legislator asserted that 'the uneducated native was the most honest, trustworthy and useful', and this sentiment has been echoed by many settlers over the decades. The status gap in a two-category social system is reinforced by an etiquette of subordination, and in this respect also practice in Rhodesia resembles that in the Deep South and in South Africa. Whites have generally withheld the titles 'Mr' and 'Mrs' from Africans, preferring to say 'boy' or use first names (for a general review cf. Rogers and Frantz, 1962: 208–22). An earlier law making punishable any 'contemptuous behaviour' on the part of an African towards a native commissioner has recently been extended to authorize imprisonment for any African who says or does anything likely to bring an official or a government department into disrepute or contempt. What constitutes actionable behaviour is not easy to define, and the effect of such legislation is often more extensive than was originally intended (cf. Franck, 1960: 105).[1] Rhodesian whites watch carefully lest educated Africans should secure exemption from the racial etiquette. Commenting upon the Europeans' 'preference for the uneducated African' one author testifies that many civil servants go as far as they can to avoid making any concession to the better-educated African. He states that the chief native commissioner told him in 1949 that it was his policy to make no distinction between educated and uneducated Africans. If any of them wanted to sit down in his office they sat on the floor (Gussman, 1962: 102). This does not obtain today (Gann, 1968).

The forces that operate to keep the colour line distinct also tend to keep it horizontal. White supremacy is dependent upon white solidarity, and this can be achieved only at a price paid by one or more of the conflicting interests within the white category. While the Deep South and South Africa show in many circumstances a clear opposition between black and white, Southern Rhodesia for many years could not afford so deep a cleavage and sought to avoid it. The metropolitan connection, with its liberal strands, was cultivated the more because of the apprehensions aroused by Afrikaner nationalism and the strength of the Afrikaner element within the white population. Yet since World

[1] Since the beginning of the century there has been a substantial increase in the willingness of Europeans to accept the idea of racial equality in certain defined respects, but some sources suggest bias.

War II the logic of the two-category system has forced events to follow the path taken by the other white supremacy societies. To further the interests of the ruling minority it has been thought necessary to subsidize European immigration very heavily indeed relative to the country's budget. To induce Europeans to come in sufficient numbers it has been necessary to pay men with little skill at artificially high wage rates, thus giving them as strong an interest as any other European in the existing order. Because the electorate has been virtually confined to Europeans, the real opposition has been excluded from political bargaining. So the only electoral tactic that offers any prospect of success is the claim to be the most effective champion of European interests against the real, if suppressed, threat of an African take-over (Leys, 1959: 292). British immigrants, whatever their previous politics, have taken over with alacrity the intransigent attitude towards the Africans, and their numbers have swamped the influence of men from established Rhodesian families, men economically and socially more secure. This growing pressure from the right influenced the governing party for many years; and since the defeat of Mr Garfield Todd as premier and the rapid succession to that office of Sir Edgar Whitehead, Mr Winston Field and Mr Ian Smith (who made the illegal declaration of independence in November 1965), it has been clear that white solidarity is to be founded on right-wing extremism. Yet further changes in the power structure are possible. It may be that, reacting to external pressure, the Rhodesian settler group may seek more actively to divide the African opposition and to detach groups willing to collaborate with them.

The etiquette that regulates race relations controls the behaviour of members of the upper category as well as the lower. To preserve their privileged position members of the ruling minority must be able to exercise supervision over their own number. The immigrant who comes out to a position of power in a new society has the opportunity to behave in a despotic and libertine fashion which can be in accord with powerful unconscious desires (Mannoni, 1956). The group therefore elaborates informal controls, chief among them being self-segregation, which not only protects its monopoly of power, but makes the immigrant more dependent upon the approval of the other members of his racial category. The standardization of relations with members of the lower category makes it more difficult for super-ordinates to deviate from the expected pattern as well as for the subordinates. Though sexual relations between members of the two categories may be tolerated at first, disapproval grows. A ruling minority often needs a mystique of being different, and this may be destroyed by a proclivity for sexual liaisons with native women. In Kipling's story *The man who would be king* a European rules over people in a distant region who believe him to be a god until he takes a wife from among them, when they recognize him for a man and revolt. The Rhodesian nationalist leader, the Rev. Ndabaningi Sithole, has said that Europeans' liaisons with African women in his country had this sort of effect (1959: 152–3); yet it may be doubted if the controls imposed by the European community are motivated by a concern for their racial mystique. The objection is more likely to stem from the undesired social consequences of such unions: the anomalous children and the difficulty Europeans would have in maintaining an impersonal distance in relations with Africans if in between times they were on such familiar terms with their sisters. Once there is a fair proportion of women in the minority community, they increase the social pressures upon non-conforming males.

In two-category racial systems skin colour acquires tremendous significance as a guarantee of the social order, and further associations are added to it. A bare statement about the white use of political power to maintain their privileges is therefore insufficient in that it does not throw enough light upon the motivations of the whites in the use of their power. They would represent their actions as guided by a desire to establish high standards of individual performance and integrity ('civilized values'), and this element is not to be dismissed as a simple rationalization. Moreover, the whites are subject to powerful cultural conditioning from their exposed political position; and this conditioning represents their objectives in an idiom that makes them seem more acceptable morally. They interpret their shared determination to defend the prevailing order as evidence of a collective 'will to survive' or 'instinct of self preservation'—a mode of expression that sounds the more reasonable in a post-Darwinian culture.

The desire to preserve their privileged position induces the minority to impose controls upon those of their number whose actions might lead to a diminution in the prestige attaching to a 'white' complexion. Thus in the early days of Northern Rhodesia (now Zambia) licences were refused to white traders with insufficient capital (Gann, 1958: 153). Elsewhere immigrants who could not live in the expected manner were repatriated by their fellows. The same consideration may affect even the cinema; in Rhodesia the quality of the films shown to Africans, almost always cowboy epics, has been very poor and the story often difficult to follow since the films themselves are sometimes heavily cut. Africans were not supposed to see Europeans behaving in a disreputable fashion, and this sometimes eliminated much of the plot (Gussman, 1962: 85). Within the upper category of a society threatened by an encircling majority there is often more social equality and good fellowship than in a society based on a class hierarchy, for this is but one mode of reinforcing group solidarity.[1] Another aspect of the same feature is the pressure for conformity (Rogers and Frantz, 1962: 121–4). This is highlighted by the popular objections to investigations by social scientists whether they examine the Africans' social life or the attitudes of Europeans. Thus a leading article in the *Central African Post* in 1953 complained:

In the name of science certain Englishmen enter this country to make exhaustive studies of the customs and habits of African tribes and in the process they conduct themselves in such a way that they lose the deference traditionally accorded to White men by Africans...The so-called scientists...who, from the very nature of their studies are usually advanced politicians, like to live as closely to the African way of life as they can...Frankly we think that much of this anthropological or sociological study is 'hooey'...When Africans see European scientific men, who are considered by them to be a better type of European, behaving as if they were Africans, then they lose their respect and deference for all Europeans...Moreover, such sociologists can disturb the political atmosphere of the country. They can give Africans 'wrong ideas'. They treat them as if they were a grown-up responsible community when they are not...We do not ask sociologists to be Tories. They can be Communists if they like, but they should behave like responsible Europeans during their investigations...(quoted Richmond, 1961: 152–3).

When two social psychologists (one an American) commenced a highly sophisticated study of European attitudes, a Rhodesian M.P., newspaper editorialists and correspondents were quick to condemn it as unscientific, to tell Americans to solve their own racial problems first, and to

[1] From the beginning, Europeans needed to stand by each other. A traveller observed in 1881, 'A Kafir who is owed money by one Englishman, perhaps the wages for a year's work, will take a letter without a murmur, to another Englishman hundreds of miles away, if he is told by his master that, upon delivering the letter, he will receive his payment' (Gann, 1965: 47).

insist that the money would be better spent 'in more practical directions' (Rogers and Frantz, 1962: 366–74). The criticism experienced by
teachers at the University College of Rhodesia and Nyasaland who
sought the kind of freedom of expression taken for granted in industrial
democracies is further evidence of the pressure to conformity on social
and political issues.

To defend their own position, the lower members of the upper
category mobilize as much pressure as possible upon any of the upper
members of the lower category whose actions appear to push the
colour line away from the horizontal. In Rhodesia the claims—or
alleged claims—of African political leaders were vehemently disparaged
by the lower whites and it became quite common for all whites to
dismiss the opposition of African leaders to federation as the agitations
of self-seekers who thought their prospects of office would be worse
under that political order. In November 1956 one of the two African
representatives of Southern Rhodesia in the Federal Parliament 'called
at the Post Office for a parcel and was told by a clerk that he must
"show his *situpa* (certificate) like all the other boys"' (Mason, 1960:
180). This incident, at a time when Southern Rhodesians hoped the
Africans would accept federation, provoked shock and concern. A new
scheme was introduced to mitigate the operation of the pass laws for
the African graduate, though it remained an offence for even the
African Federal M.P. to be without his comprehensive document.
Subsequently there were further attempts to reduce what were called
the 'pinpricks' of segregation. The pass laws were repealed. Yet the
etiquette governing interpersonal relations between members of the
two categories is not just a matter of individual goodwill; it is a part of
a system of relations and cannot be modified unless other factors are
changed too. An interracial etiquette is necessary to the maintenance
of a status gap.

It is right to recognize that 'race relations' in Africa are relations
between categories of people distinguished by more points of difference
than race, such as economic relations, cultural relations and class
relations as well. Yet the Rhodesian case shows that it is also necessary
to appreciate that the significance attributed to racial background in a
two-category social order introduces elements of much greater social
rigidity than are characteristic of these other kinds of social relations.
The sequence of events in Rhodesia, and the attitudes of the ruling
minority, are illuminated by comparisons with the Southern United

States and with South Africa. In Rhodesia Indians have been able to establish themselves as an intermediary group only by confining their activities quite closely to trading. Structurally it is a simpler pattern than that of South Africa, and more closely resembles the Deep South. Developmentally, the illegal declaration of independence corresponds not with 1772 but with the assertion of white supremacy in the South after the era of Reconstruction.

Urbanization in two-category systems

In the Deep South the colour line has moved round towards the diagonal. Why have the pressures described above not kept it horizontal? Warner represented the tilting of the line as an historical process outside the realm of sociological analysis. He did not inquire into the structural conditions necessary to permit a change in the line's angle. If the line moves from the horizontal, this means there must be circumstances in which a white man has to decide whether to interpret his relation to a Negro in colour-caste terms and treat him as a subordinate, or in class terms and treat him as a social superior. Close study of the evidence presented reveals that such a choice could present itself in urban rather than in rural communities and in business relationships, not social ones (Davis and Gardner, 1941: 53–6, 457–67). The higher posts to which Negroes had attained tended to be in new enterprises, to entail only impersonal relations with whites, or to be in positions which catered to a coloured clientele and therefore had no implications for the white community. The towns of rural Mississippi are small; both inside them and outside, white supremacy has been tempered by the flexibility in interpersonal behaviour which personal acquaintance makes possible, but, and for the same reasons, white control of Negro behaviour has been very close. The growth of larger towns has permitted the division of social life into relatively independent compartments, segments or spheres within which Negroes can attain higher positions because they climb at the expense of other Negroes and are not placed in a master-servant relationship to whites. This can happen because the norms of racial subordination are defined as regulating only certain kinds of contacts between whites and Negroes, and the proportion of contacts exempt from such norms (e.g., routine meetings between persons driving automobiles) has been increasing. In South Africa urbanization has not had this result. Blacks and whites start off from separate communities with different languages and cultures. Urbanization brings the two groups together on a segregated basis; it entails a considerable measure of economic integration and a smaller one of social integration. The more productive economic system brings the urban African a higher standard of living in material terms, but there is no tilting of the colour line, which remains firmly horizontal. The concentration of Africans in urban locations has hitherto enabled the whites to exercise a closer control over their behaviour than has been possible or thought desirable in the country districts. Possibly the segmental character of urban living in South Africa with its almost separate white and black towns will after a time make governmental control of African life more difficult, but the position does not yet show any resemblance to that described for the Deep South.

Urbanization in Rhodesia has followed the South African pattern both in its course and in its effects. It should also be noted that British colonial theory was never well adapted to the problems of urban administration. British suzerainty in Africa was represented as being for the Africans' good; therefore it was obliged to profess respect for the subject peoples' cultural integrity and to disclaim any intention of making black Englishmen of them. Hannah Arendt has observed: 'The imperialist-minded business men were followed by civil servants who wanted "the African to be left an African"', while quite a few, who had not yet grown out of what Harold Nicholson once called their "boyhood ideals" wanted them to become "a better African"—whatever that may mean' (Arendt, 1951: 130–1). A modern psychological study of racial attitudes also found, upon factorial analysis, that a belief in 'fair play' or legal justice for all races was second only to 'general conservatism' as a characteristic of the European outlook there (Rogers and Frantz, 1962: 110–11).

The ideal of preserving Africans' cultural integrity inspired an anti-acculturation policy in administration. When Africans congregated in the towns, this was interpreted as a threat to the policy, for in the towns they became 'detribalized', giving up their distinctive cultures for the less colourful pursuits of an urban proletariat. As Lord Hailey noted, in South Africa and Southern Rhodesia the urban native was regarded as an anomaly because 'he breaks the symmetry of a scheme which would divide the European and native populations into two separate spheres of activity' (1938: 543–4). The twin objectives of economic development and cultural non-interference were mutually incompatible, but in Central Africa a compromise along South African lines was attempted by regarding Africans as only temporary town-dwellers and housing them in locations separate from the permanent settlements of the whites. Urban life was to be a feature of the white way of life, not of the African. In Southern Rhodesia the fundamental legislation putting this conception into effect was the Land Apportionment Act of 1930, which divided the country into a sort of chessboard of black native reserves and white European areas. Of 96 million acres, 40 were placed in tribal trust, 36 allotted to European farmers, 10 to national parks and reserves and 10 left unallocated, though subsequently 4 of them were set aside for African purchase. The remaining unreserved land is of poor quality and can be developed only by heavy investment of capital. The Morris–Carter Commission which preceded the Act believed that for practical and psychological reasons 'the points of contact between the races should be reduced', and this was an era in which ideas of segregation appeared morally respectable (Gann, 1965: 262–82). Yet land apportionment did not bring separation in the rural districts: nearly a quarter of a million Africans are employed as labourers on European farms. Urban development could be more closely controlled, and in Salisbury today the Africans whose economic contribution to the city is so important live in satellite townships about two to five miles out. Another aspect of Rhodesian policy which restricts African participation in the urban economy is that regulating African education. In 1965 628,000 African pupils were due to be enrolled in primary schools—an increase of about 40 per cent over the last 10 years. But only a tiny percentage gets beyond the primary grades. Only 12,000 were due to go to secondary school, and there are but four sixth forms for Africans in the whole of the country.

In Rhodesia, as in other parts of Africa, there appears to be a surplus of African labour relative to the number of jobs available. The appearance is deceptive. Rhodesia, like South Africa, attracts workers from other territories who travel long distances to obtain wage-earning employment. In 1956, 48 per cent of the Rhodesian labour force came from outside the country—chiefly from Nyasaland (now Malawi) and Moçambique (on the distribution of immigrant labour in Rhodesia and Zambia, see Mitchell, 1961a: 212–31). Partly because the indigenous labour is not used economically, Rhodesia is dependent upon these migrant workers. Paradoxically, the urban situation is exacerbated by the retrograde state of subsistence farming. Effective industrial development depends, in the long run, upon the development of the rural areas, which will produce food and expand the consumer market. But capital investment that might help native agriculture has been slight. Roads and railways have been built only to serve areas that produce export crops or minerals. The young and vigorous men are drawn away from the farming districts, and in some places this imposes an almost intolerable burden on the women and older men who remain. Africans throughout Central Africa now need money for a variety of purposes (clothing, household goods, tools, taxes, school fees, foodstuffs, etc.); and when income from farming is low, wage-earning employment in the cities is all the more attractive. But in the towns, migrant workers are numerous and are not strongly attached to particular trades; thus they have been in a weak bargaining position with respect to wages, while the employers have had less incentive to economize on the numbers employed or to develop the potential capabilities of their workers. The social and political effects of the rural-urban age and sex disproportion are serious. Children grow up without their fathers, while in the urban centres prostitution, alcoholism and violence become accepted features of social life (Mitchell, 1961 b: 81–2).

The urban locations in which the Africans live are governed by officials, and the African has little direct influence over their decisions. In one Salisbury location there are government-built quarters for married people; in another about 50,000 single or separated males are crowded together. If an African loses his job he may lose his house. A recent study states that if he went into the white town the African had to take his food with him; and unless he was careful in choosing where to eat it, he might give offence. Service in the shops was provided by white assistants, and the African would usually have to wait until every white customer had been served and was then fortunate if he was treated with civility. Wherever he went, he had to carry a pass; it was an offence to be without it and a policeman could demand to see it at any time. It was against the law for him to be given European beer, wine or spirits. He was allowed only 'Kaffir beer', and that—with some exceptions—he was allowed to drink only at a municipal beer hall (Mason, 1960: 169; some of these regulations have since been relaxed). The spatial segregation of black and white was regarded as vital. Proposals to build a government house for a leading African in a white area and to admit the son of a Pakistani diplomatic official to a white school both excited forceful protests. Some white schools run by missions and private bodies admitted small numbers of African pupils, but the government has invoked the Land Apportionment Act to discourage this. Segregation enters into all institutions in which both races participate.

In industry men of the two races have to work together; segregation has been based therefore upon the reservation of certain occupations to Europeans. Such practices have not necessarily been reflected in legislation.

When a European wants to build a house in Southern Rhodesia he will, if he wants the bricklaying done cheaply and well, employ an African to do the work. It will cost him five or six times less than if he were to engage a European bricklayer. But the snag comes when he wants other craftsmen, such as plumbers or electricians, skills that the Africans have not yet been trained to perform. It will subsequently prove very difficult, even impossible to get a European electrician to wire his house if the bricks have been laid by an African. It is therefore possible for Southern Rhodesia to boast that they have no discriminatory industrial legislation. They do not need it as things are (Gussman, 1962: 101.)

Job reservation has been made even more crucial to the maintenance of white supremacy by restrictions upon the economic determination of wage levels. The differential between African and European wages was not wholly based on difference in the value of the services provided, but was affected by difference in the bargaining power of the two groups and by conventional ideas as to what was appropriate for an African. European industrialists were often willing to raise African wage levels and appreciated that the increase in African purchasing power would have a generally beneficial effect, but they were effectively restrained by the white farmers (Gray, 1960: 225–9). The belief that the African's place was in the reserves and that he was not entitled to any standard of living better than that he enjoyed prior to the European conquest, coupled with European power and the structure of European politics, depressed urban living standards. An impartial examination of this question relating to the middle 1950s necessarily concluded: 'there is really no room to doubt that from one-fifth to two-fifths of urban Africans in the Rhodesias are not earning enough to keep their families, and that of those with two children or more the majority are undernourished and underclothed' (Mason, 1960: 150).

African labour in Southern Rhodesia in the early 1950s tended, from the standpoint of the European employer, to be inefficient; productivity was low; the workers, having no security in urban society or prospect of building up a long-term career there, did not respond to the usual industrial incentives. Town life was ill-disciplined, overcrowded, insanitary, subject to the pass laws; and a man who was not gainfully employed could be expelled from an urban area even though he had been born there and knew no other home. At work, Africans were subject to supervisors 'whose chief qualifications for the post are a harsh manner and a ready flow of invective in the native tongue' (Gussman, 1953: 139). African trade unions were not recognized in law and strikes were illegal. Thus the suspicion and conflict between employer and employee was much greater than that characteristic of Western industrialism and work suffered accordingly. It was in the employer's interest to promote the stabilization of the labour force so that an urban African community might develop which would produce more efficient workers, but other interests opposed this. The European farmers have been mentioned in this connection: the European workers' trade unions feared that their interests might be threatened. The government also was apprehensive. One summary runs:

Settled labour is more efficient because, if it is really settled, it has something to work for beyond immediate needs and because the danger of unemployment provides an incentive. European employers welcome the greater productivity but they fear the social and political consequence. A settled African community would expect to enjoy the right of self-determination within the community as the cornerstone of its security and this might impinge in many ways on European sovereignty in the towns. It is, therefore, a demand which no European municipality is prepared to grant (Gussman, 1953: 143).

In Northern Rhodesia the recession of 1931 hit the Copperbelt very hard. African employment fell from 30,000 to under 7,000 (Gann, 1964: 252), and the redundant workers had to retire, with their dependents, to the reserves. The fear of another recession and the danger that there might be no secure industrial base for an urban African society, with the necessary social services, led the government there to reject proposals for labour stabilization. While the colonial administrators often defended the African against the settler, they were less liberal in anything affecting the maintenance of law and order, for this bore upon their own interests and convenience (Franck, 1960: 90). The settler outlook gradually spread among colonial administrators

271

(Fox-Pitt in Leys and Pratt, 1960: 16; cf. Gann and Duignan, 1962: 64n.). Thus European policies towards the Africans were in part the outcome of a conflict of interests within the European group.

Urbanization in Rhodesia and Zambia, therefore, did not provide the conditions under which the upper members of the lower category could climb to positions superior to the lowest Europeans, nor did it permit them to create a separate social realm relatively free from European surveillance. Contacts across the colour line became less personal and communication was impaired. Blacks and whites had less and less understanding of one another, and the repression of sexual temptations added its contribution to the other forces making for separation (cf. Gray, 1960: 324-5; McEwan, 1963: 279n.). One inquiry shows that whereas the African 'boss boy' would more naturally look for social companionship to the lower-middle group of white workers than to any others in the white community—for members of this group most nearly approximated him in educational, social and economic background and interests—in fact it was these lower groups among the Europeans who were most opposed to contact with Africans (Franck, 1960: 242: but cf. Rogers and Frantz, 1960: 124-8). A recent study in Rhodesia of urban African attitudes towards Europeans found African men more hostile towards Europeans than their wives, and their wives more hostile than unmarried women. This study shows that the more an African was in touch with the sentiments of his or her fellows, the more hostile he was inclined to be. When asked in what ways Europeans were different from them, the Rhodesians listed differences of wealth more than Africans in Ghana had done in a similar investigation. The author of the Rhodesian study concluded that the Africans were 'almost universally hostile' to the Europeans; 'this hostility was based not on political doctrine or persuasion, nor on any sense of group cohesiveness in the face of discrimination by the white minority, rather was it intensely personal, and being rooted in individual grievance and observation many times repeated'. By contrast with the situation in Ghana 'no regret was expressed at the passing of the traditional culture; the problem of how to achieve self-government and remove the yoke of the white man was too pressing to indulge in regrets for the vanishing past' (McEwan, 1963: 289, 290).

In 1965, as this essay is written, the confrontation between Africans and Europeans in Rhodesia is sharper than ever before; and a resolution of the power conflict cannot long be delayed. Urbanization instead of easing racial subordination has intensified it. In the Deep South the pattern of social relations in the rural districts constituted a highly integrated social system. Whites and Negroes had places in a single social system. Roles of all kinds were tightly interrelated and deviant interracial behaviour quickly caused repercussions over a wider area of relations. Urbanization brought a loosening of the network permitting greater flexibility. In Rhodesia the rural network of social relations was not tightly integrated in that the Europeans and Africans belonged to partially independent social sub-systems. Urbanization brought them together—on a basis of white supremacy. The pattern of racial sub-ordination bore directly upon a greater range of the everyday situations in which Africans were involved. For them to reject subordination in any context threatened the whole system. The consequences of any such deviation were therefore more serious and more immediate. The effects of industrialization, channelled by white political interests, have been to make the colour line more distinct and inclusive without moving it from the horizontal. Consequently African opposition to the racial order has become more coherent. There are no effective interest groups of a composition that crosses the colour line, and the system holds out no rewards for political compromise. The only long-term solution is for the whole society to be drawn into the ambit of some wider political unit which would stimulate a regrouping of forces and introduce greater flexibility.

Urbanization in multi-category systems

The influence of urbanization upon race relations in East Africa did not follow the same course as in the South. In the early stages of colonization in Kenya the greatest threat to the European settler came from possible Asian competition. The Europeans developed a racialist ideology which justified discrimination against Indians, but the outcome was a three- rather than a two-category system. Indian influence was strong in the towns; and after World War II Europeans feared the alliance of Indian and African councillors in elections to the office of mayor. At times neither Europeans nor Indians were certain whether to combine with one another or to seek African support against the other (Parker, 1951: 41–52). In Uganda the town of Jinja enjoyed a construction boom when work began on a dam across the Nile to generate hydro-electric power. Two years later the town's population was 800

Europeans, 5,100 Asians and 14,900 Africans. Europeans were recruited to fill the managerial posts, Asians as supervisors, and Africans as unskilled workers. Later a number of European artisans were introduced whose skills and claims to status were more comparable to the Asians' and were inferior to those of a growing élite of Africans educated in Europe. A European sub-category emerged with its separate social club (Sofer and Ross, 1951; Sofer, 1954). The white artisans were not able to mobilize the support of the upper whites to see that a status gap was enforced between Europeans and non-Europeans.

The evidence from West Africa stands in even more striking contrast with that from the two-category systems. Where the dominant category seeks to maintain a status gap, it is the upper echelon of the lower category against whom the pressure is directed. On the west coast, members of the African élite were not subjected to any constant pressure to keep them in a subordinate status, while urbanization provided them with a niche in which they could establish themselves as a group. There was no colour line in the sense in which this expression has been employed above, so that the élite's urban position was important not for tilting a line so much as for changing, by political action, the whole basis of race relations. Urbanization did not mean the founding of new towns, European in conception, but the extension and development of African settlements in which the Europeans were always a minority. By bringing Africans closer together in a denser mass under new leadership, urbanization was important to the development of African political strength.

The first step in the creation of modern West African nationalism was the formation of groups representing and developing the viewpoint of the African élite, such as the Gold Coast Aborigines' Rights Protection Society of 1897 and the West African National Congress of 1920. Through such bodies the African intelligentsia was able to work out alternatives to the pattern of colonial rule. The groups were strongest where they could be based on the leadership of educated Africans who were members of the liberal professions—lawyers, doctors in private practice, etc.—and therefore not dependent upon the colonial administration for their livelihood. These men could build up a professional clientèle only in the towns. They could hammer out their political ideas only where there were numbers of them living in close association. When, prior to independence, they were elected or appointed to represent 'native interests' on national or local councils, it was for urban constituencies; for in the country districts it was the chief who was regarded as the political representative of the people.

The colonial governments were often reluctant to recognize élite groups as representative of anyone except themselves. Thus in 1920 Sir Hugh Clifford expostulated:

There has during the last few months been a great deal of loose and gaseous talk...which has for the most part emanated from a self-selected and self-appointed congregation of educated African gentlemen who collectively style themselves the 'West African National Conference'...It can only be described as farcical to suppose that...continental Nigeria can be represented by a handful of gentlemen drawn from a half-dozen Coast tribesmen born and bred in British administered towns situated on the sea-shore, who in the safety of British protection have peacefully pursued their studies under British teachers (quoted Coleman, 1958: 156).

The colonial administrations often sought to strengthen their hold by dividing the potential opposition. Thus in the Gold Coast after World War I, some paramount chiefs were actively engaged in the work of the central government and became the allies of the administration against the Cape Coast lawyers who led the Aborigines' Rights Protection Society. Elsewhere, smaller groups like the Sierra Leone Creoles saw their interests as lying with the British rather than with the tribal Africans, and many of them served as allies of the administrations in a similar fashion. The political history of such groupings needs to be studied in detail for each of the territories, the relevant point for the present being only that because there was no inclusive colour line, the colonial governments could find allies outside the European population. Some indirect evidence in support of this argument can be derived from a comparison of the social structure of Monrovia, Liberia, with that of the other West African capitals while under colonial rule. In Monrovia the social structure has been monolithic, the same people heading the political, social and economic élites. A member of the urban society tends to have much the same social rank in all spheres and associations (Fraenkel, 1964: 197–208). The suppression of conflicts has reduced the pressure for change.

In the development of the colonial order, the position of the native élite was critical. Either the colonial government succeeded in winning the élite's support for its own policies (and the price of this support rose appreciably as the years went by) or members of the élite mobilized native opposition to the government. A recognition of the alternatives became almost explicit in Governor-General Carde's description of French educational policy: *instruire la masse et dégager l'élite*. The policy of assimilation attempted to put into effect such recommendations by offering *évolués* the privileges of the ruling group. In Senegal there was at one stage a numerically significant élite based upon the liberal professions which supported French colonial policy. Like the Sierra Leone Creoles, their energies were for long directed to obtaining from the imperial power those rights and dignities which it had promised them (Crowder, 1962: 15). After World War II its numbers increased further, competition with Europeans intensified, and the group came to express an intense reaction against colonialism, drawing heavily upon Marxist theories and elaborating a mystique of négritude. The Portuguese also offered a more privileged status to *assimilados*, but with the increased emigration of unskilled Portuguese workers and their families to Angola and Moçambique this policy seems to have been restrained. When the native élite was numerically small, its members were exposed to the contradictory expectations of the colonial masters and of their own people. Sometimes the conflicts were very severe, so that some writers emphasized the 'spiritual confusion' of the educated African (Malengreau, 1956: 632). Other writers—especially those familiar with territories where the élite was more securely established—recognized that the member of such a group might have to move in two worlds ('in his private life he is an African; in public a European'—Little, 1955: 282), but did not find that this duality gave rise to serious psychological strains.

It was often difficult for colonial governments in Africa to satisfy the élite. For example, as Africans obtained professional and higher educational qualifications and obtained positions in the senior division of the colonial civil services, the question arose of their salary scale. Europeans were paid at rates sufficient to attract personnel from overseas who were involved in additional expenses. If the government paid African staff at the same rates, they would magnify inequalities of income within the African population and impose a tax burden that was certain to increase. If, on the other hand, it fixed their salaries at a lower point, this was to open the way for charges of racial discrimination. Where, as in the then Belgian Congo, it was relatively easy to keep the African population isolated from developments in the wider world, the support of the élite could, for a time, be obtained in return for relatively small privileges. It should also be borne in mind that it was not easy for the first African nationalists to awaken a political consciousness amongst their people. European dominance was not initially perceived by the masses as a political dominance. Other modes of explanation deriving from traditional culture led Africans to interpret European power in partly magical terms. For example, an account of the clash of different assumptions in the classroom of a Uganda secondary school underlined the following factors: the prevalence in East Africa of the belief that Europeans were cannibals; the way explanations of events in terms of witchcraft could be maintained alongside the acceptance of scientific theories of causation; and the African boys' suspicion that they might not be receiving a completely genuine European education (Musgrove, 1952). In the development of African attitudes towards Europeans, World War II had a tremendous impact throughout the colonies, quite apart from the stimulus it gave to economic development. African soldiers were taught to have no regard for the racial status of enemy Europeans and Asians. Many saw Europeans defeated in battle and subordinated as prisoners-of-war. They visited other lands, sometimes lay with white prostitutes, and acquired a new image of the white man. Large contingents of British and American troops were stationed in some places. Their behaviour, like that of European seamen, often contrasted with the pukkah-sahib conventions of the colonial civil servant. After the war, the political situation within African colonies changed more rapidly. The leaders of the Convention Peoples' Party in the then Gold Coast persuaded many of their fellow-countrymen that they had remediable grievances and built the first effective independence movement. Ghana's progress to independence (legislative council with African elected majority in 1946, partial self-government 1951, complete independence 1957) greatly accelerated the pace of change elsewhere. The Congolese élite, influenced by the doctrines of African intellectuals in Paris associated with the review *Présence Africaine*, began to react against the European assumption that Africans were in a process of development from an inferior to a superior stage, and to think in terms of the contact between two civilizations (Slade, 1960: 14). The Belgians had not built up any tradition of struggle and negotiation with African representatives; hence, faced by mounting demands from Congolese leaders for a share in government and impressed by the French and British progress in decolonization, they capitulated—with results that everyone now knows.

In the early stages of the liberation movements African attitudes towards Europeans were not as simple as they may be represented in retrospect (cf. Sithole, 1959: 146–64). Much of the force behind nationalist sentiment came from the attempt to resolve conflicting feelings, such as respect for European puissance and resentment over minor humiliations of everyday contact. Young Africans' respect for Western-style norms and achievement was confounded with the experience of particular whites to generate a fundamental ambivalence (Rogers, 1960: 62–3; Jahoda, 1961: 42–3). West Africans sometimes affirmed that they had nothing against Europeans as people, but everything against them as rulers of their country. This development of a strictly political attitude to questions of race relations was reflected in an investigation in Uganda which showed that the more educated were young people, the more were they opposed to non-African participation in the government of their country (Gutkind, 1957).

In the paternalist order of the non-settler colonies, European behaviour and attitudes towards Africans were not patterned by any such simple opposition as that engendered by a colour line. They varied more, and the critical factors often derived from occupational and other roles. From a psychological standpoint, any European was in an exposed position. All the social scaffolding which in his home society was built round the values taught to children, and many of the social controls which supported the cultural norms, had been removed. Where whites were few in number, considerable determination was required to maintain at all times the norms and thereby the prestige of the imperial culture. To help him in this a man might institutionalize his own behaviour, creating personal customs and routines that reminded him of the expectations of absent others: the idea of the explorer or administrator dressing for dinner in the African bush is not really so foolish as it may seem to the stay-at-home. A club or clique of friends may provide the individual with a similar kind of support and a means of supervising the behaviour of people identified with him and whose misconduct might therefore redound upon himself. The social exclusiveness of minorities needs to be seen in this light. The European official in Africa thought it only natural that he should keep his club for himself and his fellows, as a place where he could relax without any of the awkwardness that would arise if he admitted people who did not share these assumptions. If a senior European official had had too much to drink in the club on a Saturday evening, he would not have been perturbed had this happened in the presence of a low-ranking European, who, because of his ethnic background, counted as one of the group. Nor would he have minded if an African servant had been there. But in the company of an African professional man he would have felt unable to behave with the same freedom. He might have shared more specialized interests with the educated African that he could not share with the low-ranking European, but for ordinary leisure pursuits these were of little account. Such self-segregation on the part of Europeans was bitterly resented because their circle had a wider significance in representing the social apex of the entire society. The successful African professional or businessman felt that he had made the grade and felt affronted over his exclusion in a way that he would never have done over rejection by Indian or Lebanese circles. Thus in colonies with a growing African élite the question of racial discrimination in club membership acquired a significance out of all proportion to the real desires of the parties to obtain or avoid one another's company.

Many of these European clubs in British colonies were, in theory at least, for members of the 'senior service' or some category that was not defined in racial terms. In practice, Africans were not elected to membership. As in the years before independence, more and more Africans were promoted to higher posts, the element of discrimination became increasingly obtrusive. Most of the men belonging to such clubs met Africans regularly in the course of their work and had no difficulty relating to them on an individual-to-individual basis. Because of its implications for the structure of relations between Europeans, the acceptance of African members was a problem only to the group. Commenting upon this, two authors observe that it was the character of these intra-group relations which decided how long resistance to African membership could be maintained. The protocol-minded club for higher government officials, being the most affected by outside influences and the least determined by its own inner development, was the first to capitulate (Proudfoot and Wilson, 1961: 319). In the case they studied, as in others, the title to land on which the European club stood was vested in the government. Once the Africans captured the government, they could threaten the club members with eviction. The centralized character of European colonial power meant that the social transformation at independence was extraordinarily rapid.

Another major factor determining the structure of relations within the European group was the presence of white women. In the early years of many colonies the Europeans were an all-male group and, on the west coast at least, they mixed fairly freely in African social life. When, with the improvement of communication and medical services they brought their wives out, they withdrew into their own community. The women met Africans in very few roles other than those of servants and obtained a narrower view of them than did their menfolk. The relationship between a domestic employer and servant has in most times and countries been productive of tension, especially when there was a cultural gap between the parties. African servants might not comprehend European ideas about hygiene, and the slowness and alleged unreliability of houseboys became one of the very few topics on which all European housewives had something to say. For them the adjective 'African' came to symbolize lower material and moral standards and an encircling majority with whom they themselves had no direct relationships such as to give a sense of purpose to their residence. This, together with the influence of sexual jealousy, may be responsible for the very general observation that European women expressed stronger prejudice towards Africans than the men did. They, after all, had to compete with Africans for their menfolk's attention. The stronger their influence the more exclusive were Europeans likely to be (Banton, 1957: 115–17). A study of small isolated European communities in East Africa shows how the pressures within these groups hindered adaptation to the changing political environment. European wives were involved in their husbands' work without being able to participate in it. As they were continually meeting the same group of neighbours, the women paid less attention to their appearance than they might otherwise have done. In-group gossip became the substance of their lives. Officials low in the government hierarchy were, with their wives, usually in the majority. They tended to be sceptical of imperial policy, hostile to African advancement, and to have an important influence upon the tone of community affairs. When senior African civil servants were appointed to these stations, they saw no advantage in establishing social contacts with the Europeans. Attempts to promote such contacts often only increased tension. As independence approached, Europeans became more negative about their roles in the transfer of power and their morale declined (Tanner, 1966). Once again, the source of trouble lay less in individual attitudes than in the structure of group relations.

It has been said that in West Africa antipathy towards Africans was strongest among the lowest-ranking classes of Europeans, who resented the university-trained African's claim to a higher status (Little, 1955: 276). Similar differences have been noted elsewhere. Class factors of this kind sometimes combine with the frictions of the domestic employer-servant relationship. Hortense Powdermaker specifically comments upon the wives who had never previously employed servants and never used any terms of normal politeness (1962: 813; cf. Gray, 1960: 231–2). Africans often treat domestic servants harshly, though without regarding them as an inferior race or generating the same sort of resentment. American social scientists concerned with training Peace Corps volunteers for service in Africa have noted that such personnel easily err in the opposite direction, embarrassing African domestic servants by being too familiar with them. Most of these volunteers have not been accustomed to having servants and need to be instructed in the proprieties of this relationship before being advised as to the complications which arise if the parties belong to different groups defined by race.

With a change in the structure of political power, there can be very rapid changes in the pattern of race relations. Herbert Blumer, recapitulating an argument outlined by Everett Hughes (1952: 64–5), has underlined how changes in managerial practices in the American South followed upon new policies instituted by the federal government, pressures from the national labour unions and threats of economic boycotts organized by Negro groups. There have been similar changes in the policies of European firms operating in former colonies once they have been obliged to increase the nationals' participation in management. In South Africa, industrialization has brought an intensification of racial distinctions, not because this is required by industrial circumstance, but because of governmental legislation and policy (Blumer, 1965: 247–9). Such evidence conflicts with the argument that economic interest groups will seek to control political policy. It suggests that often they wish only to be left undisturbed, and react to political changes in whatever way seems most likely to minimize interference from outside.

In Africa the transition from colonial status to independence seems generally to have reduced any feelings of hostility towards Europeans on the part of Africans. After independence the number of Europeans in these territories has usually increased because of the greater employment of specialists and technicians in connection with development programmes. An experimental study in India showed that attitudes towards the British became more favourable after independence (Adinarayan, 1953). A New Zealand psychologist who conducted an inquiry in Nigeria just before independence concluded that in acceding to the popular demand for political change 'the British have fostered a climate of good will towards Europeans which has few parallels in Africa' (Rogers, 1959: 63). In another recent investigation in Sierra Leone it was found that, in a test situation, Africans expressed less social distance towards Europeans and Americans than towards Africans of other tribes (Dawson, 1965: 224–5). Independence has also changed the relations between indigenous groups. In Zambia, for example, the Coloureds previously had an anomalous political identity. But a representative of this community became an active member of President Kaunda's cabinet and under the new régime the Coloured community has become an accepted element in the African population.

Conclusion

From a structural standpoint the simplest pattern of race relations is the two-category kind of system as analysed on the basis of research in the Deep South in the 1930s. In recent African history the closest approximation to this pattern is that of Rhodesia, though the Republic of South Africa (which has not been discussed in this essay) also shows many of the same features. Urbanization in the Deep South, by providing a niche for a Negro upper class, permitted the colour line to swing round towards the diagonal in the sense that some Negroes enjoyed a class position superior to that of some whites. Urbanization in southern Africa has brought blacks and whites closer together, but the towns have been regarded as white areas and segregation is enforced there instead of being—as in the rural districts—a consequence of cultural differences. There is very little tilting of the colour line: the structure of political interests within the white category generates pressure to keep it horizontal.

Though in colonial Africa elsewhere there was much racial discrimination, especially with respect to social interchange, this pattern was not fully reproduced. Where there was no entrenched white settler element, there were fewer and weaker forces making for the confrontation of two homogeneous and mutually exclusive social categories identified by racial signs. Even where settlers constituted an important minority, as in Kenya, the paternalist policies of metropolitan governments prevented or delayed any drift to a two-category system. At the interpersonal level, race relations in such territories were determined more by the occupations and other varied roles of the parties than by any overall pattern of racial categories. In West Africa, where the white minority was small and oriented towards the policies of the metropolitan governments, there was no colour line or status gap such as is found in a two-category system. There, urbanization provided a niche for an African professional élite; but it was important not so much in protecting their class position, as in enabling them to pioneer African political opposition.

Lloyd Warner suggested that major changes in the racial order of the Deep South would come from changes in the relation of the two categories without any change in their distinctiveness. He discussed the possibility of the colour line's swinging round to the vertical, or past it, but did not consider the possibility of its being dissolved. Although much of the African evidence does not come from two-category systems, it suggests that where members of a subordinate category can mobilize effective political pressure, it is easier to eradicate a colour line than to tilt it.

BIBLIOGRAPHY

Adinarayan, S. P. (1953). 'Before and after independence: a study of racial and communal attitudes in India', *British Journal of Psychology*, **44**.

Arendt, Hannah (1951). *The burden of our time*. London.

Banton, Michael (1957). *West African city*. London, Oxford University Press. (1965). *Roles: an introduction to social relations*. London.

Blumer, Herbert (1965). 'Industrialization and race relations', in *Industrialisation and race relations*, Guy Hunter, ed. London, Oxford University Press.

Coleman, James S. (1958). *Nigeria: background to nationalism*. Berkeley, University of California Press.

Crowder, Michael (1962). *Senegal: a study in French assimilation policy*. London, Oxford University Press.

Davis, Allison, Burleigh B. Gardner and Mary R. Gardner (1941). *Deep South: a social anthropological study of caste and class*. University of Chicago Press.

Dawson, John (1965). 'Race and inter-group relations in Sierra Leone', *Race*, **6**.

10-2

Franck, Thomas M. (1960). *Race and nationalism: the struggle for power in Rhodesia–Nyasaland*. London.

Fraenkel, Merran (1964). *Tribe and class in Monrovia*. London, Oxford University Press.

Gann, L. H. (1958). *The birth of a plural society: the development of Northern Rhodesia under the British South Africa Company, 1894–1914*. Manchester University Press.

(1964). *A history of Northern Rhodesia: early days to 1953*. London.

(1965). *A history of Southern Rhodesia: early days to 1934*. London.

(1968). Personal communication.

Gann, L. H., and Peter Duignan (1962). *White settlers in tropical Africa*. Harmondsworth, Middlesex.

Gray, Richard (1960). *The two nations: aspects of the development of race relations in the Rhodesias and Nyasaland*. London, Oxford University Press.

Gussman, Boris (1953). 'Industrial efficiency and the urban African', *Africa*, **23**.

(1962). *Out in the midday sun*. London.

Gutkind, Peter C. W. (1957). 'Some African attitudes to multi-racialism from Uganda, British East Africa', in *Pluralisme ethnique et culturelle dans les sociétés inter-tropicales*. Brussels, Institut International des Civilisations différentes.

Hailey, Lord (1938). *An African survey*. London, Oxford University Press.

Hughes, Everett C., and Helen M. Hughes (1952). *Where peoples meet*. Glencoe, Ill.

Jahoda, Gustav (1961). *White man: a study of the attitudes of Africans to Europeans in Ghana before independence*. London, Oxford University Press.

Keatley, Patrick (1963). *The politics of partnership*. Harmondsworth, Middlesex.

Leys, Colin (1959). *European politics in Southern Rhodesia*. Oxford, Clarendon Press.

Leys, Colin, and Cranford Pratt, eds. (1960). *A new deal in Central Africa*. London.

Little, Kenneth (1955). 'The African élite in British West Africa', in *Race relations in world perspective*, A. W. Lind, ed. Honolulu, University of Hawaii Press.

MacEwan, Peter J. M. (1963). 'The urban African population of Southern Rhodesia', *Civilisations*, **13**.

Malengreau, G. (1956). 'Observations sur l'orientation des enquêtes sociologiques dans les centres urbains de l'Afrique noire, d'après les conditions du Congo Belge', in *The social implications of industrialization and urbanization in Africa south of the Sahara*. Paris, International African Institute (UNESCO).

Mannoni, O. (1956). *Prospero and Caliban*. London.

Mason, Philip (1958). *The birth of a dilemma: the conquest and settlement of Rhodesia*. London, Oxford University Press.

(1960). *Year of decision: Rhodesia and Nyasaland in 1960*. London, Oxford University Press.

Mitchell, J. Clyde (1961*a*). 'Labour and population movements in Central Africa', in *Essays on African population*, K. M. Barbour and R. M. Prothero, eds. London.

(1961*b*). *An outline of the sociological background to African labour*. Salisbury, Rhodesia.

Musgrove, Frank (1952). 'A Uganda secondary school as a field of cultural change', *Africa*, **22**.

Parker, Mary (1951). 'Race relations and political development in Kenya', *African Affairs*, **50**.

Powdermaker, Hortense (1962). *Coppertown; changing Africa. The human situation in the Rhodesian Copperbelt*. New York.

Proudfoot, L., and H. S. Wilson (1961). 'The clubs in crisis: race relations in the new West Africa', *American Journal of Sociology*, **66**.

Richmond, Anthony H. (1961). *The colour problem*. Rev. ed. Harmondsworth, Middlesex.

Rogers, Cyril A. (1959). 'A study of race attitudes in Nigeria', *Rhodes–Livingstone Journal*, **26**.

Rogers, Cyril A., and C. Frantz (1962). *Racial themes in Southern Rhodesia: the attitudes and behaviour of the white population*. New Haven, Yale University Press.

Sithole, Ndabaningi (1959). *African nationalism*. London, Oxford University Press.

Slade, Ruth (1960). *The Belgian Congo: some recent changes*. London, Oxford University Press.

(1954). 'Working groups in a plural society', *Industrial and Labour Relations Review*, **8**.

Sofer, Cyril, and Rhona Ross (1951). 'Some characteristics of an East African European population', *British Journal of Sociology*, **2**.

Tanner, R. E. S. (1966). 'European leadership in small communities in Tanganyika prior to independence', *Race*, **7**.

Warner, W. Lloyd (1952). *The structure of American life*. Edinburgh University Press.

CHAPTER 9

COLOUR, CATEGORIES AND COLONIALISM: THE SWAZI CASE[1]

by

HILDA KUPER

This essay is primarily an exploration into social classifications and concepts of colour in so far as they can be related to the ideological aspect of colonialism. Colonialism may be loosely defined as a policy whereby a political power acquires or retains control over people in territories other than its own. The structural network of arrangements that extend from this policy and also the behavioural implications have been described and analysed more fully than the conceptual.

Social concepts, institutionalized in formal and informal signs and symbols, are extremely difficult to investigate by our present anthropological techniques; it is easier to avoid the difficulty by relegating this area to psychology. But the problem remains a sociological one, and social anthropologists have sought new insights through studies of symbolism (some of which have drawn deeply on psychology) and through the approach of ethnolinguistics. Symbolism has often been limited to the context of religion, but symbols are essential elements in man's techniques of communication in all social situations, including the political.[2]

Perception of colour, like perception of sound, taste, smells, is organically rooted. Through the associated receptors (sight, hearing, etc.) perceptions produce changes which are then interpreted in the brain. The sensory unit (such as the eye) enables one to derive information about 'the universe' but does not interpret or classify the result.

[1] I wish to acknowledge the assistance of Edward Leddel in the preparation of this study, and to thank him, Max Gluckman, Walter Goldschmidt, Michael Moerman and Leo Kuper for critical comments on an early draft of the paper delivered at UCLA, December 1965.

[2] The importance of symbolism has long been recognized by anthropologists (cultural and social), psychoanalysts, social psychologists, philosophers, linguists, artists, musicians and literary critics; but theories of symbolism are difficult to extend from one approach, or discipline, to another, because each contains its own implicit assumptions.

The perceived universe must not be confused with the universal, despite ethnocentric beliefs of its inhabitants.

Each universe of people, animals and things, of that which is seen, heard, touched, tasted, receives different interpretations according to the system of cultural classification. Classification orders, and delimits in time and space, the meaning that people perceive in their universe. In my discussion here I examine, within the structural framework of a particular colony, a system of classification held by the colonized in which *initially* colour did not constitute an essential principle in ordering the social universe.

While anthropologists may state that people in any society project their own concepts, based on their own cultural premises, onto a particular universe, it is extremely difficult to examine these other concepts and universes in their own right. It is easier to start with what we know about ourselves and work outwards than to have as a base of comparison notions derived from meaningful assumptions, which underlie classifications, by others. Notions are contained largely in language, 'the social side of speech' (De Saussure, 1966: 14),[1] and probably the most pervasive and revealing of symbolic systems. Each social universe is represented by its own notions, and when people of different universes come into contact with each other, their culturally different notions set the pattern for their classification of each other.

I suggest in this study that stereotyping by a particular folk notion of 'colour' dominated the perception of European colonizers, that a different set of categories initially operated among the people they ruled, and that in the process of contact, notions represented by 'colour' as a symbol reflected new classifications.

Stereotype was a term introduced into the language of social science in 1922 by Walter Lippmann (1922: 15–16),[2] who borrowed it from a

[1] It is worth quoting more fully from the same passage: 'Language is a well defined object in the heterogeneous mass of speech facts. It can be localized in the limited segment of the speaking-circuit where an auditory image becomes associated with a concept. It is the social side of speech, outside the individual, who can never create nor modify it by himself; it exists only by virtue of a sort of contract signed by the members of a community.'

[2] Lippmann assigns the term 'stereotype' to the process of 'pictures in our heads' that are essentially incorrect, inaccurate, contrary to fact, and therefore undesirable. He argues that the 'real environment' is altogether too big, too complex and too fleeting for 'direct acquaintance', and hence it is mediated by limiting albeit competing symbols made by man and ranging from complete hallucinations to the scientist's perfectly self-conscious use of a schematic model (pp. 15–16). The stereotype 'tends to

particular form of printing or rigid duplicating, but applied the term to 'pictures in our heads'. Efforts have since been made to distinguish between a 'popular' or 'layman's' image and the 'scientific description of national character' (Fishman, 1956: 27),[1] a distinction which is itself part of Western 'folk culture' with its rigidly defined and circumscribed systems of validation and its own distinctive logic (Brown and Lenneberg, 1958: 369).

It is often assumed that there is 'a human tendency for social stereotyping', but it seems to me that to use the term with reference to the categories of other people implies that they are making the same types of classification that Westerners are making. From the time of Durkheim it has been recognized that one of the tasks of sociologists is to understand the classifications used by people with other cultures, i.e., *their* idea of social reality, and it is presumptuous to assert *a priori* that other peoples have similar principles of stereotyping just as it is presumptuous to assume that other peoples necessarily have any of our other systems of classifications.[2]

In the colonial situation, classification is part of many complex sets of concepts: these include how A categorizes B, how B categorizes A, how A thinks B sees A, how B thinks A sees B, how each sees itself. The classification may be shared by all or only by some members, it may vary with situations, and in the process of interaction, classifications may change. Clearly, I am not able to deal with the situation in its full complexity and I will limit myself to gross contrasts in concepts revealed largely in linguistic classification.

The validity of isolating the phenomenon of stereotyping by a particular concept of colour and contrasting it with social phenomena based on other principles of classification should be tested in a wide range of societies, but I will restrict myself to the colonial situation in Swaziland, a small territory in southern Africa where I did intensive

preserve us from all the bewildering effect of trying to see the world steadily and see it whole' (p. 114). For Lippmann and others assume that there is an outward reality which can be scientifically apprehended and separated from the world of false ideas, that there is in fact a world that can be seen 'steadily' and 'whole'.

[1] Fishman points out that one of the chief difficulties with the concept of stereotyping is that 'there seems to be no uniform definition of what it denotes' (1956: 27). And his article attempts to define it, delimit it, and examine its overall utility (p. 27). Brown argues that 'a distinction should definitely be made between popular conceptions of racial or national character and the conceptions of social science' (1958: 369).

[2] The significance of classification in sociological analysis was emphasized by Durkheim and developed in his writings with Mauss (1963).

research (1935–40).[1] I will begin by examining classifications made by the self-styled 'whites' and then, in greater detail, because the system and concepts are more alien to English-speaking readers, Swazi classifications of a universe into which European colonizers were fitted; I then discuss the concepts as they changed in time.

Whites, mainly Dutch-speaking and English-speaking, first entered the territory ruled by the Swazi king, Mswati, in the early nineteenth century. They already carried in their heads certain notions of indigenous peoples, 'the natives', notions derived not only from personal encounters, but also from written and oral sources. The main written source was the Bible, which received a fundamentalist and exclusive interpretation, separating believers from heathens, the saved from the damned. Oral sources included accounts of varying accuracy by adventurers, slavers, settlers and traders.

In southern African, the 'natives' with whom permanent relationships were established were culturally and physically heterogeneous. Whites labelled one type 'Bushmen', another 'Hottentots', and the third 'Kaffirs'. In a colonial situation name-giving tends to become name-calling. The 'Bushmen', hunters and gatherers, were considered less than human. They proved generally unsatisfactory as captive servants, succumbed rapidly to new diseases, to kill them was not a crime, and they were on occasion hunted as animals. The pastoral 'Hottentots' were brought into more direct economic and personal relationships (mainly by serfdom and miscegenation) and were reduced to insignificance in the process of Western expansion. The Kaffirs, like other 'Bantu-speaking' Africans encountered later, were pastoralists and hoe culturalists effectively organized under chiefs; and though they lost their independence to the technologically more powerful colonizers, many chiefdoms survived and multiplied. The Dutch spoke of *mense*, *skepsels* and *uitlanders*: *mense* were people, i.e., themselves; *skepsels* were creatures—Bushmen, Hottentots and Bantu; and *uitlanders*

[1] Discussions with various African students at UCLA, more especially with Tiyo Soga, Wairimu Gethaiga Bowman and John Mhina, support my conviction that the Swazi case is by no means unique in Africa. It is possible that the phenomenon which I isolate as stereotyping may be associated with a certain level of social complexity and the stereotypes have an adaptive value for the superordinate group. But this is not the crux of the present discussion, and I am not adopting either the approach of the social evolutionist, nor the structuralist's assumption that the codification of a racial ideology is subsequent to the establishment of political domination by a culturally distinct group. My problem is of a different order—the confrontation of two different conceptual systems in an historically defined context.

were outsiders, the British. The British differentiated themselves from Boers and from 'the natives', to whom they applied more specific and also pejorative terms.

Techniques by which colonizing powers assumed control influenced subsequent developments. Where open violence was used, conquerors established a more rigid oligarchy and appointed their own 'native authorities'; where there was a 'paper conquest', by treaty, concession, or other techniques of economic warfare, a greater continuity of the traditional African political structure was superficially maintained.

The Swazi were not defeated in open warfare, but through concessions, written documents which they could not read and which embodied alien concepts. Some concessions (such as those relating to railways and banks) were outside the framework of Swazi social structure, and others (especially those relating to land usage) conflicted with established practices. Swazi talk of 'the papers that killed us'.[1] Behind the documents was the superior military force of 'Western civilization'.

'Western civilization' was a somewhat vague culture complex, or syndrome, arbitrarily bounded in the minds of the colonizers to embrace monogamy, a monotheistic religion, written languages, a capitalist economy and a wide assortment of material accessories. It was conceptualized not as Western civilization, but 'civilization' unqualified and sole. The bearers of this 'civilization' identified themselves by the symbol of colour. A 'civilized man' was a 'white man'.

In Swaziland every person in all situations was classified by the colonists primarily by colour: 'white' for European: 'black' for Swazi and other 'natives'; 'coloured' for Eur–African. These colour terms referred specifically to pigmentation of skin, but like all symbols this included other associations. With a white skin went not only other distinctive physical traits including white man's clothes but also 'white man's' behaviour—the way he ate, spoke, worked, worshipped, cursed, cured. By being seen as 'a white man' by other 'whites', he was entitled to certain positions of power and privilege. Non-whites, particularly 'blacks', were outsiders, a general referent by which whites established their identity with one another. A white who did not conform was described as having 'gone native', and was excluded from those entitled to call themselves 'the whites'.

---

[1] The historical material has been more fully presented in my previous writings, more especially in *An African aristocracy* (1947a).

'Natives' were conceptualized as inherently 'primitive' and 'back-ward' by whites drawing from a wide storehouse of notions—popular, philosophic, religious, scientific. Thus 'natives' represented to some whites a lower stage of evolution and were described as 'just down from the trees'; to others, less 'scientifically' oriented, they were simply 'like animals'. The use of analogy and metaphor from the animal world is common in Western speech, but when applied by self-conscious whites to people of different 'colour', that 'colour' was the visible symbol of such innate generalized animal qualities as violence and brutality.

At the same time, there was a common colonial cliché that 'Natives are children. They are always laughing and happy.' Missionaries, who pronounced natives to be among the 'children of God', also empha-sized their 'simplicity'. By describing them as children, the speakers implied that they themselves were adults with the right to act as mentors and inflict corrective punishment. Yet the colonizers did not really identify Africans with *white* children and were indignant when I asked if *their* children were like 'natives'. Moreover, by coupling happi-ness with childhood (in itself a self-protective and self-deceptive device of adults), whites relieved themselves of the obligation of encouraging rapid change by granting equality of rights. Housing, diet, social welfare and education could thus be differentially regulated. The assumption of black inferiority justified the retention of white privilege as 'protection' or 'guidance'.

Other favourite clichés from the white settlers' manual were 'The natives have different brains from whites'. 'They can imitate but can't think for themselves.' 'They don't know the meaning of gratitude.' 'The educated native is the spoilt native.' Further rationalizations advanced by whites for their own entrenched position were 'the inability of natives to govern themselves in the modern world', 'their incapacity to develop economic resources of the territory' and 'the despotism of traditional rulers'.

Stereotyping proceeded in two directions—generalizing from selected characteristics of individuals to arbitrarily defined categories of people; and, conversely, applying to particular individuals the preconceived image of the broad category. The latter process appeared to be more common, with the result that individuals who did not conform did not change the basic images. They were treated as excep-tions that did not prove any rule; but at the same time they had to be controlled, for side by side with the inferiority attributed to their colour category was the unexpressed fear that they might acquire the skills of whites and oust them from their privileged positions. A Swazi who did not fit the preconceived image and behaved according to white standards and adopted as much as he could of 'civilization' was not described as having 'gone white' but as 'trying to imitate the whites' or as 'an agitator who wanted the same position and rights as whites'. It was usual, but not necessary, to assume that Africans were inferior; it was sufficient to stress 'innate difference' to justify exclusion. If a non-white appeared to behave as a white, it was not conceded that he could *think* as a white; to allow identity at this level would confuse the basic assumption. The logical coherence in the system is comparable to that which Evans-Pritchard revealed in his study of witchcraft.[1]

Ideology and action operate at different levels, and the assumption of white superiority, or simply innate difference, can be expressed in a wide range of policies and actions. These depended only partly on the formal distribution of power between white settlers, black subjects and the metropole; the underlying principle of classification was at least as significant. In Swaziland, then a British High Commission Territory, policy could be described as paternalist, not tyrannous; but had the black subjects rebelled, the same colonizing power might have resorted to greater repression without changing its classification by colour. Within the mental limits of colonial rule, different sections of whites were expected to behave according to specific roles (administrator, technician, trader, missionary, farmer, etc.), so that norms of behaviour ranged from the aloof but courteous manner of officialdom to the jocular familiarity permitted the trader. Despite a permissive range of action variation, there was always a conceptually as well as a legally demarcated limit beyond which individuals could not go without meeting general disapproval or social ostracism, as distinct from formal punishment, from 'the whites'.

Marriage between whites and non-whites was not legally prohibited but morally condemned; illicit miscegenation initiated by white males was more popular and generally condoned. In the colonial context approval of intermarriage would have signified public acceptance of the most intimate and meaningful act of communication between whites and non-whites; miscegenation was a positive gesture in the language

---

[1] Evans-Pritchard (1937). Compare this with Allport's statement that beliefs have a way of 'slithering round' to justify more permanent attitudes (Allport, 1954: 191).

of white domination. At a more obvious verbal level, classification by colour was expressed in jokes, anecdotes and historiography.

In an earlier publication I wrote that colour was a uniform that individuals were not permitted to discard (Kuper, 1947 b). A white man could learn the Swazi language and Swazi ways of life, but he could if he wished still claim the legal standing of whites; and if he moved from the narrow surroundings in which he had identified himself with blacks, he was accepted as a white by other whites and differentiated from the blacks. In the present essay I emphasize the physical visibility as a symbol of mental patterns, of classification rather than of behaviour.

Western symbols express a characteristic of much of Western thinking—binary opposition: left is contrasted with right, high with low, good with bad, black with white. This is assumed by Westerners to be a universal categorization. But it has been effectively shown, particularly by Durkheim and Evans-Pritchard, that neither time nor place has any objective reality. The opposition within this relative framework has been stressed for non-Western societies more especially by Levi-Strauss, Hertz and Leach, but the dialectic within the framework indicates that opposition need not be restricted to duality.

In Western folk notions white and black are taken for granted as polar concepts, and the two colours are used as symbols for sets of opposed values—purity and sin, goodness and evil. This colour contrast with its implicit ethical equation is so embedded in Western thought that it is widely assumed to be 'natural' and 'universal', 'part of all human experience'. Let me quote a few statements from a vast body of illustrative evidence:

At all times and among all races, no matter what their color, 'blackness' has a very sinister connotation. The reason for this is probably not far to seek. As for the child, so for the primitive man, the darkness of night must always have had special terrors, for are not the dark hours devoted to the ghosts, the hobgoblins, and the magicians? 'Blackness' has been and still is associated the world over with witchcraft, devils, sin, bad luck, and all the other distressing and horrible aspects of human experience. Furthermore, the association of blackness and evil is quite as common among brown or black people as it is among the yellow or white (Berkeley-Hill, 1924: 248).

Again, MacCrone in his well-known book *Race attitudes in South Africa* wrote:

The Symbolism of white and black is simple, uniform, and unambiguous... From the psychoanalytic point of view the real origin and meaning of black as a symbol of death, evil, and misfortune remained unknown to the conscious mind since it represents the repressed or unconscious material (Mac-Crone, 1937: 296).

The writings of Freud and Jung are rich in interpretations of colour and assumptions of universal human experience; it is not only laymen, social psychologists and psychoanalysts but even the most perceptive and reputable of social anthropologists who find it difficult not to talk in a similar symbolic idiom. Turner in a brilliant description of Ndembu ritual compared Chihamba with the White Whale in Melville's *Moby Dick* and with the Resurrection of Christ in the New Testament, and concluded that '"whiteness" in all three represents "pure act of being". 'It is as though wherever men attempt to represent the act of being they have an innate propensity to use the same symbolic form, unsullied whiteness' (Turner, 1962: 96).

But ethnological data from several societies indicate that black and white do *not* always, or necessarily, have these same associations; that colours other than black and white may have major significance; and even that the concept of colour may in fact be different. Thus Conklin writes: 'Color in a Western technical sense is not a universal concept and in many languages such as Hanunoo there is no unitary terminological equivalent.' In fact, among the Hanunoo 'there is a lack of a term similar in semantic range to our word "color"' (Conklin, 1964: 189).

In a recent article Turner himself recognized that in some societies black has 'auspicious connotations', and he also added 'red' to the essential colour categories; but he still assumed the existence of a universal colour semantic system, in which colours

stand for basic human experiences of the body (associated with the gratification of libido, hunger, aggressive and excretory drives and with fear, anxiety, and submissiveness)...The color triad, white-red-black, represents the archetypal man as a pleasure-pain process. The perception of these colors and of triadic and dyadic relations in the cosmos and in society, either directly or metaphorically, is a derivative of primordial psychobiological experience—experience which can be fully attained only in human mutuality...The basic three are sacred because they have the power to 'carry the man away', to overthrow his normal powers of resistance... *Since the experi-*

ence which the three colors represent are common to all mankind, we do not have to invoke diffusion to explain their wide distribution (my italics) (Turner, 1966: 81–2).[1]

If 'all mankind' associated black with faeces, dirt, sin and evil, and white with milk, cleanliness, virtue and purity, then contact between groups (or even individuals) clearly distinguishable by pigmentation on this black–white chart would presumably have certain significant implications for their attitudes, and even behaviour, towards each other. Even so wide a slogan as 'White is right' could be a psychobiologically validated principle of action. This in fact was an important element in colonial situations where conquering colonizers called themselves 'white' and labelled the conquered subjects 'black'. And it implied an automatic acceptance by blacks, sufficiently privileged to be recognized as part of mankind.

Now I most emphatically do *not* argue that all people who follow the Western colour symbolism of 'black' and 'white' are necessarily 'racist' in action; on the contrary, men and women whose religious imagery is rooted in the Old and/or New Testament were and are among the main protagonists of 'the black man's rights'. But I argue that black–white colour symbolism far from being a 'common experience of mankind', may be a product of a particular albeit very widespread cultural tradition and that colonialism, as manifested in the expansion of 'Western civilization', is also part of this tradition.

At the time of the arrival of the whites, the Swazi were already a nation, whose rulers had brought together through conquest and inter-marriage, people speaking Nguni and Sotho languages and practising different customs. There had developed a complex sociocultural system under a dual monarchy, represented by a hereditary king and his 'mother', real or putative. Between them they shared the highest

[1] The 'universal' approach to colour is evident in the following quotation from the same article: 'Even human beings, Negroes though they are, are classified as white or black in terms of nuances of pigmentation. There is here an implied moral difference and most people object to being classified as black' (1966: 58). But what is this 'black-ness' to which 'most people object'? It is because of the moral difference implied by whites that Negroes object to being called black. Experiments by Brown, Carroll, Casagrande (see bibliography) and others reveal the relativity of colour cognition and its linguistic and behavioural associations. Some of these refer specifically to non-Western societies, more especially the Hopi and Navaho. Since writing this, my attention has also been drawn to an excellent discussion by Herbert Landar in his book *Language and culture* (1966), more especially Ch. 28.

political, economic and ritual responsibilities and privileges, and allegiance to them defined the boundaries of the nation. The king was titled *Ngwenyama* (Lion) and praised as 'Great Beast', 'Our Bull', etc., and the queen mother was *Ndlovukati* (She Elephant), praised as 'The Earth', 'The Beautiful', etc.

The white men had to be accommodated into this already existing universe with its own taxonomy and social structure. To discuss it I have used a number of Swazi terms, and given English glosses (usually in quotation marks); it will be clear that in many cases the gloss is but a crude approximation and never a definition or full translation.[1] At least four major interrelated categories, each with its special characteristics or qualities, were expounded by informants on different occasions. These categories were: *abantfu* ('people'), *tilwane* ('animals'), *abatsakatsi* ('witches'), and *emadloti* ('ancestral spirits', 'shades'). In the context of this study *abantfu* ('people') is the critical reference. The qualities of significance were *umoya* ('breath', 'spirit', 'vital principle'); *inyama* ('flesh', 'meat', 'substance'); *simo* ('character', 'temperament')'; and *ingati* ('blood', 'pedigree'). *Umuntfu* (sing. of *abantfu*) incorporated or embodied 'breath', 'flesh', 'character', and 'blood'. When the 'person' died his 'flesh' rotted, his 'breath' continued as *idloti* (sing. of *emadloti*) and his 'personality' and 'pedigree' were perpetuated in his descendants through his 'blood'.

Swazi classified themselves as *abantfu* ('people') and extended the term to members of other chiefdoms or political communities with whom they had contact prior to the arrival of whites. It did not matter that they had different customs nor even that the relationship between them was frequently hostile; the characteristics of *abantfu*, symbolically distilled in the abstract noun, *ubuntfu*, the quality of being human, were still attributed to them.

Within the broad category of humans, Swazi recognized differences of *simo* ('character', 'temperament', 'personality'). Certain qualities of *simo* were inherited from parents; others were innately specific to each individual and others were learned. It was primarily the biologically acquired qualities which determined the personality. Personality manifested itself in different ways and was given appropriate diagnostic

---

[1] I have in the main followed the spelling in Ziervogel's *A grammar of Swazi*. This grammar is useful but analyses (and forces) Swazi construction into set Western forms. Casagrande argues cogently that the success of translation depends partly on the purpose of translation (1954: 335–50).

names, and there was a definite system of classifying personalities into types. Thus some people were born to failure, others to suffer, others to be governed by uncontrollable passions, others to inflict misfortune in spite of the best of intentions, etc. The diversity of human types was explicit, and Swazi emphasized differences rather than similarities built on a core of inherited traits (Kuper, 1947*a*: 158 ff.).

Personality could be developed but not changed by learning. A generic word, *inyanga*, was applied to any specialist, whether he were a specialist in making clay pots or in driving away lightning. The term *inyanga* conveyed admiration, and the most successful specialists were believed to have been taught their skills through personal communication with the ancestors. When 'the spirit' of an ancestor was believed to enter or possess a person, that person became a *sangoma*, 'diviner', the highest of specialists. He (or she) was believed to be able to interpret the wishes of the ancestors, to discover causes of misfortune and above all to detect witches.

Ingati (blood) differentiated *abantfu abakhulu* ('big people' or 'aristocrats') from *abantfu nje* ('just people', 'commoners', also described as 'dogs' or 'wooden people'). The patrilineal clan was the furthest extension of 'blood', and the ruling king was of the senior lineage of the royal Dlamini clan. There were in all some seventy clans, and traditional political dynamics were expressed in the manipulation of alliances between aristocrats—the king, his mother, princes and heads of major clans—and commoners. All traditional national positions were determined in the first place by 'blood' and maintained by ritual. The most potent ritual symbols were reserved for the king and the queen mother; for anyone else to attempt to acquire their ritual was treason punishable by death. The rulers (described as 'twins') were considered by power of 'spirit', 'character', and 'blood' to be the greatest 'specialists' and also the greatest 'witches'; and were identified with the other powers in the universe. At the climax of a great annual national ceremony, the rulers were 'joined' symbolically with the sun, the moon, vegetation, and animal life.

Between *abantfu* ('people') and *tilwane* ('animals') there was a complex affinity. *Abantfu* were distinguished conceptually but not always physically from certain 'animals', and by definition animals did not have *ubuntfu*. To 'animals' were ascribed a variety of habits, characteristics and appearance.

Though 'people' and 'animals' were distinct at some levels, they participated in the same natural system linked by *umoya* ('vital principle', 'spirit'), and in definable contexts people and certain animals identified with one another. *Tinkomo* ('cattle') and some *tinyoka* ('snakes') in particular were cited as 'feeling with' humans. Swazi, like many East African peoples, stressed the functional necessity of cattle in all meaningful situations and incorporated cattle into the intimate human circle both in 'flesh' and 'spirit'. Thus in one of the annual rituals, cattle were sent by the rulers to the royal burial groves. Each animal was then verbally dedicated to a particular ancestor. The animals were then no longer simple 'cattle'; they embodied, in their substance, the ancestors. As such when they came back to the capital, they were welcomed with sacred songs and treated with special respect. Then on the following day the 'cattle ancestors' were sacrificed and the flesh of each was apportioned according to the special kinship relationship the ancestor held with the living communicants. Or again 'snakes' were not necessarily reptiles. On certain occasions they may have *appeared* to be snakes but in the 'real world of the Swazi' they too were 'ancestors', and to kill a 'snake', especially in a hut, was a sin which could bring terrible retribution to the killer. There was even a correlation between the type of snake and the status of the ancestor; so, for example, the mamba was the 'ancestor' of kings. Consubstantiation between men and particular animals is of course not unique to the Swazi, but its implications in contact situations are not generally recognized. It gave a new boundary to the Swazi definition of 'people'.

Whereas certain 'animals', more especially 'cattle' and 'snakes', were brought within the realm of Swazi moral relationships, other 'animals' were 'outside', and broke into the world of 'people' through the disruptive power of *abatsakatsi* ('witches', 'evil doers'). The *abatsakatsi* were the agents of harm and misfortune whose final weapon was death. Externally there was often no distinction between 'witches' and ordinary 'people', since the power of witchcraft was something internal, transmitted by a witch mother to her child; but in certain circumstances witches changed themselves into specific 'animals', sent 'animals' to kill their enemies and put the breath of an 'animal' into the body of a person so that he behaved like that 'animal'. 'Witches' could be considered by the Swazi a sort of intermediate category between 'people' and certain 'animals'.

At this point let me reiterate categories and concepts in the Swazi universe which I consider relevant to understanding the place that

Swazi assigned to whites. There was firstly the system of classification into 'people', 'animals', 'witches', and 'ancestral spirits'. These interacted through the principle of 'breath' or 'vital spirit'. 'People' had special qualities of 'personality', and within the nation 'people' were stratified as aristocrats and commoners, rulers and subjects by 'blood' and appropriate rituals.

Into this universe came the white men, but, according to my interpretation, the Swazi at that time did not see them as white men. They were perceived as beings or creatures of a different order and were not classified as *abantfu*. They were *abelumbi*. This term, which reliable informants state was the first generic term applied to whites, has a most significant derivation. *Kulumba*, the verb, describes a particular but widespread technique of sorcery—destruction from a distance. The word occurs in all Nguni languages, and in the comprehensive Zulu–English dictionary of Doke and Vilakazi is given the following meanings: (1) do wonders; perform conjuring tricks, make inventions; (2) indulge in occult practices; practise witchcraft; (3) concoct, fabricate, invent stories; tell lies (Doke and Vilakazi, 1948: 468). The main instrument of the newcomers was the gun, the most powerful mode of communication. The psychological as well as physical effect of guns on Africans, who knew only sticks, spears, and shields, is amply documented in the records of white pioneers. To the Africans the technique 'of killing by pointing a stick from a distance' was a new technique of '*kalumba*'; the practitioners were *belumbi*.

The term *belumbi*, indicative of strange, more than natural, powers, was ambivalent; and to counter it, missionaries are said to have introduced the term *belungu* from the root *kulunga*, which has several meanings, including; (1) to get into order, fit, correct; (2) be morally good (Doke and Vilakazi, 1948: 469).

Both terms, *abelumbi* and *abelungu*, have been part of the vocabulary of the Swazi for some hundred years, but it was only during my recent period of research (1966–7) that I came to realize that they were not synonymous and that *abelumbi* was used more frequently by old, illiterate Swazi. Educated Swazi, at least in my presence, used only the term *abelungu*. Ideas about whites were obviously current before there was any direct contact in Swaziland. We must remember that the Bantu-speaking people in southern Africa were not isolated from one another. On the contrary, there was considerable interaction through migration, trade, intermarriage and warfare; and though Europeans, as far as we know, confronted a Swazi ruler only in the nineteenth century, contact between Africans and Europeans had taken place as early as the fifteenth century.

Their arrival in his own country was foreseen in a dream by King Sobhuza I, *Somhlolo* (the Wonder), who ruled from 1815 to 1839. He related his dream to counsellors especially summoned to discuss its implications and significance. According to one of my oldest informants, Somhlolo reported that the ancestors had shown him *tilwane, abelumbi* (animals, wizards) entering his country. Their skin was like red corn; their hair resembled the tails of cattle. They brought new and amazing inventions (*emalumbo*), and their 'tongue' (*lulwimi*, i.e., language) was incomprehensible. They carried magic weapons that killed from a distance through a 'terrible noise of lightning'. 'They were not *abantfu* (people) like us.' They did not have *ubuntfu* (the quality of 'humanism', or 'humanity'). The ancestors then warned the king that *abantfu* should not fight *abelumbi* or there would be disaster. In later years, this dream was referred to in English as 'The Vision of Somhlolo'.

Other versions of the vision stress two specific items among the new wonders offered to Somhlolo. These were *umculu* and *indilinga*. The ancestors told Somhlolo that he (i.e., his people) must 'eat *umculu*' but beware of *indilinga*. The exact meaning of these two words is still debated; *umculu*, however, is generally assumed to be the Bible, and the injunction 'to eat *umculu*' is interpreted as to take in, or accept, knowledge or learning, and *indilinga* (something 'round and shining') symbolized money.

I suggest that in the initial encounter between Swazi and *abelumbi*, pigmentation of the skin, which is, after all, only a small part of the exposed body (and an even less conspicuous element in the totality of culture), need not have been seen as a crucial classificatory index or symbol of difference. Equally conspicuous is the topography of a face—the eyes, nose, mouth, teeth, chin, the play of facial muscles. When skin colour of *abelumbi* was commented on by informants, it was generally described as *bovu* (red) or *mpofu* (grey), and the physical characteristics that were perhaps more frequently referred to were hair and 'shoes' (as 'feet'—Swazi were barefoot people). In the initial conceptualization, such features as guns, shoes, and even *umculu*, involving a strange language and new ideas, and *indilinga* (money, or, rather, currency) were also perceived as essentially inherent extensions and assimilated into the total image of *abelumbi* cum *abelungu*. Association and identification between a person and his physical, cultural equipment, including language, operate at different mental levels.[1] *Abelumbi* was a new category of being, as distinct from *abantfu* as *abatsakatsi* ('witches'), or *tilwane* ('animals'), or *emadloti* ('ancestral spirits').

They were recognized as having *umoya* ('breath,' 'vital principle'), but it was a somewhat different *umoya* from that in *abantfu*. It was not connected with the ancestors, whose protection they did not seek and whose existence they even denied. *Abelumbi* thus had other concepts of the meaning of *tinkomo* ('cattle') and *tinyoka* ('snakes'). An educated Swazi expressed this unconsciously when he said 'I only enjoy selling cattle when I speak English'. That 'snakes' were regarded by *abelumbi* simply as reptiles was evident from the fact that they were prepared to kill any snake at any time or place.

Abelumbi were considered to have power comparable to that of *abatsakatsi* ('witches') and at the same time to be immune to African witches. *Abelumbi* could become *tinyanga* by learning skills, but were said not to be prepared to teach the secrets of their skills to non-whites. 'They showed us only part of what they knew'—a quality which linked them more closely with witches than with reputable specialists. And since they denied the existence of ancestral spirits, they could not become *tangoma* ('diviners')—the highest of specialists. On the contrary, because they did not think there were witches, they prosecuted Swazi diviners under a Witchcraft Ordinance, while Swazi who *knew* that there were witches, because they as *abantfu* believed in them, complained that *abelumbi* protected witches and condemned to death the good men, i.e., diviners, who directed their skill at discovering and punishing witches.

To the Swazi traditionalist *abelumbi* were not 'people', but creatures of a different kind. Unlike the whites who classified the Swazi by colour, the Swazi placed the whites in a new category in their complex but spatially limited universe.

The initial observable reaction of Swazi to *abelumbi* was, however, friendly and co-operative. *Somhlolo's* warning that fighting *abelumbi* would bring disaster to *abantfu* was current mythology. Perhaps the

---

[1] Ultraconservative Swazi still identify Western-educated Africans, who build themselves Western-style homes, eat Western food, and wear Western clothes, as *abelungu*: 'they even smell like whites'.

acceptance of this warning was supported by the principle that it is dangerous to arouse hatred in a witch or fierceness in an animal. Between *abelumbi* and *abantfu* was a fundamental absence of mutually intelligible or meaningful communication. The concessions, the power of aliens transmitted through words on paper, were a symbol of this difference.

At some stage the words *abamhlophe* and *abamnyama* were introduced into the Swazi language. *Abamhlophe* was applied to *abelumbi*, *abamnyama* to *abantfu*. The root *mhlophe* was translated as 'white', and *mnyama* as 'black'. There was also a general Swazi word *umbala*, translated as 'colour' with its plural form *imbala*.

These terms raise a problem of meaning that is particularly significant in the colonial situation. I struggled to understand how the Swazi conceptualized them from an examination of many contexts in which words given 'colour' translations were used. That Swazi have a keen visual awareness and their own aesthetic system of discriminating pattern, style and colour is evident in their art and clothing, especially in their decorative and elaborate bead-work. But did Swazi categories of colour match those of the colonizers? Was there perhaps a fundamental difference in range, symbolism and classificatory significance? In short, had the Swazi a specific concept of colour which we can translate in terms of black and white in a significant synonymous way? To answer these questions fully would require a more detailed investigation than I will—or can—attempt, and I am here only concerned with the two terms *mnyama* and *mhlophe* at a fairly general level of description and in so far as they are relevant to the subject of this essay.

Let me mention a few situations in which *mnyama* and *mhlophe* occurred. Enumerating various *tinkomo* ('cattle') received as bridewealth, an informant mentioned one as *mnyama*; but that same beast had been described in a previous phase of the ceremony as '*inkomo emhlophe*', literally 'beast white'. In yet another context, a beast whose hide was to me visibly black was chosen to make a person 'shine' and give him 'shadow' (i.e., an impressive personality). Similarly, Western doctors may consider the colour of medicine as psychologically and hence physically effective, but I doubt if they would describe red or green potions as 'white' or 'black'. But among the Swazi certain medicines irrespective of 'colour' were described as *mnyama* in one treatment, and in another treatment medicines of the same 'colour' were described as *mhlophe*, or by their 'taste' or other selected quality.

In a particular ritual the king's face was painted 'to be *mnyama*' but in a design described as 'full moon'; clear water was described as *mhlophe*, sea water as *mnyama*. Milk of ordinary cattle was described as *mhlophe*, but there was a special ritual herd associated with kingship and the milk of those cattle was described as *bovu* ('red'). The special hut in which the king had intercourse on ritual occasions was named *sigodlo esimn-yama*. Yet a witch sometimes painted a band of *mhlophe* around her loins when on her nefarious nocturnal activities.

Thus, even at the superficial visual level *mnyama* and *mhlophe* did not always coincide with Western concepts of black and white. And sometimes when I as a Westerner expected a colour to be mentioned, either in identification or in symbolism, it was absent; and sometimes when least expected the terms *mnyama* and *mhlophe* were applied. Literal translation into English puts the emphasis on the colour, not on that which is conceived of as a whole thing including colour. Everything—every object, person, animal—has its particular 'power' which may change its symbolic analogy in a selected 'colour' term. The colour is often not the significant element, and may not be perceived apart from the thing with which it is identified. A particular animal, or plant, or even person is a complete image which may symbolize many things not necessarily associated with its colour. Things which a Westerner would classify as white, or black, or red, or green, may not exist as such in the Swazi semantic system.

The selection of 'colours' is probably arbitrarily derived from specific relationships established by men with their universe, and reflects responses to phenomena which *we* label natural or physiological or cultural. Our natural world includes day and night, sky, sun, stars, moon, major seasonal changes associated with heat and cold, rain and drought. Our physiological world includes blood, milk, bone, urine, etc. Our cultural world, which sets the boundaries of interpretation to the 'natural' and 'physiological', includes all our beliefs and values about 'reality'. (It is significant how many of the 'Western' refinements of colour are related to minerals—gold, jade, emerald, opal, platinum, etc.—indicative of a socioeconomic market value system?) The Swazi terms *mnyama* and *mhlophe* do not coincide with the division which we may make between the natural, physiological and cultural. And the Swazi have their own notion of the relationship between the destiny of people and selected elements from a visible and external universe. Thus they do not associate darkness with evil, and daylight with good, or vice versa. Each period has its complex of potential and *ambivalent* power. Witches who work in the night have the dark as part of their 'power', but it is also at night that ancestral spirits speak to man through dreams, and, as a Swazi friend pointed out, 'sexual intercourse associated with pleasure and fertility and the essential creative act generally takes place at night'. There is a significant difference in the interpretation which is given to darkness according to Swazi concepts of sex and according to a puritan ethos in which the sex act is a necessary evil or a stolen pleasure. Again, the sun has 'power' which can be harmful or beneficial, and in its light people may behave with different degrees of virtue and restraint. 'In the day you may do good things like hunting, but also in the day people quarrel and fight.'

I do not wish to flog the dead horse of cultural relativity, but I am trying to indicate how the English terms black and white and the Swazi terms *mnyama* and *mhlophe* represent different world views and in the colonial situation have a particular significance. The ethical as well as the visual contrast between black and white does not apply to the Swazi terms, which have a more ambivalent content. Neither *mnyama* nor *mhlophe* in itself is auspicious or inauspicious. Swazi did not polarize values through colour—a bad man was not a 'black' man nor was he a 'white' man. A good man was not 'white' or 'black'. The early colonizers confronted the Swazi with a specific type of ethnocentricism which enabled them to stereotype themselves as white and superior, and to stereotype the colonized in different shades of colour [black or coloured] and inferior. It has been said that a servant always knows his master, better than the master knows the servant, for the servant can scarcely afford the luxury of the errors involved in the stereotype (Simpson and Yinger, 1953: 164). Initially the Swazi did not recognize the whites as 'people' and classified them as a different species, not necessarily better nor worse, but different, a distinctive not really human category in their universe. As communication, physical and verbal, increased, *abelumbi* as *abelungu* were recognized and incorporated as a separate sub-group in the complex world of 'people'.

I suggest that stereotyping by colour came later, promulgated by those sections of the Swazi who were most strongly under Western influence, i.e., had learned the white man's system of colour cum race classification. Some of these were converts who took over the white man's image of 'civilization' and expressed shame at their own 'heathen' and 'barbaric' customs. Others, both educated and uneducated, responded to white racialism by black racialism. The former accommodated themselves with humility: 'We were indeed fools but you have shown us the light.' The latter became aggressively 'anti-white' and produced their own battery of derogatory and not necessarily consistent stereotypes, expressed with more or less subtlety and Western sophistication. The uneducated said, 'whites have no pity'. 'Whites are full of greed.' 'They only understand lies.' 'They are deceitful and never show us their hearts.' The more educated stressed the *white* oppression, or analysed the situation in pseudo Marxist terms of a (landless) black proletariat oppressed by a white bourgeoisie.

Distinctions were made between British and Afrikaner and Jew, but these subdivisions did not destroy the basic stereotype of the white man, especially as the subdivisions were also more or less unfavourable. The position was summed up by an uneducated man: 'Whites join together like a husband who will hit a stranger who tries to help him beat his wife.' The educated were able to document their analysis of the white man as the 'enemy' from more general historical battles. Swazi also recognized a range of new roles introduced by colonizers (missionaries, traders, farmers, government officials) and of differences in the character of individuals fulfilling these roles. Personal ties based on respect and affection sometimes developed, but the barriers of colour erected by colonial domination could not be crossed by spasmodic friendly contact. A Swazi drew considerable applause at a meeting when he stated, 'All *abelungu* are alike. The missionary made us bow down, the trader woke in us new wants, and the government took advantage of our weak position and took away our land.'[1] Educated men pointed out that Europeans were entrenched in the highest posts of the government, which legislated for revenue and determined expenditure. The majority of Swazi were subsistence peasants who sold their labour to whites for the cash they required, including tax money demanded by the colonial rulers. When they performed the same type

---

[1] When King Mswati, son of Sobhuza I, died, his kingdom was more than twice the size of modern Swaziland. Swaziland's boundaries were arbitrarily delineated by Britain under the Pretoria Convention of 1884. This accounts for the large number of Swazi domiciled in the Transvaal Province of the Republic of South Africa. Then, in the reign of Mbandzeni, Mswati's son, white concessionaires claimed rights of ownership over land and minerals; though Swazi customary law did not recognize the right to alienate national assets, the concessions were validated by a white court. In 1907 two-thirds of the country, greatly reduced by the new boundaries, was owned by whites. For a more detailed account of the land situation, see my *An African aristocracy*, Ch. III.

of work as whites, their skin colour bound them to a lower scale of pay. Poverty among them was generally considered 'natural' by many whites, and accepted as inevitable by many Swazi; whereas poverty among whites was considered unnatural and wrong by spokesmen from both groups. Differential pay thus served as an indirect subsidy to 'whiteness'.

But since a black–white symbolism did not permeate the Swazi conceptual system, stereotyping by colour was not coextensive with their national membership even under colonialism. They were not prepared to accept denigration by colour, but at the same time, it was possible for them to disregard it in reaction to the culture of the colonizers. Hence, cleavages could develop within an African society which crossed the colour boundary—cleavages between educated and uneducated, Christian and pagan—and different elements could be, and were, selected by different sections from the complex of 'civilization'. Stereotyping by colour was both more recent and less rigid among the Swazi than among the whites.

Stereotyping by colour was a pervasive classificatory system of whites until the intellectual confusion between colour and race was exposed in the period of the Second World War. Granting of independence to different African societies indicates a change in the meaning of the symbolism of colour. The formula 'irrespective of race, colour, and creed' has received a different interpretation. Chief Luthuli expressed this in a Western idiom when he stated, 'in a truly multi-racial country, democracy should, by the nature of things, be colour blind' (Kuper, 1965: 369). This is conceptually easier in societies where black and white were not correlated with ethical opposites.

The axiom that man 'is both an animal and different from an animal' receives different interpretations according to the system of relating men to other men, men to animals, animals to animals. Even situational references are relative. It may appear 'universally true' that men and animals die, but the death of each receives cultural reinterpretation within a (limited) range of possibilities (rebirth, transmigration, extinction); it is also universally true that sight is one of the sensations built into the physiology of men and animals (together with hearing, taste, smell and feeling). But 'colour' is both a concept and a perception that receives the stamp of social place and social time.

Whites in Swaziland placed non-whites in a universe in which the distinction between animals and men was associated historically with a concept of 'race' and in which colour served as an ethical referent; the traditional Swazi brought the whites into a universe which was organized on different principles and had no equivalent concept of 'colour'. Whites incorporated the Swazi as inferiors within a hierarchical (vertical) social structure. Their category of 'people' was more inclusive, but their stereotype of non-whites reinforced the power of whites. The Swazi conceptualized the whites as a different kind of being, and contrasted them at a horizontal level with people, animals and witches. Stereotyping by colour was as logically consistent as categorization by witchcraft and was in fact its functional parallel. Colonialism brought into a single political framework people of the two distinct universes in which these concepts were meaningful; contact produced (limited) communication between them that changed the meaning of these systems of classification.

When the Swazi incorporated whites into the category of 'people' and developed certain reciprocal stereotypes, their terms for colour still had different connotations. In the present period of history, colour itself appears to be undergoing a change in its symbolic significance.

In this discussion, I have focused on the cognitive aspects of a particular colonial situation; I have deliberately excluded all but the minimum socioeconomic data and have oversimplified the historical perspective. I have been more concerned with attempting to understand how sets of people representing different cultural values *perceived* 'reality' than in examining any objective reality structurally or historically. I have indicated, however, that perceptions change with social experiences (the markings of social time), and that concepts associated in European historiography with colour were initially alien to the Swazi, whose categorization of the universe was based on different folk notions and experiences.

BIBLIOGRAPHY

Allport, Gordon (1954). *The nature of prejudice.* Cambridge, Mass.
Berkeley-Hill, O. A. R. (1924). 'The color question from a psychoanalytic standpoint', *Psychoanalytic Review,* **11**.
Brown, Roger W. (1956). 'Language and categories', in *A study of thinking,* Jerome S. Brunek, Jacqueline J. Goodnow and George A. Austin, eds. New York.

Brown, Roger W., and Eric H. Lenneberg (1958). 'Studies in linguistic relativity', in *Readings in social psychology*, Maccoby, Newcomb and Hartley, eds. New York.

Carroll, John B., and Joseph B. Casagrande (1958). 'The function of language classification in behavior', in *Readings in social psychology*, Maccoby, Newcomb and Hartley, eds. New York.

Casagrande, Joseph B. (1954). 'The ends of translation', *International Journal of American Linguistics*, **20**.

Conklin, Harold C. (1964). 'Hanunóo color categories', in *Language in culture and society*, Dell Hymes, ed. New York.

de Saussure, Ferdinand (1966). *Course in general linguistics*, ed. by Charles Baily and Albert Sechehaye in collaboration with Albert Riedlinger, trans. by Wade Baskin, 3rd ed. New York (first publ. 1915).

Doke, C. M., and B. W. Vilakazi (1948). *Zulu–English dictionary*. Johannesburg, Witwatersrand University Press.

Durkheim, Emile (1960). 'The dualism of human nature and its social conditions', in *Essays in sociology and philosophy* by Emile Durkheim *et al.*, Kurt H. Wolff, ed. Athens, Ohio University Press.

and Marcel Mauss (1963). *Primitive classification*, trans. and with an introduction by R. Needham. University of Chicago Press (first publ. 1903).

Evans-Pritchard, E. E. (1956). *Nuer religion*. Oxford, Clarendon Press.

(1937). *Witchcraft, oracles and magic among the Azande*. Oxford, Clarendon Press.

Fishman, Joshua (1956). 'An examination of the process and function of stereotyping', *Journal of Social Psychology*, February.

Hymes, Dell, ed. (1964). *Language in culture and society*. New York.

Kahler, Erich (1960). 'The nature of the symbol', in *Symbolism in religion and literature*, Rollo May, ed. New York.

Kuper, Hilda (1947a). *An African aristocracy*. London, Oxford University Press.

(1947b). *The uniform of colour*. Johannesburg, Witwatersrand University Press.

Kuper, Leo (1965). *A black bourgeoisie*. New Haven, Yale University Press.

Landar, Herbert (1966). *Language and culture*. New York, Oxford University Press.

Lippmann, Walter (1922). *Public opinion*. New York.

MacCrone, I. D. (1937). *Race attitudes in South Africa*. London, Oxford University Press.

May, Rollo (1960). 'The significance of symbols', in *Symbolism in religion and literature*, Rollo May, ed. New York.

Needham, Rodney (1963). 'Introduction' to Durkheim and Mauss, *Primitive classification*, University of Chicago Press.

Simpson, George E., and J. Milton Yinger (1958). *Racial and cultural min*
New York, revised ed. (first publ. 1953).

Turner, Victor W. (1962). *Chihamba, the White Spirit*, Rhodes-Livingstone
Paper, no. 33.

(1966). 'Color classification in Ndembu ritual', in *Anthropological approaches
to the study of religion* (ASA monograph, no. 3), M. Banton, ed. London.

Werner, Heinz, and Bernard Kaplan (1963). *Symbol formation*. New York.

Ziervogel, D. (1952). *A grammar of Swazi*. Johannesburg, Witwatersrand
University Press.

CHAPTER 10

~IONARY STIMULUS AND ~ AFRICAN RESPONSES

by

F. B. WELBOURN

Starting with Roland Oliver's *The missionary factor in East Africa*,[1] there has been a steady stream of writing from many parts of Africa that illustrates the Gikuyu proverb, *Gutiri mubia na muthungu*, 'There is no difference between a missionary and a settler'.[2] In origin this saying is disparaging: 'One white man gets you on your knees in prayer, while the other steals your land.' The Gikuyu thought that a missionary had done both.[3] Christianity was simply the ritual aspect of European colonialism. There is sufficient truth in this allegation to make it necessary to emphasize the positive achievements of missionaries.

The European invasion of Africa would certainly have had different consequences—and from any humanitarian point of view they would probably have been less desirable consequences—if it had not included Christian missionaries along with settlers and administrators. Thus D. A. Low has written:

It was a great advantage to the Africans of Uganda—in contrast to Kenya, where missionaries, settlers and European government arrived together— that the European missionaries arrived before the European government, so that by the time the government arrived, the missionaries had become experts in Kiganda society to whom the administrators turned for advice.[4]

More than this: in almost every case the missionaries were first in the field in the spheres of education (agricultural and technical, as well as academic) and medicine. When the Phelps-Stokes Commission reached East Africa in 1924, almost the whole educational system was still in missionary hands.[5] The first hospital in Uganda was built by the Church Missionary Society in 1897 and pioneered the training of medical

---

[1] Oliver, 1952.
[2] J. F. A. Ajayi, 1965; Ayandele, 1966; Rotberg, 1965; Smith, 1966; Welbourn, 1961; Welbourn and Ogot, 1966.   [3] Welbourn, 1961: 128.
[4] Low, 1957: 16.   [5] Oliver, 1952: 264–70; Welbourn, 1965a: 83–7.

assistants in 1917. The first government medical centre was opened in 1913 and was, to begin with, concerned largely with treating venereal diseases.[1] In the field of language, it was the missionaries who reduced vernaculars to writing, who laboured on dictionaries and produced books—even if they were no more (or no less) than translations of the Bible. Oliver has shown that, in East Africa, it was they who, more than any other force, roused European feeling against the slave-trade and thus promoted colonialist intervention.[2]

But the very fact that missionaries could influence public opinion draws attention to the possibility of influence in the opposite direction. Discussing the attitude of Anglican missionaries in western Kenya towards Africanization of the church, B. A. Ogot has described the *volte-face* that took place when the province was transferred from the Diocese of Uganda to that of Mombasa. Eager encouragement of a church that was to become self-governing, self-financing and self-propagating changed into the insistence that Africans must remain under missionary tutelage.[3] I have discussed elsewhere the near-identity, in African eyes, of missionaries and white men of other professions, and the close similarity of fundamental attitudes that made this confusion objectively possible.[4] But if the particular influence of Christian missions is to be understood, this is a factor, in the total impact of the West on Africa, that requires further attention from a rather different angle. In effect, it is impossible to isolate 'missionaries' and 'white men'; and any attempt to do so must involve an abstraction so ideal as to have little touch with African reality. If it were possible, in the Western academic tradition, to see missions as one set of institutions acting parallel to those of government and commerce, the task might be relatively simple. But this is not how it works out in practice, nor how it looks through African eyes; and it is possible that a rather different analysis may throw light not only on colonialism in Africa but also on some of the problems of the West.

Religion and society

E. E. Evans-Pritchard has described the dual causation notion of disease held by the Zande.[5] This gives rise to two interacting lines of treatment,

[1] Welbourn, 1965a: 92.
[2] Oliver, 1952: see Index.
[3] Welbourn and Ogot, 1966: Ch. 4.
[4] Welbourn, 1961: 169–73.
[5] Evans-Pritchard, 1937.

one of which requires material medicines specific to the observed symptoms. The other is directed at the 'mystical cause' without which the symptoms could neither occur nor continue. In minor cases, medicines alone are used, although witchcraft is always, in theory, an active agent. In more serious cases, both mystical cause and symptoms must be treated simultaneously.

It is possible to conceptualize this approach to therapy by recognizing that witchcraft-beliefs symbolize certain aspects of interpersonal relationships. (It is irrelevant, in this context, whether 'supernatural' beliefs are the *product* of society or of a 'real' supernatural *refracted through* social forms.) Zande medical practice thus asserts that in the aetiology of every disease there is in principle both a 'natural' and a 'social' factor; and this dual causation is recognized also in contemporary Western social medicine, which tends to use endo-psychic, instead of exo-psychic, symbols.[1]

If Zande medical notions are used as an analogy to interpret society as a whole, it can be suggested that every event has both a social and a natural component. 'Social' here stands for the experience of unique categorical demand, of the 'wholly other', which characterizes full personal relationship but is possible also in relation to things. 'Natural', on the other hand, stands for whatever—in persons as well as things—can be observed, generalized, controlled. The distinction is that of Martin Buber between 'I-Thou' and 'I-It' relationships.[2] It corresponds also to J. H. M. Beattie's observation that rituals may be either *expressive*—trying to *say* something—or *instrumental*—trying to *do* something.[3] The 'social' may be interpreted in exo-psychic ('religious') or in endo-psychic terms. But either interpretation is *expressive* of an assumption about man's place in the universe; and in neither case can one factor be reduced to the other. Both factors remain complementary, not alternative, accounts of the same event; and because of this complementarity a change in one factor is always liable to cause a change in the other. Economic development may modify, or destroy, an ancestor cult. Independent churches are suspect of political subversion. It is not possible to distinguish between 'religion' and 'politics' except as complementary co-ordinates of the same institution or event.

European society, up to the seventeenth century, had much in common with that of the Zande. There was an intensity of interpersonal

[1] Welbourn, 1969. [2] Buber, 1944.
[3] Beattie, 1966: 60–74.

relationship. Men identified themselves as children of God and saw every event as an act of God (or the Devil). But five mutually interacting forces were developing to produce a revolutionary change. These were capitalism, nationalism, experimental science, Puritanism and philosophical individualism. In Weber's words, Puritanism 'shattered the fetters of the sib'.[1] It is possible to argue that Puritanism did no more than provide a mythological sanction for the action of other forces. But Weber's account of the consequences is none the less valid. Instead of being valued as men-in-relationship, individuals became instruments in a divine purpose. The existence of society, in any organic sense, was denied; and nature came to be regarded no longer as God's action demanding man's response, but as the object of rational control in the interests of the divine order. Alleged witches were attacked because belief in their existence was not only 'despicable superstition but impudent blasphemy'. If the intense personal relationships of the Zande are symbolized in witchcraft-belief, the individualism of the Puritans is symbolized in its denial.

But there are two other consequences of relevance to this essay. In the first place, with the Puritan insistence on salvation from guilt as the essence of the Gospel, and with the growth of inner-directed men, guilt, rather than shame, began to be the driving force of an important section at least of English society.[2]

In the second place, while Puritans might find security in 'the community of faith' and *expressive* values in their assurance of salvation, they had given to 'religion' a purely *instrumental* value. Men became tools of God's purpose and God a tool of their salvation. Nature became an object to be manipulated. More ordinary men had to find community in the newly-emerging sense of nationhood and their expressive values in the assurance of being English. They were now Christian because they were English, rather than English because God had made them so.[3] 'Religion' remained expressive of moral conviction. But it became instrumental to the more inclusive purpose of making a great nation and, within that nation, of making individuals into better Englishmen.

Ideally, in the Elizabethan settlement, church and state had been two aspects—the expressive and the instrumental—of the English people. But they had been organized as separate institutions; and as separate,

[1] Weber, 1951: 237–48.　　[2] Riesman, 1950; Welbourn, 1968a: 182–99.
[3] Welbourn, 1965b: 1–3.

scarcely overlapping, instrumental institutions they had developed, till the point was reached where 'religion' might not interfere in public— Lord Melbourne said, private—affairs. The expressive aspect of both had become the superiority of English life; and this could be rational-ized as the White Man's Burden.

The extreme development of this nationalist redefinition was found in Naziism, which openly exhalted 'the People' and promoted values deliberately opposed to Christianity. But W. Herberg has argued that, in America, overt church membership is subordinated to the 'ortho-doxy' of the American way of life.[1] The expressive aspect of life becomes the assertion of Americanness; and religion is used as an instrument of making the assertion actual. (It might well be argued that, in England, much church-going is an assertion not of Christian conviction but of conformity with middle-class values.) It was precisely in this tradition that in 1900 Sir Harry Johnston (himself an agnostic) should write to the Soga of Uganda, 'We want you to learn Chris-tianity and follow our steps and you too will be great.'[2] And, to show how well the lesson was learned, in 1965 Ghana's Minister of Com-munications addressed the Ghana Methodist Church:

Out of loyalty to England's kings and queens, missionaries in colonial days used the pulpit to disseminate ideologies enhancing the exploitation of the people. The Christian Churches in Ghana today therefore should actively join a crusade for national reconstruction.[3]

But this was not the first response. It is true that the Ganda—whose expressive symbols at the clan level were the ghosts, at the tribal level the Kabaka, and who used their *balubaale*[4] in a highly instrumental way—were able, at first, to assimilate to the *balubaale* both Allah of the Muslims and God of the Christians—to experiment with the possibility that they might support, more effectively, the traditional structure. But, by and large, if an African adopted the white men's ways, he adopted also their God. If he was converted to their God, he followed their ways also. There could be no separation between what were, overtly, the instrumental and expressive aspects of the one culture. Only later was it seen that the culture itself recognized such a separation and that its covert expressive attitude was wholly unacceptable. For the time being, an African Christian became a black European. The dis-

---

[1] Herberg, 1955.
[2] Oliver, 1957: 297.
[3] *The Times* (London), 9 August 1965.
[4] Welbourn, 1962: 172–4.

covery that Europeans did not accept him as such was integral to the disillusionment that was to follow.

The impact of the missions was, therefore, an integral part of the whole impact of the West; and it was much more than a meeting of a society politically and economically strong with one which, in either sphere, had hardly started to develop. It was a meeting of men who made radically different assumptions about their place in the universe—and who made them at a deeper level than the formulations of theology. They were assumptions which administrators, missionaries and settlers were scarcely better equipped to recognize and consider than their African protégés.

When, for instance, Mumia—chief of the Hanga tribe in western Kenya—bought arms from Swahili and British, he thought he had procured a form of sorcery more powerful than that of his traditional practitioners.[1] But far more important than the fact that he was thus able the more readily to defeat his enemies was the slower and more lasting discovery of Africans that the West conceived fire-arms in terms not of mystical power but of rational empiricism. Missionaries among the Gikuyu who would allow the surgical operation of male circumcision divorced from its pagan concomitants did not realize that the rite was one: that without the mystical trappings the physical loss of a foreskin was largely meaningless. They forgot also the mystical significance of circumcision in the West. Administrators who offered to Gikuyu larger and better lands in exchange for traditional settlements coveted by settlers did not know that each range was ritually distinct.[2]

Europeans, again, stressed the importance of individual responsibility. Their readiness to serve abroad was evidence that they had shattered the fetters not only of sib but, to some degree, of the land of their birth. They were inner-directed men conscious of a great purpose to be fulfilled. If they were Protestant missionaries, they mythologized their sense of responsibility in terms of guilt. All were, therefore, put out by the discovery that the majority of Africans did not wish to take individual responsibility. Missionaries were shocked to find that they had no sense of sin.

Finally, Europeans—and, whether they recognized it or not, they constantly betrayed it in their words and actions—assumed the superiority of white civilization—an assumption which could, later, be rationalized in terms of social Darwinism. Africa had at first appeared

[1] Lonsdale, 1964.　　　[2] Welbourn, 1961: 119.

as a *tabula rasa* on which civilization (and for many this meant 'Christian' civilization) might readily be imprinted. It was a shock to find what they interpreted as a mire of ignorance, superstition and gross immorality, which must first be cleansed.

It is not therefore surprising that S. C. Neill should write:

Christian missionary work is often understood by the peoples of Africa and the East, not as the sharing of an inestimable treasure, but as an unwanted imposition from without, irreparably associated with the progress of the colonial powers.[1]

Even within its basic unity of assumptions, the missionary movement represented two different streams in British life. In one, guilt had been sublimated into the positive idealism that lay behind the anti-slavery movement, behind Venn's policy of the establishment of self-supporting, self-governing and self-propagating churches[2] and the consecration, in 1864, as Bishop on the Niger, of the African Samuel Crowther.[3] A Nigerian historian writes of the meeting between Crowther and Venn, at which the former reluctantly accepted the bishopric: 'History was made: the crowning moment, in the Lord, of mutual trust, confidence and friendship that transcended all racial feelings.'[4]

In the secular sphere the same positive idealism was expressed in Lugard's principle of indirect rule,[5] in the policies of 'pro-African' administrators, perhaps by the ideal of some of the early settlers in East and Central Africa, of setting up centres of Christian civilization from which light might penetrate to the dark continent.

But the other stream was found in missionary opposition to Crowther's appointment; by the insistence, on his death, that Africans must prove their moral worth before they were given positions of responsibility. Among all sections of the invaders it produced men who had driving consciences of their own and who were determined that all men should be enabled to stand aside from the crowd and make decisions as their consciences directed. They knew 'what was good for the Africans' and were determined to impose it with or without the consent of Africans. It was this stream that dominated all colonial dealings with Africa, whether the colonial agents were Catholic or Protestant, missionaries, settlers or government officers;[6] and J. B.

---

[1] Neill, 1964: 250.   [2] Oliver, 1952: 220 n.; Welbourn and Ogot, 1966: 21.
[3] Webster, 1964: 5.   [4] W. O. Ajayi, 1965: 92–8.   [5] Perham, 1960: Ch. 7, 8.
[6] Mannoni, 1956. Analysis of colonial attitudes in Madagascar.

Webster records how Nigerian clergy 'lost respect for African leadership in the process of an education which was as much the acquiring of English attitudes as it was a familiarization with academic skills'.[1]

Competing institutions

Of all this Africans were slowly to become aware. They had first, however, to come to terms with the fact that the missions came not as a single institution but as many—often competing—institutions. Each offered not merely different rituals and theology but different codes of conduct. Each had, sometimes noticeably, different relations with government officers. There was the fundamental cleavage between Catholic and Protestant, who could make no mutual accommodation (the situation is very different today). But there were differences, also, between the many Protestant bodies which, however they might agree among themselves to divide the field of work, adopted different policies. These necessarily contrasted at the frontiers and were in danger of coming into active conflict when African members of different religious groups met in the growing towns of East Africa or in the established cities of the west coast. Webster[2] writes that Anglican efforts in Lagos were directed towards 'the wealthy merchants, the higher professionals, and civil servants...an indigenized Christianity would leave them as uneasy in the church as their English counterparts'. This exaggerated position highlights the situation as it developed elsewhere.

At a later date the nationalists were to see the divisions of the church as a source of national disunity no less serious than tribalism. For the time being they were a source of perplexity and yet an essential clue to understanding the plural character of Western society. For some, the divided church had to be put alongside Islam. In East Africa this had been introduced by Arab traders; and it is probable that its extension was halted only by the association of Christianity with the new colonial power. By many there it is still rated as a Christian denomination—it is one more aspect of the invading religion. In West Africa it was already an important indigenous force, able to step in and claim converts once Christian missionaries and other alien forces had 'cracked the hard shell of paganism'.[3] Any estimate of the Christian missions in Africa must take into account the probability that much of

---

[1] Webster, 1964: 36.   [2] Webster, 1964: 72f.
[3] Webster, 1964: 45ff.

317

Africa was already ripe for change along the expressive dimension. If the missions had not come, Islam would have been at hand; and the instrumental changes that were to take place were closely correlated with the change in religion. In its simplest terms, neither in East nor in West Africa had Islam anything to offer in the way of formal education.

African responses

GANDA. To this complex of forces that invaded Africa in the nineteenth century Africans responded in a number of ways. At one extreme were the Ganda, whose vigorous response illuminates much that happened, in less clear-cut terms, elsewhere.[1] They belonged to an ancient kingdom. Indeed the material memorials of their kings stretched back for thirty generations. Although the clans still retained some of their earlier importance, their hereditary heads had gradually been replaced, in the administration of the country, by men who held office solely at the king's will. In many parts of Africa the British were to meet a conflict (which they did not understand) between traditional loyalty to semi-sacral chiefs and their desire for efficient bureaucrats. In Buganda it was an enormous advantage to British and Ganda alike that to a large extent the change had already taken place under the influence of internal forces. Here was a political élite who, through their experience of administration and intrigue over a large unit, were perhaps becoming already inner-directed. Certainly their characteristics made an immediate appeal to Anglo-Saxon administrators and missionaries alike. Buganda was in an expanding phase, extending her boundaries eastwards and south-westwards and in constant conflict with the Nyoro to the north-west. But she was also subject to disturbing outside forces. Arabs from the east coast had been entering the country since early in the century; and with them came Islam. White explorers appeared and disappeared. There was a constant fear of invasion by Egypt from the north; and, when H. M. Stanley visited the court in 1875 and was asked by the king to obtain Christian missionaries, it was hoped that they would bring with them guns, and perhaps a political alliance, that would help to avert more immediate threats.

In the meantime, however, Islam had made its mark. The king experimented with some of its practices. More importantly, shortly after Stanley's departure, young men about court took the new faith

[1] Low, 1957; Apter, 1961; Fallers, ed., 1964; Welbourn, 1965b.

to the point of defying the king; and at least seventy suffered martyrdom.[1] Ten years later (after the arrival of English Anglican missionaries in 1877 and French Roman Catholics in 1879) there was a further holocaust of Ganda Christians.[2] The traditional apparatus of spirits and ancestors was becoming inadequate to new political demands; the king and some of his immediate subordinates were becoming distinctly sceptical; and the monotheism—first of the Arabs, then of the Christian missionaries—was welcomed by the younger generation of Ganda as an expressive factor around which the future might be built. That Christianity was largely to win the day must be attributed not to any innate superiority but to the historical accident that the Christian Europeans, rather than the Muslim Arabs, were politically dominant. What the Ganda needed was a new mythology which would enable them to come to terms with the outside world. It was integral to their understanding of this encounter that Muslims, Catholics and Protestants were known as 'Arabs', 'French' and English'. The question at issue for them was not which religion was true but with which total culture they should make alliance.

In the long run there was to be no final settlement. After the Christian martyrdoms, Christians and Muslims alike were restored to the king's favour; and eighteen months later, when he once again tried to eliminate them all, they joined together to expel him. Armed by the Arabs, the Muslim Ganda then turned against their Christian allies; and, in due course, the latter—Catholics and Protestants together, armed by Stokes, the Protestant missionary now turned trader—came to terms with their exiled king and restored him to the throne. Catholics, Protestants and Muslims became not simply religious groups but indigenous political institutions. Through a number of agreements with the British, the Protestants gained the political upper hand; the Muslims remained a minority group scarcely recognized as true Ganda; and this religio-political tension was to spread to the rest of Uganda and to play an important part in the politics of nationalism. But, for the time being, to be a true Ganda meant to have a Christian name—and hence to have been baptized. It appeared to some as though Buganda had been converted almost overnight. What nobody recognized— whether European or Ganda—was that while the king lost much of his instrumental power under the new constitution (in the Buganda Agreement of 1955 he was, in theory, to lose it all), the kingship

[1] Welbourn and Katumba, 1964: 151–63.   [2] Faupel, 1962.

remained the expressive focus of Ganda aspirations. This was to find full instrumental outlet, during the final political manoeuvres towards independence, in the demand that Buganda should 'go it alone' and the formation of the *Kabaka Yekka* ('King Alone') party to fight the national elections of 1962. All religious forces—Catholic, Protestant, Muslim or traditional—were then called in as instruments of the secular faith; and if they failed to respond, they were seen, instead, as instruments of the old imperialism.

But from their return to power in 1889 the new Ganda leaders had taken their Christianity seriously. Slaves were freed, women were given more freedom. Chiefs accepted the responsibility of presenting the Gospel to their people; the shrines of the old gods were destroyed; and, on the whole, chiefs and clergy came from the same families.[1] Missionaries became their secular advisers; and the Protestant bishop and archdeacon played a leading part, as go-betweens with the British commissioner, in negotiating the Agreement of 1900. At the same time, leading Ganda took avidly to missionary education, visited England, built themselves two-storey houses (at a time when Europeans were still living in bungalows), began to play cricket and celebrated their weddings not only in Victorian dress but with English-style tea parties and group photographs. Seventy years later L. A. Fallers could write:

Baganda are, in many ways, extremely 'acculturated' and the leading members of society are the most acculturated of all. There are here no culturally conservative, traditional chiefs pitted against a group of young, western-educated, commoner politicians. Baganda do not see or practise politics in these terms, as so many African peoples do. Rather, Ganda society has acculturated, as it were, from the top down, and hence the new culture tends to have universal legitimacy. Indeed, from the point of view of the Baganda, this new culture, which includes Western ideas of government, Western education, Anglican and Roman Catholic Christianity, the motivations appropriate to a money economy—all this has become *their* culture in a fundamental way. They have, so to speak, 'naturalized' the foreign elements and thus kept a sense of cultural integrity and 'wholeness' through a period of radical change.[2]

In this development Christianity played an integral part. Until relatively recently, to be Christian and to be Western were indistinguishable; and the function of both was to build a new Buganda, able to meet the West on equal terms. At the same time, it was not merely a superficial

[1] Low, 1957: 12f. [2] Fallers, 1964: 9.

religion. The old practices continued—more perhaps th: chiefs were prepared to admit. Martin Luther Nsibirwa, tradition of the first Christian leaders, the 'great Chri minister' who was shot on the steps of the Protestant cathec was found to be wearing charms under his trousers. From Kabaka Mutesa II was deported by the British, there was a widespread overt return to traditional spirits and some argument that they might be compatible with Christian belief. (In one possession cult Christian initiates are made to read a Bible while possessed in order that the spirit may not later interfere with their attendance at church.) But alongside this there were many who showed by their personal attitudes and the quality of their family lives a deep devotion to the inner spirit of Christianity. The Revival,[1] for all its exaggerations, represented—not only for Ganda but for many elsewhere in East Africa—a deep interiorization of puritan virtues.

Missionary schooling and social change

One factor in development was formal schooling; and its ultimate consequences were anticipated neither by the missionaries who provided it nor by the Ganda who avidly absorbed it. But by and large these consequences were to be felt wherever in Africa missionary education was provided. There were, of course, almost as many kinds of education as there were kinds of mission; and this is an aspect of the situation that has, up to now, been too little considered.[2] Roughly it may be said that 'British Protestant' education laid stress on the development of initiative and responsibility, while 'Latin Catholic' and 'American Fundamentalist' schools were concerned more with orthodoxy and obedience. Catholic missionaries who had themselves been reared in the Anglo-Saxon tradition encouraged that mixture of independence and obedience that is symbolized by the well-known boxing club of Namilyango College in Uganda. In Buganda there developed stereotypes, clearly recognized by thoughtful members of both parties and described by one Protestant: 'Protestant boys are educated as the sons of chiefs, Catholics as the sons of peasants.'

But all over East Africa (and there is similar private evidence from British West Africa) the pattern has been the same. It is illustrated by

[1] Warren, 1954; Stenning, 1964; Welbourn and Ogot, 1966: Ch. 5, 6.
[2] Welbourn, 1965a: 155f.; 1968a; 1965b: 9f.

the very large percentage of leading nationalist politicians who are either Protestant or who have passed through some form of secular education before entering public life. In colonies of Catholic powers, Protestant Africans were regarded as rebels by nurture;[1] and the well-known policy of educating a small body of élite to the point of total acculturation was (as it turned out, unsuccessfully) a training not so much for independence as for commitment to alien rulers.

But Catholic and Protestant missionaries alike had come to Africa—whether they knew it or not—because they had perhaps more than their share of the dynamic spirit that lay behind the expansion of Europe. Whether they aimed at obedience or at responsibility, they could not fail to pass on to their charges something of their own outlook. Both sides offered schooling not merely because they wanted educated Christians but because they saw a clear need to provide educated men for the leadership also of the state. They hoped that in providing education they would also be able to form Christian character; and in this they very largely succeeded. For many years, missionary school-masters were hero-figures who provided a total culture pattern (of table-manners and cricket, as well as church-attendance and Christian morality) which formed the ideals of several generations of young Africans. Perhaps it would be truer to say that Anglo-Saxons tended to be hero-figures, while Latins would be father-figures of a traditional type. But, whatever their exact relationship, whatever their slightly differing ideals of citizenship, they could not avoid sending out into the world men and women who were trained not for African society as it was but for a society still to be moulded by its impact with the West. The effects of schooling on individuals were to play no small part in bringing about the changes.

However much they might criticize missionary education, administrators and settlers by and large abetted it. The products of Protestant schools especially were thought to be unreliable; and there were—in many parts of Africa—practising Christian administrators who thought that at this point in their development, Islam might be a more suitable religion for Africans. But settlers and administrators needed African clerks. C. G. Richards shows that the first real interest of Gikuyu in schools provided by the Church Missionary Society was aroused by the discovery of the relatively high wages paid to clerks on settler farms.[2] Administrators needed interpreters; and increasingly they sought chiefs

[1] Welbourn, 1961: 196f.   [2] Richards, n.d.

322

and minor officials who could work within a bureaucratic s
from the schools could these come; only the missionaries g
ing; and thus it came about that under the all-powerful Eu
first place in the power-structure of the new Africa was fille
tian Africans. It was they who were to execute the social chan
by Europeans, they who were to lead the way in developing a culture
in which Africa could in some way adapt itself to the forces of change.

It is important that the schools were boarding schools (partly through
force of circumstance: distances were too great for any but a few day
schools to operate effectively; partly because missionaries saw, in an
atmosphere of a boarding school far removed from tribal influences,
the best hope of promoting Christian character). Those who went to
them learnt new ideas not only from their missionary mentors but from
members of other tribes and other villages. They discovered a new,
composite standpoint from which they could begin to criticize not
merely the religious, but the total culture of their homes. They made
friendships and absorbed ideals that were to be the framework within
which they would ultimately think no longer in terms of tribes but of
one nation, no longer in terms of getting the white men's wisdom but
of wresting power from them.

But the schools were not the only factor. Government employment
also took men to other parts of the country. The need to pay poll tax
drove them to find paid employment wherever it offered. Lonsdale
has related how men returning to western Kenya from work on
settler farms inaugurated adult education classes. Traders made effective
contact across clan, and even tribal, borders, thus weakening the
strength of traditional kinship ties.[1] Some of the consequences for
village life are vividly described by G. Wagner.[2] It all amounted to a
tremendous increase in the scale of experience[3] and at a rate that caused
some of the best administrators to wish they could call a halt. Africans
must enter into Western competitive society if they were to survive at
all. The question was how fast they must move.

Godfrey and Monica Wilson have suggested that magical thinking
turns over into scientific thinking as the scale of society increases.[4] This
germinal hypothesis may well require considerable modification. But
the increase in scale, introduced by the West along the instrumental
dimension, certainly had its effect along the expressive. Gikuyu

[1] Lonsdale, 1964.   [2] Wagner, 1939.
[3] Wilson, 1945: Ch. 2.   [4] Wilson, 1945: 89.

peasants, displaced from their ancestral lands, could no longer practise the ancestor cult in the old way; and, when Jomo Kenyatta dedicated his account of Gikuyu society 'in the firm faith that the dead, the living, and the unborn will unite to rebuild the destroyed shrines',[1] he no doubt had in mind the recovery of alienated land. Despite legislation against witchcraft and accusations of witchcraft, many Africans insist that withcraft has in fact increased under colonial rule.[2] In Ukaguru 'Christian girls cannot divorce their husbands if they tire of them so they must bewitch or poison their husbands if they want new ones';[3] and Beattie describes how spirit possession in Bunyoro, originally a group cult, has become almost wholly an individual affair.[4] As the old order of kinship groups is corroded by political and economic forces, the horizontal bonds holding men together are loosened; and the vertical bonds with the ultrahuman are changed or eliminated. (It is to be noted that in West Africa, where the feeling for the ancestors seems to have been altogether stronger than in East Africa, it is still possible to pour a libation to ancestors on leaving the airport at Accra and a libation to the same ancestors on arrival at London.)

The missions, not only by the provision of schools but by their general encouragement of economic change leading to greater material prosperity, and political change leading to social order, have played their part in this undermining of kinship bonds along the instrumental dimension. They have played their part also along the expressive dimension. A reading of Evans-Pritchard or G. Lienhardt raises the question how Nuer or Dinka would eat any protein were it not for the feasts associated with religious rituals;[5] and such rituals are, in fact, the chief occasions when kin—or larger groups—come together not only for mystical purposes but, as an important by-product, for social intercourse. When their expressive aspect is condemned by the missions, the overt cause for meeting is abolished; and the ties of kinship are still further weakened. What takes their place requires examination; but, in general, the movement is towards a Western type of individualism, finding a new secular, but no less expressive, unity in a nation not yet formed, and suspecting religion of every kind unless it can be shown to serve the national purpose.

[1] Kenyatta, 1938.
[2] Middleton and Winter, eds., 1963: *passim*.
[3] Middleton and Winter, 1963: 87.
[4] Beattie, 1957: 150–61; 1961: 11–38.
[5] Evans-Pritchard, 1956; Lienhardt, 1961.

DUALA. Before going further it seems desirable to outline two other types of African response to the West. Bureau has described vividly the encounter of Catholic missionaries with the Duala; and in what follows his English summary is freely quoted.[1] Schools were established where new converts could be sheltered from heathenism. The young people were to form a new society; and the Faith could be grafted onto a basis of rational knowledge. Young girls, trained in 'schools for future wives', would ensure the setting up of Christian families. These families were gathered around the mission stations to constitute pilot zones, whose influence, it was hoped, would eventually eradicate completely the surrounding paganism. New converts were required to give up all their traditions. In particular, an important cult of water spirits came under attack; but its social functions—in initiation, inter-clan reconciliation, obedience to customary law, apportionment of fishing grounds—were unrecognized and given no alternative sanctions. Similarly, in the case of marriage, the struggle against polygamy, the emancipation of the younger educated men and women, emphasis on the importance of the element of consent—all these contributed to a progressive decrease in the authority of the elders. They tried to recapture social control by increasing the bride-wealth; and this practice, to which the missionaries had originally offered no objection, came to be seen as an abuse.

Missionary teaching and organization offered new security to the traditionally submissive categories in society. Education provided new prestige, available to all. The new religion was expected to give greater power than was obtained through the traditional rites. When conversion became general, the Duala accepted the missionaries' judgements. Many cultural traits disappeared. Christian ceremonies replaced dancing. The schools took the place of initiation rites. A Christian was 'one who abandoned the customs'—especially those connected with the water spirits. But the power of the white men was not acquired; and there was deep disappointment. Traditional institutions—especially the kinship system—more or less maimed, remained. A bishop could say, 'We manufacture Christians but life takes them away from us'. Accusations of sorcery, betraying the underlying anxiety, became more numerous. There was a general return to traditional rites. Bureau thinks that 'the native clergy will now be able to re-integrate the original common religious consciousness into today's Christian life'. But his description well illustrates Malinowski's point:

[1] Bureau, 1968: 165–81.

The Africans, again, appreciating the value and the advantages of European religion, education and technology—or startled by the novelty thereof—begin often by adopting western ways eagerly and wholeheartedly. Quite as often they end by reacting in movements completely uncontrolled by the missionary or administrator, and at times directly hostile to the Whites.[1]

MAASAI. In contrast the pastoral Maasai (Masai) have shown very little interest in anything that Europeans had to offer.[2] Their treaty with the British—often quoted by the latter as evidence of equality—has denied them their traditional pastures and the right to fight both men and beasts. Some have been valued recruits to the Kenya army and police; a few have taken to agriculture; and more recently individuals have graduated at universities in East Africa or England. But in general they have been described as 'too proud to work' (for wages). They have submitted to British administration. But a youth who went to school was 'taken by the Europeans'. He might undergo no piercing of the ear-lobes, no removal of his incisors. He would not avoid circumcision; but he might have the operation in hospital. In any recognizable sense he ceased to be Maasai. To be European was good—for Europeans. To be Maasai was necessary—for Maasai. No purpose could be served by turning one into the other; and tradition was strong enough, for all but the few, to survive not only the visits of traders, the imposition of British administration and the best intentions of missionaries. It survived also the most traumatic experience of all—expulsion from the holy land of Kinangop in the northern part of the territory which, before the coming of the British, was theirs by occupation. One of the fundamental questions, which still requires investigation, is why the Maasai—identifying closely with their cattle, strictly monotheistic, with no trace of belief in a life after death—were so resistant to all Western influences while their close neighbours the Gikuyu (a tribe with whom they intermarried and had recognized rules of war)—settled agriculturists with a rich ancestor cult—adapted themselves so readily. It is sufficient, here, to insist that both the resistance and the adaptation were to all points of Western culture. The contrast between Ganda, Duala and Maasai illustrates the point that there can be no generalized statement of the missionary impact on Africa.

[1] Malinowski, 1945: 11.
[2] Huntingford, 1953. Most of my knowledge of the Maasai I owe to Mr B. K. Kantai who, as an undergraduate of Makerere University College, worked as my research assistant during the vacations of 1962–4.

Misunderstanding chieftainship

The issue of the 'treaty', however, highlights one of the points at which the West in general was unable to understand African institutions. The Maasai traditionally have no chiefs. Each tribe is governed by agreement between elders; and in rare matters affecting the whole people representative elders from all tribes may meet to take counsel. Each tribe has a *laibon*, a hereditary office confined to a particular clan common to all tribes. He is a powerful magician; but his main function, as diviner, is to mediate between God and men in the great matters of society. In these he has to be consulted. But he can do no more than reveal the will of God. He has no political power to enforce it. This is as true of the Chief *Laibon* of the whole people as of his representatives in each tribe; and the mistake of the British was to suppose that the Chief *Laibon* in 1904 and again in 1910 had authority to make a treaty with them—a treaty which provided for the movement of half the people from the northern part of its traditional preserve. Having made the 'treaty', they enforced it. But the Maasai felt that they had been tricked. The elders had not been fully consulted; and they alone had authority to make decisions of this sort.

At the other end of the scale, in Buganda, the British had found a ready-made system of bureaucratic administration under a king whose sacral overtones were never fully understood. More generally, chiefship was a variant of that described (perhaps rather ideally) by F. M. Deng among his own people:

In all Dinka tribes there are pre-eminent clans of hereditary chiefs whose divine authority is established by myths...traced back to the original founder of the Dinka. The chiefs' symbols of authority are sacred spears...A chief is regarded as God's representative. God wills that man should live harmoniously in this world; and it is the chief's task to see this will implemented. In order to reconcile between men, the chief himself must be a model of purity, righteousness and courage...Although there are many kinds of religious functionaries in Dinka society, the spear chief...embodies the sum total of all possible spiritual powers. He is considered to have supernatural powers of life and death, but he must not exert physical force nor spill blood. For this reason, and further because he must never retreat from danger, the tribal chief never goes to war, but is expected to remain at home and pray for victory...since the chief descends from the original founder, he is regarded as the spiritual father and keeper of the tribe. As the tribal father, his home is the home of all and is open to anyone at any time, for even his time is the time of all. His property is the property of all, and is at the disposal of whoever is in need. Through rites and ceremonies he ensures the productivity of the land...Even his physical well-being is the well-being of all, and the chief must not die...he was buried alive when at the point of death; he would then leave this world while living, and continue to live in his people's memory, while his powers were transferred to his successor...Guided by their divine enlightenment, they command such great spiritual respect that disobedience to their pronouncements is almost unthinkable.[1]

Considering the impact of the West, Deng continues:

Alien religions have stripped (the chief) of his divine powers, and alien institutions have armed him with a police force. He is no longer quite the man who brings peace, order, harmony through a cool mouth and a cool heart. The educated Christians see in him some of the evils of paganism and the exploitation of ignorance in people's beliefs. Their attitudes set an example to other tribesmen, and the divine prerogative of the chief becomes a topic of conversation. He in turn makes use of his new force. He becomes suspicious of the educated *élite* who appear to claim his authority by virtue of their newly-acquired wisdom. Modern ideas turn his fatherly attitude into one of struggle for survival; the language of persuasion is replaced by that of force and arrests—authoritarianism results. It is usual for chiefs and elders to refer to the new educated class as having 'no hearts'.[2]

Ogot has shown how before the arrival of the British, even chiefs of this order were beginning to compete for suzerainty.[3] But his most thought-provoking remarks relate to the problem arising for the newly independent states in their attempts to replace, by a democratically elected president, the old institution of kings and chiefs who carried ultrahuman sanctions.[4] Traditional society requires a chief not so much as a ruler as a mediator between the this-worldly section of tribe or clan on the one hand and God or the ancestors on the other. Western society of the nineteenth century saw its kings as constitutional monarchs, its presidents as representatives of the people. Its administrators were mediators not of divine will but of bureaucratic values. This was an outlook shared by administrators and missionaries alike. It is true that in so far as they were English they thought that they had found, in such traditional monarchies as those of Buganda, an institution very much

---

[1] Deng, 1964. Cf. G. Lienhardt, 1958: 97–135.   [2] Deng, 1964.
[3] Ogot, 1964b: 284–304.   [4] Ogot, 1964a.

to their liking; and the persistent encouragement of Ganda kings by English bishops is perhaps sufficient indication of the extent to which the expressive character of kingship has remained integral to British culture.[1] But missionaries were necessarily concerned to eradicate any overtly pagan aspects of a chief's office. For instance, Low thinks that, unlike the Ashanti chiefs, the king of Buganda was able to take part in Christian rites because he had no traditional rites of his own to perform;[2] and Southwold has suggested privately that administrative chiefs in Buganda found conversion easier than did clan heads with their traditional responsibilities to, and their putative relationships with, the ancestors.[3] Where traditional loyalties to a hereditary chief could be sustained in secular form, the missions seem to have gained a distinct advantage from his conversion. This was so not only in Buganda and in the other ancient kingdoms of Uganda where the kings had a more clearly sacral function.[4] Lonsdale has noted the greater strength of missions in western Kenya in locations where they were actively encouraged by the chief.[5]

At the same time, missions were involved in the concern of administrators for efficient government. Missionaries might be reluctant to accept secular criticisms of a chief who showed them favour. But by and large they were committed to the same set of bureaucratic values and would oppose change only if they saw it (sometimes rightly) as detrimental to the true interests of their people. It was in pursuit of these values that administrators deposed traditional chiefs, or proposed as their successors educated men in opposition to those traditionally sanctioned. In Kikuyu they imposed senior chiefs onto a social system which had never previously known them; and in general chiefs found themselves in the almost impossible position of having to mediate the instructions of central government to tribesmen who denied their right to rule and despised them for their ignorance, or neglect, of custom. It was of course the mission-educated younger men who were gradually to accept the posts of responsibility and, by their influence in society at large, to foster the wider recognition of new ideals of government. But the dismissal by the Buganda government of chiefs who opposed the king after his deportation in 1953 and of senior civil servants who opposed the 'go it alone' movement in 1961–2 is evidence of the extent

---

[1] Apter, 1961: 288ff.; Welbourn, 1965 b: 28f.
[2] Low, 1957: 3f. [3] Southwold, 1961.
[4] Stenning, 1964: 265. [5] Lonsdale, 1964.

to which even such a 'modernising autocracy' is still subject to traditional values.[1]

New communities for old

Attention has already been called to the weakening of kinship bonds
by the larger scale of social relationships introduced by secular forces
and missionary attacks on rituals of kinship. In Buganda the process had
already begun, before the coming of the missionaries, through the
building up by administrative chiefs of clientages that disregarded
kinship affinities. Although it was accentuated by the large-scale movements of population involved in the wars of religion, these were based
as much on indigenous fissiparous tendencies as on imported religions.[2]
Buganda underlines the thesis that social changes were due at least as
much to secular as to religious forces. The missionaries, as the main
organizers of the schools, were important—if often enough unwitting—
agents of change. As men whose outlook was largely moulded by
Western values, they gave general encouragement to what was happening; and their influence was all the greater because they had uniquely
gained the confidence of many of their converts. At points (as described
for the Duala) when they felt that traditional kinship obligations stood
in the way of Christian ideals of marriage, they attacked the practice of
kinship rules while often enough approving kinship in principle as
integral to social stability. But thoughtful Ganda Christians have more
recently expressed the view that the whole clan system must go if it is
to be possible to realize the Christian ideal of mutual responsibility
between husband and wife. Despite sixty years of Christian teaching,
they still remain primarily responsible each to his own clan.[3]

Another way of putting this is to say that men and women must
first be valued as individuals; and this is in line with the whole of
Western—as opposed to African—culture, partly formed by Christianity, partly reflected in its contemporary forms. A Maasai warrior
of the past generation, when it seemed that he was dead, was thrown
out, as was customary, to be eaten by the hyenas. He came to in the
morning and crawled back to his enclosure. But in his coma he had a
dream that left him with a permanent sense that he must 'go out and do
something'. In due course—in total contradiction of common Maasai
practice—he became a labourer on a settler's farm and eventually

---

[1] Welbourn, 1965b: 32. For 'modernising autocracy', see Apter, 1961.
[2] Low, 1957: 10   [3] Taylor, 1958: 188.

established a shop in Maasai territory. His sons are among the most educated Maasai. In another context this is extraordinarily similar to the stories of 'calls' to the ministry told by Sundkler.[1] The fact is that whatever their ideals of changing a whole society, both secular and religious immigrant forces in Africa have had to act mainly through Africans who, for whatever reason, were already disposed to leave the old ways. The West has taken them as individuals rather than as members of traditional groups. By so doing it has necessarily weakened the cohesion of those groups; and by offering an increasing number of role opportunities it has used these individuals as the leaders through whom the whole African society would move towards the looser inter-personal structure of the West.

It has not done so without producing considerable tensions—not only the tension between roles that is common enough in the West but, more importantly, tensions within individuals between their roles in the two societies. Traditional Ganda custom (as that of many societies) involves a prolonged ritual on the birth of twins. Many educated Ganda have reduced this to a tea-party to which grandparents on both sides are invited. A particular Ganda couple, who under the influence of the Revival felt strongly the pagan implications of the twin-ceremonies, refused to hold even this simple event. Within a month the wife was admitted to a mental hospital. If this is extreme, Taylor and Ogot have described two different attitudes of revivalists towards burial services: the one attempting to turn them into opportunities for positive Christian witness, the other refusing even to touch the corpse of a close relative.[2] In general, the fact that Christians were known among the Duala as 'those who have abandoned the customs',[3] in many parts of East Africa more positively as 'readers' (in contrast to pagans, 'those who do not read'), implied that they had set themselves apart and might be disruptive of traditional society. Ngugi has described with great delicacy and imaginative feeling the consequences of this tension for Gikuyu society and the variety of new identities which, in a period of change, were available to individuals.[4] Traditional solidarity was being broken; and something had to be put in its place. If, for an increasing number of individuals, this was to become the ideal of a national, politically independent society, the majority did not think in conscious political terms and required community on a smaller scale.

[1] Sundkler, 1960.   [2] Taylor, 1958: 204; Welbourn and Ogot, 1966: Ch. 6.
[3] Bureau, 1968.   [4] Ngugi, 1965.

In Buganda the need was, of course, met by the conversion of the new churches into political parties. But, at a less complex level, it was met by bands of 'readers' collected round missionaries who gathered 'clientages' similar to those of the administrative chiefs.[1] With amazing rapidity native lay-readers established similar groups throughout the country. Ogot has quoted Bishop Willis's description of the Anglican church in western Kenya in 1916:

In not a few cases it is the native who takes the initiative into his own hands. Trained or half-trained, in a Mission school, the Convert returns to his native village, and is lost to sight. Next time the Missionary meets him he is in self-imposed charge of a little congregation of Readers, from which in due course a little group of candidates for the catechumenate emerges...Again the visitor on any Sunday to the native congregation in Kisumu will see what he will see nowhere else but in Kavirondo [*i.e.*, *western Kenya*], a drilled and uniformed congregation. Not all, but some hundreds of them, will be found clothed in a short shirt of white, with dark blue facings and a dark blue spine pad; the letters, roughly worked C.M.S., K [*i.e.*, *Church Missionary Society*, *Kavirondo*] across the breast; and on the red fez cap a blue cross on a white shield. A closer inspection will reveal mysterious buttons and stripes showing that from colonel to corporal every rank is represented...The interesting part of the organization is that it is entirely the *native* Christian's own idea. They have designed and paid for their own uniforms. They drill and organize themselves without instructions or intervention from any white man; a clearer proof of natural independence it would be difficult to find.[2]

If this was unusual, it indicates the way in which missions were able to inspire the growth of a new community to replace the old. In course of time the mission churches have increased in size and bureaucracy;[3] and the distance between leaders and the local congregations has grown. Social mobility has increased in the country as a whole, and it has become clear that the advantages of education and Western technology can be gained without the mediation of the missions. In this new climate the older-established churches have tended to become much more the ritual meeting-ground of individuals rather than a community involved from the grass roots. But Willis's description looks forward to what was later to be attempted by the independent churches with their uniforms, flags and drums and their hymns based on indigenous rhythms.[4] Lonsdale has pointed out that the old clan societies depended on a priest-like clan head, who focused the eternal order of

[1] Low, 1957: 5.
[2] Welbourn and Ogot, 1966: 24f.
[3] Taylor, 1957: 12.
[4] Welbourn and Ogot, 1966: Ch. 15.

living and dead, and on diviners, who interpreted disruptions of that order. The leaders of the independent churches have to fill both roles, with Western education beginning to take the place of divination.[1] It is not difficult to interpret the independent churches as clans within the Christ-tribe, the local congregations as new forms of lineage. C. G. Baëta has suggested that independent churches in Ghana had their instrumental roots precisely in the need to provide mutual help between individuals no longer available in kinship groups.[2]

At other points missionaries provided Christian communities. In this it is unlikely that they were consciously copying the kinship system, though they may thus have contributed to its decay. There was the situation described by Oliver:

Even the missionary who set out with a few dozen porters and tried to settle in a native village had to set up what amounted to a small independent state. He was recognised as a kind of chief by the headmen round about, and to a greater or lesser extent the Sultan of Zanzibar and the British or French consul were felt to be behind him...The men he brought with him were under his jurisdiction from the start, and, as time went on, some of the local inhabitants, perhaps political exiles, perhaps fugitive slaves, perhaps tribal misfits, perhaps religious converts, would come and settle on his land. However much he might seek in his teaching to support the temporal power already established and to preach to the people in their homes and villages, these men at least would regard him for practical purposes as their chief and look to him for economic support, for law and order, and in the last resort for military defence.[3]

Such settlements were deliberately established on the East African coast for freed slaves. Elsewhere, Roman Catholic and Scottish missions in particular actively encouraged their development as self-supporting economic communities, where the virtues of hard work ('an expiation according to divine law') might be learnt alongside protection from sorcerers, ancestral spirits and the temptations of polygamy. But

most missionaries were forced to admit after a generation of experiment that these 'centres of Christianity and civilisation' were unsatisfactory places, whether the inhabitants were freed slaves or whether they were free men who had simply changed their political allegiance. The missionary, called to be the ruler of ne'er-do-wells and malcontents, could produce results which were outwardly fair; but too often his activities were a hindrance and not a help

[1] Lonsdale, 1964.   [2] Baëta, 1962: 131.
[3] Oliver, 1952: Ch. 2.

to the evangelisation of the country in general. His pupils, lacking all the family ties and inherited traditions of free African society, were regarded as more foreign than the European himself, while the missionary's political relation to them inevitably brought him into collision with the native rulers.[1]

In cases, such as the Friends Africa Mission in western Kenya where 'Christian villages' were maintained till after World War II, conflict arose between the missionaries and elders on the one hand and the younger African inhabitants who wished to be free of village discipline on the other. Missionaries had to accept their place in an increasingly plural society and to be content with setting up congregations in the existing villages. Here, apart from the civilizing influence of schools and the effect of Christian teaching about marriage, there has been very little consequent change in traditional institutions. Perhaps the most striking feature has been that of their divisive influence. Almost from the start it was the practice in Buganda for Catholics and Protestants to establish churches on neighbouring hills. A Gikuyu Protestant, spending Christmas in Kampala during the height of the Mau Mau emergency, admitted with regret that he did not know how to celebrate it with his fellow Gikuyu Catholic from a neighbouring village.

Three examples must, however, be given of the influence of indigenous Christian movements. Taylor describes how a leader of the Revival in Buganda

has settled on his family estate...almost all the brethren that there are in the parish. If, for example, he meets...a recently converted herdman from Ankole, who, having dismissed the casual woman with whom he was living, is looking for a Christian wife, the landowner will very probably offer the young man a place on his estate, or a plot on which to build. There he comes, with the new wife he has found within the fellowship, and settles down. In two years time he is marvelling at the miracle by which he, the degraded flotsam of society, has got such a neat and prosperous little house. So a strongly integrated cluster grows up around the fatherly head. They almost forget the many different clans, or even tribes, from which they originated, because of their membership of the new community. When a girl in the community is sought in marriage, they may deny her if her suitor is not approved, particularly if he is not a member of the [Revival]. If they agree to the marriage, the brethren in the community will undertake the arrangements, provide the feast and the transport, and attend the ceremony in force. Within such a local fellowship there is a security such as no other kinship-group or association in Ganda society today is able to provide.[2]

[1] Oliver, 1952: Ch. 2.   [2] Taylor, 1958: 102.

Stenning writes of a similarly inspired movement among the pastoral Hima of Ankole. Conversion is on an individual basis. It is commonly induced by sickness interpreted (in terms traditionally familiar) as a punishment from the Lord and requiring for its cure a 'washing in the blood', which takes the form of a confession of past misdeeds also reminiscent of a traditional spirit-initiation cult. Initiation is completed at a fellowship meeting in a Revivalist village; and, in due course, the new convert goes to live there, or forms a new village along with other converts. Cattle exchanges—lengthy processes integral to Hima society—with pagans are wound up as soon as possible, except with relatives whom it is hoped to convert. The fellowship is endogamous, though clan exogamy is still largely observed. There is no bride-wealth; and the arrangement of marriages by parents is rapidly declining. Divorce is not allowed, except of wives married under customary law who have not themselves been 'saved'. The economic life of these new villages is more oriented towards a cash economy than that of traditional villages. Bull calves are reared for sale, not killed as in traditional practice. Milk is drunk only once a day, since it is regarded as the sin of greed to deprive calves of their mothers' milk. There is no blood-letting for food; and therefore banana plantations are cultivated and maize flour is bought. Villagers are more ready to buy Western goods—clothes, cycles, domestic utensils, light furniture and medicine. Villages are moved less frequently. There is a compulsive cleanliness and preoccupation with disease (privately Stenning has spoken of the use of chamber pots for children, rubber aprons for nursing, mosquito curtains over doorways and a liberal use of insecticides). Travel, which in pagan society is widely undertaken in pursuit of cattle exchanges, now takes the form of visits to hospital and religious occasions.[1]

Finally, Webster has written of the plantations started by wealthy independent Christians in Nigeria (men of a wholly different character from the independent church leaders of western Kenya). They preached 'the gospel of coffee, cocoa, cotton and work as well as the scriptures'; they opposed the uncritical acceptance of European ideas that was prevalent in the high society of Lagos; and

on the plantations the social system remained essentially Yoruba. The planter became the chief. He was arbiter and judge, benefactor and protector, and high priest leading in worship on Sundays. And he was employer. The planters believed they had discovered a system which provided the benefits

[1] Stenning, 1964.

335

of Europe without necessarily destroying the social fibre of Africa. They confidently expected the agricultural revolution...would ultimately spread over the whole of Yorubaland.[1]

Marriage and the family

Among the positive elements of African society these planters counted polygamy. In contrast they pointed to the 'self-centred small family units' of Western society. It has often enough been pointed out that polygamy has only rarely been the overt cause of separatism.[2] But, in a recent study of independent churches in Africa, D. B. Barrett has suggested that underlying all independent church movements in Africa lies a recognition, if sometimes unconscious, that the missionary attack, at one and the same time, on polygyny and ancestor cults represents a massive assault on the basic unit of the family. He finds a high correlation between the presence of these two traits in a society and the incidence of independency.[3]

Western Christian ideas of the family may not be essential to Christianity; but they have been preached by the missions, and despite sexual laxity among individuals, they have in general been approved by most Europeans in Africa. They include lifelong monogamy, consent of both parties—implying some degree of equality between husband and wife—and the primacy of the nuclear family, involving respect and often affection for kin on both sides but the right to reject kin who seem to threaten the existence of the family. In contrast, marriage in most African societies is potentially polygamous. Divorce is more readily obtainable than under Christian law. But marriage stability is protected by bride-wealth. Though marriages based on romantic love are not unknown, women in the last resort have no choice in the matter and may be severely beaten if they refuse the husband of their parents' choice. They remain minors throughout their lives; and their function is to bear children and to serve the economic needs of their husbands. In some societies (such as Maasai) men of the husband's age-grade have free sexual access to all wives of the grade, though children thus conceived belong to the *pater*.

In clan societies children belong to the clan rather than to the nuclear family; and this is well illustrated by a Ganda student at Makerere

[1] Webster, 1968: 119.   [2] Parrinder, 1953: 108; Welbourn, 1961: 184.
[3] Barrett, 1968: 117–24.

College, Uganda, the daughter of a Christian clergyman. On being asked to describe her home, she replied, 'What do you mean by my home? I've lived in so many.' From the age of three onwards she had lived mostly with a succession of relatives, while her faithfully monogamous parents received in return the children of other relatives.

The attempt to introduce Western Christian ideas of marriage was therefore a matter not of reforming the existing system but of replacing one complex with another. That many of the same elements were present in both did not reduce the difficulty of changing the whole *Gestalt*.

The most comprehensive accounts of missionary policy and African response are in A. Phillips[1] and J. B. Webster.[2] The most obvious issues were polygamy and bride-wealth; and the missionaries differed in their policies. Some demanded the dismissal of all wives but the first, who must then be married in church. Some allowed a choice between existing wives. Some permitted the dismissal of all and the choice of a wholly new, Christian, partner. Few asked seriously what would be the fate of those rejected or of their children. In the case of bride-wealth (which to many appeared as 'buying' a wife) there was a continuum of policy from complete prohibition, through permissive non-interference, to insistence that marriage by Christian rites could not take place until all customary formalities were complete.

African responses have also varied. There has been the fruition of marriages according to the best Western Christian pattern, though this has happened most often either among Revivalists or among those who, through education, have entered most deeply into Western Christian culture as a whole. There has been the overt recognition of monogamy as law alongside its almost total breakdown in practice.[3] V. Martin describes a deteriorating situation among the Catholic population of Dakar,[4] while A. W. Southall and P. C. W. Gutkind write of a situation in a slum area of Kampala where the ideal of a lifelong sexual partnership has almost ceased to exist.[5] Alongside these adaptations to the Western pattern has gone the attempt by some independent churches to argue that monogamy is a purely Western institution and that Christianity should endorse polygamy as integral to African society. Other such churches hold that polygamy must be permitted as a transitional stage.[6] Among the mission churches there is a growing

[1] Phillips, ed., 1953.   [2] Webster, 1964: *see* Index; and 1968.
[3] Taylor, 1958: Ch. 9.   [4] Martin, 1968: 362–95.   [5] Southall and Gutkind, 1961.
[6] Welbourn and Ogot, 1966: 70f., 102; Webster, 1964; 1968.

feeling that polygamous marriages must be treated with more tolera-
tion than in the past.[1]

It is impossible here, however, as at all other points, to attribute solely
to the missions the fundamental changes that have taken place. For
instance, missionary disapproval of bride-wealth, where it has occurred,
has probably contributed to a lessening of the traditional sanctions of
marriage. But missionaries, except in so far as they are themselves
products of a cash economy, cannot be held responsible for the tendency
in some areas to sell daughters to the highest bidder and to demand
bride-wealth greater than that allowed by law.[2]

With the breakdown, under secular forces, of traditional social
security and moral sanctions, the church has been able to offer only to
those most deeply committed a new pattern of marriage. Perhaps its
most positive contribution, alongside teaching, has been the encouragement through education of a higher status for women and the provision
of opportunities, through employment as teachers and nurses, to establish themselves in their own right. Their employment in commerce, in
the civil service and as ministers of government has been a natural
development of the early policy of missions. Nevertheless, even educated Africans still value women chiefly in terms of their capacity to
marry and bear children; and women themselves are so anxious to
bear children, and so aware of the need for security in their old age, that
if they remain legally spinsters, they are still likely to rear families
outside marriage. One of the unresolved problems of some African
societies is whether these children belong to the mother or to the
genitor.

With the decline in kinship bonds has gone a parallel decline in the
acceptance of responsibility for illegitimate children and orphans; and
one recent contribution of the churches has been the encouragement of
orphanages and of legal adoption and foster care. A problem to which
little attention has been given is that of the effect of child-rearing
customs on adult personality; and such studies as those of Whiting
and Erikson are of fundamental importance.[3] Africans who have lived
intimately with Europeans seem by and large to copy their total family
pattern; but whatever changes missionary teaching and example may
have effected in the relations between men and women, traditional

[1] Hayward, ed., 1963: 52, 59, 77.
[2] Welbourn, 1965a: 122.
[3] Erikson, 1950; Whiting, ed., 1963; Welbourn, 1968a.

habits of child care die hard. Perhaps this is illustrated most vividly by the feeling of Africans that European children, reared in contemporary permissiveness, are cheeky and show inadequate respect for their elders. On the other hand, Europeans ask whether many African children have a sufficiently close and continuing relationship with a single mother-figure or are given full opportunity to develop a sense of responsibility.

Initiation, identity and politics

That many have developed this sense must be attributed very largely to the common Western drive towards individual initiative, hard work and a sense of guilt. A question still to be investigated is whether these characteristics were already more clearly developed in such societies as the Gikuyu, Kalenjin and Maasai, which had for their children a well-marked system of age-grades accompanied by circumcision and temporary retirement from society for a period of intense and rigorous training before they emerged as adults. The Gikuyu were early subject to a massive missionary attack not only on the whole practice of clitoridectomy but on the 'pagan' aspects of male circumcision.[1] It seems likely that the contemporary reduction of the circumcision ceremonies to little more than a formal operation owes more to secular forces than to missionary teaching. The Gikuyu have found their outlets in widespread trading activities and in aggressive politics. The Kalenjin, far less the objects of missionary activity, have had the aggressive activities of their initiates curtailed by government and have joined the army and the police in large numbers.[2] There a district commissioner could write in 1940: 'Owing to the broadminded attitude of the Mill Hill [*Catholic*] Mission towards pagan customs, some progress is being made and its schools are fairly well attended... the anti-circumcision attitude of the Africa Inland Mission negatives any respect they may command.'[3]

It is now the educated, rather than the Christians as such, who are opposing the custom on the grounds of its brutality and adverse effects on health. Some of them feel that circumcision is still necessary (if pressed, they would say on medical grounds) but can be done medically during infancy. They wonder whether, with the loss of adolescent pain and excitement, their own sons will ever become fully men. The

[1] Welbourn, 1961: Ch. 7.   [2] Welbourn, 1968*b*: 232.
[3] Kipkorir, 1961.

Maasai have kept their rite almost unchanged and, as has already been indicated, have scarcely entered into communication with the West. There are two other cases of note. Among the Yao a highly successful attempt was made to integrate tribal with Christian initiation.[1] It is now criticized because young men living in the towns no longer undergo tribal initiation; and the Christian rite therefore seems to be archaic. On the other hand, in Bugisu, where there is no age-grade system, circumcision is still so widely valued as an entry into adult responsibility in tribal affairs that one African priest encourages initiates to attend a ceremony in church rather than the pagan ceremonies with which it is traditionally associated. Thus in some cases initiation has changed its form. It is no longer a complex of surgical operation with initiation into tribal secrets. The operation alone has become the clue to adulthood.

The fact is that through the whole impact of the West a purely tribal identity has now become irrelevant in Africa. Africans have to re-identify themselves in national, if not pan-African, terms.[2] The Christian church, partly because it was divided within itself, partly because it was too easily seen as the tool of imperialism, has failed to provide an expressive dimension around which the instrumental needs of the new situation can be integrated. Its place is taken by nationalism and the African Personality; and African Christians are left in tension between the positive qualities of nationalism and the wider commitments of their faith. This is a problem of which Western Christians are not sufficiently aware; and Warren has recently suggested that their most effective place in Africa may be no longer as professional missionaries but as servants of secular society.[3] This amounts to a recognition by a senior missionary statesman that missionaries have been as responsible as any for the present situation in Africa and that their proper place is now one of full identification with the society which they have helped to form.

It is, important, however, to try to assess the degree of their responsibility. It must not be too readily assumed that, where there is preaching of Christian ideals of personal dignity, there will develop political nationalism. In a revolutionary situation there is little room for traditional values; and by and large it is the older generation of church-going Africans in East Africa who are least at home in nationalist

[1] Lucas, 1950.   [2] Welbourn, 1965a: Ch. 16; 1965b: Ch. 11f.
[3] Warren, 1965: 185–90.

society. It is much more that having been educated, often enough in mission schools, into the externals of European culture, Africans found that they were not accepted at its core. This is true whether they were highly acculturated French-speaking men who could not find total acceptance in Parisian society and in defence formed the concept of négritude;[1] civil servants with English degrees who were not admitted to 'European clubs'; or more humble converts whom American missionaries received only at the back door. By their whole education, as much as by the preaching of missionaries, they had been encouraged to be men, only to discover that in a world dominated by Europeans the one way to assert their dignity was to become African men—to invent 'the African Personality' and to insist on the establishment of political institutions that were unquestionably African. To this all but a few missionaries have contributed little but criticism. In Protestant circles 'politics' was of the devil. This attitude was taken over by the older Christians and contributed to the alienation between them and the younger generation who increasingly found it difficult to be 'at home' in the village congregations. Among Catholic Africans, political nationalism seems to have been slower to develop; and when it did come, the attitude of missionaries appeared often to be that Catholics should enter into politics in order to ensure the Catholic presence. The end result is one of high ambivalence. On the one hand, African political leaders are deeply grateful to the church for its positive contributions, especially in education. Despite the general equation of missionaries with government officials and settlers, there is still the memory of outstanding individuals who have stood for African rights. There is still the feeling that the church can be a great moral force in the nation and that whatever may be attempted through national youth movements, there is perhaps no real alternative. On the other hand is the feeling that the church is still the handmaid of alien political forces; and this feeling is only intensified when it is seen that the main support for the church comes not so much from indigenous sources as from American and European money and personnel. 'Working within the Anglican Church in Uganda today are eighty-five professional missionaries (excluding wives) fully maintained from overseas. A conservative estimate of their cash value is £75,000 a year.' The internal budget for the whole Province of Uganda is probably not more than £12,000.[2] In these circumstances it is very difficult to forecast what will

[1] Hodgkin, 1957. [2] Barton, 1965: 222-5.

be the future of the Christian church in Africa. Certainly it must be assumed that most of the changes in traditional society, for which it has been at least in part responsible, will now undergo further change at the hands of nationalism as an expressive, as well as an instrumental, agent.

This essay has attempted to assess changes in colonial Africa as the product of Western culture of which Christian missionaries, themselves only partially free of determination by that culture, were important representatives. It has tried to select those changes in which the missions were most closely involved. But, in a complex situation which has yet to be fully described and analysed, it is difficult to present an objective picture. For there is perhaps a tendency, shared by the present Christian writer, to emphasize the Western impact of missions as opposed to that which is peculiarly Christian. The African scene, as well as the missionary spectrum, is intensely varied; and the missionary impact itself has varied from tribe to tribe. This chapter has necessarily drawn most of its examples from British East Africa, and to a large extent from Protestant sources. A somewhat different picture might emerge if use were to be made of such material as is available from Catholic areas and from other parts of Africa.

BIBLIOGRAPHY

Ajayi, J. F. A. (1965). *Christian missionaries in Nigeria, 1841–1891—the making of a new élite*. London.

Ajayi, W. O. (1965). 'The beginnings of the African bishopric on the Niger', *Bulletin of the Society for African Church History*, **1**, nos. 3–4.

Apter, D. E. (1961). *The political kingdom in Uganda*. London, Oxford University Press.

Ayandele, E. A. (1966). *The missionary impact on modern Nigeria, 1842–1914*. London.

Baëta, C. G. (1962). *Prophetism in Ghana*. London.

— ed. (1968). *Christianity in tropical Africa*. London, Oxford University Press for International African Institute.

Barrett, D. B. (1968). *Schism and renewal in Africa*. London, Oxford University Press.

Barton, J. (1965). 'From East Africa', *Frontier*, **8**, no. 3.

Beattie, J. H. M. (1957). 'Initiation into the Cwezi spirit possession cult in Bunyoro', *African Studies*, **16**.

Beattie, J. H. M. (1961). 'Group aspects of the Nyoro spirit mediumship cult', *Rhodes–Livingstone Journal*, **30**.

(1966). 'Ritual and social change', *Man*, New Series, **1**.

Buber, M. (1944). *I and thou*. Edinburgh.

Bureau, R. (1968). 'Influence de la Christianisation sur les institutions traditionelles des ethnies côtières du Cameroun', in *Christianity in tropical Africa*, C. G. Baëta, ed. London, Oxford University Press for International African Institute.

Deng, F. M. (1964). 'The impact of alien religions among the Dinka', Institute of African Studies, University of Ife, Seminar on *The high god in Africa*.

Erikson, E. H. (1950). *Childhood and society*. London.

Evans-Pritchard, E. E. (1937). *Witchcraft, oracles and magic among the Azande*. Oxford, Clarendon Press.

(1956). *Nuer religion*. Oxford, Clarendon Press.

Fallers, L. A., ed. (1964). *The king's men*. London, Oxford University Press.

Faupel, J. (1962). *African holocaust*. London.

Hayward, V. E. W., ed. (1963). *African independent church movements*. London.

Herberg, W. (1955). *Protestant, Catholic, Jew*. New York.

Hodgkin, T. W. (1957). 'The African renaissance', *The Listener*, **58**, no. 1481.

Huntingford, G. W. B. (1953). *The southern Nilo-Hamites* (Ethnographic Survey of Africa, Daryll Forde, ed.), East-Central Africa, Pt VIII. London, International African Institute.

Kenyatta, J. (1938). *Facing Mount Kenya*. London.

Kipkorir, B. E. (1961). *Christianity comes to Marakwet*. Arts Research Prize Essay, Makerere University College.

Lienhardt, G. (1961). *Divinity and experience: the religion of the Dinka*. Oxford, Clarendon Press.

(1958). 'The western Dinka', in *Tribes without rulers*, J. Middleton and D. Tait, eds. London.

Lonsdale, J. M. (1964). A political history of Nyanza, 1883–1945. Ph.D. thesis, University of Cambridge.

Low, D. A. (1957). *Religion and society in Buganda, 1875–1900*. London. (East African Studies, no. 8).

Lucas, W. V. (1950). *Christianity and native rites*. London, University Mission to Central Africa.

Malinowski, B. (1945). *The dynamics of culture change*. New Haven, Yale University Press.

Mannoni, O. (1956). *Prospero and Caliban*. London.

Martin, V. (1968). 'Mariage et famille dans les groupes christianisés ou en voie de christianisation de Dakar', in *Christianity in tropical Africa*, C. G. Baëta, ed. London, Oxford University Press for International African Institute.

Middleton, J. M., and E. H. Winter, eds. (1963). *Witchcraft and sorcery in East Africa*. London.

Neill, S. C. (1964). *A history of Christian missions*. Harmondsworth.

Ngugi, J. (1965). *The river between*. London.

Ogot, B. A. (1964 a). 'From chief to president', *Transition*, **10**.

(1964 b). 'Kingship and statelessness among the Nilotes', in *The historian in tropical Africa*, J. Vansina, R. Mauny, and L. V. Thomas, eds. London, Oxford University Press for International African Institute.

Oliver, R. (1952). *The missionary factor in East Africa*. London.

(1957). *Sir Harry Johnston and the scramble for Africa*. London.

Parrinder, E. G. (1953). *Religion in an African city*. London, Oxford University Press.

Perham, M. (1960). *Lugard*, Vol. II: *The years of authority*. London.

Phillips, A., ed. (1953). *Survey of African marriage and family life*. London, Oxford University Press.

Richards, C. G. (n.d.). History of the CMS in the Highlands. (ms.)

Riesman, D. (1950). *The lonely crowd*. London, Oxford University Press.

Rotberg, R. I. (1965). *Christian missionaries and the creation of Northern Rhodesia, 1880–1924*. Princeton University Press.

Smith, N. (1966). *The Presbyterian Church of Ghana, 1835–1960*. London, Oxford University Press.

Southall, A. W., and P. C. W. Gutkind (1961). *Townsmen in the making*. London. (East African Studies no. 9.)

Southwold, M. (1961). *Bureaucracy and chiefship in Buganda*. London. (East African Studies no. 14.)

Stenning, D. J. (1964). 'Salvation in Ankole', in *African systems of thought*, M. Fortes and G. Dieterlen, eds. London, Oxford University Press for International African Institute.

Sundkler, B. G. M. (1960). *The Christian minister in Africa*. London.

Taylor, J. V. (1957). *Christianity and politics in Africa*. Harmondsworth.

(1958). *The growth of the church in Buganda*. London.

The Times (London), 9 August 1965.

Wagner, G. (1939). 'The changing family among the Bantu Kavirondo', *Africa*, **12** (supplement).

Warren, M. A. C. (1954). *Revival*. London.

(1965). 'Church and state in Asia and Africa', *Frontier*, **8**, no. 3.

Weber, M. (1951). *The religion of China*. Glencoe, Ill.

Webster, J. B. (1964). *The African churches among the Yoruba, 1888–1922*. Oxford, Clarendon Press.

(1968). 'The attitudes and policies of the Yoruba African churches towards polygamy', in *Christianity in tropical Africa*, C. G. Baëta, ed. London, Oxford University Press for International African Institute.

Welbourn, F. B. (1961). *East African rebels*. London.

(1962). 'Some aspects of Kiganda religion', *Uganda Journal*, **26**, no. 2.

(1965 a). *East African Christian*. London, Oxford University Press.

(1965 b). *Religion and politics in Uganda, 1952–1962*. Nairobi.

(1968 a). 'Guilt and shame', in *Christianity in tropical Africa*, C. G. Baëta, ed. London, Oxford University Press for International African Institute.

(1968 b). 'Keyo initiation', *Journal of Religion in Africa*, **1**, Fasc. 3.

(1969). 'Healing as a psychosomatic event'. Centre of African Studies, Edinburgh, Seminar on *Witchcraft and healing*, 14–15 February.

and B. A. Ogot (1966). *A place to feel at home*. London, Oxford University Press.

and A. Katumba (1964). 'Muslim martyrs of Buganda', *Uganda Journal*, **28**, no. 2.

Whiting, B. B., ed. (1963). *Six cultures: a study of child rearing*. London.

Wilson, G., and M. Wilson (1945). *The analysis of social change*. Cambridge University Press.

CHAPTER 11

THE NGONI AND WESTERN EDUCATION

by

MARGARET READ

The Ngoni people arrived in Malawi more than thirty years before the British finally took over all the territory. They came from Natal in southern Africa, breaking away under military leaders in about 1820 from Chaka's Zulu empire. One section crossed the Zambezi river in 1835 at the time of a solar eclipse, and journeyed as far north as Lake Victoria in northern Tanzania before turning back to found a kingdom in northern Malawi. The other section went east of Lake Nyasa to southern Tanzania and returned to found their kingdom in central Malawi. Both kingdoms were examples of African conquest states, and they maintained their armies based on universal military service until the era of colonial rule.

The ruler of each kingdom was the Paramount Chief, called the *Inkosi*, with a hierarchy of lesser chiefs and officials under him. The system of law courts followed the same hierarchy, the Paramount's court being the supreme court of appeal. The Ngoni people reckoned their wealth in cattle, and their herds figured prominently in the ancestor cult, in marriage exchanges and in funeral ceremonies. They were a strictly patrilineal people with residence in the husband's village at marriage. The transfer of cattle from the bridegroom's family to the bride's established the authority of the father and his family over his children. The old Ngoni language was closely akin to Zulu, and was used on all ritual occasions, including the recital of the praise songs of chiefs and war heroes. After settlement among the other peoples of Malawi, Ngoni as the language of the home was gradually replaced by two of the local languages, Tumbuka in the north and Nyanja in the centre. As a result of their migrations before settling in Malawi, people of other ethnic groups became integrated into the Ngoni kingdoms. For this reason one uses the term 'people' rather than 'tribe' when speaking of the Ngoni. In their kingdoms the people of different tribal groups were recognized by their clan names.

Introduction

Walking along a footpath in northern Ngoniland I fell in with a young Ngoni teacher going to visit his father. Tucked under his arm was a book which he showed me saying he had borrowed it from the Scottish teacher at the mission station. 'You know,' he said, 'this book is all about the kind of things we talk about in our village. That is why I like it. This man has wisdom—the kind of wisdom our fathers have. Has he written any other books?' The book was Plato's *Republic*.

This encounter illustrates the main theme in the present essay: the ways in which the Ngoni people in Malawi reacted to and made use of Western education, applying their own criteria to its relevance and advantages for themselves, for their traditional culture and their existence as a people under colonial rule. In a paper to the British Association some years ago (1955: 96) I put forward the hypothesis that in the field of modern education we could recognize definite stages in the cultural contacts of Britain with the colonial territories in Africa. I suggested that this might be one way of examining certain factors in the reactions of African peoples to the impact of modern education. The approach involves both anthropological and historical techniques, beginning with the early forms of modern education, often initiated by missionary societies, and traceable through many intermediate stages to the present-day interaction of modern technological and professional training for national development with an increasing emphasis on African studies, including language, history, folk literature, etc.

The stages are, briefly, as follows. The earliest was, among many African peoples, marked by conservatism towards a new form of teaching and learning for young people. I shall be illustrating this phase from the Ngoni material. The second stage was a gradual acceptance by Africans of some of the new skills and ways of living introduced by the schools, such as reading and writing, making bricks for houses, being paid in money for work done, buying Western clothes to wear in school and in church. However, it is evident from the Ngoni material that a selective process was at work during this stage. While British culture through the schools thrust upon African peoples a wide range of foreign cultural elements, the response to these stimuli, varying in different areas, showed selectiveness in those elements adopted by Africans.

The third and fourth stages were interrelated. The Africans were persuaded or obliged, generally in mission schools, to give up certain traditional beliefs, practices and former ways of living. From many countries the verdict by Africans on this phase was, as one Ngoni teacher expressed it, 'The white teachers taught us to despise our past'. Since the introduction of schools was inevitably tied in with economic, social and political changes, leading Africans in the fourth stage began to demand that their children should have a modern education, complete in all its details. They feared, as the Ngoni did, that without it their children's development would be retarded and that they would be discriminated against in competing with Europeans.

The final stages showed a further process of selectiveness by Africans. By their own choice they had taken the opportunities offered and had built a Western school system into their society; and some had reached the final stages of full professional training. They were now released from the fear of being held back in educational progress, and they were therefore free to turn their attention to studies relating to their own traditional culture. African writing in African languages and in English, African sculpture, painting and music, the study of African history—these developments began to establish African culture alongside Western cultures in the educational system. The impetus to achieve this was fostered by the forces of African nationalism and by the desire for political independence. In the 1930s the International African Institute initiated prize competitions for essays in African languages. Some of these essays, translated into English and published after the war, show how difficult it was for African writers at that time to express their sense of values in African cultures. African novels of the last two decades, many of which illustrate the theme of 'the two worlds', express in often dramatic form the nature of the conflict in individuals and in their society between traditional values and relationships on the one hand, and on the other the impact of modern change through missionary, trading and government channels (Kachingwe, 1966).

Education, culture and society

The following conversation I recorded in the village of a senior chief in northern Malawi, a chief so respected and so senior that he was addressed as Inkosi. Two young teachers in charge of a school came to greet him and the senior men of his village who were sitting behind him on the verandah of his house. The teachers bent one knee as they gave him the customary greeting, waiting in silence till he spoke.

'How is your school?'
'The classes are full and the children are learning well, Inkosi.'
'How do they behave?'
'Like Ngoni children, Inkosi.'
'What do they learn?'
'They learn reading, writing, arithmetic, scripture, geography and drill, Inkosi.'
'Is that education?'
'It is education, Inkosi.'
'No! No! No! Education is *very* broad, *very* deep. It is not only in books, it is learning to live. I am an old man now. When I was a boy I went with the Ngoni army to the war against the Bemba. Then the mission came and I went to school. I became a teacher. Then I was a chief. Then the government came. I have seen our country change, and now there are many schools and many young men go away to work to find money. I tell you that Ngoni children must learn how to live and how to build up our land, not only how to work and earn money. Do you hear?'
'*Yebo*, Inkosi.' (Yes, O Chief.)   (Read, 1967: 2)

The Ngoni concept of education in their pre-literate society was a continuous process of socialization from childhood to adulthood (Read, 1967). Boys and girls were trained, at successive stages of their physical growth, to take their place in Ngoni society, to behave in the correct fashion to superiors, elders and equals, while the boys in pre-European days took part in preparation for training for the army. A phrase heard often from Ngoni elders was: 'War was *our* school.' Living in the boys' dormitory and taking part in cattle herding were conceived of as a process of preliminary training for the army, leading up to the formation of a regiment of age-mates, at about eighteen to twenty. The sentiments with which members of a regiment regarded each other were those of loyalty and mutual support. It was almost a transference of brother to brother relationship, so much so that marriage was at one period forbidden and later on never encouraged between children whose fathers belonged to the same regiment (Read, 1969).

The training in the boys' dormitory and in cattle herding was rigorous. It emphasized the values of physical strength and endurance, and tenacity in difficult tasks. It laid great stress on relating interpersonal behaviour to the preservation of personal dignity and the sense of shame at 'losing face'. Wisdom acquired by training and experience was contrasted with cleverness, dexterity and smartness in picking up new ways, for wisdom was equated not only with sound knowledge, but also with good judgement, ability to control others and skill in the use of speech. The end product of child and youth training—and this applied to girls as well as to boys—was to develop the traits of leadership and co-operation in tasks, and to set this objective before that of the acquisition of personal skills and brilliant individual attainments.

Modern European concepts of education emphasize the institutionalized forms of Western education: the schools, the teachers, the curriculum, the classroom equipment, examinations and inspections, the administration and financing of education as a public service. The conversation I have reported between the Ngoni chief and the schoolteachers brought out the conflict between the European and the Ngoni points of view. The young teachers, trained in a teachers' college to teach the subjects laid down in the curriculum, believed that they were 'doing education', as long as in a well-attended classroom, well-behaved children went through the process of learning certain specified 'subjects', and presumably when the inspector came round gave satisfactory answers to his questions.

The contrast between their view and that of the chief is indeed striking. The success of education policy in Western terms is measured by such factors as the number of schools in relation to the child population; the years of study followed and the converse—the wastage of pupils after the first few years; the qualifications of the teachers; the success in examinations, and so on. It is common knowledge, however, that in one colonial territory after another administrators woke up one day to find that the effect of primary-school education in many rural areas was a steady migration of ex-pupils towards towns and centres of employment, with a corresponding stagnation in agriculture and village life. The dislike of the 'half-educated African' by many employers and not a few administrators particularly in East and Central Africa was well known. This hasty and often ill-considered judgement about what constituted successful education revealed the absence of any research in the part played by the schools towards training young people to work in the framework of a changing economy.

Schools in a changing society

It is obvious that the subject of schools in a changing society is of world-wide import, and cannot be dealt with adequately in the present discussion; nor is it the primary concern of this study. Calling attention to it at this point emphasizes, however, the kind of contribution social and cultural anthropologists who are interested in this approach could make. In their view, most educational studies in the developing countries in Africa, either those undertaken by educationists or by administrators, concentrate on the development of a Western-inspired educational system, more or less as outlined in the preceding paragraph. Such studies appear to isolate the growth of this modern school system, separating it on the one hand from the changing economic and political situation in the country, and on the other hand from the cultural background of the African people and their reactions to the impact of Western influence of all kinds—political, economic, social and ideological.

On the whole, anthropological studies in Africa or elsewhere show a lack of interest in such specifically educational problems as the wastage in rural primary schools, the unpopularity of technical training at the artisan level as compared with clerical work, the drift of teachers to other forms of employment, the slow progress of girls' education.

The anthropologist who is prepared to take an historical view of the impact of Western-type education on an African society finds that he is necessarily involved in the study of a network of interrelationships. In the case of this northern Ngoniland study, an examination is needed of the relationships between missions and schools, of the position of missionaries and their work before and after the British administration took over, of the advent of traders and trade goods, of the introduction of a money economy, of recruiting for the British army after tribal warfare had been forbidden and for labour inside and outside the country. These are some of the related developments that must be considered in any comprehensive view of the reception by the Ngoni people of modern education.

A problem that is inherent in this particular study, and that opens up a new and vital field of research at the present time, is the role of the schools in acculturation to an external cultural pattern. Acculturation is sometimes taken to be an inevitable sequel to a modern educational system. Anthropologists today would find it necessary to challenge this assumption in view of the development of forms of cultural nationalism in many newly independent African countries.

The northern Ngoni at the end of the nineteenth century: a historical view

When I lived among the northern Ngoni, they were intensely interested in their history. They linked their identity as a people, as distinct from the other ethnic groups in Malawi, with their historical traditions, and especially with their original homeland in the south-east of the African continent. This attitude is recalled in their funeral rites, which included burying their dead facing south-east. They divided these traditions into three periods.

The earliest period consisted of references in songs and oral legends to the names and deeds of some of their ancestors in the south on the borders of Natal; their dramatic separation from Chaka's kingdom as a group of clans under a military leader; and the struggle to exist and the fights with enemies on their long trek north (Read, 1937). They crossed the Zambezi, according to their traditions, at the time of a solar eclipse that occurred in 1835. The second period, from 1835 to approximately 1865, began at the crossing of the Zambezi and ended when they finally settled on the northern highlands west of Lake Nyasa. In those thirty years, this strange horde of warriors armed with shields and assegais and burdened with their women, children and cattle, travelled by a route west of Lake Nyasa as far north as the southern shore of Lake Victoria before they turned back. On the journey they added some adherents and shed others, but kept their language akin to old Zulu, and preserved their traditional culture enshrined in their chieftainship, their armies, their ancestor cult and their cattle.

On the highlands in northern Malawi they established a kingdom founded on military power, conquering or receiving the submission of most of the neighbouring ethnic groups. Their political and judicial system was under a strong central authority, the Paramount Chief, with the divisions of the territory under subordinate chiefs of the royal clan answerable to the Paramount. After their final settlement there were continuous wars and raids, eastward to the lake where they came into conflict with Arab traders and slave raiders, and westward across the Luangwa river to the Bemba kingdom. The Ngoni nevertheless referred to this period as 'the time of peace' because, as they said, 'the Europeans were not here to trouble us'.

It was the arrival of the Europeans, first the missionaries and the traders, and after a long interval the British administration, which characterized for the Ngoni the third period of their history. They said of this period, 'the Europeans spoiled our country, and they came too soon, before we had finished our work'. This concept of a task to be done, a mission to be fulfilled, and the frustration of non-achievement was deeply imbedded in Ngoni attitudes. It coloured not only their relations with Europeans of every type but also with their fellow-Africans within and outside the Ngoni kingdoms. As we shall see later, it led to a curious form of rationalizing by some of the Ngoni about their sense of mission and to an attempt to correlate it with the Christian missionary purpose.

The Free Church of Scotland mission, known as the Livingstonia mission, was the first and for a long time the only one to come into contact with the northern Ngoni kingdom. The need to maintain lines of communication by the lake led to the establishment of a station at Bandawe on the shore below the escarpment among the Tonga people. While Dr Robert Laws, the leader of the mission, was at Cape Maclear farther south he had been in contact with another Ngoni kingdom in the central highlands, and had used as an interpreter William Koyi, a Xosa from South Africa who spoke Zulu. The missionaries who landed at Bandawe walked straight into a prolonged period of raiding and warfare by the Ngoni on the highlands against the Tonga on the lake shore. Dr Laws's strategy, however, was to make contact at the earliest moment with the Ngoni Paramount, and to persuade him to use his authority and power to sanction the establishment of mission stations on the highlands and to give up raiding. In January 1879 the first meeting took place between Mbelwa, the Ngoni Paramount, and Dr Laws, who was accompanied by William Koyi as interpreter and J. O. Moir of the trading firm African Lakes Corporation. Eye-witness accounts by missionaries describe this meeting between the 'two strong men'. But there was no doubt where the power lay. Not only permission to open a mission station but the lives of the missionaries were in the hands of the Ngoni.

Subsequent developments in the Livingstonia mission to the Ngoni highlands are a matter of history. (Livingstone, 1921; Elmslie, 1899; Oliver, 1952). One salient factor was the immediate and mutual respect and liking between the 'two strong men'. This strange friendship recalls that between Dr Robert Moffat and Mzilikazi, the Paramount of the Ndebele in Rhodesia, a people whose origin had many parallels with that of the Ngoni. These relationships were striking when one considers the climate of opinion among most Europeans in the late nineteenth century, as well as the views of the Ngoni about European intrusion. The majority of Europeans of that period in Africa saw all contrasts between human ethnic groups in sharp relief. People were either civilized or savage, either Christian or heathen, either educated or ignorant. The Ngoni of that period, in spite of their grudging permission to Dr Laws to allow missionaries to settle among them, resented in general the intrusion of Europeans into their country because they had 'come too soon', i.e., before the Ngoni had completed their conquests. They also resented the fact that almost all Europeans of that period, missionaries as well as the later administrators, appeared to make no distinction between the Ngoni and the other inhabitants of the region, and judged them all as being savage, heathen and ignorant.

Nevertheless the links forged between the Livingstonia mission and Mbelwa's kingdom gave northern Ngoniland more than twenty years of mission contact and the beginnings of education before the region was formally taken over by the British administration in 1904. During that period the Ngoni were the rulers of the country.

The Ngoni initial attitude to mission schools

As a result of the meeting between Dr Laws and the Ngoni Paramount, the Scottish missionaries were given permission to leave William Koyi among them, since he spoke their language, and to undertake medical work whenever a doctor could visit them. They were forbidden, however, to open schools or to do evangelistic work. In 1884 Dr Elmslie, a Scottish physician, joined William Koyi in Ngoniland, and recorded his first impressions of 'well kept villages', good gardens, and a people powerful and free' (Elmslie, 1899: 107). In accordance with the objectives of the mission, permission was again asked to open schools and to preach to the people; and again it was withheld. Dr Elmslie gave an account of the meeting of chiefs and headmen in the Paramount's kraal called to consider the work of the mission. He recorded two statements that give us some clue to the Ngoni initial attitude to schools (1899: 122, 128). The famous war leader, Ngonomo, said at this gathering: 'The foundation of our kingdom is the spear and shield. God has given you the Book and cloth, and has given us the shield and spear, and each must live in his own way.' A senior headman said: 'If we give you our children to teach, your words will steal their hearts; they will grow up cowards, and refuse to fight for us when we are old; and knowing more than we do, they will despise us.'

In 1886, seven years after Dr Laws's first contact with the Paramount, permission was given to open the first school at Njuyu near the Paramount's village, and to carry out evangelistic work in certain other centres.

These early mission contacts with the Ngoni formed the beginning of what they regarded as the third period of their history. It was a period for which there were contemporary European records by the missionaries. Ngoni oral historians talked more freely and less hesitantly about this period when I questioned them because it was within the lifetime of their parents and grandparents. The views of the senior men quoted above were part of the current folklore of the Ngoni when discussing their past in the light of their present. It was typical of their grasp of their history that after more than fifty years they understood the attitude underlying the comments to the extent of showing sympathy with them and not regarding them as the attitude of misguided and ignorant predecessors.

In several centres in northern Ngoniland I discussed with chiefs and elders, and with the younger generation of clerks, teachers and ministers, the reasons for the early opposition to mission schools. Most of the older chiefs and elders had themselves served as warriors in Ngoni regiments; and many of those who were middle-aged, including teachers and ministers, had gone as lads to carry loads for their older brothers on raiding expeditions. They knew the ritual of the summons to war, of the mobilization of the regiments, the final preparations for the setting forth of the war party (Read, 1967: 29–47), and the triumphal return.

These men with whom I talked gave several reasons for the early opposition to mission schools as expressed in the comments recorded by Dr Elmslie. The first reason was a genuine fear that if they lost their military power, the basis of their kingdom would be undermined and they might lose their freedom. Since their return journey from Lake Victoria they had had barely twenty years to establish their kingdom in northern Malawi before the mission arrived, and they relied on the success of their army and of their raids to retain and extend their conquests. They declared over and over again that the Europeans, missionaries, traders and finally the administration 'had come too soon'.

The fear of losing their military power and their independence was realized once British administration had taken over and the Ngoni kingdoms in central Malawi and eastern Zambia had been conquered by British forces. Allied to this fear, a second reason for opposition to schools was the fear of losing their economic supremacy. Warfare and raids were their means of acquiring continuous supplies of cattle, grain and captive men and women who were house servants, workers on the land and artisans in iron work. The diet of the leaders and the warriors consisted almost entirely of meat, cooked blood, sour milk curds, pounded ground-nuts and some crushed maize, with continuous supplies of beer made from sprouted finger millet. The provision of these food supplies for extensive villages and large households called for frequent replenishment and elaborate organization, and the raids on neighbouring and more remote areas after harvest-time had primarily this economic aim. The cessation of tribal warfare, as it proved, lowered the general level of living in terms of diet and curtailed the lavish hospitality of the chiefs' households.

The third reason for opposition to schools was the Ngoni belief in the efficacy and value of their own system of social and political controls. They feared lest the new learning and new ways of living, especially if adopted by the younger members of Ngoni families, would weaken the strength of their kinship system, of their legal system and administration of justice, and undermine their determination to 'stay together'. A phrase constantly used by Ngoni speakers was 'to build up the land'—with the converse, 'to destroy the land', *ukupasula* meaning literally to take the roof off a hut so that the hut became useless for its purpose. In fact, in spite of the advent of schools these traditional ties held though with some modifications. Ngoni leaders discovered in the new learning how to build up and strengthen some factors in their social and economic life.

Factors in the ultimate acceptance of schools

I discussed with Ngoni elders the reasons for the ultimate permission to establish schools and compared these reasons with the printed records of the missionaries. The chronology of the main events ran thus:

1879 First meeting of Dr Laws with the Paramount Mbelwa. William Koyi remains in Ngoniland.

1884 Dr Elmslie joined Koyi. Permission to open schools refused. Medical work welcomed.

1886 Permission given for first school at Njuyu and for extended evangelistic work.

1890 First two converts, sons of a famous diviner, baptized.

1893 Last Ngoni war raid.

1904 British administration took over northern Ngoniland.

Those older Ngoni men who related oral history to me in the 1930s had the advantage of hindsight. They expressed the belief that the Paramount Mbelwa had seen the writing on the wall, and had read in it that the days of unchallenged Ngoni supremacy were numbered. There was a tradition that just before the arrival of the Scottish mission, two of the great diviners, the *abantu benhloko* or 'people of the head', had seen a vision in their dreams of white men coming on the lake to take over Ngoniland. These diviners told the Paramount: 'Something great is coming from the sea. Receive them courteously' (Cibambo, 1942: 52). Ngoni oral historians suggested that this prophecy was the reason why the Paramount first received Dr Laws and his party. The northern Ngoni knew about the settlement of Europeans in increasing numbers in the south on the Shire highlands. Since they seemed to be invincible, it was only a matter of time before they took over northern Ngoniland.

Armed with hindsight, the Ngoni oral historians suggested that the Paramount might have foreseen the possibility of the mission's being a buffer between his kingdom and the Europeans in the south, as indeed it proved to be. The Ngoni on their highlands, so the old men related, had also evidence that the despised Tonga on the lakeshore, 'our former slaves', were learning in mission schools to read and write, and to do carpentry and other skills for which they were paid in cash and cloth. They were getting something useful, it appeared, from the Europeans.

It was pointed out in mission records and endorsed by Ngoni oral historians that the Paramount's views about receiving these missionaries were not shared by many of his subordinate chiefs and war leaders. Hence he allowed the assembly of chiefs and elders, referred to earlier, to discuss the mission's proposals and to veto the schools for another two years. When permission to teach was finally given, two additional factors came into play. Mbelwa's admiration for and friendship with Dr Laws had had time to develop, and he and other Ngoni leaders had acquired a growing respect for William Koyi and the Scottish missionaries. They paid tribute to their fearlessness in the face of threats to their life and property; they benefited from their skill as doctors; and they heard very favourable accounts of the way they treated those who worked for them. In addition, Mbelwa and the Ngoni in general had a profound respect for those who had the art of speech and song (Read, 1967: 79). The 'mouthpiece' of the chief, a senior man who spoke for the chief on all formal occasions, was one whose speech was eloquent and forceful. It followed then that ability to preach, to teach and to sing were qualities admired by a people whose speeches in law courts reached a high level, and who sang naturally in parts. In the 'Book' that the missionaries brought with them, prophets were spoken of, and the Ngoni respected prophets. Moreover the 'Book' might contain wisdom that would help them in the days of trial that were coming. It soon became clear that the Ngoni rulers, once they had given permission for schools to be opened, intended to make use of them, and of what they taught, to assist their people to enter a new age.

Ngoni historians and others who wanted to talk with me about their past tried to express in rational terms these reasons why the Ngoni rulers changed their attitude towards mission schools; and the foregoing paragraphs give the gist of their arguments. The results of the opening of schools, as recorded by the missionaries, show how rapidly the uses and benefits of school and church teaching were realized and made use of by the people. Dr Elmslie, for example, recorded (1899: 303) that in 1896, only ten years after the first school had been opened, thousands of school books had been bought by the people, and hundreds of Zulu Bibles, Testaments and hymn books. It was not uncommon for a man to give a month's labour in one of the mission stations as the cost of a Bible. In 1901 mission reports spoke of fifty schools in the northern Ngoni kingdom with a total of 7,000 pupils, many of whom were learning English in the upper classes. When Dr Laws started the Central Institution at Livingstonia, technical and commercial courses were begun in carpentry, building and printing, and later in telegraphy and electricity, as well as normal courses for teachers and training courses for evangelists and ministers.

When the administration took over northern Ngoniland in 1904, the acting Commissioner recorded that all subordinate government posts, such as clerks, telephonists, typists, interpreters, mechanics, were filled by Africans educated in the mission schools. And after Africans at the Livingstonia Institution had completed the more advanced technical courses, these trained men were in demand not only in Malawi but in East Africa, Rhodesia and the Congo.

School and church as new institutions in Ngoni social life

It has been suggested that in the course of fifty years of mission schools, the Ngoni made use of the new learning in some aspects of their social and economic life. In the period before the introduction of Indirect Rule in Malawi, that is between 1904 and 1933, the northern Ngoni kingdom, in common with the central Ngoni kingdom, was passed over as a recognizable political system. The Ngoni political system never fully recovered from this blow. Administration was carried out directly by the European officials, who used the term 'chief' for the Paramount without recognizing his central authority and his relationship with his subordinate chiefs, whom they called 'principal village headmen'. After the introduction of the Indirect Rule Ordinances in 1933, the Ngoni Paramounts in the northern and central kingdoms were recognized as such. Their subordinate chiefs were called Subordinate Native Authorities and each had his own court; and the Paramount's court was an appeal court for the kingdom. The Ngoni comment on these ordinances was 'Ha! Now they [the Europeans] see what big chiefs we have. Only our chiefs are called Inkosi.' But all the same, the scars left by Direct Rule remained.

During those years of changing political conditions when Ngoni pride suffered many direct and indirect humiliations, two new institutions were being built into the fabric of Ngoni social life. They were the village school and the district church. The latter was at first situated only at the mission stations, where also the more advanced schools and types of training subsequently developed. But as the number of church adherents grew, and as Ngoni ministers were trained and appointed, church buildings were also placed in strategic positions near centres of the Christian population. The school in all cases preceded the opening of a church, and in many instances the same building was used.

Although the outward form of the school and church was a building, put up and maintained by Ngoni labour, those buildings were a symbol of two new kinds of social grouping in Ngoni society. Moreover, they were from the beginning closely related to the power structure in the Ngoni kingdom. It did not follow that the chiefs became practising Christians or sent their own children to school, though some of them did directly patronize the schools in this way and this relationship tended to increase. Some chiefs were baptized as young men; but on entering the chieftainship if they took more than one wife, or inherited a dead brother's widows, they ceased to be church members. That did not hinder a chief from attending church services with his two, three or more wives in attendance, contributing liberally to church funds and arranging to have a Christian minister present at all important ceremonies to give a short discourse and to lead prayers and hymn singing.

This kind of situation, often difficult for outsiders to understand, was evidence of the fact that the schools, and to some extent the churches, were deliberately built into the fabric of their social life by the Ngoni themselves. The relationship obviously had its origin in the initial contacts of the Scottish mission with the Ngoni Paramount and his associated chiefs and leaders. The ties set up by these contacts, which held fast, resulted at least partly from the intention of the Ngoni rulers not to allow this new force of school and Christian teaching to disrupt the life of the community and to undermine their political authority. There were undoubtedly inherent disruptive factors in both the schools and the church. The new learning and the uses of literacy, the emphasis on monogamy, the authority of the Bible for Christian beliefs, the prohibition on warfare, on drunkenness, on trial by ordeal— these were some of the potentially disintegrating elements introduced into the traditional society. But partly because of the policy of the Scottish mission and of the fact that there were no rival missions in the area for a generation, and partly because of the tenacious hold of the early converts on their Ngoni cultural background, no major splits took place, either between the church congregations and the Ngoni power structure, or between members of families who became Christians and those who did not.

NGONI ELEMENTS IN THE CHURCH. There was some carry-over of Ngoni traditional culture into the church services. Ngoni ministers in their sermons often referred to events in Ngoni history. They illustrated their moral and ethical teaching from the pulpit with Ngoni proverbs, drawing parallels through proverbs with the way young people were taught in their homes (Read, 1967: Ch. 8). The tunes of some well-known Ngoni songs were used, generally with new words written for them, though sometimes the old Ngoni songs were used in a new context, the Ngoni minister explaining the correlation. One song in figurative language belonged to the former girls' pre-marriage ritual, and was said to be a lament of the women about the difficulties arising in polygamous households. Ngoni ministers preaching about marriage used this song as an illustration. The verses began thus, to a swinging tune:

> All the nations
> Are called together against us.
> All the nations
> Are just called together against us.
> Whom shall we ask about this?
>
> How shall we fight?
> They are called together against us.
> Whence shall we summon help? (Read, 1937.)

Another song, also from the former pre-marriage ritual, was used by Ngoni ministers in church because all the people knew it. It reflected their traditional philosophy about the common fate of human beings, mentioning in each verse one of the social groups, warriors, chiefs, nobles, royal women, common people. The ministers turned it into an introduction to the Christian concept of life after death. The song began thus:

> The earth does not get fat [i.e., is never satisfied].
> It makes an end of those who wear the head plumes.
> We shall die on the earth.
>
> The earth does not get fat.
> It makes an end of those who act swiftly as heroes.
> Shall we die on the earth?
>> Listen O earth. We shall mourn because of you.
>> Listen O earth. Shall we all die on the earth?

In addition to traditional tunes, and to the Scottish metrical psalm tunes sung in difficult partnership with the Ngoni language, contemporaneous hymns and tunes were composed by Ngoni musicians. The Ngoni believe that the seat of inspiration for words and music was the chest—*isifua*—and only those who had this gift and were thus inspired could compose or improvise. One Ngoni minister whose village I stayed in was a great hunter; and he was said to be inspired thus on his long solitary journeys in the mountains, coming back with words and music as well as a slain buck. Many of his hymns found their way into Ngoni hymn books and were very popular.

On the two most important social occasions, marriages and funerals, it was customary in the late 1930s to combine a church rite with the Ngoni one. At a marriage in the village of a prominent chief who had been but was no longer a church member, the full Ngoni marriage ritual followed the marriage in church by a minister. Everyone went to the church wedding. Then the bridegroom and his party returned to his village and the bride's party to theirs, coming back later for the full marriage ceremonial, including *mtimba* (wedding) songs and dances in the kraal. Before the marriage feast began, the minister called for silence and said a prayer, and all the people sang a hymn.

The funeral of one of the royal women, who died, a dignified old lady, at the age of 93, was conducted with the full ritual for a Paramount (Read, 1969). War dances with shields and spears, the only recognized form of public mourning for a chief, went on day and night in the courtyard of her house for three days before the actual burial. From time to time an Ngoni minister stood up and told the people to sit down and be quiet. Among the exhausted dancers there was instant compliance, and the minister prayed and read some verses from the psalms. Then the war dances were resumed. At the interment in a pit at the edge of the kraal, the minister commanded silence as soon as the body was in its prepared place, and said a committal prayer before the grave was filled in.

This acceptance of Christian participation in the Ngoni ritual that I witnessed seemed to raise no fundamental problems either for church members or others. A minor difference was made in that according to their church regulations, members drank only unfermented beer. Both the marriage and the funeral ritual emphasized certain elements of social dissolution: the bride left her father's family, the dead person left the circle of the living. The ritual was focused on drawing together the participants, two extended families in the case of the marriage, the living mourners at the funeral. The church members in both cases shared the reassurance given by the traditional ritual and added their own contribution by initiating and participating in Christian prayers and hymns.

SCHOOLS IN NGONI SOCIETY. The schools as institutions in Ngoni village life were at first something totally new; and so was the relationship between the teacher and his pupils, whether he was, as in the beginning, a European teacher, or whether he was an African, as was the case in all village schools in the late 1930s. The chiefs and the leading Ngoni had originally opposed schools because they feared that their children might be spoiled and that the country might be spoiled in consequence. Once the schools had begun to operate, the pupils increased in number and the process accelerated rapidly. The Ngoni leaders kept their eye on the schools to see that they did not get out of hand and that the boys who could read and write, and the young teachers, did not usurp the place of their elders and did not omit the customary signs of 'respect' in word and conduct—and in fact did not set themselves up as a group apart from the rest of the village.

Certain definite measures, insisted on by the chiefs and village elders, helped to maintain the integration of the school children in village society. The boys continued to live in the *laweni*, the boys' dormitory, which they entered after the appearance of their second teeth, when it was considered that they should cut themselves free from the women's influence and take their cue in behaviour and occupations from the dominant male group in the village (Read, 1967: Ch. 5). Schoolboys, as well as those who did not go to school, shared the *laweni* life and were equally subject to the rigorous kind of discipline administered by the older boys. All Ngoni boys had to take part in herding the cattle belonging to their father's and their father's brothers' group. Village school hours therefore began at first daylight and continued till the sun was strong enough to dry the dew off the grass, when the herd boys let the cattle out of the kraal and took them to the grazing ground. In the late afternoons, after the evening meal, the boys practised their 'drill' with sticks and clubs while the adult men looked on. This was a combination of marching and formation and turning, holding clubs or sticks, designed to give precision in following a leader, and instant co-ordination of the whole group with his movements. It was a distant echo of the faultless precision and discipline of the old Ngoni regiments on the march, observed and recorded by Europeans.

The Ngoni Paramount forbade his people to perform any dances that were not in the Ngoni tradition. For the young people this meant that only the Ngoni *ngoma* dance was permitted; for this the older boys and girls practised in their villages. After the harvest was in, when

363

the 'floor' in the cattle kraal was dry and fairly hard, there were inter-village competitions in dancing *ngoma*. One village challenged another; and the senior people of the 'home' village, sitting on the ant-hill in the kraal, were the judges, and also the hosts for the feast after the dance. The Ngoni used no drums in their singing and dances; drums were not, in fact, among their musical instruments and they prided themselves that they did not need them. This made their perfect timing and precision in dancing dependent on a disciplined co-ordination, arising from constant practice. The young people's 'drilling', and dancing on moonlight nights, were designed to achieve this.

I stayed for a time in one chief's village in a remote part of Ngoni-land, where this chief's father had been famous for his belligerent refusal to admit mission teachers, or to discontinue war raids into the Bemba country. An Ngoni evangelist from a distinguished clan had volunteered to go to this area and open the way for a school. The chief tried to drive him out and threatened to kill him. The evangelist stayed quietly in his hut and cultivated some land, and in the end the chief after continuous threats respected his courage and allowed him to teach and preach. When I was in the village this evangelist, now an old man, was one of the present chief's trusted councillors and an expert on Ngoni history.

In 1937 it was a conservative village in one sense, for Ngoni was still spoken as the home language and there were many Zulu books in the huts. The senior women dressed their hair in the traditional high chignon, the *idhlutu* style; and stories of the Bemba wars more than forty years ago were told as if they had happened last year. The modern element in the village was a well-built four-classroom school with an able young headmaster and a lively, attentive and enthusiastic group of schoolchildren, girls as well as boys. The chief wandered into the school now and then, and sat quietly listening to the lesson and to the children's responses. At the early morning drill for the boys taken by the headmaster in the playground, some of the elders would watch and comment on their performance. In the evenings the senior boys would come and sit by my hut and practise their English on me, ask me questions about other parts of the world and how people lived, and discuss their future. At the church service held in the school-building on Sunday, the chief and his wives, as well as several other senior men and their wives, none of them church members, attended. The convention of wearing clean and ceremonial clothes to church was observed, and the collection, as in many village churches, consisted of maize cobs, vegetables, eggs and fowls. It was in this village that I asked a boy of ten what he was going to do with a small tip I had given him for helping to unload my truck. Quick as a flash came the response: 'I shall buy oil for my father's lamp so that I can read in the evening.'

Ngoni culture and the new learning

Two books written by an Ngoni minister, Yesaya Mlonyeni Cibambo, were widely used as readers in the schools in Ngoniland. One was a history of the Ngoni, translated later into English under the title 'My Ngoni of Nyasaland' (Cibambo, 1942). Cibambo's father had been the 'mouthpiece' of one of the big chiefs, speaking for him on formal occasions, skilled in the gift of speech and in the interpretation of Ngoni law and custom. His elder brothers had been famous warriors, and as a boy Cibambo had gone with them on the later raids to carry their weapons and 'marching food'—cakes of pounded ground-nuts and crushed finger millet.

After school and a period as a teacher, he was trained for the ministry; and when I knew him he was in charge of a group of churches in northern Ngoniland, overseeing younger ministers, assisting at meetings of the elders and of the congregations, and organizing the finances of the churches, which were then virtually self-supporting. For twenty years he had been collecting different versions of Ngoni history, and on his pastoral rounds he found opportunity to check and add to his material. I travelled with him in more than one Ngoni area and could not fail to be impressed with his persistence when talking with village elders in pressing home points that needed clarifying, as well as assisting me to see the relevance of one account of an event in relation to another account.

One of the conclusions of his historical studies which he discussed often with me was the role of the Ngoni kingdom in northern Malawi, which he interpreted as being a forerunner of the work of the mission. The expression he used in his book was 'the coming of the Ngoni into Nyasaland prepared the way for the Gospel, although they were unaware of this'. Other Christian Ngoni in the northern kingdom and elsewhere held this view very strongly, and like Cibambo based it on the centralized authority of Ngoni chiefs, the internal control which allowed free travel, the organization of the people in large villages, and

the setting up of courts of justice with a recognized and enforced code
of laws. It was, of course, a rationalization of a situation that had to be
finally accepted. It was at the same time a deep-seated conviction,
which seemed to compensate in some measure for the inevitable yield-
ing to the British administration and to the new learning of the
mission. The fact that this idea was embodied in a school reader meant
that the younger generation was at least aware of these views held by
most of the leading Ngoni in the north.

Cibambo's second book (not translated into English) was an account
of Ngoni life and customs in pre-European times—again collected
from many sources and carefully checked for authentic Ngoni elements.
As a Christian minister with some theological training behind him and
with an extensive knowledge of both the Old and New Testaments,
he found himself as a matter of interest making comparisons of Jewish
and Christian beliefs and practices with Ngoni ones. He believed also
that reference to Ngoni beliefs assisted church members and especially
inquirers awaiting baptism to make a bridge between the old and the
new concepts of man and the supernatural—the new being to many of
them so very puzzling.

On two particular elements in this correlation Cibambo laid special
emphasis. One was the concept of the High God; the other was the
ideas underlying the Ngoni ancestor cult. I quote from his translation
(Read, 1969: 190):

The Ngoni believed that there was God who was chief of all created things
and the source of all. Some of the names they gave him were:

Umkulumqango	The Great Deviser
Uluhlanga	The Original Source
Umkulu Kakulu	The Greatest of All
Umnikasi we Zinto Zonke	The Owner of All Things

In these names it is clear that God was known as the Beginning of all Things,
the Owner, the One above All. They knew him as the nourisher of the
earth, sending rain and all good things, but they thought that he had little
knowledge of his people. Nor could his people know much of him, so they
did not worship him himself or speak to him. His character they did not know
and so they were not able to praise or glorify him as they were the spirits of
their ancestors, whom they knew thoroughly... When one of themselves
died, they thought that now he is a spirit with living power greater than he
had when a man on the earth... They believed that the recent spirits received

the news from their friends on earth, and handed it on until it arrived at the spirits of very long ago and now forgotten. These then delivered the message to the Creator of all.

Further arguments to justify the ancestor cult were put forward by Ngoni leaders and ministers in areas where later on there were other missions at work. These Ngoni maintained that prayers and offerings to the Christian saints also illustrated man's need for some intermediary between God and man whom people in need could address and who understood the problems of human life on earth. Others discovered certain symbols which seemed to relate the beliefs of the Ngoni to those of the Jewish people, who also, according to the Bible, prepared the way for the Christian revelation. They pointed out that both the Ngoni and the Jews had no idols or fetishes—at least in the loftier regions of their religious life; sacrifices carried out with elaborate ritual and abstinence as a preliminary to prayer had a place in both. One old historian who was a church elder likened the '*intonga*' that was carried before the Ngoni army as a mystical protection to the 'ark of the covenant' that accompanied the Jews in their exodus. Yet another found parallels between the fasting and anointing of an Ngoni Paramount before his installation with nearly similar procedures followed for a Jewish king.

Young men, the schools and the 'Dead North'

The Paramount Chief of the central Ngoni kingdom wrote a memorandum for me in 1937 on the decay of agriculture and the consequent impoverished diet in the central highlands. He wound up his argument in these terms (Read, 1938):

The foods are finished because the present day generation does not take care of these things. The reason for their not taking care is this. Formerly there was no other work than taking care of their own affairs. They were thinking about war, and hoeing, and building their houses, and drinking beer and judging cases. When the Europeans came they came with other work, adding to the work of the people, such as the tax and work to receive cloth. When they were busy with such things they forgot the cultivation of their ancestors. And when the Europeans came they did not teach the people about cultivating as they are doing today. It would be better if the people were made to remember the teachings of their ancestors.

In the pithy way in which Ngoni speakers were wont to go straight to the core of a problem, the Paramount drew the distinction between concepts of work held by the Ngoni in pre-European and European days. When the Ngoni nostalgically said 'War was our school', and looked at the results of present-day schooling, they had in mind the age-set system, and the preparation in successive stages of boys and young men to become effective warriors in the conduct of war. In pre-European days this training for the army was necessary for maintaining the Ngoni kingdom. As soon as warfare ceased, the later stages of training when the young men accompanied the regiments to war automatically came to an end. This left the Ngoni leaders with a problem that they were quick to recognize: what to do with the *amajaha*, the older youths and young men before marriage. Formerly, in the intervals between war raids, intervals which coincided with the cultivating and building seasons, these young men were under orders from the chiefs and war leaders. As need arose they were drafted to assist in house building in the villages of the Ngoni leaders, to repair fences for their house compounds and kraals, to clear new ground for cultivating. The Ngoni did not believe in leaving young men unoccupied, idling in the villages and getting into trouble with everyone.

In the days of warfare the role of the *amajaha* was clear, and from accounts such as those of Cibambo they responded quickly and with enthusiasm to the call to arms. One of the Scottish missionaries who put together the life history of an African teacher (Fraser, 1925) described how this lad from one of the leading clans was finally persuaded to attend the school and half-heartedly applied himself to learning to read and write. One day the call rang out in the nearby village that was the boy's home: '*Uyezwa-na?*' (do you hear?). It was the call to mobilize for war. Down went the slate pencil and the primer, the boy leapt up and was off to join his age-mates and accompany the regiments on the war-path. He rejoined the school later and eventually became a teacher and evangelist and succeeded his father as head of his clan. His response to the call to arms illustrated the enthusiasm with which the young Ngoni rallied to the war standard as a direct result of their training in the use of weapons. The young teacher who carried Plato's *Republic* under his arm related how in his school-days the boys always carried clubs and sticks with them on the way to school, challenging and fighting each other on the way, but hiding the weapons by the path before they reached the school. This type of fighting was a regular pastime of the herd boys when they were out on the pasture lands with the cattle. They did it to prove their ability to use clubs and sticks as weapons and to demonstrate their daring and fearlessness in giving and accepting challenges. Some of these herd boys, as we have seen, were also schoolboys for part of the day. Many found it hard to leave their aggressiveness behind and adopt in the classroom what seemed to them a passive role.

Missionaries and other Europeans in both Ngoni kingdoms recorded how the Ngoni chiefs and elders found it difficult to restrain the young men trained for warfare as the occasions for war on distant tribes and the more local raids diminished until they finally ceased. It was suggested by Europeans that many of the final raids took place because the chiefs could not hold back the young men's aggressiveness and desire to use their skills with spears and shields.

This problem of the role of the young men in a former military but now peaceful régime impressed itself on the Ngoni leaders and on the Scottish missionaries, but for different reasons. In line with what I have said earlier about European views of civilization at the end of the nineteenth century, the missionaries had always seen the schools as a preliminary step to evangelization, as well as to developing the capacities of the young Africans to assist in mission work and to build up what the mission regarded as a 'civilized' society. Dr Laws's plans for technical training at the Livingstonia Institution envisaged a new and prosperous countryside in northern Ngoniland, somewhat similar in many respects to European peasant life, with schools as the basis of training and a well-developed artisan type of industry, designed to provide good houses, furniture, better agricultural implements, etc.

The Ngoni leaders realized that the prospects of mission employment were limited to a very small number of young men, and saw no future for the remainder. In the north there was a demand for carriers for traders and other Europeans passing through the country. This, however, was the kind of work that needed no school education and was despised by the Ngoni as only fit for conquered people. The chiefs were also well aware of the dislike of their young men for agricultural work, which they considered to be the work of the women of the local tribes. Looking after the cattle, which was privileged and dignified work, could be done by boys under the supervision of the older men.

After the cessation of warfare, what was the impact of a rapidly developing economy on the young men deprived of an outlet for their energies in the army? The reference at the beginning of this section to 'working for cloth' indicated the inducement offered to carriers by traders and others and to labourers on public works. Cloth was at first the reward which supplied an economic need, only met to a limited extent in pre-European days by Arab traders. Ngoni leaders used to exchange ivory with the traders for heavy dark blue and black cotton cloth. At that time the local people wore bark cloth, the Ngoni women mostly finely dressed leather skirts and the men and boys a short kilt of skins, the toga-like cotton cloth being reserved for the senior men. The clothes worn by the Europeans were admired and coveted by the younger men. To possess such clothes was a goal. How could it be achieved?

Two situations were in conflict here. One was the need of the young men for an outlet in varied occupations whereby they could earn money wages and satisfy their wishes for clothes and other European goods. The second was the absence of a government policy of development in northern Ngoniland and the neighbouring areas that would have furnished opportunity for the young men to find wage-earning employment. Dr Laws on more than one occasion pressed on the government in Zomba the need for a development policy, but without any effect. And so it came to pass that Ngoniland and the rest of the northern area was known as 'the Dead North'. The success of the educational advance among the Ngoni and their neighbours in the Dead North left no option for the majority of the young men except to leave the area and seek work for wages elsewhere.

Reference has been made to two outlets for the young men in Ngoniland who had been through the mission schools and had some additional training. When the administrative district of Mzimba was created in 1904, all the subordinate posts whether clerical or mechanical were filled by local men. The second outlet was the demand from outside Malawi, in East Africa, Rhodesia and the Congo, for young men trained in the technical departments at Livingstonia. The first outlet was limited and quickly reached saturation point. The second showed the main trend of the future, partly though not entirely at an unskilled level. The industrial and urban development of Rhodesia and of the Rand Mines in Johannesburg created a demand for labour which apparently could not be satisfied in their own territories. The government at Zomba gave permission for agents to recruit a quota for the Rand, and 5,000 men were recruited from the northern highlands in

1904. In 1906, 1,700 passes to work in Rhodesia were issued from Ngoniland. This exodus to work, whether encouraged by government permits to recruiters, or undertaken on their own initiative by Africans, became the dominant economic feature of Ngoniland and of the Dead North in general. And there was no doubt that at least in Ngoniland there was a direct correlation between school education, the exodus to work outside the area, and the kind of work preferred and the level of money wages sought.

This conclusion is based on an inquiry I made in 1939 at the suggestion of the Malawi government into the effects of emigrant labour on village and tribal life. The methods of inquiry and the results are described in Read (1942). One of the areas selected was in the Mzimba District of the Dead North, and I was able to get as assistants during school holidays some intelligent young teachers who not only learned quickly how to collect accurate data but who took a lively interest in the problems revealed.

One Ngoni village was typical of several others (1942: 15):

There are now three generations of educated people, and all the men and some of the women have had four to five years in school. Of the houses in the village, all are well built and in good repair and many have several rooms; the cultivated land, though not very fertile since it is on a sandy ridge, yields, with careful husbandry, enough for all the households to have two good cooked meals a day; and the standard of cooking and variety of diet including the use of milk and milk products is high. But from this village 75% of the adult men (i.e., those over 18) were away at the time of the survey. The good clothes, houses and furniture, including a number of books and lanterns to read by at night, are all made possible by the money earned and sent home by the men away.

I included in the survey data on the standard of education reached and the kind of work done by the men then away as well as by those in the village who had returned after one or more spells of work away, including the few who had local jobs. I made a category of 'skilled workers' in which I included teachers, clerks, ministers of religion, store boys, boss boys, police, sergeants in the army, carpenters, bricklayers, dairy owners, and all occupations for which a certain degree of school education or a special technical training involving literacy was required. In northern Ngoniland twenty-five per cent of all those working were in this category of skilled workers—a higher percentage than anywhere else in the areas surveyed.

One obvious conclusion in this survey was the close correlation between educational level, a rising standard of living and emigration. In other words, the survey showed that in the Dead North it would be impossible to find a village where a number of inhabitants had good houses, furniture and clothes and other goods, and where none of them had been away to work. 'Wherever men have been to school, they want, sooner or later, those goods which denote to them a higher standard of living, and they tend on the whole to seek employment where wages are higher' (1942: 22).

Some problems of an Ngoni élite

In pre-European days there were clearly defined principles determining the status and recognition of an 'élite' in northern Ngoniland. These principles had three origins: Ngoniland was first of all a centralized kingdom and the Paramount and those who exercised power under him formed a political élite; secondly, it was a military state, and those who commanded sections of the army and those who distinguished themselves in fighting formed a military élite; and thirdly, the Ngoni were an aristocratic minority among an ethnically mixed population, and those who belonged to old Ngoni clans formed an élite based on birth and kinship.

In the days of warfare the military élite was the most broadly based and comprehensive, for it was open to all warriors whether they were Ngoni or members of a conquered tribe incorporated as young men into a regiment. It was therefore based on individual achievement and recognized as such. The war 'heroes' and the great war leaders had their own individual song and dance—*ligiya*—which they performed in the Paramount's village when the regiments returned from a raid and reported to the Paramount. This *ligiya* was a type of praise song, belonging exclusively to an individual but always performed in public. After all warfare had ceased a war-dance, *ligubo*, was held from time to time in the Paramount's village as a means of drawing all his people together. On such occasions former war heroes performed their individual *ligiya* at intervals during the *ligubo*.

There was an extension of this 'individual achievement' song-dance connected with the killing of a lion, which I saw more than once. After a big lion-hunt the actual killer of the lion, the one who planted the fatal stab with his spear, came with his fellow huntsmen carrying the lion slung between two poles, first to his own village, where he gathered his friends and fellow-villagers, then to his chief's village, and finally to the Paramount's village. It was part of Ngoni law that all lions killed had to be brought to the Paramount. Armed with their spears this company danced the war-dance of warriors returning from a campaign, while the hero improvised a song describing his exploit. The party was then entertained by the Paramount with beer and beef—the traditional welcome for heroes (Read, 1967: 136).

While the military élite was open to all, the political élite and the aristocratic élite were necessarily limited. In northern Ngoniland the royal clan to which the Paramount belonged was also the clan of the subordinate chiefs. The great officers of state as a rule belonged to other aristocratic clans. Those of the royal clan who held no office were sometimes accused of claiming undue recognition, especially if they were visiting other areas than their own and expected to be given beer and food just on account of their clan name.

Universal recognition of the position of the group of élite based on birth was seen in the marriage of their daughters. This had two aspects: dynastic marriages arranged between leading clans; and the amount of *lobola* demanded and given, i.e., the number of cattle handed over by the man's family to the girl's family at marriage, girls of the royal clan having the highest *lobola*.

In a younger stratum of Ngoni society the senior herd boys of leading clans demanded and received respect and obedience from their fellows in the *laweni*, when out herding, and in all village occupations (Read, 1967: Ch. 5). They nevertheless did not rely only on their clan name to command respect as an élite. They too reckoned on some individual achievement, such as their knowledge of cattle, their skill at stickfighting, and their leadership in dancing *ngoma*.

During my field-work from 1935 to 1939 I found that in the villages the concepts of a political élite who held the reins of power, and of an aristocratic élite who demanded respect due to their clan name, were still current. At the Paramount's and the chief's villages the order of walking in processions and of seating at a ceremony kept strictly to the accepted status pattern. But the new learning was in process of creating a new élite among those who had entered the European-controlled world through the schools and the labour market. In the course of discussions concerning the problem of the young men in Ngoniland it was suggested that they despised the work offered as carriers. An early report in 1904 by the commissioner in Mzimba said that the Ngoni avoided engaging themselves for road work, plantation work and as carriers—all work in fact that could be done without school education or training.

The migrant labour study showed the correlation between standards of education reached and the categories of 'skilled' workers who were either in the villages at the time of the survey or away at work. The study showed also that ex-schoolboys who left Ngoniland to look for work had definite preferences in the jobs they sought. They aimed at work that gave them or would eventually give them authority, dignity and responsibility. Talking with boys in the schools I found most of them wanted to become a *capitao* or boss boy, or a sergeant in the army or police. In such jobs they would command other men and be given respect and honour. Such aims arose from the process of socialization in Ngoni villages and families, and particularly from the training given in the herding and *laweni* system. One man whom I interviewed in an Ngoni village had reached the top of the village school, and had picked up a good deal of English during eight years' work in Blantyre. He was a head houseboy there in a European house with six other servants under him, and was ready to find places for boys from his village who wanted to learn housework. By virtue of his position and his ability to pay several cattle for the *lobola* for his wife, he had married into a leading clan. His view was that a head houseboy with 'good' Europeans who trusted him was a distinguished job—an 'élite' job. He had control of servants, of supplies, of money; and his relations with his employers gave him status and dignity, as well as responsibility.

In order to achieve the kind of work which the young men preferred, and of which their fathers approved, the Ngoni were as far as possible selective in the schools to which they sent their sons. The two top standards in the earlier school system, Standards V and VI, which ensured a good command of English, were only, at that period before World War II, found in boarding schools at mission stations. In northern Ngoniland there was more than one such school, but in central Ngoniland, the leading Ngoni families would only send their boys to the 'School of Scott'—the Scottish Mission boarding school in Blantyre. The fees for these boarding schools were high in terms of village expenditure—£5—but the Ngoni leaders sold cattle to find the fees, or encouraged their sons to go and work in Blantyre until they had saved enough money to pay the fees.

One group of children in northern and central Ngoniland, whose fathers were ministers and headmasters of schools, were always given the chance of a good education. This came out clearly in the village surveys, where a minister or a senior teacher often restricted his expenditure on such items as clothes and furniture in order to pay for his children's schooling.

This new élite, who had behind them all the education that the schools could give them, were not found in any numbers in the villages. Here and there a man with a good education who had been away at work for many years was called back to his village as headman, or to act as a counsellor to the chief, or to enter the chieftainship himself. I found none who regretted this return. In many cases they had less money to spend as well as greater demands on their hospitality. But they had achieved a position of influence and authority among their own people which was in their eyes of greater value than anything they could achieve in the European-controlled world.

Educated Ngoni in urban areas

The town of Blantyre was the headquarters of the Scottish Mission in south Malawi, and the chief commercial centre for the whole country. The capital, Zomba, forty miles away, was almost entirely an administrative centre. During my field-study on the Ngoni from 1935 to 1937 I followed up some who had left the northern and central kingdoms and had settled in Blantyre and in the peri-urban area. This urban Ngoni study also formed part of the migrant labour survey in 1938–9. It included a study of the social and economic aspects of urban food habits, in connection with the nutrition study being carried out at that time.

There were further opportunities of face-to-face contact with educated Ngoni. During the Victory Parade in London in 1946, Ngoni NCOs and other ranks talked to me in the King's African Rifles camp in Hyde Park about their experiences in Egypt, India, Burma and London, and discussed their ideas about their own future and the future of Malawi. In 1947, while on a government commission to Malawi to look into girls' education, I found many occasions for discussions on education in general, on education in relation to jobs and standards of living, and on the prospects of higher education for Malawi citizens.

In 1949–50 the first Malawi teachers were sent to London to do an

advanced course in education, to prepare them to take up posts as
assistant education officers. This year and subsequent years provided
many opportunities for continuing discussions in London with teachers
and others on education in a developing country and on its contribution
to social, economic and political advance. Finally, in 1964, when I went
for the celebration of Malawi Independence, there was opportunity
to visit some of the Ngoni households I had known in and around
Blantyre and to talk with both the older and younger generations.

In 1939 the most burning educational question, brought up again and
again by the Ngoni in the towns, was the need for a secondary school
in Malawi. As they reminded me, the first primary schools in northern
Ngoniland opened in the late 1880s. In 1939 there was still no secondary
school in the country. The majority of Ngoni and of other Africans
who discussed this with me wanted a government secondary school, to
overcome the divisions and dissensions caused by different missions
and to bring up the young men of the country, the future leaders, all
together in one school. Hitherto there had been no government schools
for Africans, with the exception of an abortive attempt later abandoned
to run one among the Muslim Yao. While the Africans of that day
were by no means unsympathetic to the missions and indeed largely
manned and supported both the churches and schools, their increasing
sense of Malawi nationalism led them to demand a secondary school to
which all would be admitted irrespective of religious affiliation. This
point of view was rejected by the government; and two mission secondary schools, one Protestant and one Catholic, were opened in 1941
and 1942, respectively.

MAIN TYPES OF NGONI SETTLEMENT AROUND BLANTYRE. In 1939
Ngoni who came to settle in the Blantyre area had before them three
choices. They could rent a site in the government location and build
their own house on it, in which case they might or might not have
relatives or other Ngoni families next to them. They could rent a
small plot of land in the township area from a European landowner at a
high rent and build their own house; or rent a larger tract of land from
a European landowner at some distance from the town, where they could
build more than one house, raise some crops and keep cattle. The third
possibility was to ask for a plot and build a house on Native Trust land,
holding it under the Yao chief. The two characteristic types of Ngoni
settlement were 'tribal villages' on Native Trust land, and family

'estates' in the peri-urban area rented from a European landlord. The latter type were owned by educated Ngoni who were in regular and well paid jobs and could therefore afford the rent asked by European landlords, which was in some cases £5 and more a year—a high rent by the economic standards of 1939.

I visited three Ngoni 'tribal villages' that had been gradually built up on land held under the Yao tribal authorities who collected government taxes from the villagers and to whom the customary tribute of beer was given. Each of these villages was connected with an Ngoni chiefdom, one in northern Ngoniland and two in central Ngoniland. They formed, as it were, social outposts in the peri-urban area, though they had no political significance, since they recognized in the manner just described the authority of the Yao chiefs who owned the land. The purpose of the outposts was partly to protect the interests of other Ngoni immigrants from the home area; partly to superintend the sale of cattle and other goods such as tobacco and maize sent to Blantyre to be marketed; and partly to provide a place where the Paramount or other Ngoni chiefs could stay when visiting Blantyre. Here, in the outpost, they received hospitality and were treated with the respect to which they were accustomed in their own areas. The headmen of these Ngoni villages derived no pecuniary benefit from the work they undertook on behalf of the Ngoni leaders from up-country, work that was often exacting both in time and money. In fact they welcomed such work, since it conferred additional prestige on them among their own people and gave them an outlet for their interest in the organization and direction of social and economic affairs among their people.

LINKS WITH HOME VILLAGE. It was largely the result of lack of opportunities of employment for educated Ngoni in rural areas that drove them to emigrate to the towns in southern Malawi as well as farther afield. My studies in 1939 showed that in several respects the educated Ngoni in the towns maintained links more or less close with their home village. Those who wished to be free of all obligations to their kinship groups could always leave the country and take up work and residence elsewhere. A few individuals had severed all links and were regarded as lost (machona), but most men kept those links intact and many sent back money to their relatives at home. In one small section of Mzimba District in northern Ngoniland, for example, £3,387 was received in postal orders alone in the year 1938–9 in the post office at Ekwendeni, built by the Africans in 1933 in order to facilitate the receipt of money sent through the post. This money came from southern Malawi as well as from Rhodesia and South Africa.

It may be convenient here to summarize the most typical forms of these village links. Most Ngoni families settled in the urban and peri-urban areas of Blantyre were 'a receiving and forwarding depot' for members of their kin group and for fellow-villagers who had decided to leave the rural areas in search of work. If a kinsman arrived to look for work in Blantyre, his Ngoni relatives or fellow-villagers would take him in and feed him until he found a job, and he often continued to live with them until he married. If such a man wanted to emigrate to Rhodesia or South Africa, his Ngoni relatives or fellow-villagers housed and fed him, and often clothed him, until he left; and on his return they received him on his way back to his home. Sometimes he had been successful and might give them a present of money to acknowledge their former help. Sometimes he was sick in mind and body and in need of rest and rehabilitation before returning to his home, and was afraid of going back as a failure.

The second category of links with the home village covered sending money to a man's father or older brother to pay the taxes for older relatives who were not earning. Men sent money as a present from time to time to meet clothing or other expenses. On the subject of sending money for cattle to be bought to add to the family herd we shall have more to say later. The third category of links arose from the Ngoni ideas about training children. On the one hand, several urban families I knew sent their marriageable daughters back to their home villages to marry in Ngoni fashion, with exchange of cattle establishing the girl's and her father's status and ensuring the custody of children on the patrilineal side. Some families sent their younger boys back so that they might learn how to herd cattle and experience the rigours of life in the *laweni*. On the other hand, this desire to have their sons 'grow up like the Ngoni' conflicted with the desire to put them into a good school at the right age, and on the whole, Blantyre schools were better staffed and more efficient than those up-country. For this reason, many children of up-country relatives were sent to Blantyre to attend school there; and it was taken for granted that an urban family would receive these children, house and feed them, clothe them and pay their school-fees. This was a heavy charge on urban family budgets. One mission employee I knew had fourteen children in his house—eleven of them from up-country relatives—and the result for him and his wife was a chronic anxiety about making ends meet.

The last category of links depended on the status and role of a man's father in the home village. If he were a headman or a chief, and his son or sons were working in Blantyre, the elders of the village, on the father's death, consulted together and might ask the son in Blantyre to return and 'enter his father's place'. This proved to be a difficult decision for the urban wage-earner, who would not only be deprived of his income from his job, but would also have to abandon many of the comforts and conveniences of urban living. The man could refuse, but only at the cost of losing the esteem of his older relatives in the village. My village studies of emigration showed that where a village had a relatively high level of education, and the higher standard of living which accompanied it, the town-dweller as a rule accepted with less reluctance the call to take up his father's position. This often depended, however, on the prestige and responsibilities of the man in his urban job and on the type of settlement he had embarked on, especially if he had over the years built up a 'family estate'.

EDUCATIONAL LEVEL AND URBAN WAYS OF LIVING. In 1939 leading Ngoni in Blantyre owed their economic position and, with certain exceptions, their social position to the fact that they had been educated as far as the education available could take them. They had either trained as teachers for two years after Standard IV or they had completed Standard VI, the highest class in the primary school. They all spoke, read and wrote English easily, and habitually read newspapers published in English. Some of these leading Ngoni held senior clerical posts in banks, trading companies and government departments. Others were employed as senior assistants in the mission, in the hospital, in the schools and in the agricultural department. All these positions carried considerable responsibility in the job as well as authority over other employees. Senior mission employees, who were in the £3 to £5 a month salary class, were paid at a lower rate than the senior employees of banks and trading concerns, who were in the £10 to £12 salary class.

A marked difference in salary rate, though it determined to a large extent the standard of living of the respective families of the men employed, did not affect the social standing of these mission-employed Ngoni heads of families. Social commitments of much the same kind were undertaken by men who were on the lower as well as on the higher-salary scales. Several of the younger mission employees on the lowest rates of pay taught themselves skills such as photography and watch repairing in order to add to their income. All of them found means of raising food crops on rented land or in their home villages in order to supplement their money income. A reluctance to depend on money incomes to supply the basic cereal food supply was a marked feature of most families with whom I was in contact, and was not by any means limited to the families in the low income group. Discussions about family budgets, with selected groups of men who were heads of families, revealed the problems faced by well-educated and less-educated men alike in adjusting to urban conditions of living. Mr Micawber's 'misery budget' became one of the current jokes in these sessions.

NGONI FAMILY ESTATES. There were two outstanding directions in which educated Ngoni in the high income class made effective use of their money, their training and their desire to exercise authority. One was in the family estate. This was a typically Ngoni method of adjustment to urban conditions. The land, rented from a European landlord at a high rent by standards current at the time, was made use of in several ways. The owner built himself a brick house with several rooms where he entertained business acquaintances at week-ends. Other houses, of brick or village-type mud and thatch, housed his married sons or other relatives and the employees on the estate. The government at Blantyre showed some opposition to the expansion of an 'estate', often started by the Ngoni owner ostensibly as a place to retire to eventually, into a 'village'. Ngoni owners were well aware of this, and succeeded as a rule in quietly camouflaging the purpose of the estate and not advertising its expansion by boasting about it. They did this by several means. They used part of the land to grow food crops for their own family, and for sale as surplus crops in the market. They improved the grassland and bought cattle and grazed them there, also with a view to sale in the markets. They began to employ men and women to grow the crops, boys to herd the cattle, as well as women to work in the big house. These 'retainers', often émigrés arriving from the up-country home village or area of the owner, built a house for themselves, received wages and a food allowance, and were usually given a small plot to cultivate their own food crops. The children of the owner of the estate and other children from his relatives up-country went to school in Blantyre, later got good jobs in the town and had the option of building themselves houses on their father's or uncle's estate.

NGONI AS ENTREPRENEURS. The Ngoni in the higher income group had some choice before them about the disposal of any surplus income they might have after meeting their current expenses and taxes. The alternatives they discussed with me were either deposits in European banks, or buying cattle, or embarking on an enterprise which involved growing crops and marketing them. Most of them divided their surplus about evenly between deposits in banks and investing in cattle. The latter process usually meant sending money to relatives up-country to buy cattle and keep them there; and they relied on these relatives to take care of the cattle and to sell them advantageously. Cattle were quickly convertible into cash if ready money was wanted; and if they did not die from disease, a regular increase in the herd could be expected. This increase some Ngoni cattle-owners regarded as equivalent to interest on investments. There was, however, some feeling that this method of using, or 'investing' money, though it conformed to traditional Ngoni ideas about the prestige value of owning cattle, could not be easily controlled from a distance by an urban wage-earner. Ngoni with money to invest had learned by hard experience to be shrewd in their estimation of what control of an enterprise involved. I was able to see some of the account-books in which certain Ngoni urban salary-earners kept records of their 'investments' and expenditure. These records showed the use they had made of their formal education in the first place, as well as their subsequent training and experience in banks and trading companies where they had to keep ledgers and accounts for their European employers.

One Ngoni man who held a responsible and well-paid post in a European trading concern had a roadside 'canteen' up-country, selling tea, scones and plates of meat and rice. In the same area he had ten acres of maize, five acres of English potatoes and a herd of ten cattle; in another, five acres of tobacco and eight of cotton; and in a peri-urban area near Blantyre he had three acres of maize and beans. He employed fifteen people in these enterprises, which were supervised in one area by his brother, in another by his sister, and near Blantyre by himself. He knew where he was making a profit and where he was losing money. He had no difficulty in getting and keeping labour up-country, partly because he paid them at the same rates as those paid by Europeans, and partly because he took a paternal interest in their affairs and helped them when they were in trouble. It should be noted here that this kind of enterprise involving investment in equipment and employees' wages was not unknown up-country. In one Ngoni area where the making of *ghee* had started, the head of an Ngoni clan had built up a 'dairy industry', buying milk from local herds, investing in separators and employing local labour.

SOCIAL PRESTIGE AND RESPONSIBILITY. We noted earlier in this section that the Ngoni in senior posts in Blantyre had all reached the most advanced stage of education which was available for Africans in 1939. We have also seen that some of these senior Ngoni were employed by the mission at much lower salary-rates than those in commercial and government employ. In the assumption of public responsibility, within their own Ngoni community as well as in wider spheres, the social prestige attached to such roles depended on the level of education reached and the recognized 'character' of the man: *makhalidwe* indicating his behaviour as an adult as distinct from *mabadidwe*—the qualities he was born with and inherited from his parents (Read, 1967: 46).

Since the majority of Ngoni from northern Ngoniland had been educated in mission schools, they were church members, though some had left off being active members and some had been 'disciplined' and suspended from membership. The role of the elders in the church was an important one in the eyes of the public. They shared with the minister the responsibility for church affairs, including finance and the collection of church dues, and for the instruction and discipline of church members and young people. Leading Ngoni in well-paid jobs, as well as leaders of other tribal groups, shared with mission employees the onerous duties of elders and the prestige and authority attached to their election.

The 'Native Clerks' Association' was the initial form of a 'white collar' trade union among clerical employees of all kinds. It was not well-liked on the whole in colonial government circles, where it was regarded as an attempt by Africans to have some say in the terms of their employment. It had an important role nevertheless in training senior Ngoni and other Africans in arriving at some measure of internal agreement among themselves on conditions of work and in collective bargaining, though on a very limited scale, with the three categories of employers of educated men: government, mission and commerce. The handling of money in the form of subscriptions to the Association was the responsibility of its officers, among whom Ngoni senior men served, using the experience they had gained in their individual enterprises.

A third type of association, responsibility for which conferred prestige for its officers, was the Ngoni Highlands Association, limited mainly but not entirely to Ngoni from central Ngoniland. It began in 1926 when a group of central Ngoni working in Blantyre collected money to build a tomb on the site where Paramount Gomani I had been killed by British soldiers in 1894 because he had refused to walk as a captive to Zomba. The tomb was built and consecrated by an Ngoni minister of the Scottish Mission; and an annual meeting, one of which I attended, was held at the site. The main business of the Ngoni Highlands Association, however, was conducted in Blantyre. Regular subscriptions were collected and meetings held every quarter. The minute book was kept with great care and showed how the meetings were planned, discussion conducted and decisions taken. The average attendance at meetings was between 60 and 80. At the one to which I was invited there were 15 committee members, 60 other members and some 8 or 10 headmen of Ngoni villages. The business at the meetings was divided between discussion of local Ngoni concerns, the future of Malawi, problems of education (particularly the secondary school issue), and 'mutual aid', such as attending funerals of members and looking after widows and children who might be destitute.

The role played in 1939 by the Ngoni in church affairs, in the trade union and in the Ngoni Highlands Association was largely that of the senior men. These institutions, however, were supported by the younger men, and proved to be a training-ground for handling public affairs.

FAMILY LIFE AND DOMESTIC PLANNING. A demographic study of seventeen villages in the peri-urban area of Blantyre made in 1958 showed a population of 33·9 per cent Ngoni in the total sample with five villages in which the Ngoni formed the majority. The survey found that 68 per cent of Ngoni women married Ngoni men and that they appeared to make more stable marriage-partners compared with women of other ethnic groups. Out of a total of 188 adults born else-where in Malawi, 103 were Ngoni; and this was related to the fact that 'the Ngoni immigration into the area is still proceeding or is of recent origin, especially among women' (Bettison, 1958).

This survey was made nearly twenty years after my study of Ngoni families settled in and around Blantyre. It did not cover any of the peri-urban areas in which I had contacts. But the two factors quoted in the previous paragraph bear out two findings of my own. The first was the tendency of Ngoni immigrants in peri-urban areas to cluster together in villages and settle near other Ngoni. The second was the tendency for Ngoni women to marry Ngoni men and for these marriages to be relatively stable. In the 1958 survey there was unfor-tunately no correlation in the data between tribal affiliation and scholastic achievement.

On the subject of the education of women and girls I heard much discussion in the villages in both northern and central Ngoniland, and this topic was in the forefront in my visit in 1947. There were two contrasting points of view in the villages in Ngoniland about educating Ngoni girls in schools, one positive and one negative. It was notable, particularly in northern Ngoniland, that Ngoni teachers and ministers took it for granted that their daughters would go to school as well as their sons, and that they would take some further training in nursing or teaching before their marriage. Some of the Ngoni chiefs and heads of clans (*alumuzana*) sent their daughters to school; others did not. In any case these girls had a very strict home training (Read, 1967: 139–47). The majority of Ngoni villagers took a negative view: girls' education had to be paid for as well as boys', but girls, since they married early, did not bring in any reciprocal return as the boys did when they took up wage-earning employment and sent home money to their father. In the father's eyes, therefore, girls were not worth educating—with one exception. The *lobola*, or handing over cattle before marriage, was traditionally reckoned, and agreed on by the two families, in terms of the aristocratic standing of the girl's father, and sometimes also of her mother. There was evidence in the late 1930s and in 1947 that the education achieved by the girl formed an element in the bargaining that went on about the amount of the *lobola*. Hence some Ngoni fathers who were at first hesitant about educating their daughters sometimes thought it would be worth while, as they could demand more cattle at their daughter's marriage.

On the other hand, the young Ngoni potential husbands were torn in two directions. If they wanted an educated wife who knew how to dress well by Ngoni standards and to keep the house and prepare food in the manner of urban families, she would often demand help in the house, and certainly refuse to do arduous agricultural work such as hoeing a garden. She would therefore be expensive on two counts: she would not 'work'—i.e., hoe in the gardens—and she would demand money for her clothes and the children's, for furniture for the house, and for wages to pay field labourers and household help.

The same kind of controversy about educated wives was prevalent in the towns, particularly among the younger men in government and commercial jobs. When I talked to the well-dressed young women in the peri-urban area, their replies to my questions about hoeing were reminiscent of Eliza Doolittle's famous remark in Shaw's *Pygmalion*: 'What? hoe? me? not bloody likely' (in the vernacular: '*Nanga kulima? Ine? Ha! toto ine*'). The dilemma of the younger Ngoni educated men looking for a wife in the towns was a real one, and was connected with their problem of how to make a small salary meet the needs of a family and maintain an urban establishment without getting hopelessly into debt.

On both the higher and lower salary scales the Ngoni urban families whom I studied showed a fairly uniform pattern of marriage with a wife who had had from four to eight years of schooling. Though some of these wives came from the rural areas, most were born in the urban areas. Some of the Ngoni men had married non-Ngoni wives who had been to school. In these instances the Ngoni fathers insisted on the Ngoni family pattern being maintained. They refused to send their children to the wife's maternal relatives to be brought up, as was the usual procedure then in Yao, Nyanja and Lomwe households, and they encouraged their married sons to settle near by or on their family estate, and in many cases their married daughters, too.

In urban areas the role of the educated wife of Ngoni men was evident in several ways. In the first place, she was expected, and she wanted, to keep the house and its furnishings up to the standard her husband demanded. This included mosquito nets and clean linen in the bedrooms; tables and chairs and curtains and rugs and cushions in the sitting-room; often a small 'study' with bookshelves, sacred to the husband; and chairs on the verandah for entertaining friends. Visitors were frequent in these town households. Local visitors dropped in in the evenings or at week-ends, when they were offered tea to drink, unless they had been formally invited to a meal. The other common type of hospitality we have already considered, namely, taking in relatives and fellow-villagers from the host's home village whether they were children to be educated or transients looking for work. The educated Ngoni wife might see her tea, sugar and milk disappearing fast, or several days' supply of food bought in the market eaten at a single meal by unexpected guests. But she never questioned her husband's right to invite guests, and did her part in maintaining his reputation as a generous man. Generosity was always a highly-prized value among Ngoni men and women.

In the second place, the educated wives listened to and tried to put into practice the advice given in the mission clinic and hospital about diet in general, hygiene in the household, and the care and feeding of children in particular. They went short of money to spend on new clothes for themselves in order to dress their children suitably for school and for church on Sundays. They took their babies regularly to the clinic and attended ante-natal clinics when pregnant.

In the third place, the Ngoni educated women showed outstanding skill in catering for a big occasion like a wedding, even though at other times they were baffled, as their husbands frequently were, by the problems of relating expenditure to income. The households were very few where the husband told the wife what his income was, or discussed with her how to lay out whatever weekly money he gave her for household needs. The Ngoni men said the extent of their 'wealth' whether monthly income or investments could be communicated to their brothers, but not to their wives. The educated women disliked asking their husbands constantly for money. It was undignified, and to express their feelings they used to quote to me the Ngoni proverb about begging: 'Give, give: that is to snatch. The child of a free man only gives' (in the vernacular: *Patsa, patsa, nkulanda. Mwana wamfumu patsa yekha*). Even the women with several years' schooling found themselves perplexed by the handling of money. 'Money is something strange' (in the vernacular: *Ndarama ndi za cilendo*), was a remark constantly heard. On the other hand, a husband occasionally said to me: 'My wife knows very well how to arrange things. I give her all my money, and she spends it or saves it, and knows exactly how much we have. She is careful and very clever.'

I went to two Ngoni wedding-feasts in the peri-urban area, both on

village schooling showed the way in which they evaluated wage earning outside the country:

If we stay here in the village we lack one thing: money. We do not see it. If we go to Blantyre to get work they give us 6s. a month. That is something but if you want to help your family it is not enough. If we go to Johannesburg we must get a pass to look for work. If we find work we can get £2 or £3 a month, and then we can send some money home to our family. But that country in Johannesburg is not our country. The people there are bad. Our home is here in Nyasaland. Here in our homeland (*Kwathu*) we are free and there are no passes.

This sense of a homeland in Nyasaland, in a wider sense than only in Ngoniland, and the recognition, by comparison with South Africa, of the relative personal freedom in Nyasaland, was I believe one of the elements in the third way in which education promoted acculturation: the adjustment to urban living. One result of the failure to develop the Dead North economically, and of its relatively extensive spread of primary education, was to force enterprising younger men to settle permanently in the towns of southern Malawi. Not only were there jobs available for educated men and schools for their children, but there was an outlet for the Ngoni interest in constructive social and economic planning, primarily for their own family and kin group, but extending to public responsibilities in a wider range of contacts.

THE FRUSTRATION OF EUROPEAN DOMINATION. Education through schools, even though in 1939 they were as little developed as were African schools in Malawi, was nevertheless a common cultural element in African and European society as a means of bringing up children and equipping young men for wage-earning jobs. But the gulf between the kinds of schools, the skills of teachers and the range of the curriculum in African and European schools was enormous. Africans who went to work in Rhodesia brought back stories about the European schools in Salisbury and elsewhere where European children from Malawi were sent on government scholarships. The opportunities open to young Europeans were a constant topic of discussion among educated Ngoni in the towns and villages.

Formerly discussions among adult Ngoni men took place at the gate of the kraal (*pasangweni*), where no woman could venture and children were excluded. In many up-country villages in Ngoniland in

1939 the older men still tended to congregate by the kraal, to eat there the food sent by their wives, and in the late afternoon to glance over the cattle when the herds were driven back into the kraal by the herd boys, and to receive the boys' reports. The majority of discussions which I listened in on, however, concerning wider issues than a man's cattle and other village affairs, took place on the verandahs of chiefs' or headmen's houses and of court houses up country, and in the towns on the verandahs or in the sitting-rooms furnished in European style. The same kind of discussion took place during my visits in 1947 and in 1964, and echoes were heard in my university office in the 1950s.

Most of these discussions began or at least ended up with remarks about European domination. I referred in my article on labour migration (1942: 25) to the evidences of social maladjustment and tension in Malawi before 1939. These verandah discussions touched on many questions and illustrated the reactions of educated and of some illiterate Ngoni to the changes going on inside and outside Malawi, and their intense frustration at the continuing and stifling effects of European domination. One of the questions concerned their reactions to taking part in European wars. In Ngoniland villages the grandfathers of the educated men often drew attention to the disparity between the prohibition of tribal warfare and the encouragement and recruiting to enlist in the King's African Rifles to carry out campaigns in the British army against other African tribes. These old men's memories went back to the campaigns against the Ashanti in 1900, the Somali in 1900 and 1902, the Nandi in 1905 when the first battalion of the King's African Rifles had an all-Ngoni company. There were more vivid memories of the 1914–18 war and of the miseries of the campaigns in Tanganyika. The older men kept on referring to the promises made at recruitment which were not fulfilled—promises allegedly referring to development in the Dead North and to prospects of earning better wages. Echoes of some of these bitter memories I heard in the King's African Rifles camp in London at the Victory Parade in 1946. Ngoni NCOs came to my university office and talked about their, to them, amazing experiences in Egypt, India, Burma and then London. A leit-motif running through these talks was: are we African soldiers just pawns in the hands of these European nations? Where does the real power lie? Is education one of the chief means by which we can gain power? And how can we get that kind of education?

A second question illustrated the sharp divergence in the attitudes of the older Ngoni men and the younger educated men towards their future. The older ones—'the kraal-gate discussants' and some of those sitting on the verandahs of the chiefs, their backs up against the house walls, their Ngoni togas slung round their hunched shoulders, taking snuff with a disdainful air—these men saw no future for the kind of life they had once enjoyed. 'We have no power, finished is everything today' (*ife tiribe mphamvu, zatha zonse tsopano*). This was their judgement reiterated many times. The younger Ngoni men whose village primary schooling had earned them jobs in the south had acquired thereby new and wider ideas about their relationships with Africans and Europeans inside and outside Malawi. When they went south for work they made contacts with the Ndebele in Rhodesia and with the Zulu and Swazi in South Africa through understanding their language. On the verandahs in my hearing they often compared the behaviour of different groups of Europeans they had seen and worked for in South Africa, in Rhodesia, on the Copperbelt in Zambia and in the Congo, and in their home country in Malawi. Identification with Malawi instead of only with Ngoniland was evident, as well as a mounting sense of frustration and of being muzzled by colonial domination. Already in 1939, and to an even greater degree after 1945, Malawi nationalism had become far more important to the educated Ngoni than Ngoni tribalism.

BIBLIOGRAPHY

Bettison, D. G. (1958). *The demographic structure of seventeen villages in the Manchester, Blantyre-Limbe peri-urban area*. Rhodes–Livingstone Institute.

Cibambo, Y. M. (1942). *My Ngoni of Nyasaland*. London.

Elmslie, W. A. (1967). *Among the wild Ngoni*. Edinburgh, reprint (first publ. 1899).

Fraser, D. (1925). *Autobiography of an African*. London.

Kachingwe, A. (1966). *No easy task*. London.

Livingstone, W. P. (1921). *Laws of Livingstonia*. London.

Oliver, R. A. (1952). *The missionary factor in East Africa*. London.

Read, Margaret (1936). 'Tradition and prestige among the Ngoni', *Africa*, **9**.

    (1937). 'Songs of the Ngoni people', *Bantu Studies*, **11**, no. 1.

    (1938). *Native standards of living and African culture change*. Memorandum XVI. International African Institute.

Read, Margaret (1942). 'Migrant labour in Africa and its effects on tribal life', *International Labour Review*, **45**, no. 6.

  (1955). *Education and social change in tropical areas*. London.

  (1968). *Children of their fathers*. New York (first publ. 1960).

  (1969). *The Ngoni of Nyasaland*. London, reprint with new preface by the author (first publ. 1956).

Spindler, G. D., ed. (1955). *Education and anthropology*. Stanford University Press.

CHAPTER 12

POLITICS AND MODERN LEADERSHIP ROLES IN UGOGO[1]

by

PETER RIGBY

I attempt in this essay first to give a brief historical description of political roles and political structures in Ugogo,[2] from the period immediately prior to colonial penetration in the area until the present, when Ugogo is part of the independent Republic of Tanzania. I then try to assess the legitimacy and integration of these roles and structures in terms of Gogo society as it was in the past and as it stands today.[3]

Most of the political roles and structures described here may be classed as 'modern' in that they owe their existence in Ugogo to cultural norms and sources of authority both spatially and socially removed from the 'traditional' organization of Gogo society. The problem of central interest is therefore the distinction between the *legality* of these roles in terms of a wider context of legal rules, and their *legitimacy* in terms of their operation in the context of Gogo society, which is our reference point.

For the first part of this problem, the conventional interpretation of Weber's distinctions of the bases of legitimacy is insufficient (Weber, 1947: 130–32; 1948: 78–9, 294; and *passim*). In spite of the heuristic

[1] I did field-work among the Gogo people of the Central Region of Tanzania from September 1961 until the middle of 1963, first under the auspices of the then Colonial Social Science Research Council, and then as a Fellow of the East African Institute of Social Research. The first draft was written in Ugogo in May 1963 and was later revised in Cambridge while I was at King's College on a Crawford Studentship. To all these bodies I am deeply indebted. The form which the paper takes is, of course, my responsibility. My greatest debt is to the Gogo people, and particularly to Mr Madinda ala Mutowinaga, without whose assistance the material presented here could never have been recorded.

[2] Ugogo is the country of the Wagogo people, and Cigogo is their language. In this study I have omitted most of the prefixes, however awkward this may sound to 'Bantu' ears, as it does to mine.

[3] Some aspects of Gogo social structure and politico-religious organization are described in Rigby, 1966a, 1966b, 1967a, 1967b, 1967c, 1968a, 1968b, 1969a, 1969b. An analysis dealing primarily with Gogo political structure and processes since independence is given in Rigby, 1969b.

value of differentiating between the traditional, charismatic and rational-legal bases of legitimate authority, it is clear that in the empirical case none of the 'pure' types appear; and an emphasis on one may lead to obscuring the presence of the others. A useful development of Weber's analysis is the distinction drawn by M. G. Smith between legitimacy and legality (Smith, 1960: 20-1). Although I am unable to see fully the value of restricting the concept 'political' to action which is concerned with influencing 'decisions of policy by competition in power' (Smith: 1956: 49; cf. 1960: 15-18), as opposed to 'administrative action',[1] the point that legitimacy *always* refers to some 'traditional moral system' must be emphasized. Thus, 'legality' may exist where 'legitimacy' does not. This is particularly the case when two political systems of whatever order are brought into unavoidable relations with one another, as in a situation of conquest, or revolution (cf. Weber, 1947: 130).

In such a context, therefore, 'governments are constituted on bases which do not adhere to previous conditions of legitimacy, but do reflect the distribution of power' (Smith, 1960: 26). I show in this study that such a statement adequately describes the relation between Gogo society and the colonial governments in the earlier stages of the latter's imposition.

The second part of the problem, however, must also be faced. Our definition of the 'non-legitimacy' of the various legally constituted roles we analyse stems from within Gogo society and its values, for this is the unit with which we are primarily concerned. But if such a situation is maintained over time, however this is effected, new patterns of legitimacy begin to appear. The pre-existing authority structure is 'retained, revised, or replaced' (Smith, 1960: 26). In order to isolate these processes, a diachronic approach is essential. Hence, this essay also attempts to examine in some detail over time the various structures and processes involved in Gogo politics.

Because a considerable time period is telescoped in this analysis, I use the present tense to refer to what is still extant, both of the traditional and imposed systems, and the past tense for what no longer exists as described. Although the discussion is concerned much of the time with

---

[1] As Southall rightly points out (1965: 119): 'The determination of policy is always an important arena for competition in power, but it is not the only one. Empirically, a great deal of competition in power is not concerned with influencing policy but with achieving administrative roles. It is here concerned with the way persons move in the system, not the way they change it.'

historical events, these are not nceessarily presented in chronological order.

Further, the study may appear to contain some unsupported generalizations; this is a limitation set by the subject matter. There are numerous difficulties in the way of formal inquiry into many of the topics considered, not only because of the rapid changes that have taken place especially in the past few years, but also because some of them are outside the scope of normal sociological investigation within the time available.

The 'traditional' system

The Gogo are a 'Bantu-speaking' people who numbered some 300,000 persons at the 1957 census.[1] They inhabit a part of the eastern Rift Valley where it spreads out to form the dry plains of the central region of Tanzania. They subsist primarily upon agriculture, and cultivate several kinds of sorghum, bulrush millet and other crops; but the area is economically marginal due to short and unevenly distributed rains and recurrent droughts and famine. The population in general is highly mobile; and many Gogo own large herds of cattle, sheep and goats which represent the main medium of exchange in the society, and in terms of which most values concerning wealth and prestige are expressed. Gogo do not inherit land, and thus livestock form the major part of heritable property. The search for good grazing and water is a major reason, amongst others, for the comparatively high residential mobility. Thus Gogo society may be classed as 'semi-pastoral'.

The whole area occupied by the Gogo people is traditionally divided up into a large number of ritual areas or countries (*yisi*) with definite boundaries (*mimbi*), each of which is associated with one of over eighty-five patrilineal clans (*mbeyu*).[2] Members of these clans have a relative numerical preponderance in the areas within which they have ritual precedence; but generally other members are dispersed at random over most of Ugogo, and each ritual area is inhabited by men and women of a great variety of clans. Only the shallow lineage holding the ritual objects is in any sense localized. Not all clans have such ritual connections, but most do in at least one ritual area. Although there is a great

---

[1] Tanganyika Census, 1957: East African Statistical Office: the 1967 Census has no 'ethnic' breakdown in the materials thus far published.

[2] See Rigby, 1969 *a*: Ch. III.

deal of variation, the population of any Gogo ritual area seldom exceeds 4,000 to 5,000 persons.[1]

Members of clans may be further subdivided into what may be called subclans (*milongo*), which are associated with avoidance objects (*mizilo*). Each clan has ritual control in its area by possession of the rain-stones (*mabwe gemvula* or '*zimvula*'), stool (*igoda*), and other ritual objects which are the centre of rain and fertility rituals. Clan elders are also the repositories of the history justifying this possession and occupation. The clan member who is currently the possessor of these objects is called *mutemi*[2] or *munyaligoda* (lit. 'the possessor of the stool'), and succession to this office is theoretically within the clan by the rule of patrilineal primogeniture.[3]

The functions of this office were primarily ritual and hence I have not translated the word *mutemi* as 'chief', although Gogo use the same word for government chief and ritual leader. But they do distinguish in most situations by referring to the latter as *mutemi weligoda* and to the former as *mutemi wenghofila*[4] ('chief of the cap', as government chiefs were given caps as a sign of office), or simply as *mutemi weserikali* ('government chief': *serikali*, 'government', Sw.).

Any homestead-head coming to live within a particular ritual area must accept the ritual leadership and precedence of the mutemi and other elders of his clan. Even today attempts are made to exile people from a ritual area when they refuse to abide by the ritual interdictions of the mutemi and his diviner to ensure good rains and fertility. The

[1] For reasons which appear later, the boundaries of subchiefdoms set up during the time of the British administration under subchiefs (*wapembamoto*—see below) to some extent corresponded with the boundaries of traditional Gogo ritual areas. A community development census taken in 1962 in one chiefdom revealed that the populations of subchiefdoms ranged from 751 at the lowest to 6,055 at the highest, with an average of 2,721 adults and children. The 1957 census figures do not give the populations of areas then designated 'subchiefdoms'. The population of government-constituted chiefdoms is discussed below.

[2] A similar term, *mtemi* or *ntemi*, is used for 'chief' by several other Tanzanian peoples, including the Nyamwezi and Sukuma. The commonly accepted derivation of the term is from the verb *kutema*, which means 'to cut', and thus refers to 'he who first cut (cleared) the bush', i.e., settled in a particular area (cf. Wilson, 1958: 48; Oliver and Mathew, eds., 1963: 191).

[3] I say 'theoretically' because there is an element of selection from several candidates for the succession. Some Gogo clan histories even tell of cases where the stool was inherited by the sister's son (*mwihwa*), either by a trick or other unfortunate circumstance. The ritual leadership thus passed to the clan of 'sister's sons' (Rigby, 1969a).

[4] *Nghofila*, from Kiswahili *kofia*, cap, to be distinguished from Cigogo *ngalanda*, skin cap worn by warriors to protect ochred hair.

ritual leader does not (and did not in the past) allocate the usufruct of land and other resources but could on occasion, for ritual reasons, prohibit the exploitation of any of these in parts of the country. Elephant tusks (*mbali zanhembo*) and the scales of any pangolin (*nyamung'umi*) killed in his area were brought to him; these have ritual and medicinal associations.[1] In the past, clan members of the ritual leader's clan usually had a monopoly over slaves and captives (*wawanda*), but in practice any rich man could have these prerogatives also. Adoption of strays as dependents into Gogo homesteads (and eventually into the network of kin relations through their dependents) still occurs.

However, the secular political, military, and judicial functions of the ritual leaders are severely limited. Even in ritual matters the mutemi is to some extent dependent upon his association with a diviner (usually in another ritual area), and no rituals can be initiated without prior divination. Gogo say that the power of divination (*wuganga*) and the possession of ritual authority (*watemi*) are mutually exclusive in any clan (Rigby, 1969a). In the settlement of disputes, the mutemi takes no precedence, and, indeed, Gogo maintain that in the past he would not even attend the informal courts of elders, where most judicial activity took place. He preferred to let his 'representative' (*mundewa*) do so if necessary.

In the case of homicide or witchcraft accusation, the accused could escape the wrath of his victim's kin by taking refuge in the ritual leader's homestead (*ikulu*) until compensation or an ordeal could be arranged. In these negotiations the ritual leader played an important role; and it was a respected fact, elders say, that no violence was permissible in his homestead.[2] But these functions again may be seen as aspects of his ritual status rather than his judicial authority; he did not make any

---

[1] It may be that the bringing of tusks to the ritual leader was an innovation dating from the time caravans began to go through Ugogo (about the middle of the nineteenth century). Mnyampala (1954: 46), talking of a 'chief' in Nondwa, northwestern Ugogo (which was one of the routes), and describing the extent of his influence, says, 'They used to take him the tusks of elephants', as a sign of his influence. Elders today, although mentioning that pangolin scales and the hearts of lions used to be taken to the mutemi, do not mention the tusks. It is certain, however, that there was no kind of tribute or taxation.

[2] Violence at the homestead of a village headman, over a case between husband and wife, was strongly condemned by elders who were present. In this particular case the village headman concerned had usurped considerable ritual authority from the local ritual leader, who was a rather weak man. It was clearly stated that this was a case of violence at the *ikulu* and was therefore thoroughly to be condemned.

final decisions and had no means of carrying them out if he did. Military organization in the past was based upon an age-group system that cut across the boundaries of ritual areas and clans, and the mutemi was not a war leader. If the signs interpreted by diviners and the elders are inauspicious, the mutemi can even today prevent the performance of circumcision rituals, which are the means of recruitment to age-sets and groups. But he is not necessarily the prime mover in opening them in any year unless his children are involved.

A few minor leadership roles such as those of song leaders, war leaders, hunters, or elders who simply had the reputation for wisdom, wealth and authority could be classified as 'achievement' roles or acquired statuses. These were believed to be at least partly dependent upon medicines and other widely obtainable supernatural supports, and this is still true today.

The ritual area is the only permanent territorial unit in Ugogo. There are scarcely any geographical units that may be termed 'villages'. Gogo live in large homesteads (*kaya*) scattered at considerable distances from each other on the thorn-scrub plain that comprises most of their country. Homesteads are grouped into smaller clusters (*vitumbi*), occupied by closely related kin and affines, and these in turn are grouped into larger socially defined neighbourhoods called *matumbi*.

Gogo have an ideology of patrilineal descent which is normally followed in inheritance and succession, but genealogies are remembered to a depth of only three or four generations, and corporate lineages do not form the basis of local groups. The heads of adjacent homesteads are sometimes father and married sons (at one stage in the family cycle) or brothers when the father is dead, each set of full brothers living with their mother. In most contexts, a large variety of kin, affinal, and other links form the basis of several networks of ties within a neighbourhood at any one time (Rigby, 1969*a*).

The picture, then, is one of a 'grid' of ritual areas with definite boundaries, linked to particular clans which are not, however, necessarily localized, save for the minimal lineage group in actual possession of the ritual objects. Over this grid moves a highly mobile, but not nomadic, population of livestock-owning family groups of various stages of development, in search of good grazing, water or grain in times of famine; or who may (for example) be avoiding witchcraft or sorcery in the area from whence they came. They usually move to, and settle in, an area where they have affinal or kinship links, or can establish them, provided they accept the ritual precedence of the clan which has it in that area. Membership of a territorially defined political unit at its widest is thus expressed in terms of ritual affiliation.

External contact and the German colonial period

Long before the imposition of European control, the Gogo people had intermittent contact with foreigners. From the middle of the nineteenth century, caravan routes crossed Ugogo from Mpwapwa in the east to Kilimatinde in the west. Along these routes, caravans had occasionally wrought havoc upon food supplies and the often scarce water resources of the people, until in some areas the Gogo organized themselves sufficiently within each small country or ritual area to extract taxes from the caravans for the use of water and the collection and sale of food.[1] This may have given some ritual leaders political and military power they did not possess previously; but Gogo political organization remained essentially the same until the arrival of the Germans, who then imposed an alien structure of 'administration', concerned initially with the collection of taxes and the 'pacification' of the area.

The early German base at Mpwapwa (1887) was destroyed, and it was not until German influence was consolidated in about 1890 that attempts at control were initiated in Ugogo. The Kilimatinde 'boma' (administrative centre) in the west of Ugogo was not established until 1895 by von Prince.[2] But it was von Sperling[3] who effectively established the system from Mpwapwa, becoming the first effective German administrator in Ugogo. A British administrator, writing in the late twenties (*Dodoma District Book*), states:

Little progress was made [in administration]...until von Sperling—in general estimation the best administrator among the Germans—was sent to take charge...Most of the standing orders in the Jumbe's books are those

[1] The behaviour of some travellers through Ugogo did not augur well for good relations between the caravans and the Gogo people (cf. Oliver and Mathew, 1963: 444–5; Peters, 1891: *passim*; Stanley, 1872; Speke, 1863; etc.). Southon went through Ugogo in 1879, using a more northerly route, and found that although he had to pay tolls, he had little trouble in his relations with the Gogo, in contrast to the reports of the 'insolent Wagogo' on the more southerly route (Southon, 1881: 552–3).

[2] Remembered by Gogo elders as 'Sakarani', a name given to him by his Sudanese soldiers and by which he was known wherever he went in Tanganyika. See Hans Schmeidel, 1959, trans. Anne Wahmhoff.

[3] Gogo have a great number of stories about von Sperling, who is remembered as 'Sipelenje'.

made by von Sperling...No administrative officer will ever capture the imagination and become such an influence amongst the Wagogo as von Sperling.

The German system was based upon appointed *majumbe* and *maakida*, who were mostly non-Gogo and often Muslim Africans and Arabs from the coast. Mnyampala states that after the Germans built their first boma at Bagamoyo on the coast, the following events took place:

When they came from there, they fought some battles in Ugogo and then built their first boma in Ugogo at Mpwapwa (Mhamvwa). All the 'rulers' (Kiswahili *watawala*) of Ugogo arrived at that time to be given 'recognition' ('caps') and books (tax books) for their various areas—that they should become so-and-so ruler of such-and-such a country, and they were called 'majumbe'...then there were instated *maakida* (tax clerks) to be their representatives in affairs concerning the government (...*mambo ya serikali*).[1]

Bates (1962) confirms that what the Germans did was to adopt the Arab technique of using maakida (African or Arab assistants) for the lower levels of the administrative hierarchy in most of Tanganyika. They were appointed generally because they could write, sometimes spoke the local language, and had some organizational ability. She adds (1962: 402): 'but they seldom came from the area they administered, and they had no role in traditional African society'.

The few Gogo who were appointed were sometimes of the clans of the ritual leaders, but more frequently their 'slaves' were put forward for the job. At any rate, these individuals were never the ritual leaders themselves. The latter have throughout remained in the background, and in this way managed to survive more or less unscathed throughout the period of German and British rule, right up to the present and independence. Most still operate as ritual leaders in their areas, much as in the past (see above), although their functions are considerably diminished. A brief case of the way in which Gogo handled this problem when the Germans established their rule will illustrate this:

Senzi was a ritual leader in office at the time of the arrival of the Germans. He had many sons in senior houses, one of whom would normally succeed to the ritual office. He also had a son Kamoga who had been born of an unmarried girl, and for whom Senzi had paid the adultery fine and *ndima*

---

[1] Mnyampala (1954: 11). The Germans actually *rebuilt* their boma at this time (see above).

payment for rearing the child.[1] When Senzi died, one of his senior sons succeeded to the ritual office. He was pointed out as 'chief' by the people to the Germans, who beat him and nearly killed him. The people decided that the Europeans would destroy the ritual office in this way and cause havoc, so they decided to put Kamoga up as their 'representative' (*jumbe*). He was instated by the Germans and took all the beatings and other troubles for the non-payment of taxes, etc. When the Germans departed and the British arrived, the other sons tried to demand the 'government chiefship' as well, but Kamoga refused. Since then the descendants of Kamoga have had the government chiefship while the descendants of Senzi's other sons have the ritual office.

This was important, for it set the pattern which existed until the end of 1962 (when political chiefship was abolished) for the relationship between government chiefs and ritual leaders. In a few cases in later years under the British, one individual sometimes fulfilled both roles of government chief and ritual leader, but this was the exception rather than the rule.

The German system was based upon the principle of external force, and deviants from the rules were simply eliminated. This was not conducive to the integration of an alien centralized administrative system with any elements of Gogo society, nor did it encourage the growth of new *authority* roles from within the society to deal with the situation (cf. Bates, 1962: 402 and *passim*). Authority was in the hands of 'foreigners' (Cigogo *wakonongo*), both African and non-African. But it is clear that new intermediary or 'representative' roles developed which did not participate in the institutions and values of authority legitimation in Gogo society. They were legalized as 'authorities' by the colonial government; but they were legitimate only as 'intermediaries' in Gogo society.

The structural network of kinship and affinal ties, together with the local organization I have briefly outlined in a previous section, remained relatively untouched by these changes. So too, the institution of ritual leadership partially retained its functions and effectiveness, and this is still true at the present time.[2]

---

[1] When an unmarried girl becomes pregnant (a strongly condemned event), the lover is made to claim the child and must pay *ndima* for the child's upbringing (lit. 'the herding') and the adultery fine. He is then normally given full rights of inheritance in one of the houses of his father's wives. A married woman's children always belong to her husband (Rigby, 1969a).

[2] In other parts of Tanganyika, the role of primarily ritual chiefs was sometimes secularized and took on the new functions of government, thus diminishing in ritual

The British colonial period

The British took over with a military administration in 1916. The functions of the earlier officers in Dodoma were simply to reorganize and control a country torn by the Anglo-German war, famine and epidemic. The worst famine in Gogo living memory is that of 1918–19, called *Mutunya*. During the war, large areas of Ugogo had been devastated and depopulated. Gogo cattle, donkeys and crops were commandeered by force, and young men were forced into labour corps for the armies of both sides. Consequently, from 1916 until 1920, when civil administration was established, and until 1925, administrators were concerned with settling claims for loss of relatives during the war and trying to reunite lost families with their kin. In 1925, an administrator in Dodoma estimated that 30,000 had died in the famine and influenza epidemic of 1918–19 (*Dodoma District Book*). Bates (1962: 403) suggests that at this time in Dodoma District, the Gogo 'had almost entirely left the area; remnants of the tribe could be found in five neighbouring areas'. This is certainly the impression gained from the notes in the *Dodoma District Book*. But judging from the accounts given to me by the elders, it is safe to assume that this is slightly exaggerated and that Gogo ritual areas and clans remained much as before (cf. Mnyampala, 1954: 14–15).

The early British administrators also relied upon non-Gogo personnel to carry out the collection of taxes and maintain 'law and order', and the system for a time was admittedly based upon what the Germans had left behind. On the plea of 'continuity' in administration, von Sperling's dicta were followed. The system of *maakida* and *majumbe* was continued, but courts were set up to assist them. The administrators' main problems were to prevent their own military personnel from extorting wealth from the Gogo people and abusing their positions, and in the meanwhile to establish a system of workable courts.[1] An administrator wrote in 1925:

importance, although rituals associated with installation, etc., were continued (Richards, ed., 1960: *passim*; Abrahams, 1967).

[1] It is clear that these outsiders were unpopular and their administration one of 'rough invective and rude homilies' (*Dodoma District Book*). They presided as 'registrars' in the tribal courts; the latter 'arose easily and immediately from their own (the Gogo) councils of elders where all serious cases were heard from time immemorial'. It has been shown that Gogo elders' courts were the primary centres of judicial activity in the traditional system, and still operate as such. These, however, were not the courts which took over the enforcement of 'reforms'.

with such a backward people as the Wagogo...the pace must be slow[1]...
But a short experience of [them] will soon force an administrative officer to
realize that with the striking exception of *mgeni*,[2] there are no natural
leaders...The influential man in each jumbeate is usually the jumbe's
father[3] called the Sultani or Mtemi. The Sultani makes the rain and drives
away the birds, fructuates seeds etc....His instincts are all against advancement as his income shrinks *pari passu* with enlightenment amongst the
tribesmen (*Dodoma District Book*).

There is an awareness here that there were ritual figures related to those
who had been put forward as 'jumbes', but little further notice was
taken of how Gogo society was organized. The same administrator
continues:

[The Watemi] cannot well be removed however as the WAGOGO particularly
are fanatical clansmen and will not accept as tribal head any man who is not
'of the blood'. We have therefore to keep to the old families. In an endeavour
to obtain better results we have:—(*a*) educated the most promising sons of
chiefs (*b*) set up native courts so that a tribesman has some sure and easy
redress for any arbitrary injustice by his chief (*c*) cut the country up into
akidats and at convenient centers set down intelligent alien natives who can
convey the few government orders and see that they are obeyed...[con-
cerning mainly] taxes and revenue.

We are not told how an alien could possibly be a 'tribal head'. Nor
does the writer show any awareness that the Gogo ritual leaders had
absolutely no 'arbitrary' judicial or political powers whatsoever. The
people most responsible for arbitrary action were the 'intelligent alien
natives' or *akidas*, as appointed under the old German system, whose
power was virtually unchecked.[4] But this period, in which the British
colonial administration was forced to find or create new authority
roles, is probably as critical in the development of politics in Ugogo as
the later Indirect Rule policy.

[1] In this case 'backwardness' was apparently equated with 'lack of chiefs' or the absence
of any immediately identifiable figure of authority.
[2] The word *mgeni* simply means 'stranger' in Kiswahili and this must be its connotation
here. It is also, however, a personal name in Swahili.
[3] Cf. pp. 400–1 above, and cases described below. The statement here confirms as general
for this period the relationships described between the government representatives
and the ritual leaders in Ugogo. The term 'father' as used here could, of course, refer
to any member of the classificatory category of 'fathers'.
[4] I have recorded many stories about this from old informants who remember these days,
or who had been told about them by their fathers. These are not recounted with any
bitterness, and there is no reason to question their accuracy. Bates (1962: 402) says for

Indirect Rule and beyond

In 1925 the 'theory' of Indirect Rule became the basis of administrative policy in Tanganyika.[1] In Ugogo it was found that the units which bore some resemblance to 'traditional political structure' were far too small and too numerous for the implementation of this policy without their being merged into larger units. It was stated by the administrative officer in charge at that time that there were nearly 150 'independent headmen' in Dodoma District (which then included part of what is now Manyoni) and 51 in the primarily Gogo areas of southern Mpwapwa District, all 'claiming authority direct from the boma'. They 'had to be fitted into new positions under their tribal councils' (*Dodoma District Book*).

Writing in the early thirties, an administrator summed up the position at the inception of Indirect Rule:

As a start under the new regime seven headmen were selected from each of the four areas of Dodoma North, Dodoma South, Mpwapwa North and Mpwapwa South and placed in authority over their respective areas and Councillors.

There is no mention of what these 'respective areas' were, nor of how boundaries were drawn; but it is mentioned that the headmen were selected:

either with regard to their birth, the size of their respective districts or their individual ability but in nearly every case however, they happened to be members of the old ruling Wagogo families.

This was the first attempt to integrate, on some consistent basis, the administrative activities of tax collection and the courts with Gogo society, by filling the offices with individuals drawn from the local community. But even these offices and the councils had no basis in

Tanganyika in general: 'In some areas the akidas proved efficient and useful, but in most sections of Tanganyika the people were soon smarting under their tyranny.' Exaction of tribute and bribery in court cases are only two of the accusations made frequently against them.

[1] A great deal has been written about this policy. In Tanganyika it was introduced by Sir Donald Cameron, and the Tanganyika Native Authority Ordinance became the model for similar systems elsewhere (Mair, 1958: 195). Bates says (1962: 405–6): 'this...system of using African authority to support colonial authority was dictated by lack of men and money on the part of the colonial power, but Lugard in Nigeria and his followers throughout the British Empire elevated the policy into a theory and even a mystique.'

traditional institutions. They were neither stable nor successful in carrying out their functions. The same administrator remarked later:

By the end of 1926...there was a distinct awakening on the part of the tribesmen that the Native Councils had been placed to rule various areas... There were four councils gazetted as Native Authorities...in 1927 (*Dodoma District Book*).

Subsequent reports are full of the difficulties experienced in preventing friction in the councils and between them, and trying to get them to perform their functions. The main administrative problem was to 'amalgamate' the smaller units under the leadership of suitable individuals whose authority would be accepted. It is important to see how this affected Gogo ritual areas. A clear idea may be gained from a case study of the process which took place in Mundemu (then Makutupora) 'chiefdom', in north-east Ugogo (see Figure 4).

In 1927, as a result of 'amalgamations', sixteen courts were established in Dodoma District (*Dodoma District Book*; Mnyampala, 1954). Makutupora was amongst these and has until the present remained an administrative unit, first as a 'chiefdom' and later as a 'division'. On a map made in 1927, the whole chiefdom is marked as being under the ruling clan called the Pulu.[1] The Pulu, however, were the ritual leaders in four adjacent and much smaller ritual areas in the south-eastern part of the present unit (see Figure 4). The rest of the 'chiefdom' was composed of autonomous ritual areas associated with the clans given on the map. Each of the Pulu areas had its own stool and boundaries, although the ritual leaders in all four were clan agnates. On the creation of the office of government chief, the area of influence of the Pulu clan was extended to cover parts or all of the other ritual areas indicated. Much later, Cilungulu, which was originally amalgamated under the government chiefship of the Nyanghwalo clan at Bahi to the south-west, was also incorporated. All of these ritual areas still have their own *watemi* with ritual control within their respective boundaries, although a Pulu headman has managed to usurp some ritual authority in part of Cilungulu areas, which is associated with the Deje clan.

These amalgamations were carried out explicitly as an extension of

[1] All Gogo clan names begin with the prefix *Wa-* in the plural and *Mu-* in the singular. Thus Wapulu/Mupulu. I have omitted these prefixes for clarity. Vowel-commencing stems modify the *-a* of the prefix through assimilation. Thus Igoso would be Wegoso in the plural, and Mwigoso in the singular; and so on.

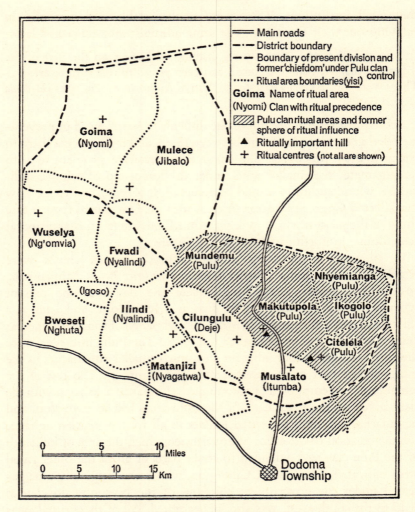

Figure 4. Some ritual areas in Ugogo, and the extension of clan influence under the government chiefdoms.

the Indirect Rule policy. The whole district was toured in the late 1920s and 'questions were put to the people' as to whether they wanted amalgamation and how it could be implemented. This was finally accomplished (in the words of an administrator) 'by asking the families of headmen to unite'.[1] The administrator described the process:

[1] *Dodoma District Book*; cf. Mnyampala (1954: 18–19).

It was found that every Mgogo had certain perquisites, the possession of which stamped him as a true Mgogo. The first of these was his family name or Mkungugo and the second was his totem name or Mlongo. Many groups possessed the same Mkungugo and Mlongo and lived each in his [sic] little country or *nchi*,[1] and in some cases these nchis were situated next to each other...Once the ideas of family amalgamation were suggested, all the difficulties fell away at once, and the natives, especially in Dodoma, were quite enthusiastic about recognizing the true family head. Other *watemi* readily accepted their family senior and fell into their proper niche in the family tree as *wapembamoto*.[2]

This statement was not strictly accurate, either as to the picture it presents of Gogo ritual areas or of the continual conflicts that subsequently took place (as the writer himself later admits). There were few connections, apart from joking partnership links (*wutani*), between most of the clans (Rigby, 1968*b*). Elders say that most of the amalgamations were unenthusiastically accepted. But even here the ritual leaders themselves made no attempt to object, for fear of coming too much to the notice of the colonial government—although their clans and close agnatic kin were involved in the implementation of these changes. In some cases the boundaries of ritual areas became those of the sub-chiefdoms, but even this was not always the case (see Figure 4).

I cannot here record in detail the amalgamations, redistributions and boundary disputes that have characterized local authority government and local courts in Ugogo until the present. It must suffice to draw the broad outlines. But it was out of these early councils and council meetings that the Dodoma Local Authority (and the local authorities of Mpwapwa and Manyoni) developed (*Dodoma District Book*). In 1928 the councils of Dodoma 'expressed a wish to unite under one council, to be situated in the vicinity of Dodoma'.[3] When this central council was formed, chief Mazengo of Mvumi in central Ugogo became president.[4] He held this position in slightly varying statuses (at one

[1] A Kiswahili word meaning 'country'; cf. Cigogo, *yisi*.
[2] A word derived from Cigogo and meaning literally 'the lighters of the fire' (*kupemba*, to light; *moto*, fire), but here used exclusively in a new sense to mean 'sub-chief'. The implication (so the elders told me) was that they were responsible for introducing new 'customs' and changing tradition. This is discussed elsewhere in more detail.
[3] The council, together with its executive, was referred to as the *hazina*, a Kiswahili term emphasizing its financial activities as a 'local treasury'. The financial independence of these councils really dated from about 1948, when efforts were made to make them 'more democratic' and 'financially competent' (cf. Bates, 1962: 464).
[4] Mutemi Mazengo had been made 'chief' under the Germans. A member of the

stage he was known as 'Paramount Chief') until the removal of chiefs in 1962–3, when the Dodoma Council was reconstituted as a District Council with authority over all persons residing in the area and not only over members of the Gogo tribe as it had been in the past (cf. Mnyampala, 1954).

The local authority and court systems eventually settled down into a fairly workable pattern. One of the greatest obstacles throughout was that of finding suitable personnel to fill the 'responsible' positions of court clerk and tax clerk in the chiefdoms, and finding literate chiefs. In the earlier phases, most of the latter were illiterate; later on it was difficult to attract people of a fairly good standard of education to these posts because of low salaries and limited privileges.[1] The only way in which a government chief could make his position viable was to have enough influence with kin and affines within the chiefdom, and also to have enough pull outside the chiefdom, to manipulate his position, increase his wealth, and thus gain a new kind of prestige. Most government chiefs who stayed any length of time in office managed to accumulate large herds and often resources enough to buy cars and build houses of brick and corrugated sheeting.

The chiefs' main functions were to carry out government directives at the chiefdom level and, in the absence of the local magistrate (*hacimu*),[2] to sit as head of the local court (*baraza*), together with two assessors who were usually village headmen or other local government officials. The court also had messengers (Kiswahili *matarishi*) who had power to detain offenders and who acted as local authority policemen. All this was entirely new in conception to the Gogo and was the creation of the colonial administration.

About five or six years before the attainment of independence on 9 December 1961, other forces were beginning to make themselves felt at the level of local government and the chiefdoms. Amongst these was TANU (Tanganyika African National Union), which, on coming to power and gaining independence for Tanganyika, was to introduce radical and sweeping changes in the formal structure of local govern-

Nyamzura clan, who are the ritual leaders in a small part of what later became Mvumi chiefdom, Mazengo was not, however, ritual leader himself.

[1] Cf. Richards, ed., 1960: *passim*. The Dodoma District Council was, however, one of the first local authorities in Tanganyika to appoint a university graduate as Executive Officer, which had a considerable effect upon increased authority and autonomy being allowed the *hazina*.

[2] Kiswahili *hakimu*, judge: appointed by local authority in Dodoma.

ment, in Ugogo and in the rest of the country. TANU also linked itself with the development teams and projects on the rural areas from before the independence; and through this, in Ugogo, took a large part in forming new types of leadership and providing for their expression in the villages and the 'chiefdoms'. These are described in a later section. In the series of changes the TANU government was to introduce in an effort to make local government more democratic, one of the central acts was the abolition of the office of government chief. This was in spite of the fact that government chiefs, at least in Ugogo, had been making strenuous efforts to identify themselves and to co-operate with TANU (see below).[1] The chiefs were officially informed of the decision at a meeting in Dodoma in July 1962, but most of them knew already what was happening. All of them terminated their chiefly duties at the beginning of 1963. The full effect of these changes cannot as yet be gauged or predicted, as most of them are so recent and there are many further changes upon the horizon.[2] But certain elements of continuity and predictive value will appear in the following analysis of the way in which old authority and leadership roles have been dispensed with, and the new roles adopted which have been designed by government to take their place, mainly at the level of the village and the division.

I have dwelt on these historical factors as it is essential to see the broad outline of events before a sociological analysis of the roles concerned, and recruitment to them, is possible. In this way, the types of roles or offices available to aspiring leaders may be placed in their historical perspective. Starting with that of 'chief', I now try to describe briefly these roles and their relation to Gogo society.

Government chiefship and its operation

It has been noted that the local government chiefs and subchiefs were the only members of the new system of administration who had links

[1] The system set up by the British had always been considered by TANU as reactionary and based upon a policy of 'divide and rule' (cf. Bates, 1962: 408). Its dissolution was probably essential; and certainly in Ugogo the British system, as I have shown, had no 'traditional' justification other than the adjustments made by operating for a number of years (see also Bienen, 1967).

[2] For example, new 'villagization' schemes involving reorganization of settlement and thus of leadership and authority roles were put into operation, with new development projects. These are still being re-assessed (cf. Rigby, 1969b; Bienen, 1967).

both with the local community and the ritual leaders. One case has already been given of how Gogo handled the problem of putting forward representatives to be recognized by the colonial intruders. But it is relevant to give a more detailed example in order to place the role of government chief more clearly in the context of Gogo social structure:

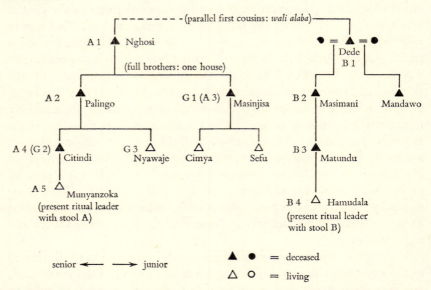

Figure 5. Succession to ritual office and office of government chief in the Pulu clan, Makutupora (Mundemu) chiefdom. A 1...A 2...represents the order of succession to Ritual Office A (see text), or *wutemi weligoda*. B 1...B 2...represents the order of succession to Ritual Office B. G 1...G 2...is the order of succession to government chiefship under the British administration.

In the country of the Pulu clan, already referred to, there are two 'stools' (sets of rainstones) in the main ritual area of Makutupora. This divides Makutupora into two areas, Madako and Songanghali (Rigby, 1969 a). The stools have long been the centre of conflict between two closely related groups of agnates of different 'houses' (*nyumba*) [see Figure 5]. Nghosi was the founder of one house with the stool now in the possession of Munyanzoka. Dede, Nghosi's younger parallel cousin (their fathers were half-brothers and at this point the segmentation occurred), also passed on a stool of ritual authority through Masimani and Matundu to its present possessor, Hamudala.

The office of government chief (i.e., of 'the cap', *wenghofila*) originally became a source of conflict when Palingo was made *jumbe* by the Germans. (At this time, Nghosi was still alive and his son was put forward as representative while he retained the ritual office.) When Nghosi died, the British administration had taken over and was attempting to set up its structure of government chiefs. Palingo, an eldest son of the senior house, had succeeded to the office of ritual leader. Nghosi's house was felt by the elders to be the senior one (in relation to Dede's). Thus, either Palingo or Masinjisa, his younger full brother, would have been put forward as 'chief' and given recognition by the British.[1]

Mandawo, Dede's son by a junior house, decided, on the instigation of his close agnates and other supporters, to claim the government chiefship when the British took over.[2] Thinking that Palingo would be given recognition, Mandawo asked him to come to his homestead to drink honey beer. Palingo became drunk and fell asleep. Mandawo and his associates strangled him and threw his body into the well called 'Mwinjila-cipwi' (the one who enters naked).[3]

After searching for the ritual leader for two days, during which time the people at Mandawo's homestead denied having seen him, some elders and a *jumbe* from a nearby area, suspecting foul play, went to Dodoma. There they told the administration that Palingo might have been killed by Mandawo. Mandawo was arrested, and he and his associates admitted under questioning that they had killed Palingo. Asked why he had killed Palingo, Mandawo replied, 'I had a quarrel with him over the chiefship (*wutemi*), because I also wished to be mutemi'. He was executed, and Palingo's younger brother Masinjisa was put forward and recognized as the first government chief under the British.

When Citindi was old enough, he succeeded to the ritual office.[4] Later,

---

[1] I have stated, and given reasons for, the fact that Gogo ritual leaders were reluctant to put themselves forward to the alien administration as representatives. In some cases, however, this did not occur and ritual leaders became government chiefs when the British took over. In this case it was even more likely, as Palingo had been recognized by the Germans. Later, government chiefships or subchiefships were usually separated from the ritual office, either through manipulation by the elders or by the administration itself. The latter did not want to be bound by a rigid rule of descent. The two roles became characteristically distinct. The account I present here of the Pulu clan was given to me by elders. It is consistent with the few points made by Mnyampala (1954: 50) for this area, who states that Masinjisa was the first chief (under the British) in Makutupora.

[2] It is not clear whether at this time Masimani, his elder half-brother, had already succeeded to the ritual office in this lineage, or whether Dede, their father, was still alive.

[3] Gogo dig very large and deep wells (*masima*), and there are constant accidents over people (particularly children) falling into them. Adults have also to be very careful at night, particularly after a beer party.

[4] Some informants stated that at one time Masinjisa held both ritual and government office. If he had the stool, it would have been as 'regent' until Citindi could be installed

Masinjisa was deposed from the government chiefship by the administration and exiled to Usandawi in the north. He instructed Citindi to take over the government chiefship also. This arrangement proved unsatisfactory. After a very short time, Citindi went to the administration and said he was willing to do the job of chief, but Gogo 'chiefs' had ritual functions to perform and, as Masinjisa was the eldest living member of this kin group, he should be allowed back to help in this.[1] The district commissioner allowed this, but soon after, Masinjisa died. Citindi was unsatisfactory as chief to the administration (actually Masinjisa had in effect been government chief all along). Nyawaje took over the government chiefship, which he occupied until the chiefs were removed from office in 1962. While Masinjisa was still alive and in exile, Nyawaje had in effect acted as chief in the local court. Thus Citindi, the ritual leader, was government chief for a very short period, and even during this period did not actually perform the functions of government chief.[2] Citindi died and his son Munyanzoka succeeded to the ritual office.

The processes represented in this case are fairly typical for the whole Gogo area. The most consistent common element was the purposeful separation of the offices of government chief and ritual leader, preferred by the people and accepted by the administration, although they always remained fairly closely related. Ritual leadership perforce remained firmly embedded in Gogo values and institutions. But the offices of government chief and subchief, if they were to be effective, had to depend principally upon other (alien) criteria and institutions for their power and recruitment. It is to these factors that I now turn.

During the period when the local authority system based on chiefs functioned most effectively, between about 1935 and 1961, the administration's aim was to make the office of chief more and more bureaucratic, to recruit educated, or at least literate, leaders. At the time of the removal of the chiefs, most of the fourteen in office in Dodoma District were literate in Kiswahili. Their level of education ranged probably

---

    as ritual leader. An heir who is too young cannot be installed until he is married (and most usually) until he has a child.

[1] Even though Citindi now had the stool, Masinjisa was the senior living member of the stool-holding lineage, by generation, and was classificatory 'father' to Citindi. His attendance at all rituals concerning the country was essential.

[2] The administration had already taken pains to give Nyawaje a primary education at the old 'school for chiefs' at Tabora. Thus the choice was mutually satisfactory to everyone, although some elders still remark that Nyawaje 'snatched' the (government) chiefship from his brother Citindi, and have to be reminded by others that ritual leaders were not government chiefs, and that anyway it was undesirable.

between Standards IV and VI. One (the youngest) had reached Standard X. But the government put forth little effort to make the position more attractive to better educated aspirants. It was thus obliged to maintain the system by appointing individuals who had local ties and authority, and who could make the office effective by manipulating both old and new sources of authority. This made most chiefs unpopular and led to the idea current in Ugogo at the time, that if one wished to be successful in a case at the *baraza*, one had to be wealthy enough for bribery, or be a relative of the chief.[1] The chief's wealth enabled him to establish a wide range of affinal ties and cattle trusteeship links (*kukoza*) with a comparatively large number of homestead-heads in his area, creating ties of mutual obligation. Such ties still have strong currency in terms of Gogo values. But this did not interfere with the traditional system of ritual leaders being associated with wealth (in cattle and wives, and therefore indicative of fertility). One of the richest men (in cattle) in the chiefdom discussed above was a ritual leader of another clan in the north. His younger brother held the government subchiefship until 1962. But while government chiefs showed their wealth in their new kinds of possessions, a ritual leader in Ugogo cannot be distinguished from any other homestead-head by dress, by his homestead or any other visible signs.

Although the chief appeared to derive most of his authority and power from alien sources in terms of alien criteria (and was therefore unpopular), he was often able also to manipulate traditional ties to his own ends. Chiefs usually dressed in Western or 'Swahili' clothes, built better homesteads; some had motor-cars and were constantly attending meetings and functions in Dodoma. But they also made attempts to attract to themselves some characteristics of the old ritual leaders. I have shown how closely related they were to some of the ritual leaders, and they were almost always of the same clan. In one case the chief refused to move his residence some five miles to a new site for the *baraza*. The site had been chosen by the administration for reasons of health and administrative convenience. The chief gave as his reasons that he had established home and fields where he was, and also that he was on the

---

[1] Chiefs were heads of courts (*baraza*) in their own areas. Towards the end of the period of government chiefship, local magistrates (*hacimu*) were appointed, but even then there was close rapport between these officials and the chiefs. If conflict occurred between them over the conduct of affairs within the chiefdom, and it did not lead to the prosecution of the chief in the district magistrate's court, the affair usually ended in the removal of the local magistrate to another area and his replacement by another.

main road and therefore within easier access to Dodoma. But it was generally known in his area that he had refused to move because, in the past, ritual leaders could not move their homesteads out of a restricted area where the clan had first established its ritual control and where the gravestones of past ritual leaders were. Such an area is called *matemelo*. The government chief himself did not possess the rainstones, but he was in close contact with the ritual leader (his classificatory son, *mwanagwe*), who lived at the original site. The government chief compromised by moving one of his wives to a homestead at the new site.

Many chiefs and subchiefs, as a result of their school education and as part of the social equipment necessary for their positions, adopted Christianity and were baptized with Christian names. However, their positions were also said to be gravely open to attack by witchcraft. Further, their wealth and their ability to become chiefs and wield power laid them open to accusations of witchcraft themselves. One powerful and successful Gogo chief had a widespread reputation for witchcraft power and was said to owe his position and wealth to this attribute. People said that if any of his colleagues went against him, he simply had to point his finger to bring down illness, misfortune, or death upon the offender. This was linked also to the fact that he belonged to a clan whose members are notorious throughout Ugogo for their ability to stop the rain through witchcraft. The chief in question is a close agnatic relative of this clan's ritual leader, who lives nearby.

Because of this reputation and because of the possibility of attack by witchcraft, most government chiefs would not eat in others' homesteads. Nor would they stay the night away from home, except with certain categories of close kin or affines. In Gogo theory, non-kin do not usually bewitch each other. But certain categories of kin (such as MB/ZS)[1] are also thought to be incapable of using witchcraft or sorcery against each other. In one area the government subchief, when attending meetings or other functions in villages other than close by, would spend the night and eat only in the homestead of his cross-cousin (*muhiziwe*, in this case FZS). He would also stay with the local 'Indian' storekeeper, who was a friend and outside the system anyway, and therefore incapable of wanting to kill him.

When the chiefs were removed, a village headman told me:

---

[1] The letters here and throughout stand for the normal kinship terms, i.e., F = Father, M = Mother, B = Brother, Z = Sister, S = Son, D = Daughter.

The Gogo people will now stop bewitching each other over the problems of [government] chiefs, because they know now that even if one bewitches his colleague, he will not get the chiefship. What would they bewitch each other for?

I asked my informant if this was why government chiefs did not like staying with others, and he said:

Yes, the government chiefs fear witchcraft a great deal; even if you are strangers [i.e. non-relatives, whom, in Gogo theory, it is difficult to bewitch] they are afraid to eat, because they think that if they go and eat with a non-relative, perhaps another government chief would have given that person witchcraft to kill him.[1]

The authority position of the government chief was thus thought to be insecure and full of danger. The fact that government chiefs were also thought to be able to *expand* the area of their influence (see above: the process of amalgamation of areas) was added incentive for them to bring these forces into play. The office carried judicial and political authority created by an alien system; it was not sanctioned by an hereditary principle; there was no right to sacrifice to the spirits which influence the country; it was excluded from the power of divination in combating witchcraft; and the ritual leaders, with whom some kind of relationship had to be maintained, were present in large numbers.

When the chiefs were deposed in 1962, it was evident that until the new rules and offices were actually effective, they would still continue to have considerable influence over the conduct of affairs in the newly named divisions. This was confirmed by the part some of the deposed chiefs continued to play in the new local government (see below).[2] It was widely recounted in Ugogo that, when a central government minister made a personal call on a long-standing and successful government chief, the old man is said to have remarked, 'I knew this would come. But choose carefully those whom you put to rule the country, for you will see trouble between the old chiefs and these new people'. Even if this were not actually true, the fact that it was recounted with obvious belief is significant. My own impression was that, in spite of

[1] The problem of commensality is, of course, strongly linked with witchcraft and sorcery accusation situations, and is an indicator of relationships where such accusations are likely or unlikely to occur (cf. Middleton and Winter, 1963: 163, 242, and *passim*).

[2] Cf. Mair, 1958. But in making comparisons, it is important to note that in most cases the chiefs with whom the newly independent governments had to deal were fulfilling 'modernized' *traditional* roles whereas in Ugogo this was not the case.

the early election of village committees (*halmashauri*) and in spite of the unpopularity of the chiefs amongst the Western-educated élite, the chiefs were fully in control of all meetings concerned with famine relief, community development, elections, and other matters. This continued until the presidential election in November 1962, and even until the resignation of the chiefs in January 1963. The following case (one of many) illustrates this:

Just before Independence Day in 1961, the TANU secretary for a chiefdom (an extremely energetic and clever young man from southern Tanzania) called a meeting in a subchiefdom to discuss arrangements for the day of independence, and to make a collection in cash or in kind from homestead-heads in order to provide food and entertainment. The meeting was very poorly attended (only about 150 people came) and the response to the appeal for funds was even worse. The TANU secretary's explanation was: (a) that the village headman concerned had not turned up (he was actually 20 miles away in search of good grazing for his cattle) and (b) the subchief had been unable to attend because of illness. The only headman who attended had never been successful in his office and was considered incapable of carrying out his duties.

This kind of situation was frequent until the end of 1962.

Few of the chiefs and subchiefs in Ugogo were educated or qualified enough to be offered posts in either the central government or the new local government, as were many in other parts of Tanzania. Four from Dodoma District were offered positions as division executive officers, assistant executive officers, or local magistrates. Only one took up the post of local magistrate, in the area in which he had previously been chief. The fact that so few executive officers in Ugogo were Gogo was pointed out by government and party speakers at village meetings towards the end of 1963. The points made were that: (a) so few Gogo were qualified for these positions and therefore people must make an added effort to 'raise themselves up'; and (b) in view of the increasing rumours about the ritual state of the country since the 'chiefs' had been 'insulted', it must be remembered that the government had not exiled the chiefs. They therefore retained their ritual functions and had merely handed over their administrative functions to the executive officers. It is clear that there is also a growing awareness in the new local government that at least some of these ex-chiefs, who are individuals with some abilities in carrying out various administrative tasks, can and must be made use of. The reasons for this development appear in the following analysis.

The subchiefs had official positions until April 1963, when they too were removed from office at the same time as the village headmen. Through this period from the removal of the chiefs until the deposition of the subchiefs and headmen, the only official administrative instruction was that village headmen and subchiefs should no longer hear cases before they went to the local court. This was simply an attempt to enforce a ruling that already existed. The only official court in the chiefdom was that of the local magistrate.

The fact is that most cases *still* begin at neighbourhood level in the informal court of elders, and many are settled there. Even with the removal of village headmen and the subchiefs, this procedure continues as at the end of 1965. The settling of cases in this way avoids the payment of the relatively high court fees at the *baraza*, and the transportation of litigants and witnesses sometimes up to forty miles for a case. Furthermore, litigants need not be checked for tax defaulting and other offences as they would be at the local court:

In a recent case (1963) in a division in southern Ugogo, a dispute was settled by elders at the ex-subchief's homestead. The latter was also a ritual leader. A young man was accused of being the lover of an older man's wife. The wife admitted that he was her lover, and the court ruled against the young man, who was ordered to pay an adultery fine. The youth, who still had his hair plaited and ochred in traditional Gogo fashion (now illegal), said he could not accept the judgement and would take the case to the local court some 42 miles away. The elders advised him against this, telling him that he would pay a fine and have his head shaved before they even heard the case at the *baraza* (which was quite true). He agreed to pay the fine, and the case was closed. (A further case of assault, settled in this manner in 1965, is given later.)

In this context it should be noted that many cases that would have been heard in the past when the chiefs were still in control of the courts are rejected now. For example:

The people of one division (which corresponds rather closely with a ritual area) decided in early 1963 that a diviner living in the area was stopping the rain because he had not been consulted. They took the case to the local court, but no action could be taken. The opinion of all was that, had the ex-chief still been in charge (he was present at the *baraza* throughout their attempt to bring a case), their complaint would have received a more sympathetic hearing.

The village headmen

In the following sections, I describe the role of village headmen as it was until abolished in April 1963, when village executive officers were elected and the composition of village committees was raised to twenty or more members.

As with the chiefs and subchiefs, the formal rewards of office for village headmen were very limited.[1] The tenure of duty for headmen was often short and unstable, and clan affiliations were seldom taken into account (by the administration, that is) in the appointment. In actual practice, however, most of the village headmen in any area were kin or affines of the chief and subchief, and frequently related to one another. Individuals were put forward by the elders and the chief, and elected at a public meeting by show of hands. In one case, the most influential headman, one of four in a subchiefdom, was of the same clan as the chief of the whole chiefdom, but not a close agnate. He was also cross-cousin (FZS) of the subchief, and related to the ritual leader of the area, who was his classificatory grandson (*mwizukulu*, actually MBSSS). He was also related to the other two village headmen in the subchiefdom, one of whom was his classificatory cross-cousin (FMBSS). Such networks of kin relations are important in Gogo social structure, and the mutual obligations engendered by them assisted the individuals occupying these imposed authority roles in carrying out the functions of administration (Rigby, 1967*b*, 1969*a*).

In this context, the 'village' was defined by the administration and was usually based upon a minimum number of taxpayers. Although the village headman's office was a part of the official hierarchy of local administration, and thus rested upon 'native authority' rules and regulations, it approximated more closely the Gogo ideas of leadership than any other office in the system created by the British colonial government. In the past, founders of neighbourhoods were recognized as having some precedence over those who followed them, and were often rich men with large herds and homesteads. Those who did follow them often attached themselves to the homestead of the founder before establishing their own. The neighbourhood founders had no authority over the allocation of rights in land, grazing, or other resources, other

---

[1] In the 1930s, subchiefs' monthly salaries ranged from shs. 5/- to shs. 30/-, and village headmen earned comparatively less. In 1962, village headmen were paid shs. 25/- a month to about shs. 40/-.

than individual water rights in wells sunk by themselves. They were, in a literal sense, 'builders of neighbourhoods' (*wazengamatumbi*) (cf. Cory, 1951). The sons of founders, as long as they had other suitable qualities, continued to enjoy this prestige. Of the village headmen mentioned above, one was the son of the founder of the neighbourhood (who had established the new settlement some forty-five years before), and another the son of an early rich settler. Several of the present homestead heads in the neighbourhood had originally attached themselves to the founder's homestead before establishing their own (Rigby, 1969 a).

Nevertheless, most of the government village headman's modern functions and authority were based upon alien institutions. He was responsible (together with a tax clerk) for the collection of taxes and the implementation of government directives at village level. Whereas in the past the *muzengatumbi* had been simply *primus inter pares* in such activities as the settlement of disputes between homesteads in the neighbourhood, the government headman was set apart, given officially defined functions, authority and salary. A *successful* village headman during the period of colonial administration was usually a man of some wealth (in cattle), personality and presence. Ability as a speaker and knowledge of law gave him a prominent position in the informal (and officially unrecognized) elders' court. There were, however, many 'unsuccessful' headmen.

As with the chiefs, wealth, strong personality and the successful wielding of associated authority were all linked in the minds of people with the possession of witchcraft, or sorcery medicines. Witchcraft was also said to be used against a headman, and the position was considered a ritually dangerous one. One headman told me in early 1962 that he had been in office for seven years. He had been about thirty-eight years old when he took over the government headmanship, and he was the senior son of one of the founders of the neighbourhood. His father had not been government headman and was dead when he took over. He said:

When I took headmanship I was still very young...When I went into it, some people used witchcraft against me a great deal. There are a great number of witches in our country; I know because I dreamt it. They wanted another headman.

He went to a diviner to get medicines to 'close the body' (*kudinda umuwili*), and now all the people in the chiefdom want only him as headman.

Many successful headmen, who had been elected and appointed by the local authority in conjunction with the administration, began to take on some of the ritual functions more usually associated with the ritual leaders and the members of his clan. The headman quoted above, even after his removal from the government office, now has considerable influence over rituals concerning the fertility of crops in his area. He even goes on trips to a diviner some forty miles away for medicines for the country (*kujenda gandawega*, or *lamali*; see Rigby, 1969*a*). Although he has no rainstones, there is a tacit understanding that he has a sphere of ritual influence (*yisi*) apart from that of the ritual leader who lives some six miles away. The latter is a weak man who made little attempt to prevent this development, even though the headman concerned is of a different clan.[1]

When the chiefs resigned, many headmen (most of whom were illiterate and therefore could not hope for positions in the new system) thought that they too would be removed from their posts and sought to resign. But they were not removed from office until April 1963. Village committees were originally set up to advise village headmen on various matters; but as I have noted, they had little impact while the headmen were still in office. Even while they still occupied their positions, however, some of the older headmen felt it difficult to work with the young, mostly literate, people who were elected to village committees. They felt that their positions would soon be taken over by younger, literate people. This proved correct, but during this period it was clear that, in the absence of the chiefs, the whole system of tax collection, administration and development work rested upon the village headmen.

It is clear, then, that although so much depended upon these offices in terms of the functions of administration, when the changes detailed were brought about, these offices were destroyed, together with the adjustments that had been made to link them, however tenuously, with Gogo social institutions. Although these roles were imposed from outside and legalized by an alien system of authority, a certain degree of integration in structural and functional terms had been reached through the various mechanisms described. A new and more democratic system has now been introduced to fill the gap left by the

[1] The usurpation of ritual authority is common in Gogo history and is still going on; but in this case it was definitely linked with the position of the individual concerned as government headman.

dissolution of these roles. Before we look at this new system, however, it is relevant to note briefly one or two unforeseen results of the changes that took place in 1962–3.

Administrative changes and the origin of myths

Gogo recognize that a proliferation of rumours is indicative of events which produce unrest and social tension, particularly in times of famine. But this awareness does not prevent the dissemination of rumours in such a situation. At the approach of the first rainy season after the removal of the chiefs and the installation of the village committees, stories began to circulate in at least one part of Ugogo (and I heard evidence of it elsewhere) to the effect that there would be a drought, and that crops would be destroyed for a third year running. In an area where the subchief had also been a ritual leader before the introduction of these changes, an elder stated during a discussion:

This year there are many bees, and those bees portend famine, because all the chiefs (*watemi*) have gone.[1] Now, when they left their posts they became angry. They did this because they were mourning their countries. All the rituals which they usually carry out when 'the year is finished' [i.e., just before rains] they are not going to do. And so the rains will be small again; it will not rain. So, if it does not rain in all the countries of Ugogo, surely famine has befallen us? This is the way they are destroying us.

Another elder added that he had been told at the cattle market that Dr Nyerere had said all chiefs must be returned to their positions all over Tanganyika, because he had seen that where the chiefs had been removed and thus offended, the rain had not come.

Rumours also took forms with less explicit reference to rain and fertility. They suggested that some Gogo were using their witchcraft and sorcery to combat the many changes and new regulations which seemed to threaten their identity and culture. At this time, a regulation was being enforced that Gogo women should not wear the heavy brass arm and leg rings (*wudodi*) and ornaments they are so fond of, parallel to the rule already mentioned that men should no longer wear ochre and beads. The following is one informant's version of a rumour that was widely discussed by the elders in the area in which I was living:

---

[1] This was in spite of the fact that it was recognized that only the government chiefs had been removed from office. But it was the clans concerned, whose members included the ritual leaders, who were thought to be offended.

Two women from Cigwe[1] came to a cattle market in central Ugogo, with their brass rings on. When they arrived at the market they met up with the people going around cutting off brass ornaments, who told them, 'Take off your brass rings! Why are you still wearing them?' They replied, 'We will not take them off'. They then got hold of some metal cutters, which immediately broke. They brought another pair, and that also fell apart. So they said, 'Very well, bring a knife'. Others gave them a knife and they began to hack angrily at the bangles. When they had cut off one lot they saw the little hand of a child had fallen on the ground.[2] They began cutting off the bangles of her companion also, and again they saw the hand of a child. And the person who was doing the cutting, there and then his mouth twisted to one side and his neck became arched! He just shrivelled up and they had to take him to hospital.

Brass ornaments were still an issue in 1965. I attended an electoral campaign meeting in Dodoma North constituency during the September national elections. The division executive officer, after explaining the procedure for the presidential vote in the election, said he had a couple of 'local issues' to raise. He said he had found a woman who had just brewed beer for a communal work party of women for 'winding the brass ornaments' (*wujimbi wakutinya uwudodi*). This, he told the meeting, was extremely bad. It encouraged women to waste money, not only on the beer, but on the ornaments, instead of buying their children good clothing and food.

I have given these examples of rumours which, although present at all times in Ugogo, were in these cases retold in the context of an 'awareness' of the uncertain ritual state of the country. They arose from examples in a more traditional idiom, concerning famine, but commented upon current political and social events. They were indicative of unease at the disruption of a political system which, however alien and imposed upon Gogo society from 'outside', had been in operation a number of years. It had thus adapted to some kind of *modus operandi* and integration with the more traditional ritual institutions and offices of Gogo society.

Local government officers and party officials became aware of these

[1] Cigwe is near Cinyambwa, western Ugogo, where women are notoriously attached to their brass decorations, but where men gave up using ochre and sheep fat many years before the present rules were promulgated.

[2] This was a mark of sorcery and witchcraft; and an omen of danger which the 'alien offenders' were thought unable to recognize. The implication here is that the sorcery medicines or witchcraft of the Gogo are still effective and operate against all modern innovations.

factors and began explicitly to combat them in public meetings. It became increasingly common for both the division executive officer and party official in one area to insert into their speeches a reference to the fact that it was *only* the government chiefs who had been deposed. Their secular functions had been transferred to the new offices, but the ritual leaders were still there, free to perform their traditional duties. I heard this at several meetings, particularly in areas of Ugogo rather remote from the district centre.

The village development committees

In the past, village headmen were assisted in their duties by people occupying two types of unpaid offices: the *mulugaluga*,[1] who acted as messenger, calling litigants to cases at the headman's homestead or informing people of meetings, and the *wacili*,[2] who represented the village headman in the other 'villages' of the cluster over which he had governmental authority. The messengers usually received informal payments[3] from litigants who brought cases to the elders' court, but the *wacili* received no *direct* benefits. The latter were, however, thought of as potential successors to the headmanship, and kept in close touch with their headman. Both these roles have now disappeared, as they depended to a large extent upon the patronage of the village headman. Their functions have now been taken over by the village committees.

The village committees were originally elected to advise the village headmen, but this arrangement was purely a transitional one. Since the removal of the village headmen, the membership of the committees has been raised to twenty or more. A chairman is elected, but none of these positions is paid. Village development committees are elected by the several 'villages' and function within an area approximating the old subchiefdoms. These are grouped into 'divisions', which are the old chiefdoms with minor boundary re-alignments in some cases (although

---

[1] Derived from the Kiswahili term *mrugaruga*, 'an irregular soldier...also messenger or retainer of a chief' (*Oxford Standard Swahili Dictionary*). In Nyamwezi the chief's body-guard were called *warugaruga* (Abrahams, 1965), but in Ugogo the word was intro-duced only in the context of 'messenger'. The chief had little control over military groups (see above) in Ugogo, at least until the intrusion of alien influences.

[2] Derived from Kiswahili *Wakili*, 'agent' or 'representative'.

[3] These payments were called *vitalu* (lit. 'little sandals') and were settled by the litigants in discussion with the messenger before the latter went off to call witnesses or defen-dants, etc. When the case was settled, the litigant who lost was usually held responsible for these payments, which were thus considered part of the 'costs' of the case.

this is still going on). The chairman of TANU organization in the divisions, and the division executive officers, play a major part in explaining and instituting these changes, as well as development directives, etc. A village executive officer is elected for each village committee area, and this is the lowest-paid position in the new local government hierarchy (cf. Bienen, 1967).

The village development committees, then, are designed to take over all the functions of day-to-day administration which in the past were performed by subchiefs, headmen and their assistants, excepting the collection of taxes and the settlement of disputes. They will also have new functions which, at least ideally, are the more important ones: those of creating new settlement patterns and thus new kinds of communities, and the implementing of development and 'nation building' projects. In these committees and their associated offices, new processes of adjustment are beginning to emerge, operating to ensure the adaptation of Gogo values and concepts of legitimacy to the present administrative and political structures. I explore these processes fully elsewhere (Rigby, 1967a, 1969b: cf. Bienen, 1967; Hyden, 1968), and therefore do not discuss them further here.

Rural 'élites' and Gogo politics

A final category of roles I must examine are those of the local government officers and private individuals who run the various services based upon the division headquarters in each division (or 'chiefdom' in the past). These roles are distinguished occupationally, but in their context as leadership roles they may be considered as a single category. I discuss primarily their role relationships with one another and with the local Gogo populations. It must be kept in mind that the activities and attitudes of persons in this category are also undergoing rapid change, and that much of the present analysis may already be outdated in some parts of Ugogo.

These individuals, with Western education and orientation, with their special skills, are mostly non-Gogo, although this situation is also changing at the moment. But their cultural affiliations are important principally in a negative sense. The members of this élite view themselves as leaders in the wider context of Tanzania society, but they do not form a *group* in this wider context; rather, a category, with roles defined and recognized at the 'supra-ethnic' level. But at the level of the communities with which I am concerned now, they form exclusive groups at the local level, both consciously through associations and in other ways, through which they keep their identity separate from the local communities in which they live.

In this sense I refer to them as an external élite, when viewed in relation to the categories of Gogo society. Their roles do not grow out of a proliferation of Gogo social institutions; and consequently, most Gogo, until very recently, did not consider participation in them as a possible choice. This may appear a truism, but I think it is important to keep it in mind when comparing the situation in Ugogo with that in other parts of Africa, or even in other parts of Tanzania. The social structure has frequently adapted itself more easily to the integration of this type of role, and the comparison is relevant in an examination of the interrelations between Gogo society and the categories of new élites and leadership roles available in terms of the broader national society (cf. Lewis, 1958).

One such group is described in this section. The rather 'informal' data were recorded mostly before independence, but what is described probably remains substantially unchanged (cf. Bienen, 1967).

The present administrative headquarters of the division used to be a village in the chiefdom. The site is a little over twenty miles from Dodoma, the government district centre, by an almost all-weather road constructed when the health centre and clinic were built in the division. It contains a secondary school (which used to be a middle school, that is, Standards V to VIII), a primary school, a veterinary centre for half the district, a community development office, the *baraza* or local court, two Indian-owned stores and an Arab one. Most of the buildings housing these activities, except the stores, have been built since 1955. There is a wind-driven water pump that supplies the community with water some of the time.[1]

With continual minor changes the inhabitants of this settlement include basically the following officials:

9 teachers, 3 in primary school and 6 in the middle (secondary) school, all men in the latter, one woman in the former
2 medical assistants and a dispenser
1 health inspector who runs the health centre
1 midwife and her assistants

[1] A reliable water source often determines the siting of such a settlement in Ugogo—an area where water even for drinking is often a difficulty during the prolonged dry season.

2 community development assistants (when the local government has enough money, otherwise 1)

1 veterinary assistant who has responsibility for this division and several neighbouring ones, and 2 other junior veterinary assistants

2 court clerks and the local magistrate (*hacimu*, now usually a peripatetic magistrate who handles 3 or 4 divisions).

Added to this group is a division TANU secretary who is also a member of the development team at this level, and a village executive officer who administers several 'villages' in the ritual area immediately to the south-west of the settlement.

A large number of these people are not Gogo and are between the ages of about the mid-twenties to late forties. The court clerks, magistrates, one school-teacher at the secondary school, and one at the primary school, are Gogo. Recently the two community development assistants were Gogo, one man and one woman, but all previous incumbents of this office were non-Gogo. The previous TANU secretary, who was Ngoni, was transferred to another division and was replaced by a local man in his mid-thirties, who is Gogo. He was previously an adult literacy teacher in a nearby village.

This was the position in 1963, but the turnover in personnel is so high (a point discussed below) that it is impossible to keep abreast of the changes if one is not resident in the settlement itself. From September 1961 until 1963 there had been three different community development assistants, two veterinary assistants, and two medical assistants. In addition, the previous local magistrate had fallen out with the government chief while the latter was still in office, and was transferred. He was replaced only after the chief had been removed.

Of the shopkeepers, the Indians divide their residence between the settlement and Dodoma. The Arab is resident more often. There is always at least one vehicle a day travelling each way between the settlement and Dodoma. The local court messengers act as mail carriers. Two of the messengers are Gogo, the other of Congo origin, born and brought up in Ugogo.

All the people listed so far are literate in Kiswahili, and a good number are literate in English as well. Two primary-school teachers, the messengers and the resident magistrate did not know English.[1]

---

[1] This situation has now changed radically with the rationalization of the court system in Tanzania. The younger men now filling the office of local magistrates are literate in English.

Kiswahili is the principal medium of communication, not only within the group but also between them and the local population.

Spatially, the whole settlement is seen as one of well constructed metal-roofed buildings somewhat isolated from the surrounding flat mud homesteads—a physical impression paralleled by social distance. The group is set apart from the Gogo population by dress, language, housing, and an expressed feeling that they should be so distinguished.

Since the secondary school was established, there had existed intermittently in the settlement a 'Public Servants' Association', which died three times and was resurrected twice. In late 1963 it was defunct. The aims and reasons given for the formation of this association are somewhat similar to those given for 'ethnic' associations in urban areas, although the membership, of course, does not have a common ethnic base. The ethnic affiliation is wide. At one time it included Pare, Kaguru, Nyaturu, Hehe, Nyamwezi, Nyasa, etc.; but 'tribal' affiliation is important only in the sense that most of the individuals are non-Gogo and therefore have no ties of kinship or other obligation with members of the local population. Gogo members of the group were not, of course, excluded from the association, but those with local ties were usually not members. For example, the government chief or the local magistrate would not have been particularly welcome, even if they had considered associating themselves with the group.

The expressed aims of the association, both constitutional and unofficial, could be summed up as follows: (a) the raising of funds in case of an emergency affecting any of the members or their families, (b) to act as a pressure group for exerting pressure on the various departments in Dodoma (especially the local government, which employs most of the individuals mentioned) with the purpose of improving conditions of service and living in the settlement, (c) to furnish entertainment in the form of concerts, also useful for raising funds,[1] (d) to speed up personal correspondence by having a box in Dodoma through which members could receive their unofficial mail, (e) to provide drinking facilities for the purchase of bottled beer at a slightly higher than standard price in order to raise funds, and (f) to provide a discussion centre for the modern-educated people living in this 'backward' rural area.

[1] One member suggested that they should put on a concert in Dodoma in conjunction with the students from the secondary school in order to raise funds and 'let the people in Dodoma know that we are here'.

The member who was in possession of the association's books (which have been kept intermittently) told me that the association had collapsed in 1961 due, the new members suggest, to the apparent fact that the office bearers were not energetic enough to fulfil their duties. It was re-formed in 1962, and members decided that one man of energy and enough interest was needed to keep it going. Subscriptions were fixed at shs. 5/- for entry and shs. 1/- a month. At a meeting, potential members elected a chairman (the headmaster of the primary school, a middle-aged man with a large family, who comes from Malawi) and a treasurer (the veterinary assistant, who left the area a couple of months later) to collect subscriptions. The secondary-school teachers remained somewhat aloof (they constitute the most highly educated sub-group). The senior medical assistant did not attend because he was studying for his school certificate and did not drink. In fact, for reasons suggested below, the association collapsed soon after this early organizational stage.

The motives for re-forming the association were given variously as, 'We must have some place to discuss things, for the educated people of this area' and 'This is a very backward place and however short a time we stay here we must press for better conditions'. The idea was also expressed that, however little the association might help these individuals personally, there would be something for their successors to take over in order to make life more bearable. It did not occur to anyone that the association was having an intermittent existence possibly because of the high turnover of personnel in the settlement. This, I suggest, was because the main significance of this association lay not in its expressed constitutional functions (it did not serve these) but in the attempt to form an exclusive voluntary association in response to the exclusiveness of this group in the local context, and its isolation from the surrounding community. It gave members an opportunity to state their distinctiveness from the values and institutions of Gogo society.

I do not suggest that this situation can be found in other parts of Tanzania, where there may be a greater degree of integration between the modern élite and the local community. But in the case under consideration it is illustrative of my hypothesis that these modern roles remained external to the categories of Gogo society, and therefore as roles unavailable (due to the historical and structural reasons outlined) to the majority of the members of Gogo society.

Apart from the association, the exclusiveness of this group showed itself in other areas, such as that of language, already touched upon. All the members of this group used Kiswahili principally in everyday conversations and attempted to use it in their work situation as well, except for the secondary-school teachers, who used both Kiswahili and English in their teaching. Only one secondary-school teacher was Gogo and liked to speak Cigogo. None of the others made much attempt to learn the language, in spite of the fact that many Gogo do not know much Kiswahili, particularly women. The health inspector felt that the local population were deliberately spiting him by speaking Cigogo when he addressed them in Kiswahili. The medical assistant knew Cigogo, but always began his questionings in Kiswahili. The exception was the young Ngoni TANU secretary who made every effort to learn Cigogo and so improve his relations with the people. But he used Kiswahili at meetings, necessitating translation by one of the court messengers.[1] The two later community development assistants, however, played upon the fact, when they addressed meetings, that they were Gogo and they spoke Cigogo.[2]

All the individuals described in this section belong to the category of modern-educated Tanzanians, but none had degrees. The highest standard of education among this group was School Certificate. All felt themselves only temporarily in this type of post and area, where they felt they could not give full expression to their abilities. It is clear that when thrown together and isolated from the local community they form a group, recruitment to which is based upon criteria totally alien to the local population. This isolation is facilitated by close residence, common interests and language, and is buttressed by voluntary associations. There is no attempt at identification by the group with Gogo society, except in the case of a few fringe members.[3]

Certainly, relations between the group described here and the Gogo

[1] During the 1965 campaigns for the national elections, the contestants were permitted to use only Kiswahili in their speeches; but when local officials explained electoral procedure for the parliamentary and presidential elections, they frequently used Cigogo (Rigby, 1967a).

[2] Sixty-nine Standard VII and VIII students at the local secondary school were asked to express their opinions on their linguistic habits. Forty-nine (71 per cent) said they spoke their own vernacular languages most at home (forty Gogo and nine non-Gogo): fifteen (22 per cent) said they spoke Kiswahili most at home; three (4 per cent) said they usually spoke English at home; and two did not respond.

[3] My own partial acceptance in the Gogo community, in a neighbourhood several miles from the settlement, was viewed with tolerant amusement by this group.

population were of an authoritarian kind at the time these observations were made. This was particularly so in the past when the members of the group worked in conjunction with the chiefs, in spite of the fact that they seldom had close relations with the chief outside the work situation. For one thing, the chief was really a member of the local community and therefore was not completely accepted within the exclusive group; and secondly, in terms of group values, the institution of chiefship was considered archaic and undemocratic. They described the chiefs as unprogressive and authoritarian and resented the power they still had in the areas in which they worked. Most were relieved when the removal of the chiefs became certain.

In rural Gogo values in general, at the present time, these élite roles are neither attainable nor desirable. At most, Gogo see them as being filled in the future by their youngest sons, now going through school. But this itself presages for Gogo elders the total destruction of Gogo social institutions. One middle-aged friend of mine expressed it to me in terms of property:

The youngsters these days will not care for wealth (i.e., cattle) because they are simply incapable of appreciating it. There is a young boy of mine reading school (secondary school). I have thrown away huge sums of money on him; last year I paid out shs. 200/. But also, we *are* throwing it away. Even when he has left school and come home, when I have died and left him cattle, do you think he will herd them properly? He'll sell the lot! Simply to wear a little flashy clothing! He is capable of taking the cattle to market, and then all the property is gone, in shoes and clothes; he'll return empty-handed. And then what will he herd? Then, when he has returned to the homestead he will want to take another beast; all the cattle could be finished in a year. But look at our friends the Baraguyu and Masai: they still adhere to their traditions and customs. Even when a Baraguyu dies and leaves his cattle to his children, they can look after them properly because they do not have an idea of modern finery as our Gogo children do.[1]

Even though the standard of literacy required for some of the positions in the new hierarchy is not high, the majority of Gogo do not as yet view literacy as a legitimate criterion for leadership or authority. This situation is changing rapidly at present. No more can be said about it here. But even for the students at the secondary school, membership

---

[1] I.e., Baraguyu youths do not wish to identify themselves with the educated élite by wearing Western clothes, and still have 'traditional' ideas of finery obtainable in more traditional ways than getting rid of all one's cattle.

of the local élite represented in the division headquarters had little attraction as an ideal for status and position after the students had left school. They apparently hope for higher offices elsewhere, as do the members of the local élite I have described here. Forty-eight (68 per cent) of the sixty-nine students in Standards VII and VIII were Gogo in 1962, and many of the others had been born in Ugogo.[1] Thirty (44 per cent) had no lengthy experience in towns, even small towns like Dodoma. Forty-four (65 per cent) expressed a first choice for an occupation *not* represented amongst the educated élite in the settlement under discussion, although these were on the list from which they were asked to choose. Only thirteen (19 per cent) expressed a preference for any of these occupations, of which four (5·8 per cent) wished to be pastors in the church and one a shopkeeper, and are thus not truly indicative of positive attitudes towards these occupations and statuses.

Postscript

Finally, a case I observed and participated in in 1965 substantiates the continuance of widespread informal judicial activity in Ugogo and its relations with the formal court hierarchy, which remains much as described for 1963 above, and in Figures 6 and 7.

James, a young man of twenty-six, is a very close friend of Ndahani, his age-mate. On polling day in 1965 several people completed their voting and went to a beer party at a homestead some three miles from the polling booth.

During the course of discussion and drinking, James and Ndahani began to joke and taunt each other (both were slightly drunk). They picked up their sticks[2] and, challenging each other to a friendly contest, went around to the other side of the homestead. No one present thought anything of this; a friendly stick contest is a common game among young men in Ugogo.

On this occasion, however, one of the friends lost his temper, and they began fighting in earnest. They drew blood and broke each other's sticks. Ndahani came round to join the rest of us with blood on his mouth and clothes. James, who by this time was very angry, followed Ndahani round, picked up a heavy pounding pole (*mutwango*), and struck Ndahani a

[1] In 1962 I conducted a survey of the backgrounds and attitudes of all the students in Standards VII and VIII in the secondary school in the area. The results of this will be published elsewhere.

[2] All Gogo men carry sticks at all times when out of their own homesteads. These sticks (*nghome*) are quite heavy and designed for protection against animal and human attack.

(fortunately) glancing blow on the side of the head. Ndahani fell unconscious and James, thinking he had killed his friend, fled.

Ndahani was unconscious for several hours, had difficulty in breathing, and we had to take him to a clinic some miles away. Thus the medical assistants at the local court came to hear about the affair.

Such assault, especially where close friends are involved, is a serious offence. However, the elders on both sides (including Ndahani's father) decided that taking James to court would only get him locked up for several months, and do no good. They settled the case in informal local discussion (*calo*), James giving Ndahani one ox for the assault, and a young ox 'to cure the injury' (*kumudesa*). Neither the police nor the local magistrate's court was involved at any stage.

This illustration of judicial activity at the local level confirms, I think, the analysis I have presented in this essay. It indicates that the same kinds of change and re-adjustment that had already begun in 1963 were continuing in 1965. It also shows that political and leadership roles at the local level are still very much in flux in the modern context of Gogo society.

Conclusion

I have attempted in this discussion to describe and analyse some of the modern leadership roles introduced or emerging in Ugogo since contact with wider political systems began, and as those systems themselves changed. I have dealt in more detail elsewhere with the position since independence (Rigby, 1967a, 1969b). The present analysis is based primarily upon an examination of the operation of these roles in actual role relationships, but reference is made also to the characteristics of these roles which have a bearing upon their integration in Gogo social structure. The proliferation of these roles has not been a coherent historical process; nor are they amenable to analysis from a purely synchronic structural perspective.

From the earliest contact between the Gogo and alien groups which were, or were potentially, politically disruptive, new roles have emerged. But these roles were primarily of an 'intermediary' or 'representative' kind, not fully participating in the system of legitimate authority within the society. This was probably true of both the earlier phase of contact with Arab and European travellers and traders, as well as of the German colonial period. Towards the end of the German period, the Gogo had made some adjustments to externally imposed *authority* roles. This adjustment was re-inforced during the critical period of the Anglo-German war and the consolidation of the British colonial régime. It was pivotal to the whole political process during the later indirect rule phase.

It was, however, during the period of 'indirect rule', a period of about thirty-six years, that the political roles and statuses 'legalized' in terms of the colonial government and the broader polity began to attain some measure of legitimacy. This was assisted by several factors: a more reasoned government policy, new bases for the legitimation of authority becoming apparent to Gogo themselves, and the transference of some of the traditional characteristics of legitimacy to the new offices and roles. Under a colonial system, however, all these roles were ultimately authoritarian; their final sanction lay with the force that could be brought to bear by the colonial government.

After the attainment of the Republic, these roles were abolished in conformity with the ideology of democratization and the participation of the general population in the processes of local (and national) government. No general assessment can yet be made, in terms of Gogo society's changing values, of the legitimacy of these new legal offices and roles (cf. Rigby, 1969b). The material presented in the latter part of this study shows that new adjustments are being made to this situation by those directly involved: that is, the younger men and women with modern education who have no leadership qualities in terms of Gogo institutions. They are a small minority in Ugogo and the means available to them at the moment for legitimizing their new roles vis-à-vis the rest of the Gogo population (of all age-levels) seem very limited. The idea of an educated élite leadership and concomitant roles and statuses current in the broader Tanzanian society is not yet an integrated part of Gogo concepts of leadership, just as the possibility of attaining such roles is not realized by the majority of Gogo. The values of the latter are still very much tied to the ideals of Gogo society: of wealth in cattle and children and the headship of a large homestead; the wisdom of age, and the value of political egalitarianism in a society primarily lacking in roles of secular political authority and leadership. Despite the ideology of democratic local government, the actual performance of administrative tasks may well fall back upon authoritarian roles created under a different system. The great increase in number and variety of these tasks may encourage this. An effective political leadership has yet to make its appearance in Gogo local communities in the modern context.

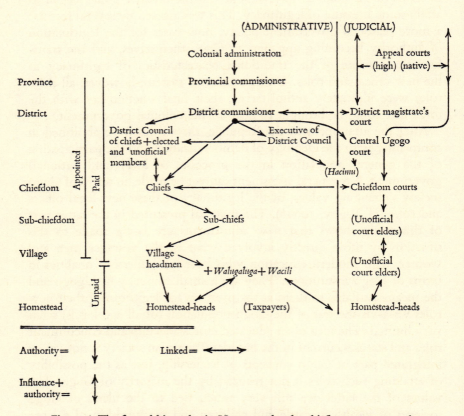

Figure 6. The formal hierarchy in Ugogo under the chiefly system set up by the British and dismantled in 1962–3, not including indigenous Gogo institutions.

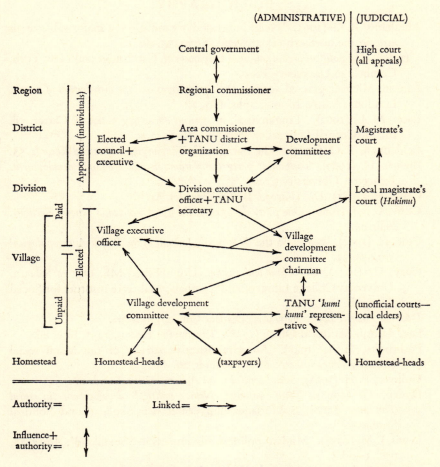

Figure 7. The formal hierarchy in Ugogo under the new system of local government set up by TANU and the District Council, from late 1963.

BIBLIOGRAPHY

Abrahams, R. G. (1965). 'Neighbourhood organization: a major sub-system among the northern Nyamwezi', *Africa*, **35**, no. 2.

— (1967). *The political organization of Unyamwezi*. Cambridge and New York, Cambridge University Press.

Banton, Michael, gen. ed. (1965). *Political systems and the distribution of power*. London. (A.S.A. Monographs, No. 2.)

Bates, M. L. (1962). 'Tanganyika', in *African one-party states*, G. Carter, ed. Ithaca, Cornell University Press.

Beidelman, T. O. (1960). 'The Baraguyu', *Tanganyika Notes and Records*, **55**.

Bienen, H. (1967). *Tanzania: party transformation and economic development*. Princeton University Press.

Claus, H. (1911). *Die Wagogo*. Berlin, Baessler Archiv.

Cliffe, L., ed. (1967). *One party democracy: the 1965 Tanzania general elections*. Nairobi.

Cole, H. (1902). 'Notes on the Wagogo', *Journal of the Royal Anthropological Institute*, **32**.

Cory, H. (1951). *Gogo law and custom*. Unpublished MS. Dar es Salaam, University College Library; and Kampala, Makerere Institute for Social Research.

Dodoma District Book. Tanzania, District Office, Dodoma.

East African Statistical Office (1958). *Tanganyika Census, 1957*. Rev. ed.

Fosbrooke, H. A. (1948). 'An administrative survey of the Masai social system', *Tanganyika Notes and Records*, **26**.

Gulliver, P. H. (1963). *Social control in an African society*. London.

Hyden, G. (1968). *Tanu yajunga Nchi: political development in rural Tanzania*. Lund, Bokförlaget Universitet och Skola. (Lund Political Studies 8.)

Lewis, I. M. (1958). 'Modern political movements in Somaliland', *Africa*, **28**, nos. 3 and 4.

Mair, L. P. (1958). 'African chiefs today', *Africa*, **28**, no. 3.

Middleton, J. (1960). 'The Lugbara', in *East African chiefs*, A. I. Richards, ed. London.

— and E. H. Winter, eds. (1963). *Witchcraft and sorcery in East Africa*. London.

Mnyampala, M. E. (1954). *Historia, Mila na Desturi za Wagogo wa Tanganyika*. Dar es Salaam. (Custom and Tradition in East Africa Series.)

Nadel, S. F. (1957). *The theory of social structure*. London.

Nye, J. (1963). 'Tanganyika self help', *Transition*, **11**.

Oliver, R., and G. Mathew, eds. (1963). *History of East Africa*, Vol. 1. Oxford, Clarendon Press.

Peters, C. (1891). *New light on dark Africa*. London.

Richards, A. I., ed. (1960). *East African chiefs*. London.

Rigby, P. (1966a). 'Dual symbolic classification among the Gogo of central Tanzania', *Africa*, **36**, no. 1.

(1966b). 'Sociological factors in the contact of the Gogo of central Tanzania with Islam', in *Islam in Tropical Africa*, I. M. Lewis, ed. London, Oxford University Press for International African Institute.

(1967a). 'Ugogo: changes in local government and the national elections', in *One party democracy*, L. Cliffe, ed. Nairobi.

(1967b). 'Time and structure in Gogo kinship', *Cahiers d'études africaines*, **7**, no. 28.

(1967c). 'The structural context of girls' puberty rites', *Man* (N.S.), **2**, no. 3.

(1968a). 'Some Gogo ritual of "Purification": an essay on social and moral categories', in *Dialectic in practical religion*, E. R. Leach, ed. London and New York, Cambridge University Press. (Cambridge Papers in Social Anthropology, No. 5.)

(1968b). 'Joking relationships, kin categories, and clanship among the Gogo', *Africa*, **38**, no. 2.

(1969a). *Cattle and kinship among the Gogo*. Ithaca, N.Y. and London, Cornell University Press.

(1969b). 'Local participation in national politics: Ugogo, central Tanzania', in *Micropolitics in Eastern Africa*, A. W. Southall, ed. (forthcoming).

Schaegelen, T. (1938). 'La Tribu des Wagogo', *Anthropos*, **33**, nos. 1 and 2.

Schmeidel, H. (1959). 'Bwana Sakkarani—Captain Von Prince and his times', *Tanganyika Notes and Records*, **52**.

Smith, M. G. (1956). 'On segmentary lineage systems', *Journal of the Royal Anthropological Institute*, **86**, no. 2.

(1960). *Government in Zazzau: 1800–1950*. London, Oxford University Press for International African Institute.

Southall, A. W. (1959). 'An operational theory of role', *Human Relations*, **12**, no. 1.

(1965). 'A critique of the typology of states and political systems', in *Political systems and the distribution of power*, M. Banton, gen. ed. London. (A.S.A. Monographs, No. 2.)

Southon, E. J. (1881). 'Notes on a journey through northern Ugogo, in East Central Africa', *Proceedings of the Royal Geographical Society*, **3**.

Speke, J. H. (1863). *Journal of the discovery of the source of the Nile*. London.

Stanley, H. M. (1872). *How I found Livingstone*. New York.

Weber, M. (1947). *The theory of social and economic organization*. Trans. by A. M. Henderson and Talcott Parsons. London, Oxford University Press.

(1948). *From Max Weber*. Trans. and ed. by H. H. Gerth and C. Wright Mills. London.

Wilson, M. (1958). *Peoples of the Nyasa-Tanganyika corridor*. Communication from the School of African Studies, University of Cape Town.